To my dear Karola Piotrkowska

WEIMAR AND NOW: GERMAN CULTURAL CRITICISM
Martin Jay, Anton Kaes, General Editors

1. Heritage of Our Times, by Ernst Bloch

HERITAGE OF OUR TIMES

Ernst Bloch

Translated by Neville and Stephen Plaice

University of California Press
Berkeley and Los Angeles

First published as *Erbschaft dieser Zeit*
© Suhrkamp Verlag, Frankfurt am Main 1962

This English translation © Polity Press 1990.

First published 1991 by Polity Press
in association with Basil Blackwell

University of California Press
Berkeley and Los Angeles, California

Library of Congress Cataloging-in-Publication Data

Bloch, Ernst, 1885–1977.
[Erbschaft dieser Zeit. English]
Heritage of our times/Ernst Bloch; translated by Neville
Plaice and Stephen Plaice.
p.   cm.
Translation of: Erbschaft dieser Zeit.
ISBN 0–520–07057–7 (hard)
1. Germany—Civilization—20th century.   2. Germany—Social life
and customs—20th century.   3. Germany—Social conditions—
1918–1933.   4. Germany—Social conditions—1933–1945.
5. National socialism.   6. Middle classes—Germany—History.
I. Title.
DD239.B713   1990
943.08—dc20   90–11013
                                                          CIP

Printed in Great Britain

1 2 3 4 5 6 7 8 9

The paper used in this publication meets the minimum requirements
of American National Standard for Information Sciences—
Permanence of Paper for Printed Library Materials,
ANSI Z39.48–1984

CONTENTS

TRANSLATORS' INTRODUCTION

The first edition of *Erbschaft dieser Zeit* was published in Zurich in 1935, during Ernst Bloch's five-year period of emigration from Nazi Germany in various European capitals before his final emigration to America for ten years in 1938. The book thus appeared roughly halfway between the publication of the first edition of Bloch's major literary work *Spuren* ('Traces') in 1930 and the beginning of his herculean labours, covering almost the whole of his period of American exile (1938–49), on the vast three-volume work that was to form the keystone of his philosophy, *Das Prinzip Hoffnung* (the English version of which – by the present translators with Paul Knight – was published as *The Principle of Hope* by Basil Blackwell in 1986). The structure of the book reflects a further development of the open pattern of short, often challengingly cryptic and intensely poetic texts employed in *Spuren*, while also prefiguring in the brief preliminary section 'Der Staub' ('Dust') and each of the subsequent three major parts the structural progression used in *The Principle of Hope* from these densely evocative introductory passages towards longer stretches of direct cultural, social and political analysis. *Erbschaft dieser Zeit*, which sets out to explore the true legacies of our present 'age of transition', thus itself also plays a crucial transitional role in the structural and philosophical development of Bloch's work as a whole, culminating in his wider theory of the world as open process and the concept of the Not-Yet-Conscious, the preconscious dimension in past, present and future, at the heart of his comprehensive philosophy of hope.

The bulk of the book was written in the early 1930s, although the oldest sections go back as early as 1924 (all dates given in the text are those of the original versions of the respective pieces). The enlarged and revised edition translated here, most notably incorporating the essays that formed Bloch's central contribution to the literary controversy in the late 1930s that has come to be known as the 'Expressionism debate', was published in Frankfurt in 1962, shortly after Bloch had decided to remain in the West, after the erection of the Berlin Wall, and to accept a guest professorship at Tübingen university. Bloch's bitter disappointment with 'socialist' developments in East Germany, where he had been obliged to retire from academic life, is clearly apparent in his 1962 Postscript to the Preface to the first edition of the book, expressing an open disillusionment with the narrow totalitarian system he had just escaped (particularly with its official cultural policy of 'socialist realism'), which belies the superficial right-wing caricature of Bloch as a blinkered apologist for Marxist orthodoxy.

It was precisely against the dogmatic advocates of 'socialist realism' that Bloch made his courageous stand in defence of the artistic avant-garde in the vehement debate in the 1930s concerning the relative merits of Expressionism and realism. His particular adversary was the Hungarian literary critic Georg Lukács, one of his closest friends in younger days, who had sought to trace a direct link between Expressionism and National Socialism in his essay 'Größe und Verfall des Expressionismus' ('Greatness and Decline of Expressionism'), first published in an issue of *Internationale Literatur* in Moscow in 1934. But the Expressionism debate proper did not get under way until over three years later, sparked off by two essays in the September 1937 number of the literary magazine *Das Wort*, a major organ of the 'Volksfront' (a popular front of intellectuals of various political persuasions, united in their opposition to fascism). The first of these essays comprised an attack by Klaus Mann on the Expressionist poet Gottfried Benn's complicity with National Socialism, and the second, by the hard-line functionary Alfred Kurella (under the pseudonym of Bernhard Ziegler), also employed the example of Benn to support the thesis that Expressionism was a logical precursor of fascism. Other writers and artists were quick to spring to the defence of Expressionism by pointing out the tremendous political diversity of its major exponents, and the consequent absurdity of condemning the movement lock, stock and barrel as a homogeneous enterprise. There was indeed a strongly progressive, implicitly anti-fascist strain in the best Expressionist writing and art, dwarfing the work of a writer like Benn – writers of the calibre of Johannes R. Becher, Georg Heym, Else Lasker-Schüler or Ernst Toller, to name just a few.

Bloch himself had been an active exponent of this progressive vein of Expressionism in his first philosophical work *Geist der Utopie* ('The Spirit of Utopia') published in 1918, so his subsequent defence of the movement was sharpened by an element of direct personal and political commitment. His first major contribution to the Expressionism debate was the article 'Diskussionen über Expressionismus', first published in *Das Wort* in 1938 and later revised for inclusion in the enlarged edition of *Erbschaft dieser Zeit*. As a glaring topical example of the antipathy between Expressionism and fascism, Bloch could point to the Nazi exhibition of 'Entartete Kunst' ('Degenerate Art'), containing works by almost all the great Expressionist artists, which opened in Munich in the summer of 1937 and which Bloch had already pilloried in the slightly earlier essays 'Der Expressionismus, jetzt erblickt' ('Expressionism, seen now') and 'Gauklerfest unterm Galgen' ('Jugglers' Fair beneath the Gallows'), both also later incorporated at different points into the enlarged edition of the present book. Coincidentally, this exhibition was organized by the would-be artist, Hitler's crony and President of the Reich Chamber of Art, Adolf Ziegler, his surname ironically identical with that of the time-serving Communist anti-Expressionist Kurella's adopted pseudonym. This chance echo highlights the fact that deep-seated cultural philistinism was not the exclusive preserve of the right at that time. Stalin's cultural *Gleichschaltung* (bringing into line) had been effected, and the truly revolutionary legacies of Russian Expressionism and Constructivism had already been sacrificed to sterile socialist realist conformity. And naturally this line was dogmatically followed by Communist parties all over Europe. It may indeed even be argued that the convergence of the artistic policies of right and left at this time irrevocably halted the development of a genuine revolutionary aesthetic in Europe.

As Bloch rightly points out in his first detailed riposte in 1938 to Lukács's essay of four years earlier, it does not refer to a single Expressionist painter and contains only the sketchiest of allusions to actual Expressionist writers, confining its attention almost exclusively to the programmatic statements of theorists of the movement. It is above all Lukács's underlying conception of literature as a closed totality, his admiration of the classical tradition (echoing the strong neo-classicist element in 'socialist realism'), which Bloch attacks and counters with his own unorthodox Marxist vision of art as future-orientated, necessarily fragmentary (giving rise to the radical innovatory technique of montage), at its best reflecting the light of a world that is not yet there (illustrated by the very concept of 'Vor-Schein' that lies at the heart of Bloch's aesthetic theory, with its double connotation of 'pre-appearance' and 'shining ahead'). In contrast to Lukács's stubborn allegiance to the mainstream literary tradition of bourgeois realism sustained by a writer like Thomas Mann, Bloch champions modern experimental writers such as Bertolt Brecht, who incidentally also himself took issue with Lukács's narrow definition of realism in a series of private notes which he decided not to publish at the time in an attempt to avoid any further exacerbation of the virulence of the debate. For Bloch, Brecht is a supreme modern example of those artists who stand on the very Front of their age, from where they can anticipate future developments.

For all their differences, Bloch's dispute with Lukács is unmistakably based on a mutual respect grounded in their early close friendship. In retrospect, it seems astonishing that such a similarly open debate as a whole was possible in Stalinist circles at this time on questions of literary theory. But it was the tolerant atmosphere of the 'Volksfront' – the united struggle against fascism embracing a vast spectrum of left-wing and bourgeois liberal opinion – which made this possible. This openness was soon stamped out again in East Germany after the war, as Bloch was to experience at first hand, and fittingly it was Alfred Kurella himself – a leading instigator of the whole controversy over Expressionism – who played a dominant role in this fresh cultural repression, from his appointment in 1957 as cultural commissar in the GDR up until his death in 1975.

Underlying the clash between Bloch and Lukács over the respective virtues of Expressionism and realism was the deeper question of cultural inheritance. Whereas Lukács saw only bohemian decadence symptomatic of an age of capitalist decay – and hence nothing worth inheriting – in the work of the modern artistic avant-garde, Bloch passionately believed there were positive elements to be extricated and claimed from cultural developments in all ages (not just that of classical bourgeois art favoured by Lukács), including the current 'age of transition'. Indeed, the primary task he set out to accomplish in this book was to readdress the real target of fascism, to rescue positive elements of the genuine German cultural tradition of both past and present from the thieving magpie grasp of Nazi ideology, and to claim this inheritance for the future. As a demonstration of his commitment to contemporary experimental departures in the arts, Bloch also used montage as an organizing principle for his own book. It is a heterogeneous patchwork of ideas and insights, juxtaposing segments of acute social and political analysis with others of critical perception and broader cultural vision. The book cuts and pastes from across the whole spectrum of high and popular culture, setting Wagner alongside colportage, for example, in order to rescue a hidden legacy of colportage from the portentous composer, drawing on the undiminished cultural energy of the fair and Karl May alongside Proust and Joyce, and even extracting positive images for the future from the nineteenth-century parlour. With its combined wealth of culturally specific reference and transcendent philosophical perspective, the content thus mirrors the style of the book in its exemplary embodiment of the heritage of our times.

One of the key philosophical concepts Bloch develops in the book is that of 'Ungleichzeitigkeit' (non-contemporaneity), the obligation to the dialectic of which is explored in a significantly central section. Social and cultural structures of the past continue to flourish in the present alongside contemporary capitalist ones and those pregnant with the future. Bloch believed that the anachronism of large parts of the peasantry and petite bourgeoisie in the modern capitalist world was not exclusively a negative phenomenon but also the source of potentially fruitful contradiction. It was largely the scornful wholesale rejection by vulgar Marxists of these seemingly anachronistic and irrational features of earlier social modes which had surrendered this whole fertile and influential area to the Nazis without a struggle, and had thus allowed them to occupy the positive, genuine elements of non-contemporaneity along with the negative ones. Bloch's book is ultimately an appeal for the cultivation of the dialectic sparked by these non-contemporaneous contradictions alongside the contemporaneous dialectic spearheaded, in his view, by the proletariat.

But of course one of the most fascinating aspects of the book is that it also reads as a contemporary observation of the rise of the Nazis. It probes their bogus roots in German history and mythology at the very moment the ludicrous ideologies of Blood and Soil and the Blond Beast are actually taking hold of the German people. Reading these essays today, it is sometimes hard to believe that many of them were written either from within Germany long before Hitler came to power, or from the distant standpoint of exile in the thirties, long before the rest of the world had begun to grasp the full horrors of the National Socialist regime. Though he subsequently had the opportunity to add to and to revise this collection of essays in the postwar period, there is no question of hindsight. Bloch's original analysis of developments in Germany was astonishingly prescient, literally before its time, and brilliantly anticipating the welter of post-war analysis of the phenomenon.

Bloch focuses not so much on the proletariat in this work, as on the petite bourgeoisie, the ground-swell of Hitler's support. He lays bare the rising political consciousness of this class, its negative and positive heritage, the legacies it inherited or failed to inherit from German history, and shows how at this crucial point it took the wrong road, towards fascism. But the analysis is not confined to the rise of German fascism, its implications are much wider. It springs immediately into new significance for the late twentieth century, when the lower middle class, albeit by other means – technological, monetarist, corporate means – are once more in the ascendancy. It is particularly appropriate that an English edition of *Heritage of Our Times* should appear at the end of the first decade of the political hegemony of that class in America and Britain – since many of the cultural reflexes Bloch identifies in the 'Golden twenties seen differently' may be reidentified in 'democratic' disguises in the consolidating reaction of the 1970s and 1980s. It was a depressing confirmation of the view that the new-found West German allegiance to democracy is little more than skin-deep to glance through the visitors' book at the recent exhibition in Munich to mark the fiftieth anniversary of that grotesque Nazi show-trial of modern art, of 'Entartete Kunst', and to discover that many contemporary Federal German citizens still share the same barbarous Nazi perception of the 'degenerate' nature of some of the very finest achievements of twentieth-century German art. The post-war European democracies have been patently unable to enter upon the heritage of the revolutionary avant-garde which Bloch defended so staunchly in this book, largely contenting themselves instead with a diet of American realism and the increasingly synthetic products of the Hollywood dream-factory.

The events of 1989–90 in Germany, the demolition of the Berlin Wall, the economic reunification of East and West, the recreation of a Greater Germany, lend Bloch's assessment of the rise of Nazism a fresh significance for our immediate times. His analysis of the cultural antecedents in German history of the idea of the 'Third Reich' and of the will towards racial and economic supremacy is rendered topical once more. Such analysis is of crucial importance at a juncture where the reunited and once again democratic German state will inevitably emerge as the dominant economic power in the European Community. The events of 1933–45 may now be viewed retrospectively from a platform of peace amongst the Western democracies which Germany has rejoined. But Bloch's work does allow us to assess how fragile and unsteady that platform may be and what 'non-contemporaneous' cultural mythologies and dangerous unclaimed heritage might still lie beneath it, not only from Germany, but from all those democracies currently congratulating themselves on the global success of the capitalist system.

Yet, alongside this negative perspective on our own period, we are also being offered here the positive legacies of the 1920s and 1930s, the unclaimed ideas and images that Hitler and Stalin tried to eradicate, and which post-war Europe and America continue to repress. Indeed, the pre-appearance and reappearance of Bloch's book itself certainly forms a perfect example of its central thesis that a genuine anticipatory heritage is not just to be claimed from the conveniently closed, safely packaged and neatly labelled ages of the past but also from the open, experimental and transitional cultural process of our own times.

Neville Plaice
Stephen Plaice

PREFACE TO THE 1935 EDITION

A broad view is taken here. The times are in decay and in labour at the same time. The situation is wretched or despicable, the way out of it crooked. But there is no doubt that its end will not be bourgeois.

The New comes in a particularly complex form. It is here considered as such, even in what hinders it. But above all in the involuntary crack and some of its shimmering signs. These are, as goes without saying, definitely found only in the victims, the deceived and intoxicated ones. The dupers themselves, the actions of those who preside over Germany, do not shimmer. They only have the character and function, for the capital that called them, of producing the most expedient degree possible of terror and confusion. There is no novelty here, not even a crack that could be used as a handhold. The powers which still *rule* today are united in spite of everything.

But those among whom they deceive are a different case. The peasants and the susceptible petit bourgeois who are not 'satisfied' in more senses than one today are in a partly obscured, partly strange unrest of a kind which was never seen before the crisis. There thus remains the question of their susceptibility or of a New which is at any rate complex even in what really or apparently hinders it. There is also an anti-capitalist 'drive' outside the proletarian stratum, although the latter, theoretically and practically, carries forward the real development, although proletarian liberation and hence, ultimately, that of all human beings can only be the work of the working class itself. The tenor of these pages, the position from which things are examined, is specifically Marxist. But precisely within this tenor another question arises, indirectly, concerning the ideological movement of the lower, and especially the upper, middle-class cultural stratum. It is this: does the declining bourgeoisie, precisely because it is declining, contribute elements towards the construction of the new world, and if so what are these elements? It is a purely indirect question, one of diabolical application; as such it has, as it seems, been neglected up to now, although it is thoroughly dialectical. For a dialectically useful 'inheritance' can be contained not only in the revolutionary rise or in the vigorous blossoming of a class, but also in its decline and the various contents which the disintegration itself releases. Seen as such, directly, the flickering or intoxicating deceit of fascism serves only big business, which thereby diverts or dims the glance of strata becoming impoverished. But indirectly there appears in this diversion the shallow crack of a previously even more shallowly closed surface, in this irrational intoxication vapour from chasms which are useful not just to capitalism alone. Apart from nastiness and speechless brutality, apart from stupidity and panic-stricken deceivability, which are illustrated by every hour and every word of the Germany of terror, there is an element of an older, romantic contradiction to capitalism, which misses things in present-day life and longs for something vaguely different. The susceptible situation of the peasants and employees has its different reflex here, and not merely one of backwardness, but occasionally one of genuine 'non-contemporaneity' as well, namely of an economic-ideological remaining existence from earlier times. Today the contradictions of this non-contemporaneity exclusively serve the forces of reaction; but in this almost undisturbed usability there lies a particular Marxist problem at the same time. The position of the 'Irratio' within the inadequate capitalist 'Ratio' has been all too abstractly cordoned off, instead of its being examined from case to case and the particular contradiction of this position possibly being concretely occupied. That is why dogs and false magicians[1] were able to break into large, formerly socialist areas undisturbed. That is why these areas are not only quiet corners and arsenals of reaction but are in danger of remaining storm corners even for later on, even for victorious Marxism. It is high time to knock these weapons out of the hands of the forces of reaction. Especially high time to mobilize contradictions of non-contemporaneous strata against capitalism under socialist direction. The 'Irratio' must not be ridiculed wholesale here, but occupied: and from a position which has a rather more genuine awareness of 'Irratio' than the Nazis and their big business partners. This purpose is served in the book, after the short introductory section 'Dust', after the differently preparatory 'Diversion' which employees have already experienced, above all by the section 'Intoxication'. One chapter of 'Intoxication' (that is, of National Socialism), 'Non-contemporaneity and obligation to its dialectic', stands at the orientating centre.

But the astonishing times are not thereby exhausted. For even the declining upper strata produce elements, or release them, which do not

---

1   As elsewhere in this introduction, Bloch has Mephisto in Goethe's *Faust* in mind here. Mephisto appears as both a dog and a false magician in *Faust*, Part I.

absolutely belong to them. The fact that each latest machine which late-bourgeois technology produces is the best is not contested by Marxists. Yet almost no inheritance whatsoever is acknowledged in the ideological manifestations and products of the late period. Apart from 'objectivity' as a technoid and at the same time apparently collective form, the final spurt is not taken into account, although it is full of curiosities. Some of these are certainly, even indirectly, totally insubstantial or only 'sociologically' interesting: but a few of them, such as above all the strange late-bourgeois 'montage', undoubtedly carry more than decline. For montage breaks off parts from the collapsed context and the various relativisms of the times in order to combine them into new figures. This process is often only decorative, but often already involuntarily experimental or, when used, as in Brecht for example, voluntarily so; it is a process of interruption and thereby one of intersection of formerly very distant areas. Precisely here the wealth of a cracking age is large, of a conspicuous mixed period of evening and morning in the 1920s. This extends from visual and pictorial connections which have hardly been like this before to Proust, to Joyce, to Brecht, and beyond, it is a kaleidoscopic period, a 'revue'. This content is served by the section 'Objectivity and montage'; at the same time it contains the specific 'Irratio' of the upper middle class itself, the cunning and refined weariness of 'empty mechanics'. The bourgeoisie prepared this lyrically and philosophically for thirty years, partly as an emergency fund, partly as a cracking place of its own fatigue. Capital now occupies these cracking places with armed petit bourgeois in the fight against the proletariat; if properly occupied, they could be breaches or at least weakenings of the reactionary front. 'Life', 'soul', 'unconscious', 'nation', 'totality', 'Reich', and similar anti-mechanisms would not be so one hundred per cent usable in reactionary terms if the revolution did not merely wish, with justification, to unmask here but, with just as much justification, concretely to outdo, and to recollect the ancient possession of these very categories. The ancient possession: which does not mean that it can be the modern one unchanged since the days of the young Marx. But the obligation to examine and occupy possible contents exists here too; this book is a scuffle, moreover in the midst of the susceptible, indeed in the midst of the enemy, in order to rob him if need be. It is confined to topical features, names and the symptom that is posited with them; the background is concrete-utopian, here also composed of the colours, which are still so involuntary, the heirlooms of a not-to-be-forgotten phase, of its end and transition. The present work contains its share of late-bourgeois temporal content, for the most part in ambiguous form and thus dialecticized.

This begins with something small, first hears its way in as it were. Always pounces on the instances anew, advances with interruptions, as is proper today. Both linguistically and thematically, until the pace is reached to cover the large questioning stretches themselves. The book was essentially written during the times it examines; and in Germany. Its theme is in fact the dust-spreading bourgeoisie in decay, and in strata and periods one behind the other: thus the 'diversion' (1924–29) is already over, the 'intoxication' (1924–33) still in full swing; but both continue to have an effect in transition. 'Objectivity and montage', as the contradictory condition of the upper strata, encompass even temporally the two lower manifestations of the transition. The accent lies not only on the unmasking of ideological appearance, but on the scrutiny of the possible remainder. Of course, the way of dealing with witches[2] is not lacking, indeed it is the critical music of every beginning, but it is in fact more important to take out of the bankrupt's estate that which appears to be susceptible and usable in mediated form, and to neutralize that which is dubious. One more word to hinder misunderstanding, which likes to make itself comfortable. Even if this work speaks not only from above, even if it also considers all kinds of evil or glittering confusion, it still does not extend its so-called little finger to the devil.[3] But hopefully – with considerably more effort than that of the little finger – he is relieved of his lying weapons and his dazzling delusions. But this does not occur through the proof alone that the petit bourgeois rebel only crookedly and dully: we knew that long ago, in any case. The fact that with them there exists 'nothing but petit-bourgeois opposition': there is no argument about this part of the assessment, for what should the petit bourgeois have at their disposal other than, at best, petit-bourgeois opposition? But more important today than this interesting, only somewhat stereotyped, assessment is differentiation and reconnaissance, is a campaign which does not underestimate the opponent, who is above all intent on booty. On booty of people who have become restless, of the frequently ambiguous, indeed revolutionary material which solely in its ambiguous capacity can serve the 'anti-capitalist' deception. We notice there is a new formulation of the question here, it does not articulate petit-bourgeois opposition itself, nor upper middle-class infection or whatever else sings the song of the old barrel-organ. Instead both conditions are only indirectly located from a Marxist position and their dialectical character noted, provided it exists – in the midst of the mere, insubstantial rottenness of decay – as one of transition. Nor has this formulation of the question the slightest thing in common either with social-democratic dilution or with Trotskyite obstructionism; since what the party did before Hitler's victory was completely correct, it was simply what it did not do that was wrong. The

2   Mephisto in *Faust*, in the Witches' Kitchen, Part I, 2517.
3   Bloch is here playing on the German proverb which reads literally, 'If you extend your little finger to the devil, he'll take your whole hand', the English equivalent of which would be, 'Give him an inch, and he'll take a mile'.

tendency destroys that which stands in its path, it inherits that which lies along its path.

This was seldom more due than today. Of course the aunt whose estate one wants to inherit must first be dead; but one can have a very good look round the room beforehand. Of course once the revolution has occurred it will liquidate a whole series of questions and apparent contents which today still count as such; but not all that is still 'irrational' is simply dissolvable stupidity. The hunger for – let us say – complications remains or it would be the first to have been appeased by the withdrawal of nourishment. The damned clearly surveyable talent has no place even in 'heaven on earth', there are questions and contents which precisely the really concrete concept does not automatically dissolve, but to which it does justice beforehand. The case is admittedly different with regard to the degree of the 'rescue' of such contents, or rather of their robbery for a different purpose. For once anyone has tasted Marxist criticism, he is not just disgusted for ever by all ideological claptrap, but also that which possibly remains after the criticism is not for him a happy end at all costs or the miserable logic of the Yes-But. Yet there often ensues only the warning of a dangerous, of an enduringly seductive quiet corner and storm corner of an irrational kind, in no uncertain terms. And the indirectly 'positive' inheritance which remains appears all the more strongly for consideration or as doubtful consideration; this 'rescue' then provides material for a Marxist problem or for propaganda among the susceptible or for neutralization. If we want to understand and overcome the remedies that are dished out precisely against genuine revolution to a bourgeois citizen becoming impoverished, then we must go – diabolically – into the bourgeois citizen's land, or rather on to his ship. He has only one ship left; for it is the age of transition. May this book play its part in determining the longitude and latitude of the final bourgeois voyage, so that it really is a final voyage.

Locarno, 1934

POSTSCRIPT, 1962

Since then almost thirty years have passed. But the times from which the present book emerged are still vividly in the air. Their vividness is even growing, precisely among young people who never experienced them and who miss them in an almost sentimental way instead, in keeping with the term 'Golden twenties' and the other, incidentally older exaggeration that until the night of 1933 Berlin was the intellectual capital of the world. But the *age of transition*, illustrated by the 1920s, has undoubtedly remained one, at least in its predisposition, and certainly in its appeal. This transition from one society to another did not blunt the class fronts, but stood in the way of any hardening into a fixed pattern. The more than interesting character of such a mixed shipping period is merely concealed in the modern West by surprising prosperity and extensive boredom, and in the modern East by equally surprising non-prosperity and monolithic boredom. The transition in the modern East, in so far as inhuman distortion and undialectical hindrance has occurred there, has even been ensnared in grim narrowness and stereotyping. The celebrated eleventh thesis on Feuerbach by Marx states: 'previous philosophers have only interpreted the world in various ways, but the point is to change it.' But above all in Franco-type countries on the eastern side this was practised to the following effect: The point is only to interpret unanimously the world decreed from above, it is forbidden on pain of downfall[4] to change it. This not even partially socialist and nevertheless, or rather therefore totalitarian system still certainly lacks much more, something distinctly different from the heritage of the transition. The hindrance there comprises far more than the merely sectarian narrowness which then promoted the débâcle of 1933. Far more than the connection missed at that time with the several dust-

---

4 Bloch is perhaps also thinking of his own fall from grace in East Germany here.

potentialities (diversion, intoxication, montage) out of collapse. With the
conscious-unconscious element of proletarianized but not proletarian
strata, then with the hypnotized experimental gaze of highly susceptible
cultural upper strata. So-called socialist realism continued to do its bit
as kitsch long afterwards to demonstrate both the aridity and the full
showy backwardness in such narrowness. But what is this in comparison with the differently lacking element whereby the greatest liberation
movement, which had been intended as definitive, could become so
alienated from itself? Capitalism with the product of two world wars
and with fascism has no need to advertise itself, but the corruption of
what is better becomes no clearer despite pharisees who often do not
even have the right to be right. The ring of freedom in the old impetus,
in the implied goal, is lacking, the inheritance of 1789, with the Ninth
Symphony which can no longer be revoked. The inheritance of corrected Natural Right is lacking, as the sought-for facultas of walking
upright, 'honoured in individuals and secured in the collective' (Natural
Right and Human Dignity).[5] And – in this respect a foil to the more
central lack of ideas in the modern West – the development of theory is
lacking, most urgently in economic terms, a reformatio literally in capite
(which does not mean 'Führer') and in membris (which certainly does
not mean an apparatus with lackeys). But what exists and is still not yet
lacking is that which made the greatest liberation movement in the
world, formulated, though not securingly thought through, appear as a
scourge of fear instead of a breaking of the last chain; that which
endowed it with the archetype of the wall instead of the 'leap from
necessity into freedom'.[6] Nevertheless, at least the aridity and narrowness are connected with that sectarian pseudo-enlightenment which
made people in the twenties so helpless against the deceitful intoxication
but also so unappreciative of an experimental art. This latter lack of
appreciation, which has remained official, is in fact called socialist realism, due to absence of both elements. Thus from this viewpoint too, it is
instructive to glance at the so little surmounted luring ground of the
Nazis, but then at the strangeness and dissolving density, now become
so homeless, of works which even today totally lack the smug gallery
tone, which still challenge their century – in so far as even their montage
is one of rhetoric, and precisely for that reason. 'Heritage of our times'
therefore, of the continuingly influential times of montage above all: if
the book devoted to this subject appears in a new, little altered edition,
then that which is dismissed and converted in it should even seem like
present times in places, negatively and positively. Together with several
pieces written at the time, which have further been inserted into the

5   A further work by Bloch himself, published in 1961.
6   Cf. Engels in *Anti-Dühring* on the 'leap of humanity out of the realm of
    necessity into the realm of freedom'.

montage of the book itself. 'The Golden twenties': the Nazi horror germinated in them, and no light fell down below here, experimental art drew its lines into unheard of regions and found nothing it can hold on to – may that be different one day. Hollow space with sparks, this will probably remain our condition for a long time, but a hollow space which allows us to walk undisguised, and with sparks which increasingly model a figure of direction. The paths in the midst of collapse are layable, right through the middle.

Tübingen, March 1962

DUST

HALF

We still are. But it only half works. The little man holds too much back.
He still thinks, for himself alone.

MUSTINESS

We live with it more than ever. Children are not taken out of the mustiness. They continue to absorb it or suffer until they become like their father. Even those who are not listening take notice of the conversations of the bourgeois conformist; so propping up the table remains, the gossip, the visitors, the false laughter and the real poison they strew amongst each other. The close, stale air still greets even those who are not breathing it. It seeps down to the young man, and up to the beautiful people. Keeps him good and quiet, them good and deaf.

GOSSIP

No one believes it could be done to them. Those with little positions would not put up with it, namely from others like themselves. The little man has no desire whatever to rebel upwards, except in quite general terms, against red tape and the like. But he lets out what is tormenting him all the more readily at home; inauthentically, as a dispute with those weaker than him, as gossip versus the neighbours. Even the peasants know Gossip, a sweet expression on his face, leaving a stink behind. But country life never lets him feel as much at home, never lets him become as much the neighbourhood itself as he does in the block of flats. The worms crawl out of this place every day; they come out of the flour that is lacking, out of the borrowed pots, out of the many morals which are there for the purpose of having offended against them. Gossip crawls up and down the stairs, holds these people together by keeping them apart. He is the crooked way of being dissatisfied, the wrongly addressed way, the desire to fight without squaring up to the opponent. If he squares up, however, hands on hips, then it is clear just what a limited person is made of. Where he is, you can never do anything right by him.

KNOWING EYES

Occasionally little people still get up satisfied. Sometimes there is enough for this, only for this and only just. But the meagrely paid man has never got beyond doing sums, and he seldom splashes out. Strange then that he finds this limited life not only cheap, but also proper.[1] That he begrudges the stratum below him anything to spread on their bread; and the top brass are doubly respected if they save. As for the beggar, he is not allowed to get beyond pennies; the coinage he is entitled to is small and, above all, it is only for bread. It pains the generous donor when poor children buy sweets with his penny; woe betide, then, the beggar who drinks away his mite that is no match for any misery. Because alms demand that the receiver is even more modest than they are themselves.

But even little people sense that they have nothing to laugh about. And they console themselves about this, namely with the illness of others which supposedly follows pleasure. It is quite in order then if enjoyment revenges itself on those who have it. The 'dissipated' young man belongs here, and especially also the 'knowing eyes'; the latter usually occur in adolescents and then preferably with dark rings around them. As if the body, of all things, were doing the creeps the favour of seeing to their business for them. As if even a hangover did not come from bad schnapps, but from riotous living. But the petit bourgeois never stop undermining their own kind, let alone those who are not their own kind, with illnesses which their revenge-drive mined in the first place. When a dancer dies, she has died of the ever wilder stimuli of her life, and the hack compounds these with consumption. Her delicate, childlike body was not up to the stresses of her way of life; a sad ending, he says, to a life without inhibitions. To the satisfaction of the

1   Bloch is playing on the German expression 'billig und recht' – 'right and proper'; 'billig' also carries its other connotation of 'cheap' here.

reader, who has in fact got vices, but still has not learnt any vices. Whereby it is precisely the petit bourgeois who are most ill, because in their fear they first infect themselves with the illnesses and pass them on. This sense of being burdened, of diseases running in the family does not occur at all in less respectable circles. The middle classes talk less about consumption among the proles than about that of the dancer, although here there usually is a truly sad ending. They see only the colds which supposedly come from the fresh air, from the same air which they basically long for themselves.

FROM NEAR AND FAR

To read a lot, the average man says, is not healthy either. Harassed fathers have nowhere to sit at home in any case. The room belongs to the housewife who cleans it, not to the man who simply yawns and eats there. The dreary home and the escape from it thus began with the middle classes, long ago, not higher up. They while away the evening among the regulars at the local with rumours and prattle, learn only from others like themselves, rack no brains. Above all, no false passion compels them to want to know more than is needed for business or pleasure. The little man knows nothing more about business than whether it is going well or badly, according to the 'times'. As far as pleasure is concerned, however, and particularly flicking through the pages, there is also the aversion of the older petit bourgeois to profitless arts, the reluctance to take them seriously. So-called brooders end up in the 'asylum', far removed from healthy common sense. Free living revenges itself on physical health, but superfluous thinking on the mind: this then is the other myth of the petite bourgeoisie. Thus it was already superficial and spouted forth, as still the full coherent body of know-ledge everywhere. It is not only the evening in the family circle which does not invite the average man to collect his thoughts. For a long time 'Die Woche',[2] with lots of pictures, also satisfied his intellectual needs, when educated circles still very definitely read coherently. From the petit bourgeois who prattles and flicks through, diverted life, often in baffling fashion, got going.

---

2 *Die Woche*: an illustrated periodical founded in Berlin in 1899, which achieved a sensational success through the new techniques of illustration and layout. It ceased publication in 1944.

KITSCH THAT WRITES

Here even what is insipid readily comes together. It writes for unalert people in the style they wish for themselves. The inside of the readers is itself squashed here, their outside they perceive is not the one in which they really are. A writer who did not deal in cut-and-dried feelings would not find any place here, in a stratum which lives by lying to itself and being lied to, which not only wants, but is itself largely kitsch. Of course if one remains in the parlour and in what it pretends to itself, then our little yesterday can still be said. This sayable stuff has both its market here from which it lives, and its so-called fount from which it draws. Bright young feeling and similar expressions, none of which is bright, young or felt any more, teem from the fount. The end remains fervent kitsch, which does not exclude filth; love's young dream and the craze for budding flesh are thus well suited for contemplative hours. These heroes do not lead us into any provocative life, but simply to grope in the dark. There is again little scope here, rummaging around in the mustiness.

UNCHECKED

Something becomes different. From below a thrust runs on. The centre now at least realizes it is poor. In fact it is a false realization; because there is a difference between never having had money and having lost one's money. But sometimes too the unique situation arises that bourgeois conformists want to renew life. Here the air is perhaps not quite so heavy as before. But it does not blow yet, it just raises dust.

PART I
EMPLOYEES AND DIVERSION

THE JADED MAN

He has had enough. But he can never see how and where. So the dependent man allows himself to go on being used. Thinks he is a different person than the one he is.

THE COLLARS

No one would come of his own accord. But later he adjusts himself. Those who sell themselves do not always give themselves completely of course. The workers are hostile to what is done with them. But the employee corresponds completely to the image that his masters fashion from him, which he allows to be fashioned from him. The way the girls lead their dreary lives (and the evening only numbs them for the next day). The way the men remain subordinate, disgruntled to themselves, cheerful in company; the way no one ventures beyond the unindependent limit. In the collar of the day, in the cheap pleasure of the evening that is specially set for them, they feel themselves to be citizens. With a sense of duty, from which there are no pickings to be had, they still polish their chains patriotically. In small towns they are still only living from the viewpoint of yesterday, but in large towns they have processions, falsely glittering pleasures too. Thus they are no longer the limited little people of dust-spreading mustiness, but new people, existing beside themselves, distracted. Who allow themselves to be diverted, by cinema or race, so that they do not collect themselves. Disperse, policemen shout in difficult times in the street, circulez, messieurs. The white-collar workers[1] sort this out quite happily by themselves, allow themselves to be sorted out.

1 Bloch uses the English expression in the original here.

SMALL TOWN (1924)

Everything is quiet here, scarcely still breathing. The blooming country-side, with peasants, stretches into the place in vain. Few like living in smaller towns, these themselves are hardly living any more. And become totally dreary when the autumn comes.

The empty streets, not even the wind feels at home in them. An old tram clatters from the station to the market-place; the light inside illuminates tired faces which do not become more cheerful, because they all know each other. Paltry shops are bursting with pots, cheap clothes, rubbish from the big city; far too many tinned preserves are ageing between them. The stationer's – soon there will be cotton-wool snow on display in the shop-window, three candles, writing paper with sprigs of pine, some silver foil. Fewer and fewer characters permeate the small town, less and less language still stewing in its own juice, less and less country loaves, good old days in the newspaper. Instead, yesterday's cliché rules, and just as the shops have their tinned preserves, public opinion comes ready set, freshly churned, as dross from Berlin. An unspeakable sadness permeates the small town with the autumn, the poorly illuminated evenings; it makes the people who are interned there fruitlessly embittered. The summer sustained the image thus far, a scent of mountains and meadows wafted in, the sky was high. But the autumn has just as constricting an effect as evening in the train, when you no longer see any landscape, only the few faces under the lamp in the compartment. There are of course exceptions, small towns with people who have set themselves up, who find truth in wine and the big wide world in the cinema. But most backwaters are so spiteful today, dead and conventional like an unhappy marriage. There is early ageing here and so little room that there is not even real emptiness, except the inward kind which the manual worker, the employee, the boss while away in separate clubs, united sentiments. Many bowls roll, everyone throws their own, but they all aim for the king-pin. Only the one down the road of course, to whom one must give a false smile.

ARTIFICIAL CENTRE (1929):

on Kracauer's *The Employees*[2]

Elsewhere the day has simply got louder, not fuller. Life in the big city foams more, swindles all the better in return. Dupes the poorly paid man, who has to pay for everything pretended to him. The workers are outside in the factories, the employees inhabit the shops, offices, streets of the big city itself. By day grey life, in the evening diverted life determines their image, fills them.

Kracauer travelled to the centre of this way of not being there. With a solitary glance which penetrates where others only report, or simply chat. In a language which can say what it sees, which sticks, with a certain sober colourfulness, closely to the recognized matter. The beginning is placed several paces ahead of the usual scientific one, and thus manages, over the whole race, to get just as far beyond the theoretical end, namely by tendentious means. Here the real situation of the employees is hit on the head or rather on the false consciousness which it has of itself. The masks which the employees put on or allow to be put on them are shown and recognized as such.

Strange though, how easily the average man allows himself to be duped about where he lives. The employees have increased fivefold in the same time in which the workers have only doubled their numbers. And their situation has also become a completely different one since the war; but their consciousness has not increased fivefold, the consciousness of their situation is in fact totally obsolete. Despite miserable pay, conveyor belt, extreme insecurity of existence, fear of old age, debarment from the 'higher' strata, in short, proletarianization de facto, they still feel they are the bourgeois centre. Their tedious work makes them more dull than rebellious, authorization papers nurture a caste-

---

2 Siegfried Kracauer, 1889–1966, cultural critic and writer, a regular contributor to the *Frankfurter Zeitung* (see 'New slave morality of the newspaper', n. 69).

consciousness which has no real class consciousness behind it at all; only the external formalities, scarcely the contents of a vanished bourgeoisie haunt any longer. In contrast to the worker they are integrated into production much more remotely; that is why economic changes are perceived only later or easily misunderstood. Only a third of employees have organized themselves into trade unions, and of these a third are social-democratic (only the most progressive are communist). The second third are democratic, the final third have been nationalistic for ages, have caste ideology (the way things are cast at the moment), are a kind of core-group for the so-called National Socialist of today. This false consciousness (false even in revolt) also extends among peasants in fact, and students add the fancy garb;[3] but it is employees who chiefly succumb to it. The unspeakable rabble of older bourgeois conformists stirs in its instincts, not folkish[4] ones at all, but malicious, fossilized, downright unfounded ones whose only notion of anti-capitalism is to beat the Jew to death as a 'usurer'. But distraction plays the greater role here, acquiescent distraction from real life. It dams life back to nothing but youth, to inflated beginnings, so that the question concerning the Where To never arises. It promotes sport and the evening sheen of the street, the exotic film or the differently glittering kind, indeed even the 'new objective'[5] facade of nickel and glass. Nothing lies behind this except dirty linen: but it is precisely this which is supposed to be concealed by the glassy openness (just as the abundance of light only serves to increase the darkness). Cafés, films, Lunaparks[6] show the employee the direction in which he has to go: signs, much too illumin-ated for them not to be suspicious, indicating how to evade the true direction, namely that towards the proletariat. With which the employee now shares everything: deprivation, worry and insecurity, only not the clear consciousness of what his condition actually is. Of course distrac-tion, precisely as a colourful street-fair, has another side to it, one which does not favour closed mustiness. Of course this side throws up dust too and this time already interrupting, sparkling *dust to the power of two* as it were. But that does not prevent the fact that, directly, the whole evasion simply amounts to deception which is supposed to con-

3 Bloch is alluding to the ceremonial uniforms of the reactionary student fraternities in Germany, which were hotbeds of anti-semitism.
4 A National Socialist concept of an original Aryan people entitled to racial supremacy in Germany.
5 'Neue Sachlichkeit' ('New Objectivity'), an architectural and artistic move-ment in the Weimar Republic. Generally seen as a reaction to Expressionism in its emphasis on 'objective reality', it was in fact as much a realist offshoot from Expressionism as a reaction against it. A major exhibition of 'Neue Sachlichkeit' was mounted in Mannheim in 1925.
6 A term for an amusement park (probably derived from the name of such a park at one time in Berlin).

ceal the place and ground on which it occurs. The culture of the employees, says Kracauer in a telling sentence, is escape from revolution and from death. And the masters, the master supervisors at the top (as one employee called them before the criminal court), are subject to the very appearance they pretend. They borrow it from the employees, present bathing glamour in films and the ever more amusing press, incapable of having and printing any other content here. Everywhere the same joke (even if enjoyed much more fully at the top), life as 'business': as tedium by day, as escape at night. The new centre does not save, does not think about tomorrow, diverts itself and soon everything.

THE DAZZLING FILM STAR

Clearly, this new breed has become lighter. Otherwise it could not endure its life, its fleeting life. Sport already loosens up, the film supplied a feeling for gesture. The type has veered with the wind, not to say like a sailor; in fact, he does not want to be a type at all, but a character, and he captains his own ship every evening. The living person rebels against the dependency and degradation of the conveyor belt; here however not as an oppressed class, but as a caste which has seen better times, as a character cast for the part. Through this lived-out appearance people hope to keep themselves at the top, and copy precisely those who caused them to plunge to the bottom, namely the genuine masters, the genuine characters of today. These are the individual managers themselves, the actual mechanizers of life; but the victims join forces with them, not with the proletarian comrades. The shop-girl can easily carry off the rose-tinted or suntanned lady, but the male employee fails to carry off the master. Because the lady also blooms in the erotic field, not just in the social one, and a well-groomed exterior can make up for a great deal here; but the so-called master-man[7] is far from one today when posing as the master of profit. Indeed, the employee cannot even assume the 'aura' of the boss (because the latter mostly does not have one); so the new type develops through the film, allows his feeling for gesture to crystallize into the mere film character. So that the maliciousness of the earlier petit bourgeois towards dancers, people who enjoy life, and the like, ceases; on the streets what Ernst Blass[8] once sang becomes a reality: the gentlemen come as if from operettas. The appre-

7 'Herrenmensch', i.e. a member of the *Herrenvolk*, the Nazi concept of the master-race.
8 Ernst Blass, 1890-1939, Berlin Expressionist poet and author of *The Nature of the New Art of Dance* (1922). In the Expressionist period he also edited a Heidelberg review, *Die Argonauten*, to which Bloch contributed.

ciation of the Führer also first began in front of the film; supremely the hero up there stands out from the crowd, supremely he is illuminated by rotten dazzling highlights. Extraordinary too the erotic effect which precisely these false characters had on those who are equally false. Fraudulent bundles of nerves were admired as baby-dolls; amorphous heaps of fat had popular appeal as gentle giants. The really beautiful or victorious film star in particular cast the spell that befits him. The more life deteriorated and the more fraudulent the plot which replaced it, the more easily the petit bourgeois became the gushing girl in the presence of champions. Through boxers he drew himself up physically to his personal height, through film heroes mentally. The boss had wanted him to leave the prole behind him, and respect for himself commanded him to obey. After all, so many heroes likewise come from humble beginnings in order to rise out of them all the more beautifully: make way, if no longer for efficiency, then for happiness.[9] Only Chaplin remains as poor as before and trips the masters up, modestly. But he too is seen as funny, and the masters from whom the poor devil escapes in a really fairytale way dazzle in the film right alongside him and are by no means refuted, let alone exploded. Even the colportage-like paths which lead from the hut to the drawing room remain a game. Beautiful gestures, naked shoulders, swiftly mushrooming and lucky beggars, but they still entice in vain.

9 'Make way for efficiency': cf. Chancellor Bethmann-Hollweg's speech to the Reichstag, 28 September 1916.

BELOW THE BORDERLINE[10]

Here too, how idle things are. There was not much energy left to read anyway. Only people who have done nothing all day are mentally alert in the evening. In fact, if the glance strays below the borderline, then immediately this is no longer that relevant.

Not merely the reader is to blame for this, but also those who supply him. Of their own accord, of course, most businessmen do not go beyond the day in which they flourish. And they unwind in the evening: thus we see the tired man who comes home from work and only reads the yawning newspaper. The life he has is printed large, another life which diverts him and is nothing to do with him is gossiped about. But of course the men who reflect life below the borderline in the newspaper by cutting and scribbling certainly do their bit to turn it into fun, veeringly and versatilely. Partly they seem good for nothing other than copying out or checking through all kinds of things they do not know. Partly they overrate themselves, shack up grumpily in their job, ready to leave at any opportunity of becoming authors. For the centre, which has chosen its profession and fills it, few seem cut out here.

Thus there is a gradual descent into fun, the latter becomes increasingly arbitrary. The business section of a good bourgeois newspaper is still half true, occasionally it roughens up laundered reports. The political section has character, so to speak, namely that of the publisher's capital and of the large advertisements. But even the reports in this section grow all the more fantastic the further away the scene of events gets, the thinner therefore actual knowledge of their subjects becomes. Thus the feature section begins precisely in Mexican, Indian

10   In this section Bloch is using the phrase 'Unter dem Strich' which literally refers to the old German practice of ruling off the entertainment section of the newspaper with a line. Figuratively it has come to mean 'not up to scratch'. We have rendered it here as 'below the borderline'.

and Chinese regions, i.e. wherever there is an unclear market and no familiar capitalist plane. To become out-and-out entertainment below the borderline: entertainment from events that do not really disturb the businessman, which are above all portrayed as harmlessly or as 'colourfully' as possible. Here the captioned cartoons stand unconnected side by side, indeed even the instructive has to be entertaining. There are exceptions in two or three old papers; otherwise there is the art of evasion everywhere, aversion to the real matter.

Such pens can and must dance around everything. Overblown bourgeois consciousness overblows itself once more. For the average reader the emptiness in which he has to live is boarded up with nothing but inexact little pieces. The man of means however, who actually conducts business out of the emptiness, makes himself immune even to poison, the modest poison of a Toller[11] for example, by taking it from his paper in stimulating doses. And for the time being the scribe may say everything, because he has nothing to say.

11 Ernst Toller, 1893–1939, Expressionist poet and playwright who was also leader of the Munich Soviet Republic in 1919 which lasted for only one month. Though imprisoned for five years for his part in the Republic, he was later criticized on the left for his liberal humanitarian stance and hedonistic life-style.

A VICTORY OF THE MAGAZINE (1929)

Further and further afield now effort is omitted. The newspaper is cheerfully laid out, in order to be skimmed over all the more pleasantly. On the way to the office, during the breaks in a life that hardly comes to its senses in bed. Even the periodical is either no longer one or it perishes where it wants to remain one.

Not five lines are printed about poems, never mind people being given these to read themselves. A novel must be reviewed in no more than thirty lines unless it puts the bourgeois himself, the way he would like to see himself, into the bookcase. Essays, which in France for example, as an undiverted bourgeois country, immediately magnetized negatively or positively, are printed here just as if they never existed. Stresemann[12] once complained in vain that the periodical as supplement of the daily paper was dying out and gave him no opportunity to inform himself about the intellectual life of the country. In France the bourgeois are even less advanced in the consciousness of their ideological decay; so people like Briand[13] are informed over there. But the advert controls German printing space: the cigarette is illustrated sometimes ethereally, sometimes voluptuously, a stir is created about considerably less than an omelette, and only the writers lack space. If we put the printing space of cosmetic and tobacco advertising together, then Germany could have a periodical in comparison with which the 'Neue Rundschau'[14] would be a mere publisher's brochure. In France the sharp

12 Gustav Stresemann, 1878–1929, briefly German Chancellor in 1923, Foreign Minister, 1923–9.
13 Aristide Briand, 1862–1932, Foreign Minister of France, 1925–32, signed the Treaty of Locarno with Stresemann in 1925 agreeing to observe the demilitarization of the Rhineland.
14 Founded in 1890 as a weekly periodical in Berlin called the *Freie Bühne*; from 1894 it became a monthly called *Neue Deutsche Rundschau*, finally acquiring the name of *Neue Rundschau* in 1904. It appeared in Berlin up to 1944, was then published as a quarterly in Stockholm (1945–9), and from 1950 in Frankfurt.

commentary still exists, the space-creating essay; in our country even formerly great reviews seem like 'cream which takes the bite out of the wind' or 'like the miracle of the perfect mixture which makes our Arabian blend so palatable'. Thus they can be replaced by Mouson and Reetsma;[15] but who can help Stresemann? Quod licet Jovi, non licet bovi.[16] Only the President of the Reich has the right not to have read any books since his cadet training.[17]

At the same time papers still exist, some really fresh, some not quite faded. A typical example of the former would be the 'Weltbühne',[18] of the latter the 'Neue Rundschau'; there are also more distinguished ones, they still preserve the times when people spoke about poverty as the great radiance from within and thought nothing of it. Left-wing periodicals are read by shadowy people, oily ones who need some vinegar, Jewish and other malcontents who use wit or the caustic tone as a release. The writers of these things often understand the art of always being in the wrong place on time, some are turncoats by nature who do not really want to arrive at all. Activists are on the market whom no one hires, journalists are themselves sometimes the type they are fighting, whom they equally entertain with possible and impossible jokes. This fosters a certain feeling of jubilation on the left, often useful and preserving space for more exact things, often quite abstract and without substance. There is of course a degree of light over this, so that it can be said: just as the great democratic press remains (who knows for how much longer), even though the democratic party, not to mention its outlook, no longer exists, so too in the plus which a man like Ossietzky[19] gave to the 'Weltbühne', the USP[20] has been preserved and

15   Cosmetic and tobacco manufacturers respectively.
16   'What is allowed to Jove is not allowed to the ox.'
17   The president of the Reich at this time was Hindenburg, a military figure not renowned for his wide reading.
18   A socialist political weekly which began as *Die Schaubühne* ('The Stage') founded by Siegfried Jacobsohn in 1905, renamed *Die Weltbühne* ('The World Stage') in April 1918. The most influential journal in the Weimar Republic. Banned in 1933, but continued to be published in various European cities as *Die Neue Weltbühne*. Revived after the war as a weekly journal in the GDR. Bloch was a frequent contributor to *Die Neue Weltbühne*.
19   Carl von Ossietzky, 1889–1938, pacifist writer, who became editor of *Die Weltbühne* on the death of Jacobsohn in 1926.
20   USPD (Unabhängige Sozialdemokratische Partei Deutschlands), the Independent Social Democratic Party of Germany split from the SPD (the Social Democrats) in 1917, as an anti-war party. The party went into alliance with the Spartacists, led by Karl Liebknecht and Rosa Luxemburg, and supported the extra-parliamentary soviet system during the failed German revolution of 1918–19 in Berlin, Munich and elsewhere. The remainder of the party eventually remerged with the SPD in 1922. Bloch is suggesting that elements of it were preserved in the spirit of *Die Weltbühne*.

better things than this radical construct of war — or rather of peace. But as far as the *arts* periodicals à la 'Neue Rundschau' are concerned, they no longer have any current stratum at all behind them, only one from yesterday that is vanishing. Previously there was a centre here of educated business people and property-owning academics; this centre cultivated a certain art and education in the home. Alongside the soil of fat profit some garden earth blossomed; in good families a more refined art of language papered over the crack of the second generation. But along with the subscribers to this culture its writers have disappeared too; and all that has remained is a mere blurb of the times which has its neutrality in the routine fare of 'trends' and 'observations'. Quite right then that this disappears; the place of the falsely coherent muses is taken, as is only fitting, by the incoherent magazine. An American construct that has long been appropriate to the lower level of the middle class there; with this, good honest fun also begins, fun taken to its logical conclusion. Of course the diverted are running away from real life, but those who collected themselves in a merely artistic way were not any closer to it. Let alone the amount of education that even today, through lecture and radio, as a finished product, is displaced and left incomplete, reified for a second time. A consciousness which ignores the everyday so studiously is worse than diversion. Which, when it ignores the everyday and is used as distraction from it, nevertheless likewise contains its emptiness. The fairground of diversion distracts and numbs, but even so it is still — a fairground. Images from all over the world, while entertaining the employee, sustain the flow in which he finds himself.

APPEARANCE THAT DESCRIBES

A fresh glance is welcome here. The price being that the writer who has it reaches his readers only in appearance. Younger portrayers, no longer willing, nor even able to provide educated appearance, seek another instead; that of youth in itself, for example, or of what it has 'experienced'. This subject-matter was the war for a time, more precisely the experience of the front in it, the comradely, dangerous existence far from home. On the strength of which they sought to extricate themselves from merely central-bourgeois questions by setting them in the trenches. The subject-matter of war thus came, ten years after the war, just at the right time to replace, for literary sons of the bourgeoisie who wanted to remain so, the rejected appearance of their class. But significantly (so that the appearance would not be punctured) war remained a merely emotional subject-matter for them, although the spiritual must have been the least important part of it. The war-content was a different one from that of experiences at the front of an abandoned, desperate, communal or heroic kind. The stalemate is demonstrated, in so many experiences, also by the fact that war hardly contributed to bourgeois subject-matter anything that would not have been there already in pre-war times. At the same time this is true, by a long chalk, of the literary conquest of the so-called big wide world and of the means of getting out into it. Of course there is less soul here, less In-Vain of terror, more the generously accumulating glance which the car, the aeroplane and the travel ulster bestow. Yet even the travel books, whether written by Hauser,[21] whether by the still available Edschmid,[22] stand in refreshed appearance. They too only collect abroad in order to divert all the more exotically at home; without the wilderness of colpor-

---

21 Heinrich Hauser, 1901–55, travel writer who specialized in sea stories.
22 Kasimir Edschmid, 1890–1966, Expressionist writer of exotic novels and
   short stories.

tage and yet without precision. Such books call out the circulez, messieurs! only in literary terms or filch subject-matter which in this way
becomes educated finery. Even subject-matter of misery, bloodhounds,
slaughterhouses, paddy-fields and no sweetmeats would be worth something only amidst real brothers. Amidst diversion nothing moves from
its place, yet of course it becomes fluid.

SUBSTITUTE AND NEW

Not everyone plays along here. Certainly not the peasant, the manual worker and retailer only a little. But the new centre does so all the more, it seeks a life which it intends and cannot lead, in substitute form. Petit bourgeois never call each other such amongst themselves, not even as an insult. This too is connected with the substitute which they are now striving for, above all in their predominant stratum, that of the employees. Anyone who does not join in the dance with them is not called a petit bourgeois but a stuffy conformist, and has indeed passed on.[23] Versatilely, the employee gazes after empty, distracting sheen in his empty street. So that the sedate bourgeois runs after him, gets up from his regular table, is confusingly on the way. In the evening, when lit, the dust of the day looks really colourful and alluring. This entices, but does not fulfil, does not create the desire for more genuine things, but for things that are always new.

23 Bloch is alluding to Matthias Claudius's classic poem 'Death and the Maiden', in which the skeleton Death dances with a young girl: 'Pass on ! Oh please pass on! Go, frenzied man of bones!'

PART II
NON-CONTEMPORANEITY
AND INTOXICATION

THE DARK ONES

Do not want to go along any more. Often only because they are not fit for it. So the embittered man is completely left behind here, bloody and dark. More and more people are becoming both together today.

LEAP BACK

Feel quite a lot in the process. Lash out around them, particularly down below, where they are in danger of sinking. This new kind of centre turns away crookedly, turns in gloomily on itself, but aggressively in both cases. It can still definitely be distracted, yet no longer towards something, but rather against something and in the wrong direction again of course. Those people shout out to it: Stop thief, who are this themselves. A distinction is made between grubbing and bubbling money, the one in Jewish, the other in Aryan hands. The one is to be abolished, because the small investor is not one any more, the other to be preserved because it pays for the movement. We would see those calves who choose their butcher themselves here, if the smell of many of these calves were not precisely that of butchers. But it is also odd what the centre thus became capable of; the hitherto dullest stratum is steaming. We see impulses, so brutal and crazy, so little bourgeois, that they are hardly human any more. Something wants to make its leap here. Does not know where it comes from, where it will land, what it will take in its teeth.

RAGE AND MERRIMENT (1929)

It even throws down all kinds of things for itself. Life is hard, the people need thrills. New are those which are drawn from the life of those who are even worse off. It is even nice to hound poor bastards just like the rich do to oneself. Brutal, but also merry rage then lets off steam. Passes on the kicks from above to those down below.

Resourceful minds make this possible for everyone today. Here is an example in passing, it stands (quite soon perhaps) for more. The Festival Hall in Frankfurt organized for two weeks and longer a so-called International Continuous-Marathon-Dance-Championships. The technical direction lies in the hands of a company into which one would not like to fall. Ross Amusement Co.; it sounds as if it has been dragged out of the stable by fat Wallace.[1] About 25 couples have to keep dancing day and night, 45 minutes per hour. The other 15 minutes are intended for resting, relieving themselves, eating or sleeping. Dancers who go to the toilets during the dancing period receive three minutes off, for which they have to dance on for five minutes during the break. The competing couples have to keep their feet in motion during the whole duration of the dance; one hand of one partner continually resting on the other, as if for pleasure, as if in the drawing room. This has nothing to do with the benefits of sport, but all the couples are to preserve 'a socially dignified appearance'. The dignity of the tight patent-leather shoes, the collars, the evening dress; Spanish boots[2] are drawn from this dignity and a gag for contorted faces which thereby become twice as merry. The winner of the championships is the couple which is the last to collapse on the dance floor. Around twenty couples have already laboured in vain, some

---

1 Ross means 'steed' in German, which is why Bloch uses the image of the stable here.
2 Spanische Stiefel: an instrument of torture for crushing the legs, also with the figurative meaning of a forcible restriction of freedom.

after over 300 hours of dancing. They carry off nothing but a bad heart and the whistles of the gallery.

The couples are just stepping forward again. Staggering on to the terrible oval of the dance floor, shoved by invigilators. In the vast hall stand two tents, of prison canvas, with little clouded glass windows in them. Beneath these the dancers have been spending their fifteen minutes, for weeks, in a stinking atmosphere day and night, with bleeding feet, tortured eyes and a body like lead. The management gives 1000 RM[3] to anyone who can prove that one of the male or female dancers has exceeded the rest period of fifteen minutes. Music, loudspeakers, a compère's speeches laced with humour fill the break outside. Whistles are already burning a hole in the rest period; the jolly dancers do not hear them. They have to be beaten until they come round; trumpet blasts in front of the tent door, a rapturous hall. But the resurrection of the dead occurs softly, and they form up, for the old routine. Bear their courtly love on to the dance floor, socially dignified. Breaking bodies hold one another, one partner's hand on the bleeding flesh of the other. The pot begins to shake again, from which the jackpot ticket is to be drawn.

One dancer certainly will not get it. No 1000 RM after twenty days of dancing, not even 60 RM, which will go to the one who comes sixth, the lucky beggar. 'But Pitou', says the brochure, 'is so tired, the state of his feet is so bad, that he could drop out at any time. His partner has now also become very tired from all her encouragement and it can be expected that she will also drop out soon too.' The fellow certainly looks as if he were staggering out of the torture chamber to the scaffold; red-hot tongs would bring him round. But this way his head is dropping, his eyes are closed, saliva is flowing, his arms are dangling or lying heavily on a poor, blonde, unhappy partner. A Goya mask has risen from unutterable sleep, and more than this: Ross Amusement Co. presents the materialization of one of the damned. The layer of haze from the other world hangs about him in wisps, curdled, whitish and disgusting about a moving sorrow. Suddenly the fellow grows wild, the wisps of sleep which had trailed behind him or in which he was shrouded melt away, he breaks free and even at the end of the dance, indeed while the music has already stopped and the couples are promenading, he storms all over the place with his partner on a crazy flight, to nowhere, lifts her up like an animal with which he is fighting, like a crowbar against invisible enemies, until he is completely woken by the roaring of the three-thousand-strong hall and smiles at the judge, terrible and saved, as a bloodhound at least of this world. And the band begins to play cheerful tunes again, a few couples even dance genuine figures, and the girls are uniformly fresher and neater than the men. But

3   Reichsmark.

the figures soon cave in again, and when the couples, as planned for the last day, have to spend their rest period on the dance floor itself, when the audience 'is given the chance to see how the dancers sleep and are looked after in this period', then nothing but corpses lie on the shavings of this floor. The numbers of the dancers are sewn on to them with a scrap of canvas at the bottom of their right trouser leg. The audience are invited to support their favourites, which they need more than ever during the final stages of the contest. When large ships sink and now lie down below, the water fills all rooms and flows through with a light motion: thus it is easy for every raiser of the dead to imagine how the corpses of the passengers have risen in the dining saloon and dreamily sway past one another, always in a circle, forming couples, forming figures, swaying and nodding, the gentlemen in dinner-jackets over their stinking flesh, the ladies in evening dress and always in a circle. What would be in the water there, would be in the air here and made of wood, if the couples were not still alive and Ross Amusement Co. did not have the whip in its hands, for the perpetuum mobile of agony.

The dancers have voluntarily agreed to this. As voluntary as unemployed people are today who provide this spectacle for others of their kind. The unemployed, petit bourgeois and proletarians take up three quarters of the hall, are fooled into viewing the torture down there as sport. As sport which has no other goal than the collapse that is postponed the longest, no other laurels than those for the longest suffering. A third of the voters are Nazis today; here in the hall more than half of them must set the tone. If not in terms of numbers, then in terms of the instincts which they have brought into the crowd. Outside stand a few dozen average motor cars, which must admittedly belong more to the business world than to society. 'Society' does not yet need this dry slaughter, it only hires out the festival hall for it. It still has masses enough beneath it who are worse off than it is and whom it can disembowel in the daily Colosseum. What Greeks are we who have such a marathon, and what a message is brought from it.[4] What nastiness and boring brutality in these circuses, what stupidity and ignorance even in their long-stemmed title. Prague and other cities are said to have banned Ross Amusement Co.; in Germany the police control the smooth admission. What the soul of the people is cooking up here[5] will shortly be served up in quite an acceptable form.

---

4   Pheidippides, the first 'marathon' runner, ran from the Athenian army to Athens to announce their victory at the battle of Marathon against the Persians in 490 BC. He died of exhaustion upon reaching the city and delivering his message.
5   Bloch is playing here on the phrase 'die kochende Volksseele', 'the seething (lit. cooking) populace'.

SAXONS WITHOUT FORESTS (1929)

Live and let live, this often looks easy. But if business is not running as usual, then the wit becomes sharp. Hates all those who sell the same product, seeks to oust them more than ever. Now many shops next door are Jewish, some perhaps also better run. Hatred thus becomes particularly rewarding, and transparent too: Jews out, namely out of the other shop. And if one hits Jewish capital and uses this as a distraction, then perhaps one will rescue one's own. Since the bell on the door has been rusting, the shopkeeper's gaze is particularly blue.

But many are bettering themselves now, with blond hair, inwardly too. The little man likes to feel noble, that makes up for the lack of something to spread on his bread. He feels considerably better behind his desk and shop counter since he is Nordic or fully recognized in his blondness at least as regards his blood. Primarily looking down in his blondness, he equally looks up to himself; Teut[6] makes him proud of his nakedness and strengthens narcissism under his clothes, in his meagre post. Racial pride becomes the noble crest of the roturier,[7] serves more than ever the craftiest demagogy: it completely encloses the slavedriven individual in his ring of blood, gives him German honour for bread, thwarts the class struggle. But it makes the racially interpreted 'nation' just as personal, into the self-esteem of the individual blond body; so that the Teuton, satisfied with his blood, does not crave a share in the ownership of the other riches of the nation. It is just strange how precisely the average German so likes to celebrate his blood. If nothing but Friesians lived here, then at least the racial talk would come from exactly the same mouth. But Germany is, as is well-known, particularly varied, also fruitfully mixed and certainly for the least part Nordic. For

6 Teut: the fantasy notion of an old Germanic God, which arose in the eighteenth century (conflating the name of the god Tuisto with that of the Teutons).
7 A person not of noble birth.

the petit bourgeois the Nordic nobleman is perhaps necessary to sustain his false consciousness, but he himself is no such thing in terms of his blood. Celts, Romans, even 'Ostians'[8] live in the west and south of the Reich; the east is almost totally Slavonic, a thin, not even explicitly Nordic stratum of conquerors and immigrants lies over it. Indeed, the Nordic racial cliché is so little patriotic that, when it crowns the Nordic as the noble race, it could almost be an ideology for treason. England, Scandinavia, even Northern France are more Germanic, above all more North Germanic than the large mixed race of Germany. 'Germania' is a chunk of the International, and its ecclesiastical state lies rather on the Thames than in Colonia Agrippina or even in the town of Zabrze, which is now called Hindenburg. So the folkish crew would have to throw not only the Jews but the greatest part of Germany out of it in order to be in their 'Germany'. In the flesh they are themselves mostly 'sinners against blood', and have been so for hundreds of years: that is how dubious 'race' is, if one is not a Viking or not a – Jew.

On the other hand the Jews are silent, who are precisely the last who need to be silent here. They leave every racial book undisturbed in its anti-semitism: all Aryans noblemen and only depicted thus, all Jews master crooks – as if the master crooks had to be shy of servile churls; as if there was not also the finest, the most well-cooked racial image in Israel. The Jews permit the nonsense that such a countless mixed race in Germany posits itself as one hundred per cent, to slander Israel, a race moulded for centuries, as a pariah. To be of mixed race like most Germans is basically no misfortune and no inferiority; but the nastiness and stupidity stink to high heaven when this very mixed race considers itself superior to the race of the Bible, as if the Jewish grandmother were a venereal disease. A faceless rabble not only abuses the rabble in the old Jewish race, but raves against the character of this race, from which it once received the Bible; indeed, if we remain for a moment in the sphere of racial ideology, then it must be said: only 'canaille' can rage in this way against 'race', real race would have to honour the other, if it is (in the opinion of the anti-semites themselves) as strong as in the case of the Jews. The Jewish bourgeois, the empty intellectual is another story, one which he shares with nothing but Aryans, because it does not belong to the annals of race but to the ledger of capitalism: but 'foreignness' to the Jew, to the Jewish character ab ovo? To all those who still call themselves Christians, or at least to their forefathers, the biblical world was after all once very familiar and they put their trust in Jesus. What bright lights precisely the anti-semite might surround himself with,[9] and how

---

8 An Alpine race.
9 Bloch is here playing on the phrase, 'jemandem ein Licht aufstecken', 'to put someone wise', the idea here being that the anti-semite is putting himself wise.

supremely high indeed he would illuminate, if the history of his people had become the devotional book of the white race; instead of him now repressing this fact from his consciousness, with astonishing success. But even the conscious renouncers of the Bible, the honest neo-pagans of the land, thrive on Jewish proximity, *copy* (as infertile as the anti-semite wishes and makes the Jew out to be, and wholly without understanding the meaning) the category of the 'chosen people'. The nation as an object of patriotic feeling begins only with the French Revolution, of course, with the victory of the French bourgeoisie, which smashed the arrogant International of the nobility; la grande nation of Louis XIV still by no means included the 'roture', and Friedrich II of Prussia by no means felt German. But however powerfully the German feeling for the fatherland came through later and however much medieval Romanticism embellished the states of the high protective tariff, especially of imperialism: the myth of the chosen people does not come to the Germans from their bourgeoisie, not even from the Romanticism of the old Reich. But it clearly comes from the Bible, and it is the only thing which still connects the wild olive tree of the German pagans with the genuine olive tree of Israel, on to which it was once grafted. When the Aryan went off to Palestine in the Crusades, he first beat Israel to death at home; if the swastika crusader wants to be the chosen people, he must slander the original today, crush it under his boots, make it into a 'world plague' and exterminate it, in order to be 'chosen' himself, to have any 'race' at all. The race of a non-Jew, which he now has of course; for Saxons without forests, for the many present Saxons of the Reich it has become blood and forests. There is certainly no German *culture* without the Bible; the best Germans have 'assimilated' themselves to it no less than the best Jews have done in turn to German culture. That very culture which has the Bible at its heart, and which extends from Eckhart to – Mahler. But in point of fact, as far as race is concerned: race in the organically well-cooked sense is more certainly manifest in the Jews than in most Germans; and race in its only value-sense: as an impetus to proper humanity[10] – has been taught distinctly enough precisely by Jews not to have it confused with stockbreeding. Or with the fighting league of the commercial middle classes or with the money-grubbing gestures, 'predatory' gestures of late capital. In view of the fact that many Jews are drones, there is no reason to spare them, but also none to checkmate them differently from the Aryan exploiters. In view of the fact that many Jews in the city have become intellectual, this flatly clever, abstract, non-committal element, there is just as little reason to tolerate this kind of intelligence, but certainly none to over-

10 'Menschenähnlichkeit': the Blochian concept of 'menschenähnlich werden', 'becoming like proper human beings', posits the utopian condition of man in his fully realized humanity.

look capitalism as the basic essence which is singing its swansong here too and uniting the harm of Joseph with the harm of Teut very effectively. But the fact that so many Jews apply themselves to this spirit of haggling (yet no longer as the 'gravediggers' of 'German faith and honesty'): this deterioration certainly cannot be straightened out from the standpoint of Stinnes,[11] but only from that of – Marx the Jew; and those who stand with Marx are the least acquainted with this deterioration, precisely as Jews. Many a German man will perhaps turn to them when his warriors have done enough Jewish advertising. When people desire in vain to obtain a piece of bread, a mouthful of truth in the emporium of the Nazis (which promises to stock everything).

11   Hugo Stinnes, 1870–1924, a prominent German industrialist.

ROUGH NIGHT[12] IN TOWN AND COUNTRY (1929)

Until recently the peasant was not foreign to anyone. The path into town, and out of it, was nearby or had points of transition. The fat country itself, one plunged in as into sleep, into collecting, colourful sleep. Those who had to paint, to write, learned to love the silence from another side too. Like the peasants, the painters did their day's work, often very early on; something rose from the sap. The soil sprouted, its various fruits were sold in the town.

Whereas now the soil is irritated, its people and itself. The economic causes are not obscure, their effects all the more astonishing. The average town is today, partly, just desolate, but the country throws up mud. The average town is partly populated by the educated, who feel uneasy in the ploughing up of the usual world and who therefore cultivate inner values. But the country stands out qualitatively against the times, digs under beeches (no Jewish beech is among them)[13] for rotten treasures. The average or plush town has only remained somewhat outside on the path of Berlin, yet still does not leave behind any *pathetic* corpse, with the significant exception of Munich. Whereas from the country old sap rises into long-forgotten shoots, it nourishes National Socialists and folkish mythologists, in short, arises as *pastorale militans*. Before the war, we said, it was related to everything that was sprouting, no matter to what end and on which floor it was growing. The germinating power from the soil was strong, but neutral as it were; images and ideas, although they were gladly elaborated in the country, acquired no ideology from it. The painters of the first Expressionist document, the 'Blue

12 A reference to the period of the twelve nights from Christmas Day to Epiphany that constituted the old Germanic pagan festival surrounding Wotan and the Wild Hunt.

13 'Judenbuche': a reference to a famous *novelle* by Annette von Droste-Hülshoff, 1797–1848.

Rider',[14] lived in Upper Bavaria, and the Murnau glass pictures[15] were no folklore for them, but witnesses to their own, highly topical fantasies. Today, however, precisely the windcheaters draw their dullness from Swabia and Bavaria, even though spotted with mildew, and the 'forces' which come to light from homeland and folksiness exclusively serve petit-bourgeois reaction. The Murnau glass pictures (pars pro toto) have become memorials of a reactionary regional art or basement windows of a romanticism of the earth which Marc's and Kandinsky's Blue Subject-Rider certainly did not intend. Antiques in the country are no longer seen as a piece of native Tahiti, loved as cooperative wonderlands as it were, by people in the direction of Gauguin, but they have become 'old German wine taverns' again, at best decorations of grim spookiness. Pan, in particular, is no longer bucolic as in the olden days, at the time of Beethoven, at the time of the Rousseauesque, joyful love of nature. The pastorales of Beethoven and Schubert, even of Bruckner and Mahler, were still congenial initiations into stream and field, into the unirritated soil of our southern Germany. The demon Beethoven composed, when he went out into nature, 'cheerful feelings on arrival in the country'; here was an *idyllic* circulation of Pan, and his *sublime* one stood, despite the storm which was appropriate to the demon Beethoven, in the Christian god. The less demonic but folkish Pfitzner,[16] if he wrote pastorales, would like to compose nothing but cadaveric poison, an anti-Berlin and this without light. In short: if the average town was only a communications zone, the country has become a front against Berlin; and the situation of this front is the strangest of all.

Namely because it is so well and evenly prepared in the previously easy south. At the risk of becoming mythological ourselves, we must still give credit to the Swabian and Bavarian *location* as well. For more than anywhere else a kind of faith – albeit thoroughly interested – is still at work here which is not only capitalist, but which rather seems to draw additional force from older ideologies, indeed from the soil itself, at which these were directed. Even landed property here in southern Germany and in Switzerland is not just capital, not just the (very much older) guarantor of personal freedom, but a corner of the church of the earth as it were, a piece of mythical *enchantment by the soil*. The spell is admittedly shrewd enough not to go back any further than the desire for property and freedom of the average peasant. It is certainly not so archaic as to disturb the family egoism, the 'Natural Right' of parcelled-

---

14 A group of artists founded in Munich in 1911 including Kandinsky, Klee and Marc.

15 Kandinsky often visited and painted in Murnau (a Bavarian market town on the Staffelsee) in the years leading up to the First World War and extended the Murnau tradition of glass painting with glass-pictures of his own.

16 Hans Pfitzner, 1869–1949, composer.

out landed property, for example; the archaic element does not recall really archaic conditions, communal property or common land. But the spell also blocks every recent rationalization statically enough: the whole of Alemannia-Bavaria is obsessed with the earth, and its writers and ideologists all the more so the more Christian they seem. Hebel[17] too was a friendly country spirit, his characters are journeymen from Segringen in the big wide world; even Gottfried Keller,[18] if he can be mentioned at all in this context, transposed Switzerland as it is; he causes an incessant fairytale light, hence a strange and wondrous light, to play in it. Yet the arch-Alemannic Gotthelf[19] already mirrors nothing any more, least of all into the distance, he preaches without further addition precisely *Bernese spirit* against the spirit of the times; and the location of Berne already denotes a reactionary-mythical content on the title page itself. The spirit of Frankfurt or Nuremberg would never be automatically antithetical to the spirit of the times (in the sense of movement) in this way; the urban type of Berlin would be conceivable in Franconia, but never in a country where the sheer *geography*, as in Gotthelf, already signifies a kind of cult of the soil, indeed cult of the earth. Switzerland was also undoubtedly very congenial to the great mythologist Bachofen;[20] 'in the confinement of the valleys and land-scapes that native sense develops whose intensity is unknown to the inhabitants of broad plains'. Indeed, wherever Bachofen portrays pat-riarchal conditions and cults of the earth, there is also a tinge of love for his Swiss 'mother country'; even Dionysus is closer to Demeter for him than to wine. Consequently rootedness has been posing here for a long time as the strangest in-rootedness, limiting fate as chthonic fate, just as if the soil itself were still saturated with ancient earth cults and held – with a kind of objective romanticism – its inhabitants tight. From this perspective, Alemannia-Bavaria seems like a Catalaunian[21] battlefield in which slaughtered myths or myth-contents are still circulating after the real battle, and not only aesthetically, but in the spell of the ancient location. There is a kind of lasting field here with the strongest peasan-try and almost no city, apart from the special case of Munich; the very earth contents of this field now also benefit the rough justice[22] against 'civilization' again. As if an idol under certain constellations should

17   Johann Peter Hebel, 1760–1826, poet.
18   Gottfried Keller, 1819–90, Swiss novelist and poet.
19   Jeremias Gotthelf, pseudonym of the Swiss writer and parson Albert Bit-zius, 1797–1854, author of *Die Schwarze Spinne*.
20   Johann Jakob Bachofen, 1815–87, anthropologist and historian of Roman law, principally known for his work on matriliny, *Das Mutterrecht*.
21   The Catalaunian Fields near Troyes (Champagne), site of the battle in which Aetius beat the Huns under Attila in 451.
22   'Haberfeldtreiben': Bavarian popular courts meting out summary justice to offenders.

receive magic forces again, there now also shines – in the precisely defined ideology of this 'circle' – a phantasm of house cult and conservation, of hatred of distance and hatred of 'mind' again. 'The demons of the place also assert their claims', says Bachofen, and he means the chthonic persistence, here so particularly strong: paganus the peasant, paganus the pagan. This double meaning of the word paganus recalls even today the late and dogged effort to 'open the door' for Christianity in the rurally closed circle of enchantment. The peasant everywhere resisted the Christian rupture, the rupture with the ideologically substantial relationship which his technology and way of life had with given 'nature'; he resisted the alertness and the reworking consciousness of Christianity. Even when Christianity had long been accepted, indeed when it had even combined with the agrarian-elemental conditions of the Teutons more easily than it had previously done with Roman civilization, Jesus was all the more narrowly converted to a household and field god again, Pan was as little played out against the homo spiritualis as today, beneath other stars, against the homo faber. Wherever the locus of this Panic bond may be, whether it is merely ideological or whether a piece of nature itself plays a part here, an interacting part, which the earth cult had once invoked and mythologically denoted, from this bond there comes even today persistence and dullness, a deep antipathy towards moving into the unknown, a reluctance to subjugate the earth (completely), a hatred of rationalization, and an ideology of sacred landed property which suits the transparent interest down to the ground anyhow, as if springing from the soil itself. Modern sobriety and modern atheism are naturally to be found here too; only they have not expelled and elucidated the myth of the soil nearly as much as the faith in the other world. Thus the country forces of reaction seem literally well founded, not just economically but also 'chthonically'. And this sunken mother-house lies revealed again today, with all the instincts, all the remnants of its spell. The secret Germany of such observance (or anti-Berlin) admittedly has no strength any more for peasant furniture or votive pictures, but on the gable of its house there are crossed horse's heads, and myth guards the parlour. This secret Germany is a gigantic, a seething container of the past; it pours forth from the country towards the town, towards the proletariat and bank capital 'simultaneously', it is suitable for every terror which bank capital needs. Rootedness in the soil which has become mythical thus not only produces false consciousness but strengthens it through the subconscious, through the really dark stream.

Other pagans or those who need them now draw on this too. Feelingly the *town* gradually approaches, even its plush, its merely backward plush, becomes like false moss. The weekend in particular is increasingly liberating itself from mere diversion: the wish to become healthy through bathing simmers as a cry and protest. The country had defended itself against a mechanized condition with which it is as yet wholly unfamiliar, and which it had rejected not because of its dreariness but above all because of the expected Communist consequences. Whereas the employees of the town flee from the empty mechanics which capitalism has already completely bestowed on them, and in which since the growing desolation of their work, since the growing crisis, they feel so little at home any more that they jump over the ditch of arrogance between town and country for the first time, that they let the earth myth into their world: namely as an 'organic' machine wrecking, which takes the place of capitalism for them. Only now, as with the peasants, has the Jew invented the crisis; indeed crisis, capitalism and Marxism are lumped together in fantastic, almost intentionally fantastic, ignorance; the town razes itself to the ground. In all its ruins we can see today how broadly the 'drive' against the 'mind' is circulating here as well, the blood drive, wild drive which is the only 'country' of the town-dweller. This contrast is also circulating among those who have never read about it in their books, who know nothing of a Klages[23] or other new calls back to nature. Rousseauism as this stratum is reviving it – as a song often without words – thrived in the whole of the nineteenth century; but it was either harmless in a bourgeois conformist way and a holiday philosophy of life, or conversely an affair of the avant-garde which, in Nietzsche!, derived no peasant dullness from it. Nietzsche stood by Offenbach[24] and the breakthrough of Carmen, not by the sons of Teut; he stood by utopia, even though a burnt reactionary one, not in the stasis of Gaia. Just as Gaia herself was unirritated, more colourfulness than spell, more dialect than earth, so in fact old Bavaria still seemed to be, with mountains which lay deep in Catholicism, not in a National Socialist province, with the crystal of the Alpine peak diagonally in front of the statues of the gods of the Zugspitze[25] massif, the wholly unmythological statues – here for once were forces from which everyone could draw only something good and a field precisely for 'Blue Riders', not for the ruins of a superstitious architecture. Whereas today town and country are beginning to become *superstitions together*; even in the town the soil has triumphed over motion and a very old space over time. What there is of motion, what so infinitely understandably seeks support, grabs falsely, desires 'the great old powers of life', which for the most part have remained only as spooks. The desperate humans wear animal masks, as usually only intoxicated peasants do in the Bavarian-Austrian 'Rough Night'; ardour with grotesque faces appears as the season of Advent.

It does not become one for the country which merely lashes out. With blows which always only strike the wrong one and are paid by the

23   Ludwig Klages, 1872–1956, the mystical right-wing German philosopher.
24   Jacques Offenbach, 1819–80, composer of operas and operettas.
25   The highest peak in the German Alps.

right.[26] The German fascio is the grim answer of the centre, the precise answer of big business to a crisis which cuts to the quick. The revisionist swindle of the social democrats and its upper house – the democracy of illusions of a people's state – no longer cut any ice with the masses. So capital, under extreme threat, resorts to a new deception, a mythological one, and gives rewards to all 'non-contemporaneous' stocks which frankly nurture this deception or are encapsulated within themselves, alien to the times, unconscious. The impoverishment of the peasants and of the middle classes joins that of the proletariat; fascism thus becomes necessary to oppress the proletarians completely and to separate the newly proletarianized elements from them ideologically. This succeeds: since those who are discontented are already too different in their grouping to be able to fathom their situation together; and the urban centre in particular, just as it does not stand directly in production itself, so it conceives nothing but unanalysed links, and also ancient forms, in which unaired instincts dwell and all the contradictions of individual and collective as well, of being a cog, being a hero and state dictatorship at one and the same time. Precisely these ancient forms distinguish the proletariat and proletarianized elements superbly; which is why they are rewarded by big business with such success, in both town and country. The folkish doctrine of family, caste and nature thus lacks every connection with the way of life of the workers, just as conversely the way of life of the employees, their instincts and remaining stock are not accommodated in proletarian materialism. This is a strange, a disastrous circle: precisely the capitalist factory dams up 'soul', and it seeks to flow away, indeed to explode against dreariness and dehumanization; but precisely vulgar Marxism, which employees first encounter and which is actually not that rare, cordons off their 'soul' for them again, even theoretically, and thus drives them back to a reactionary 'idealism'. In this way remaining stock from very different versions of 'Once upon a time' (but no fairytale begins with this, only a myth) triumphs all the more. The quiet book increasingly portrays the moral discipline of our fathers; the lights of Hollywood, which only got into your dreams, are followed by the goose-step parades of Potsdam, which also get into your blood; pleasure pulls – with the new seduction of Thusnelda[27] – its skirt over its knee and Father Rhine has long since conquered Valencia. Films which until recently only showed silly cheerfulness of fascinating drawing rooms set out on wars of liberation with the aim of far more exact distraction. Lützow's[28] wild, daring hunt and other autarkies on a war footing transform the unemployed into cannon fodder; revolution

26 Bloch is using 'right' in the political sense here.
27 The wife of Hermann der Cherusker (Arminius, the prince who beat the Romans in the Teutoburger Wald in AD 9). Thusnelda appears in Kleist's *Die Hermannsschlacht*.
28 Adolf von Lützow, 1782–1834, Prussian major-general (founder of the Lützowsche Freikorps).

in particular is forgotten among war-drums of its own accord. Thus the emptiness of diversion (in which nobody had believed) now becomes one of intoxication, with exoticism at home, with a national myth (in which the National Socialist completely believes); it is filled with kitsch and a myth which has its fantasy not in the distance but, as it were, vertically beneath the native soil. Indeed, the stale force of the reaction is so great that in the wake of kitsch it serves up the nineteenth century of the portières again, in fact directly. What was seen looming in only wanly, like ruins from our childhood, what the Surrealists portrayed as the most uncanny discovery, namely the 'unburied corpse of our parents', this is now naively built into the reaction, naively offensive and charged. Just as the lost rider in Sealsfields's[29] 'Prairie on the Jacinto' finally finds a trail, and follows it to its campsite only to see that it completely disappears (for in fact the lost rider had ridden after his own trail, and the campsite was his own from five days before), so much cultural reaction of today makes it seem as if not days but fifty years had never been, and one was coming to a halt again in the parlour of a generation ago. Big business itself admittedly leaves the retreat to the middle classes, sticks to its 'objectivity' and façade, has no faith in fatherland and primeval times, merely cultivates all kinds of experiments of 'montage' and takes a look at them. But together with the National Socialists it has still become inquisitorial, sensitive to every kind of 'cultural bolshevism' which could clearly give rise to the other sort; it has made itself formidable in its emptiness, has completely blocked not sceptical relativism but rather the old sceptical tolerance. Big business has no Dionysus of mustiness, like the urban associations which it whistles up, but it protects and formulates it all the more consciously. Thus even in the city the reaction goes back to the 'chthonic' stock of prehistoric times; hence where one would have least expected it. Indeed, it goes back – differently than in the anciently sober, settled, earthbound country – to the berserker and his totally dark running-amok. Even if the latter always – in the case of the petit bourgeois at least, as the bulk of the movement – provisionally ends in the parlour of yesterday and the day before yesterday.

The question is whether wildness which stops up emptiness does not also rip it further open. For the centre has literally lost its mind and the young do not merely want to return home to mustiness. For their urban wildness it is not fifty years which disappear as with the magic of the parlour, but as in the country centuries seem to evaporate, St Vitus's dance begins in the streets. One definitely sees of course that there is no 'Germany awake'[30] whatsoever in it; Nazism rather forms a shelter for

29 Charles Sealsfield (real name, Karl Postl), 1793–1864, writer of adventure novels.
30 'Germany Awake' ('Deutschland Erwache!'), the slogan emblazoned on the swastika flag which formed part of the Nazi standards designed by Hitler himself.

the contradictory unrest so that it should not awake. Yet the question at least remains: whether the incipient disparateness and 'irrationality' of the National Socialist spectacle may not also estrange the capitalist Ratio even in the town, precisely there, so much does it encapsulate the contradiction to capital and mythically stop up the hollow spaces. Let us leave the most obvious point to one side for the moment: namely that the *progressive* proletarianization of the centre will break through the National Socialist mist anyway, i.e. with the right leadership; it has after all no cash value in economic terms and cannot have any. But even now capitalism cannot totally keep the peace with two 'truths': with an irrational one on the one hand, for its populace, with an abstract-mechanical one on the other, in the factory. Capitalism had no other choice than that which it has excellently made with fascism up till now; yet it would certainly prefer old liberalism to romantic 'anti-capitalism' (without which business could admittedly no longer be done in Germany). The blood myth, and intoxication as a whole, is not the most desirable servant of capitalist *reason*. Indeed, to look further, to do complete justice to the 'mist broken through' sooner or later and the Communist conclusion: the mist will still perhaps present a good many things to solve not merely to capitalist reason but also to communist *good sense*. Not from the angle of 'irrational' backwardness and stupidity, let alone from the angle of open deception. But there are in fact, as was noted, certain underground cellars in the hazy National Socialist structure, and also certain sunken superstructures whose content, not yet totally 'resolved'[31] even in Communist terms, seriously remains to be examined. There is, as was remarked of the peasants, not only false consciousness here, but a deep unconsciousness of an early, even prehistoric kind. There is thus the threat here, even if ten five-year plans of good sense are completed, and especially if the whole alleged 'godlessness' should have remained, of *storm corners* of possible reaction. Romanticism has no other future than at best that of the undisposed-of past, of course. But it does have this kind of future, and it ought to be 'resolved' for it, in the precise dialectical multiple sense of this term.

31 Philosophically, 'aufgehoben' can mean both 'resolved' and 'lifted'. It can also carry the sense of 'removed'. Bloch has all three meanings in mind here.

AMUSEMENT CO., HORROR, THIRD REICH (september 1930)

However rough things are, just as crazy men emerge. Up to now the mob, as it was called, was only on the left, now it is on the right as well, even the centre is not safe. It drags itself further and further into the wilderness, its gaze becomes fixed, its face flushed, dull, determined. The unrecognizably familiar, which previously flew after false light, burrows its way into all the more excited gloom. The sturdy knife drifts from the country into the town, from the parish fair into the brawl, and this one stabs bleakly, suffused with blood. Drives are at work here which only expose deprivation and the false consciousness of it, but which are not of today. But a piece of fossilized moon shines, beneath it is a path which one strangely recalls.

Against that which approaches on it not only Jews had bolted their doors. Old grotesque faces eerily arise and yet they are real: the Nazi for instance, who on the arrival of Böss danced all night in front of his house, in a yellow fur coat down to his feet, was just as wild and witty five hundred years ago when Jews were beaten to death. He danced in a fur coat, swayed and raged all night, because Böss, the mayor of Berlin, was also involved in an affair to do with furs; but the stench of this scene is age-old, despite the miserable joke, the shabby stupidity of its allusion, age-old and terrible as if from a nightmare and the depths it touches on. And in other respects too: while Communist excesses, emerging from a new stratum, mix in little German folklore, National Socialist ones are very often reminiscent, even if they do not attain the heavy-handed cheerfulness of the dancer, of revived olden times. Here are medieval lanes again, St Vitus's dance, Jews beaten to death, the poisoning of wells and the plague, faces and gestures as if on the Mocking of Christ and other gothic panels. This kind of popular depth has probably dried up in other countries; only the lynchers in the southern states of America, Ku Klux Klansmen, awaking Magyars and the like go along with it. If Spengler[32] predicted the fascist period, he was still wrong to see it starting out coldly, mechanically, from the civilized cosmopolitan cities, in short, from a totally wakeful and late consciousness. But with our fascists Munich, not Berlin, started it, the 'most organic' capital city, not the mechanized one, and the violence emanates from the 'people' (in the highly undemocratic sense), from butcher's dances and the crudest folklore. This above all makes inroads into the acquisitive fear and the resentment of the petit bourgeois; it still garnishes the neo-Rome of those industrial bosses who pay for the butcher's dances and thereby strengthen their very highest law of the jungle. The primitiveness admittedly extends no further than the grotesque face of the rabble on Crucifixions, but it has preserved this face very well.

It cannot be denied that alongside this crudeness there is also an undercurrent of very old dreams. The strongest is that of the 'Third Reich', the very phrase already shrouds the petit bourgeois in premonition. Music on the square piano, bands in beer gardens sang out to him, when there had already long been a Kaiser: 'A crown lies in the deep, deep Rhine'. The Prusso-German Reich had long been founded, and the crown of this petit-bourgeois music was still hidden, and whoever raises it 'will be crowned in Aachen that very same hour, as Kaiser of the future, as Prince of the Rhine'. As Kaiser of the *future*: uniquely today a 'future state' is proffered all the more to the proletarianized petit bourgeois and at the same time blocked, by the Kyffhäuser line.[33] And uniquely a mere number in a historical count (old Reich, Kaiserreich, Third Reich) is connected with the very familiar triple character of the fairytale (which with the number three always also contains the decision, the end, the happiness ever after). But above all, age-old images are revived in the 'Third Reich', nobler ones than those of the fur-coat dance, more easily pervertible ones, all the more astonishingly sparkling ones. The term 'Third Reich' accompanied almost all revolts of the Middle Ages, or as it was then called, the 'Reich of the third gospel' – it was a passionate image of distance and carried with it just as much Judaism as gnosis, just as much revolt of peasant minions as the most aristocratic speculation. After the gospel of the Father in the Old Testament, after the gospel of the Son in the New, comes the third gospel, that of the Holy Spirit: so the abbot Joachim of Fiore in the thirteenth century, indeed even Origen, the Church Father, had heralded the better future, and so had the prophecy remained alive in the Peasant Wars.

---

32 Oswald Spengler, 1880–1936, philosopher of history, who wrote *The Decline of the West*, a book which greatly influenced Nazi thinking.
33 Kyffhäuser: according to legend, Emperor Frederick Barbarossa was enchanted to sleep in the Kyffhäuser mountains between the Harz and Thuringia.

Today only the empty phrase lives on, but to the same extent that deprivation has risen in the old strata, and that beery haze became explosive,[34] the phrase has ignited, and a ghostly procession of perverted memories moves through the semi-proletarian 'folk memory'. Among the bourgeois intellectuals who knew their Ibsen, the 'Third Reich' was Hecuba, a small symbol which they were content to leave in Ibsen's drama, at 'Emperor and Galilean'.[35] The Third Reich of the 'noble characters', as conciliatory centre between antiquity and Christianity – how the connection with the mystical tradition is severed here. All the more powerfully, of course, Dostoevsky was a literary mediation for the old dreams (and one for literature with political-archaic dreams); the Dostoevsky of that Byzantine music which had preserved its Origen within it and believed in the return of the Holy Spirit. 'Third Reich' was thus ultimately the title of a book by a 'Dostoevsky German', by the name of Moeller van den Bruck,[36] and this has now become – in a wild crash of reaction – the basic book[37] of the National Socialists, the deceiving space, and also the believing space of their dreams. The beaters to death, differently from Ibsen's intellectuals and noble characters in the theatre, now feel the old fanaticism of the phrase; it is therefore for this that the empty phrase has drunk blood and lives.[38] Certainly in this new 'folk base' there remains nothing precise from, or only the opposite of the preachings which haunted the whole of the Middle Ages since Joachim of Fiore, which extend as far as Lessing, as far as his 'Education of the Human Race'[39] and his completely liberal spirit. But a basis of reaction is unmistakable precisely in the 'backward rejuvenation' of today; it creates a reinforced echo in the chthonic base which glows so mysteriously. It creates the *music* for today's St Vitus's dance, though without earlier content, indeed with the opposite of the revolutionary content of love and mind in the 'third gospel' or pneuma. It was thus that reaction itself was able to commit itself to this Pentecost, to the dense chaos which once permeated Germany, that aristocratic and caste mythology which all previous 'folk dreams' had assailed. Yet there is an age-old structure even here, revived and perverted; if the brutality previously gazed at us as in Crucifixions, the old 'Third Reich' is now

34 Bloch is perhaps here referring to the beer-hall *putsch* in Munich in 1923 in which Hitler played a prominent part.
35 Henrik Ibsen's *Emperor and Galilean* (1873).
36 Arthur Moeller van den Bruck, 1876–1925.
37 'Grundbuch': Bloch is also punning on the primary meaning of this word, 'land register'.
38 In the *Odyssey* the spirits in Hades have to drink blood before they can speak to Odysseus, and Bloch is envisaging the Third Reich as such a shade here.
39 In this work, *Die Erziehung des Menschengeschlechts* (1780), Lessing prophesies a third secular stage in moral development when people will do good for its own sake.

reflected in the eyes of the crucifiers and mercenaries. With furor teutonicus, lost contact with real revolution, copied Christian ideology; the
lord of blood stands for Jesus, the warlike state for the congregation.
Thus these people are spellbound, something rages and dreams mur-
kily within them. A piece of German brutality strikes up in them again,
has in fact a subconscious or unconscious impetus, instead of a class-
conscious one; posits not only folk and fatherland as a substitute for
their own sinking caste, but fills the frame with very old pictures. The
berserker strikes out who marches in every direction where things are to
be destroyed; his crazy cruelty reinforces the revenge-drive of the petit
bourgeois. Germany, unlike France, was always without the influence of
women, without Mary; now it has become totally anti-flower. Hereditary memory of a brighter kind is also a factor, precisely as the myth of
the Third Reich; but it has no power to have light in its fire as well. The
abstract brutality is rather becoming stronger and giving the myth of the
Third Reich an odour of blood which is in keeping with its corruption.
Age-old regions of utopia are thus being occupied by St Vitus's dancers,
the Germanic Romanticism of blood has gone down well with the petit
bourgeois, has bugled up a whole army of vehme murderers[40] and
'Guardians of the Crown'.[41] Volsungs' blood,[42] which previously had
only musical infusion or boiled philosophically in Klages, has suddenly
become 'concrete', namely in the arrears of sinking strata, with a wealth
of memories in their sinking. Their sinking lowers these strata into the
proletariat only in socio-economic terms, but ideologically it brings no
inclination towards dismantling, towards analysing the situation, towards uncovering the causes and 'grounds' of today. Instead the sinking
abandons even more the thin layer of reason of the 'modern age',
brushes in falling very old modes of drive, ways of life and superstructures, and thereby provokes 'Irratio'. So roughly and so full of warlike
eroticism, so usefully as well for the darkest forms of imperialism, one
of these young Nazis exclaimed: 'You do not die for a programme you
have understood, you die for a programme you love.' It is unnecessary
to stress the bad Irratio in this exclamation, the reluctance to demand or
to betray a programme where none exists at all, the heroic ignorance of
backward strata which sooner desire death than insight into their own
contradictions. It is necessary for us Marxists, of course, to see the dark
fanaticism of this exclamation as well, which is not only maintained by
ignorance, and its differently 'backward' backgrounds; precisely in these
there shines an archaic-emotional remnant never wholly accessible or

40   A reference to the old German 'Vehmgericht', a medieval secret court
     which operated in Westphalia.
41   A reference to an unfinished novel *Die Kronenwächter* (1817) by the
     German Romantic writer Achim von Arnim, 1781–1831.
42   From Wagner's opera *The Valkyrie*.

exorcizable for all too present analysis. It is not the 'theory' of the National Socialists but rather their energy which is serious, the fanatical-religious strain which does not merely stem from despair and stupidity, the strangely roused strength of faith. This streak could in fact, like every recollection of 'primitiveness', also have turned out differently, if it had been militarily *occupied* and dialectically transformed, on the 'enlightened' side, instead of merely being abstractly cordoned off. But since Marxist *propaganda* lacks any *opposite land* to myth, any transformation of mythical beginnings into real ones, of Dionysian dreams into revolutionary ones, an element of guilt also becomes apparent in the effect of National Socialism, namely a guilt on the part of the all too usual vulgar Marxism. Large masses in Germany, above all the young (as a strongly organized and mythically intertwined condition), were able to become National Socialist precisely because the Marxism which presents them does not also 'represent' them at the same time. As certainly as the proletariat is the class which is alone historically decisive today, it is just as certainly quite remarkably intertwined with the bourgeoisie (much more than the latter was with feudalism); and just as certainly it is not only the latest machine and the last phase of imperialism which is important to it, but also the National Socialist decay and the other transitional phenomena of late bourgeois ideology. Important in the sense of disarming and plundering, of the critique both of revolutionary appearance and of the dialectical linking of all its (pre-bourgeois) contradictions with revolutionary theory and practice. The Dionysus of mustiness and the Third Reich within the framework of capitalism are such contradictions for example, it has produced them itself; but Dionysus and the Third Reich cannot be made concrete in vulgar Marxism *alone*, otherwise they stray into reaction again. The fruit is there and the formula thus irrefutable: the success of National Socialist ideology is countering, for its part, the all too great progress of socialism from utopia to science; in Engels it was conceived totally differently. In this way the enemy triumphs with wild cries of jubilation and undisturbed Irratio, despite its revolutionary situation which makes its victims susceptible at least in socialist terms. In this way an archaism develops which more than understandably blocks the transition to the proletariat. The vulgar Marxists keep no watch over primitiveness and utopia, the National Socialists owe their seduction to them, it will not be the last. Both hell and heaven, berserkers and theology, have been surrendered without a fight to the forces of reaction.

But every advance against the top should be used, no matter how it comes. One can of course believe that the growing movement will bear to the left by itself, and the remainder will perish. This is the hope not just of the social democrat, who always allows everything to occur above his head, and for whom everything passes 'by itself'. Communists too, powerfully involved, believe in a decline of the active parts of the NSDAP, in one which will be all the swifter the more Hitler has to serve capitalism, which has summoned him as the last rites. A bulletin of 1930 already reads as follows: 'In the Berlin headquarters of the KPD the confidence prevails that sooner or later they will draw the lion's share from the bankrupt's estate of this political monster speculation. They reckon in the foreseeable future on a slackening of the binding force between the National Socialist and the socialist element of the movement, as soon as the pressure of economic deprivation dispels the mist of phraseology and reveals the patchwork of compromises and illusory façades in all its wretchedness.' Thus emergency positions are already being constructed here which are to absorb Hitler's crumpled battalions one day. Thus there is a hope that the SA proletarians and a section of the other pauperized elements will land up as Communists, the remainder will become German National[43] and the whole thing was a big boast (like so many better movements in Germany too). However, we consider this hope in its entirety to be premature, not because of the anti-capitalist contradiction but because of the equally anti-mechanistic one which the movement contains. The first contradiction, that to capitalism of the middle stratum becoming impoverished, can certainly soon be cleared up and used; it is of course not yet a clearly conscious one, but rather an irrational one which was likewise produced by capitalism and can hardly remain comfortable for the Ratio of capital in the long run. The second contradiction, however, the general one to 'mechanism as a whole', means that Communism can also still be represented to the employee as empty mechanics, as a process of depersonalization and rationalization, indeed as the mere reverse side of capitalisms. There thus arises – in a crazy yet tenacious confusion of the capitalist and Communist 'Ratio' – an anti-mechanistic 'irrationality', which is fed by a thousand refinements of the uppermiddle-class Irratio and furnishes at least as powerful a contradiction to the usual vulgar Marxism as it does to capitalism. For the proletarian, who has grown up together with the forces of production, these are no enemy, he sees through them; but the petit bourgeois stands today, on a new level, almost inevitably at the machine-wrecking stage. This is why semi-proletarian existence produces false consciousness beyond all measure; this is why thrusts and contents, which are equally those of catching up with capitalism as they are capitalist decay, become encapsulated in fixed ideas. It is not these that are important but rather the region of blood and haze in which all this has become revived again and stands in contradiction to vulgar Marxism, indeed even to the mechanically presented 'world-picture' of Marxism. Since Marxists do not as yet set any

43 Reference to the Deutschnationale Volkspartei (German National People's
    Party) which existed from 1918 to 1933.

varied and outbidding language in motion here, the anti-mechanism benefits the forces of reaction, balances the other contradiction in which the 'irrational' stands to capitalism. If therefore all National Socialists had already gone over to Marxism, indeed if the commune were well on the way to being realized: there would still remain, as we said above, a *storm corner of possible reaction* here, namely a danger zone of the 'remnant' which had not yet been represented in Marxist terms. In Russia they accommodate the peasants with harvest festivals and Lenin's tomb, replace the church for them with the collective and with young symbols; in Germany Marxism abandons all these points of contact to the forces of reaction. In Germany the winning of the impoverished centre and the activation of its 'non-contemporaneous' contradictions to capitalism would be just as important as the winning of the peasants in Russia was; nevertheless, there is hardly a tactical approach and adherence to Lenin which decisively disavowed the pseudo-enlightenment of vulgar Marxism. Pseudo-enlightenment is abstraction, not totality and *opened* irrationality within it; if it does not yet seem the time to rouse a totality which has largely fallen asleep in socialist terms, then surely it is time to use the portent of National Socialism in the matter of a lasting Irratio. History is no entity advancing along a single line, in which capitalism for instance, as the final stage, has resolved all the previous ones; but it is a *polyrhythmic and multi-spatial entity, with enough unmastered and as yet by no means revealed and resolved corners.* Today not even the economic substructures in these corners, i.e. the obsolete forms of production and exchange, have passed away, let alone their ideological superstructures, let alone the genuine contents of not yet defined Irratio. It is precisely this which supplies the material for the romantic anti-capitalism, moreover for the realistic-romantic kind as it were, of these strata; this tempts them to the nonsense of seeing in liberalism and Marxism only 'two sides of the same coin' (namely those of abstraction and mechanization). And even later, when all substructures will be levelled out, when no reactionary class interest will force people into romanticism any more, a rationality which thought it had done enough by causing capitalism to overturn will rediscover the omitted, still irrational matter; no longer in an economic crisis, but rather in a 'religious' one. Capitalism has been so little able to drain the irrational that it has become ever stronger precisely as a 'contradiction' to its objectivity and rationalization; and vulgar Marxism certainly will not reduce this hunger by viewing it on all sides merely as backward. National Socialist romanticism stands with bad directness enough as regards modern civilization, namely directly opposed to it, and in this respect it is a Jacobinism of myth. Yet genuine revolutionaries have just as directly rejected this bad directness, have as yet by no means mediated it with the whole of modern reality, nor even with remainders which have announced themselves so monstrously. Petit-bourgeois horror and merely backward stupidity are a clear component in themselves, but it does not exhaust the entire National Socialist complex. Differently 'non-contemporaneous' wildness and demonic mythicizing also exist and possibly have a dialectical hook, are at least in strange 'contradiction' to capital and the spirit of capital; this contradiction must be helped along.[44]

44 Bloch is here echoing the final line of Schiller's play *The Robbers*: 'That man can be helped along.'

INVENTORY OF REVOLUTIONARY
APPEARANCE (1933)

When two do the same thing, they do not do the same thing. Especially when one copies what the other is doing, in order to deceive. So it is today, when the Nazi cannot yet reveal the way he really looks and what he really wants, and thus disguises himself. He pretends to be rebellious, as we know; the most dreadful white terror against populace and socialism which history has ever seen camouflages itself as socialist. To this end its propaganda must develop sheer revolutionary appearance, garnished with thefts from the commune. The business of deception could not be done more cheaply any more; for even the slogan of master-race nationalism would not go down well unless – apparently meeting the real need of the people – it first poses as an anti-capitalist one. Whereby the anti-capitalism of the Thyssens, Schröders[45] and other employers of Nazism understandably cannot hunt up enough masks so that Little Red Ridinghood should not recognize it. The burning of the Reichstag alone is not sufficient, the populace must also believe that Nero is the early Christian in person. Thus hell mocked right from the beginning with a grotesque mask of salvation, again and again.

1 First they stole the colour red, stirred things up with it. The first declarations of the Nazis were printed on red, this colour was enormously extended on the fraudulent flag. The posters gradually grew paler and paler so that they no longer frightened the financial backer. The flag itself bore its crookedly coiled, slantingly distorted symbol from the beginning anyway, and it is named after it, not after the colour. But when an efficient worker cut the swastika out of it, there still remained metres of red appearance on the cloth. Only with a hole in the middle, gaping like a mouth and totally empty.

45 German industrialists. Fritz Thyssen was head of the Steel Trust, Baron Kurt von Schröder a Cologne banker who contributed to the funds of the Nazi Party.

NON-CONTEMPORANEITY AND INTOXICATION 65

2   Then they stole the street, the pressure it exerts. The procession, the dangerous songs which had been sung. What the red front-line soldiers had begun, the forest of flags, the marching entry into the hall, precisely this was copied by the Nazis. The Parliament day of Potsdam, on 21 March 1933,[46] steered the would-be revolutionary image more into the usual, military channel again, but 1 May 1933 made up ground with stolen magic all the more shamelessly. In Offenbach they erected the maypole, the old Jacobin symbol of liberty, and danced around it like members of the White Guard, indeed Hindenburg in person celebrated the world holiday of the proletariat. And the business concerns advertised for the first of May in the newspaper that nothing but 'workers of the brow and fist' were employed in them, and shared in the celebrations in honour of the day. The life of profit even stole his festive day from the worker too, laid down derision as its trump card.

All in all they pretended to be merely workers and nothing else, thus distorting boundlessly. Took the word in the wishy-washiest sense, and so spread a nebulousness in which nobody knows who is the guest and who the waiter any more. So the 'Völkische Beobachter'[47] writes about the pimp Horst Wessel:[48] 'He was a worker in the truest sense of the word, a worker on himself, a fighter with his self, and thus he gained inner firmness and strength.' With such a truest sense of the word there are of course no exploiters, class struggles, let alone exploited people; unless one is not a worker on oneself, but one for others, like all proletarians up to now, unfortunately. Only the word proletarian is not adopted by the Nazi, any more than the word crisis, for which even in the Weimar Republic the image 'undulation of economic life' was substituted and in the Third Reich, with even better speculation in human stupidity, they simply say 'November crime'.[49] The 'workforce' at any rate becomes an extraordinarily cordial mush, the basic contradiction between capital and work, which the petite bourgeoisie has not understood anyway, is totally blurred with it, and the fraudulent monster is nevertheless, or for this very reason, called a 'Workers' Party', causes the murderers and their victims to greet one another as comrades and

46   The ceremonial opening session of the new Reichstag in the Garrison church in Potsdam, a shrine of Prussian imperialism. The chosen date for initiating the Third Reich was also symbolic, since 21 March was the day on which Bismarck had opened the new Reichstag of the Second Reich in 1871.
47   An anti-semitic Nazi propaganda newspaper acquired by the party in 1920. It was turned into a daily paper in 1923.
48   Horst Wessel, 1907–30, an SA leader who was made into a Nazi martyr. The 'Horst Wessel Lied' (1933) was a Nazi anthem, written by Horst Wessel to an old music-hall tune.
49   The signing of dictated peace terms by the Germans in November 1918 in a French railway carriage in the forest of Compiègne.

even poses, by practising Marx's resolving of the proletariat with shoot-
ings and concentration camps, as the real stuff of socialism. Whereby the
Nazi, for he is human and his first of May already displayed this
embracing power, is naturally also an expert over and over again at a
stifling kind of 'deproletarianization'. It is the surest sign of his petit-
bourgeois nature the way 'the depths of the people', from which the
king of bourgeois conformists Hitler also emerged, are to be raised, the
way proletarian class consciousness is aborted and 'caste consciousness'
forced through. With the task of stifling the class struggle in that general
wishy-washy drivel which is called petit-bourgeois consciousness and in
which, as Marx says, 'the contradictions of two classes simultaneously
blunt one another'. Only even here the deception would not be so
widely successful if the Christian-social non-seller of 'deproletarianization', which Hitler is bringing back into favour, his supposed national
community were not embellished in highly socialist terms again, indeed
actually with nothing less than the classless society itself, just as if it
already existed now. Thus in the fraudulent Nazi world from the Thyssens to the lowest donkey-worker there is only a single classless 'work-
front', and the 'Reich Peasants' Day' in Goslar likewise recognizes no
differences any longer between big landowner and little peasant, apart
from the insignificant ones which are denoted by are and hectare and are
of no consequence before the Father of all at harvest festival. Whatever
constitutes village poverty and urban proletariat is merely described by
Hitler as faint-heartedness, which can be removed by operation in
purely psychological terms, precisely through inner elevation out of 'the
depths of the people'. For it is self-evident to the Nazi that the proletarian feels himself to be exactly as the petit bourgeois regards
him, namely as a leavening force behind the people which ought to be
ashamed of its existence, as a single inferiority complex. Thus the
working classes must be downright feudalized, namely into a 'fealty',[50]
together with the employees as the other feudally faithful noble
Teutons, in order, according to Hitler's patent remedy, 'to kill off their
inferiority complexes and also the boredom from which heretical ideas
and thoughts arise'. Consequently for Hitler the 'prerequisites of
Marxism' are solely the proletarian's misfortune in not being a petit
bourgeois, combined with the boredom of the proletarian horde which
is to be cured partly in the barrack square (also in the factory as barrack
square), partly with hullabaloo. Hitler's concept of proletarian consciousness, proclaimed during Goebbels's May Day celebrations, is thus
unbeatable: 'We are determined not only to eliminate Marxism externally but also to deprive it of its prerequisites. For the centuries to come
after us we want to eliminate the prerequisites for this mental confusion,

50 'Gefolgschaft': Bloch is using the specifically Nazi word for workforce
here, with its feudal connotations.

and they include the arrogant feeling which grips the individual and
makes him look down from above as if – manual work were a disgrace.'
The individual is the National Socialist petit bourgeois, and the 'Völkische Beobachter' goes on to add: 'Through this festive day the German
worker is to become a fully qualified member of the German national
community again.' Or as the leader of the 'work-front' (the occupied
trade unions) puts it: 'The German person must understand that when
he works for the people he then also has the right to be proud of his
achievement. Therefore, my Führer, as the strongest representative of
your nation take the weak son under your patronage.' So far has the
proletarian come in the 'general workforce' that he who up to now
could feel himself to be the historically decisive class, the representative
of the future, has now become the weakest son of the petit bourgeois.
Wretched, but elevated he stands under the 'patronage' of the king of
bourgeois conformists, just as this patron is now in turn patronized by
capital finance. We have really reached the trump card here after a
hundred years of the German workers' movement: a monster has come
true and is committing the proletarian in chains to the Thousand-Year
Reich, to capital finance as national community.

3   And finally they pretend to think of nothing except what will
change things. This sounds almost formally Marxist, recognizes no
intellect in itself, but places it instead in the service of politics. Goebbels
expressly declared the film 'Battleship Potemkin' to be a model for the
German film, so far does the formal consent go, as the crook and
thieving perverter imagines it.[51] What is important, according to the
latest dramatic guidelines of these shabbily cunning plagiarists, is not
how good or bad the performed play was but the mood in which the
spectator leaves the theatre. The pleasure in theatrical performance for
its own sake, the problems of the private sphere and the ivory tower, the
development of unpolitical themes, are all rejected; Goebbels desires no
romanticism, unless it is 'steely' (an admittedly strange alloy); he wants
tendency in the theatre instead of l'art pour l'art. All this seems, undoubtedly, as deceptively anti-contemplative as a forgery can only be
which confuses the Marxist application of theory to practice with the
patter of a con-man. Further parallels of dazzling illusion can also be
discerned; thus a not even fascist university paper writes: 'It is inevitable
in times like the present ones that the last word then belongs not to the
university, but to the state. This and nothing more, not the fact that
politics and learning are simply mixed anyhow, is what politicization of
the university means.' It is important here to observe the paths by
means of which precisely the copy of the Marxist relationship between

---

51   Goebbels deliberately plagiarized Eisenstein's techniques when he assumed
     the role of film director for several Nazi propaganda films during the
     thirties and the Second World War.

theory and practice seemed attainable to National Socialism in a particularly easy, particularly 'modern' way. To tolerate not only no intellect in itself, but no intellect at all, except on the commanding heights of profit, this constitutes the chloroform practice of Hitlerism. 'Justice is, truth is, what benefits the German people', that is, benefits German monopoly capitalism: this scandalous pragmatism of the Nazis is ultimately not just the ape of the Marxist relationship between theory and practice, but its total perversion. For in Marxist terms the primacy of theory is definitely found in this relationship, i.e. something is not true because it is beneficial, but because it is true it is also beneficial. The eternally identical and ignorant arias which Hitler sings to his petit-bourgeois followers do not become any better when the university whore which he found (just as Wilhelm II found her in 1914) latinizes the kitsch and improves the deception with refinements à la Schmitt[52] or Freyer[53] or Heidegger.[54] National Socialism, apart from clueless despair and rampant stupidity, also has many corrupt professors on its side, but no theory which could bring with it any other practice than deception and murder. Its stolen relationship between theory and practice is hence in reality the mere relationship between false siren song and genuine laceration, between the abdication of reason and the raid of gangsters in the night thus produced. All this ultimately in the name of a 'theory-practice' which abolishes Mammon by christening it 'working capital', and satisfies the 'anti-capitalist longing' by kissing the Aryan arse of Old Nick.

Thus the enemy is not content with torturing and killing workers. He not only wants to smash the red front but also strips the jewellery off the supposed corpse. The deceiver and murderer cannot show his face other than with would-be revolutionary speeches and forms of combat. The petit bourgeois sees socialism in them, the member of the upper middle class possesses a backdrop in them, and for capitalism it was high time for both. For the democratic sham of Weimar social democracy no longer concealed their reality from the impoverished masses. So the sham had to be replaced and to pass from social-democratic 'socialism', with nationalization committees, into the much more radical seeming illusion of the Nazi kind. But of course, not even this illusion would succeed, and the deception with it would not be necessary, if in fact a continuing revolutionary situation did not exist, which is prevented from becoming acute by the theft of its emblems. We have to go back to Luther in the Peasants' War to encounter a similar deception by means of perverted revolutionary slogans (at that time they ran: Freedom of

52 Carl Schmitt, 1888–1985, right-wing political theorist.
53 Hans Freyer, 1887–1969, sociologist and philosopher.
54 Martin Heidegger, 1889–1976, the influential existentialist philosopher, publicly came out in support of Hitler in 1933.

the Christian Man);[55] and even the Judas in Luther is being far surpassed by the Satan Hitler. But the awakening from the National Socialist ecstasy will be all the more instructive for its masses, the more
promising in anti-capitalist longing the ecstasy was and the more 'strikingly' it turns out that its contents fail in the worst possible way on the
credited Nazi foundation. Hitler roared that he had stabilized his Reich
'for the centuries to come after us', and 'in ten years there will be no
Marxism any more'. In ten years the Thousand-Year Reich will instead
have completely gone to the devil – the dog is dead, the conjurers will
not call up any spirit[56] any more. Only the writing on the wall will be
left; woe betide any dictatorship which does not heed it.

55 *Freiheit des Christenmenschen*: the title of one of Luther's most influential
    works during the Reformation.
56 See Preface to the 1935 edition, n. 1.

NEW SLAVE MORALITY OF THE NEWSPAPER (1934)

The Brownshirts are honest in one thing. In the art of not telling the truth. They admit this in a manner which almost verges on pride. Not only the lowest official now has to be cunning so that his business remains shady even when it comes to light. Not only the newspaper man, on pain of downfall, has to find a lie as soon as he sees to the bottom of things, to blood and soil.[57] But, as the result of new instructions, the lie becomes not only the morality but also the science of the Reich. Implicitly so in the regulations governing the law for editors, explicitly so in the official science of journalism. Since the German editor has assumed the 'responsibility' for writing the opposite of truth, the subjective dirty trick is made easier for him and objective so to speak by being public. The editor lives in all respects on this side of power and is a poor dog who lies down. But after the great transvaluation of values, slave morality, as soon as it writes, also stands beyond true and false.[58]

As is prominently confirmed in a textbook of lies. The new professor of journalism in Leipzig, by the name of Münster, published it under the title: 'The three tasks of the science of German journalism'. In it Münster 'felicitously sums up for the knowledgeable reader the present

57   Bloch is punning here on the Nazi notion of 'Blut und Boden'.
58   Bloch is ironically referring to Nietzsche's philosophy here. Firstly to the central concept of the 'transvaluation of all values' which appears in the latter's *Genealogy of Morals* (1887) and which he used as a subtitle to his main philosophical enterprise, *The Will to Power*. (The origins of the concepts of moral good and bad are located by Nietzsche in the master/slave structure of ancient classical culture.) Secondly to his idea of 'beyond good and evil' which furnished the title of an earlier work (1886). Nietzsche, of course, was often hailed as a prophet and claimed as a forerunner by the Nazis, and indeed by Hitler himself, who was apt to quote him at the dinner table. But their interpretation of his work was, to say the least, tendentious.

conclusions in the burning glass of the new way of thinking'. It is not knowledge, whether of the historical or even the economic kind, which prevails in first place here; why should it? It has its moratorium, and not even a pleasant one. In first place stands, expressis verbis, 'the task of performing the work of general political education and developing the appreciation of the necessity and nature of propaganda. This preparatory study is followed, as the second special task, by the historical knowledge of *national influence* and intellectual national leadership *in all times and nations.*' Only then does there follow, as the third task of the science of journalism, the theoretical element, so to speak, and even then only, in Münster's commendably restrained definition, as 'assistance in the training of up-and-coming German editors'. As that training which 'corresponds to the requirements of the law for editors and imparts knowledge about the German nation in connection with the requirements of newspaper practice'. So it is only in this respect, bowed beneath the basic purpose of 'national influence', obedient to the basic goal of also placing a printed radio alongside Goebbels's propaganda, that science comes into question, the brand of economics and history, depraved in any case and merely running around in quotation marks,[59] which is taught at German universities today. For not only the newspaper man is to be trained, but also the propagandist of film and microphone: the truth is that which is useful to Thyssen.

Thereby, as the Nazi believes, the bourgeois newspaper now leaves the stage. So little does it do this, of course, that with the new regulation it has merely lost its final sense of shame. The shame which had still held up the old threadbare robes of the good bourgeois conscience, at least of the factual report, in front of the interest of the proprietor and the advertisers. From times when the bourgeoisie still believed in the blessings of capitalism and literally held out the hope that at the same rate as one's own pocket was filling up those of others would also have to be favoured with a suum cuique, and the general sail of general civilization would have to billow as a whole. Now no Thyssens believe in a harmonious course of business, unless it is the business of treading over corpses:[60] and the nation, even if exploitation and later war may need certain of its movements, must in political terms at least be the corpse over which capital treads. Ideology had earlier aspired to something similar, but it was still mixed subjectively with a relative *unconsciousness* of deception and objectively with a sheen of civilization; both veils are superfluous today. Thus the final bourgeois shame of the

59 'Auf Gänsefüßchen', 'in quotation marks', but Bloch is punning here on the literal meaning, 'on little goose feet'.
60 We have rendered the expression 'über Leichen gehen' literally here because it is used as an extended metaphor. An English equivalent would be 'to sell your own grandmother'.

newspaper disappears, it disappears together with that 'reviewing element' or 'imperishable charm of correctness' which in one or two major
liberal papers sought to provide a sort of Baedeker's guide to events.
Capital needs consciously cynical deception instead, with the perishable,
yet obscene charms of incorrectness; it needs journalists with the patter
of white slave traders, preferably with a diploma from a school of
pick-pockets as well. The revolutionary appearance of National Socialism is more exhausted anyway than any appearance has ever managed.
And with it the possibility of its early days to seduce in some copy of
the old popular broadsheets or even of the revolutionary Messengers of
old.[61] What remains is only 'national influence' in the confessed sense of
schooled cunning; the journalist, who in olden times was called the
ignoble brother of the poet, has been elevated to the noble one of the
crook.

Two means are combined for this purpose, the more recent one
enlivens the older one. One is advertising, with which struggling sales
yell how hard a time they are having. Today still forbidden to doctors
and lawyers, and even in the business world having reached established
stores only slowly with growing competition, it is totally new for
statesmen to be using it. No corn lotion has been as deafeningly praised
for its own 'gigantic achievement' as occurs at the cabinet table, as soon
as a head of the triple monster opens; and does not even lay claim to the
name of Doctor Bloodless.[62] The other means of influence is considerably more old-fashioned, in fact in liberal times it was solely a school or
theatre remnant. It is rhetoric, namely that genuinely sophistical discipline which does not work with truth but with surprise. With arrangement, momentary bluff, psychological not logical distribution of light
and shade, in short with contempt for the listener and a total cynicism
of means. There is also a sound rhetoric which does not stem from the
sophists, not even from decorators; the great Philippics of Demosthenes,
which believe in themselves, are its unforgotten model, and the parliamentary speeches of the two Pitts also belong to this category, as well
as forensic examples which blossomed with Zola and Labori[63] in the
Dreyfus trial. But the rhetorical speeches of Demosthenes, O men of
Athens, are themselves those of men to men, have a soldierly aspect, are
by no means a rhetoric in the traditionally sophistical sense, but rather
logos before equals, like all such speeches, up to Mirabeau,[64] Robert

---

61 Bloch has revolutionary pamphlets such as Büchner's *Hessische Landbote*
    (The Hesse Messenger) of 1834 in mind here.
62 A reference to the Third Reich. Doctor Bloodless is clearly the quack who
    promises to cure all ills without drawing blood. Bloch is thus saying that
    the Nazis have no such scruples about bloodletting.
63 A champion of Dreyfus.
64 Comte Honoré de Mirabeau, 1749–91, French statesman and orator.

Blum[65] and Lenin, honestly covered, kindling and illuminating with real light. The opinion of the speaker and the opinion of the speech are identical here, form and content homogeneous. Whereas the dubious rhetoric which really deserves this name, the sophistical and later Roman-decorative kind, has no homogeneity at all between form and content, even its baroque element stands at a crooked angle to the truth and driving only towards the purpose concealed in the whole speech. Jesuits published the best textbooks of this waking hypnosis, up until the middle of the last century, and all fallacies, from the quaternio terminorum[66] to the heterozetesis,[67] found a refuge here. With snakelike beauty Antony makes the best of such speeches, not Brutus, the honourable man and honest republican; beaming with sophistry Fiesco[68] beguiles with this one piece of antiquity, while Verrina, the other one, remains silent and ultimately, instead of a crafty trick, only performs a flick of the wrist. False rhetoric always presupposes simpletons who are believed, or at least one's own promises or colourings which are not believed; hence its false tone, hence the disagreeable element even in theatrical form, when bloated language and the mouse of a petit-bourgeois content behind it do not match one another to the point of being comic. Hence also the totally different aspect of genuine, subjectively and objectively covered, glowing language, its character of never being solely rhetoric, any more than the manly eloquence of Demosthenes or Lenin. But rigged rhetoric is the only 'rational' instrument of despotism, so long as it is not yet in the saddle or – as in Germany – so long as the machinery of repression is not yet sufficient alone. Alongside the trembling terror there then stands the sweet one of demagogy; whereby Nazi rhetoric differs from the advertising which it takes a share in using, both through the magnificent scale of its mendacity and through the fact that its customers get to the bottom of the product only when it is too late to exchange it in any case. The real situation, the character of reality cannot themselves be 'influenced' by the lather of clichés which pulls the wool over people's eyes. For rhetoric is not a theory which leads to concrete practice; on the contrary, it is the dazzling which prevents the breakthrough of reality into consciousness

65 Robert Blum, 1807–48, politician, leader of the left in the Frankfurt National Assembly of 1848, executed for his part in the Vienna Revolution.

66 *Quaternio terminorum*: a false logical conclusion in a syllogism, when the middle terms in the major and minor premise are not the same, leading to four terms (together with subject and predicate) in the conclusion instead of three.

67 *Heterozetesis*: false reasoning with arguments foreign to what is to be proved.

68 Fiesco, Verrina: references to Schiller's play *Die Verschwörung des Fiesco zu Genua* (1783).

and practice. But by turning white into black and red into brown, it ultimately gives the victim the same insensitivity to the truth which the duper already professionally calls his own. With the difference that the latter certainly evades all truth, but does not lose from his technique the sensitivity to his profit during operations for a moment.

For this purpose, therefore, and to this end the editor also studies world history ('historical knowledge of national influence in all times and nations'). A great deal of personal addition will be unavoidable. For all previous scented candles of adulation only burnt down once, on the principle that lies have short wings and do not return so freshly alive the second time. Or otherwise behind the machinery of influence repeating several times or even constantly, like that of the church for example, there stood a very great versatility and cultivation of means, and above all a great deal of deviousness of control, by virtue of the compensating other world. Whereas National Socialism weakens itself first by the *monotony* of its repetitions (in keeping with the stereotype and the illiteracy of its phrasemongers). But then even the most stupid man gradually has a *control* at his disposal if he compares the 'gigantic achievements' and the self-satisfaction of those whose pockets have been lined by the 'revolution' with his own catastrophe and the absurd overall situation of Germany. The Nazi editor seeks in vain to create for himself a kind of temporal substitute for the other world and its uncontrollability by prophesying – with a mixture of vaingloriousness and despair – a thousand years, if not hundreds of thousands, for the 'total success' of National Socialism. Hunger is of today and the only thing in hard cash which the Nazi empties from his sack of promises; hence the 'Frankfurter Zeitung'[69] calls the optimism which its kind of newspaper now has to disseminate 'almost foolhardy'. Caligula, also a pet lover, and Nero, also an artist, were almost easier to praise than Hitler. Thus the journalist, illuminating prescribed lies or even adding some of his own invention which not even Goebbels has thought of, has a hard job, especially today. It is already at the point where, just as he is properly learning the art of lying, the art of being lied to is rapidly[70] being lost.

69 The first number of the *Frankfurter Zeitung* appeared on 16 November 1866, having developed out of a business newspaper the *Frankfurter Handelszeitung* (1856), founded by Leopold Sonnemann. It originally championed the liberal democratic aims of the 1848 revolution and opposed Bismarck. The paper was later viewed by right-wing extremist circles as an organ of the Jewish world conspiracy. It rose to European and world stature after the end of the First World War, attaining a powerfully independent influence during the Weimar Republic. The paper was forced to abandon its independent line after the takeover of the Nazis and finally banned in August 1943, ostensibly because of paper shortage!

70 Bloch is also ironically echoing the phrase 'reißenden Absatz finden', 'to sell like hot cakes', in his use of 'reißend' here.

JUGGLERS' FAIR BENEATH THE GALLOWS (1937)

Let us speak quietly, there is someone dying in the room. Dying German culture, it does not even have catacombs at its disposal inside Germany any more. Merely chambers of horrors in which it is to be exposed to the derision of the mob; a concentration camp with visits from the public.

It is getting crazy and ever crazier. What is an honest, a talented person to do in this country. His simple existence is a danger to him, he must conceal it. Every kind of talent endangers the life of the person who possesses it, apart from that of cringing. Artists, who are such, are openly threatened with castration or prison; this is no joke, such mouths do not make jokes. People have learnt to take the ridiculous seriously.

Nevertheless, they refrain from going into details. The 'Frankfurter Zeitung' writes of Hitler's speech on art: 'The Führer has given the theory and standards which are alone appropriate for the high founda-tion of a temple of art.' Führer and standards speak for themselves, they are not inviting, although as the same newspaper remarks, the house painter's aesthetic lecture had been given 'both with the weapons of sharp irony and with the means of philosophical discussion'. The demands are different; what seems like irony to one person appears to another to be revenge of the rejected art student of former days. An irony which declares that certain painters experience the meadows as blue, the skies as green, and the clouds as sulphurous yellow has also often existed before in the gazettes of cultural backwaters; though without the actual sharpness which is necessary for castration. And as far as philosophical discussion is concerned, the equally correct categories flowed from the correct source of supply; the philosophizing Führer has the floor: 'A radiantly beautiful human type, gentlemen, you prehistoric art-stutterers, is the type of the new age, and what do you produce? Misshapen cripples and cretins, men who are closer to animals than

human beings – and this is what these most dreadful amateurs dare to
present as the expression of that which shapes the modern age and
stamps its hallmark on it.' Naturally the philosophical discussion turns
away from such allusions to the present and from its hallmark and finds the
following about itself and its kind, who would not have been regarded
as human among the Greeks: 'Never was humanity closer to antiquity
in appearance and in its feelings than it is today.' As we noted, a
commentary on the Führer's speeches is no business of ours, while there
are still doctoral dissertations in the Third Reich, and their topics, so we
hear, are limited. Recently a dissertation is said to have appeared on the
topic 'Life and activities of purveyors to the court', and another one on
'Signposts in the age of national migration'. A chair of astrology was
even 'recommended' by the Führer to the Berlin faculty of science.
Given this desperate academic state of affairs, sweet fruits can be picked
even from the Munich speech, the German Nobel prize is in the offing.
'Streicher[71] and Hellas' – a worthy topic, a truly philosophical discussion; this above all would be capable of furnishing the standards which
'are appropriate for the high foundation of a temple of art'. They grow
potatoes in Boeotia, breed owls in Athens,[72] but Greek cannibals are
unknown up to now.

Meanwhile the Munich temple has been officially opened. 'This object', says the man who commissioned it, 'is so unique and original that
there is nothing to be compared with it. There is no building of which
one could claim that it was the model and this one here was the copy.'
Others call the same thing brutalizing neo-classicism or Aurora in oils.
But nothing has yet come to light about the style in which the opposing
concern – the hall of 'degenerate German art' – is built, although here
we really have an object with which there is nothing to be compared.
The very juxtaposition of this 'temple' and this 'hall' is unprecedented,
and nothing has been heard of the temple sinking without trace in
shame. The man who commissioned it could indeed lay claim to origi-
nality here: a similar proximity of evil and good, of corruption and
future, of kitsch museum and picture-gallery has not as yet existed in
the world. Since there has as yet been no such government in history,
there has been no such reversal of values. In the 'temple' unspeakable
banality (the one or two better older works, there are very few of them,
stick out like Schubert in the Dreimäderlhaus).[73] Whereas in the 'hall'

71 Julius Streicher, 1885–1946, leader of German Socialist Party in Nuremberg, founder and editor of the anti-semitic paper *Der Stürmer*, later joined
the Nazis. He was sentenced to death at the Nuremberg trials.
72 An allusion to the proverbial German phrase 'Eulen nach Athen tragen',
equivalent to 'carrying coals to Newcastle'.
73 *Dreimäderlhaus* ('The House of the Three Girls'), a musical play by H.
Berté, with music by Schubert.

near the gallows hangs everything which has given a new lustre and name to German art, masters of world repute, above all Franz Marc, the pride of Germany, the great admirable artist, first a war victim, then the victim of a Marsyas who finally flays Apollo.[74] Franz Marc's marvellous work 'The Tower of Blue Horses', together with Nolde, Heckel, Kirchner, Pechstein, Beckmann, Kokoschka, Kandinsky, Schmidt-Rottluff, Chagall, Feininger, Hofer, George Grosz, Campendonck, Paula Modersohn, Klee, and Otto Dix, illuminated the chamber of horrors in which the whole of Germany finds itself, and endure the inscriptions which shabby stupidity and demagogic vulgarity have pinned on them. If Picasso, and indeed Cézanne, van Gogh, and Manet were Germans, if Grünewald were not already long dead, these masters would undoubtedly also have found accommodation here; it would be quite in order. A state which only survives by stultifying, degrading and demoralizing the people will tolerate no standard by which it could be measured; the most putrid kitsch is good enough, it does not stand out. Even the gangster loves an oleograph over the sofa on which he is snoring; even the philistine is not without a sense of beauty, his daughter plays A Virgin's Prayer, and Courths-Mahler[75] tugs at his heartstrings. Franz Marc is no match for this of course, in the gentle mystery of his animals the banal Nazi beast is judged; before the mirror of George Grosz the whole of the new antiquity recoils. What a homely effect, however, the clownish figures of Grützner, Defregger[76] and the newly arisen parlour have on it. How comfortably the bourgeois conformists and their king make themselves at home here, not lost at all, with insolent cool – let no one moan away about displays of spite, whatever people say they are displays of might.[77] But in a different way from that in which Goethe intended this and was able to intend it, the spiteful man has gained mighty power today, is erecting temples for himself and taking it out on others. Beneath every picture of real German art sticks a placard with the inscription: 'Paid for out of the taxes of the working German nation'. But the temple of kitsch cost nine million marks alone, the battle between Defregger and Cézanne has been won with the deployment of large resources.

We are not moved by what is going on in the victor. If the very lie of the Nazis is worthless, their personal truth is even more so, it can be seen just by looking at them. But it is always important to ask, even

74 Bloch here ironically reverses the Greek legend: Marsyas was a pipe-playing Silenus who challenged Apollo to a musical contest and was finally defeated by him and flayed alive.
75 Hedwig Courths-Mahler, 1867–1950, a popular sentimental writer.
76 Eduard Grützner, 1846–1925, a German painter, mainly of humorous genre pictures. Franz von Defregger, 1835–1921, painter of Tyrol peasant and historical pictures.
77 Goethe, 'West-östlicher Divan: Wanderers Gemütsruhe'.

here, what intentions lie behind it, why and for what end these boundless insults? 'Miserable wretches, daubers, prehistoric stutterers, art
swindlers' – these are tones which have previously only rung out from
such mouths against Jews, Marxists and émigrés. All credit to resentment; but how does it have time for itself, in the midst of economic
distress, a shortage of raw materials, the struggle between Church and
state, and Spain? When Wilhelm II officially opened the Avenue of
Victory[78] with a very similar aesthetics, along with the 'gutter art', social
democracy was to be destroyed as well, and along with poor people's
painting, the poor people's movement. Social democracy is finished
today, in its place there is so-called German socialism, German peace; of
course it does not mean what it says. Well, the (let us say) neo-
classicism of the Führer's heart means itself, or simply aesthetic objects
in general, almost just as little as this. Instead, the attack on art is firstly
a new trap for bourgeois conformists, it flatters bad taste and malicious
stupidity at the same time; philistine tones and hunting whistles mingle
in an exceptionally demagogic combination. But secondly behind the
slogans 'antiquity' or 'cultural bolshevism' (and also 'Stone-Age art', it
does not matter that precisely) lurk the differences between Rosenberg[79]
and Goebbels, the same ones which had already become apparent in the
argument about Barlach.[80] They are the differences of a demagogy
which seeks to have an effect, now through the plush sofa, now through
youth, the campfire, and 'Irratio'. The plush sofa is the one side, it has
always been part of this 'revolution'. In the meantime it had likewise
been furnished with youth, bourgeois storm-trooping, expressio and
primeval times, perhaps even more effectively. Alongside the parlour
there was the lure of an irrational drive, as we know; the aversion to a
thoroughly rationalized existence had intensified it, certain 'non-
contemporaneous' features in backward strata were fundamentally congenial to it. The drive ranges from the vague longing for women, through
berserkerism, to those wild feelings, that conscious Unconscious, to
which Benn[81] gave lyrical, Klages philosophical, and C.G. Jung medical
expression. Paganism lives in these wishful images, the Greek kind as
well, not just the barbaric kind; a Greece, however, interpreted by the
blond beast, not by Hölderlin and by humanitarianism, and of course
not by the plaster-figure or bull's-eye pane antiquity of the ignorant
bourgeois conformist either. Our diluvial Benn has been 'out of order'
for a long time, but the fact that the alternative between primeval times
and 'decent art' (as the Führer says) had still not been decided in the top

78 The Siegesallee in Berlin.
79 Alfred Rosenberg, 1893–1946, Nazi politician and 'philosopher', executed
    after the Nuremberg trials.
80 Ernst Barlach, 1870–1938, Expressionist sculptor and dramatist.
81 Gottfried Benn, 1886–1956, Expressionist poet and doctor.

clique is proved precisely by the Munich speech, by the highly personal decision of the High Court supremo. Even in its afterbirths Expressionism still contained rebellious elements among the archaic ones; it represented the 'second revolution', as it were, among art students and young people who were interested in that kind of thing. The 'archaic', the 'primitive', is still desired today, as sadism, in concentration camps, and – as furor teutonicus – naturally in the coming war, continues to have an effect in the swastika, in 'victory runes' and the 'Odal',[82] in 'thingsteads'[83] and wherever decorative humbug seems to be in order. But however well-disposed big business was towards the swastika as long as it ensnared the masses, it equally never reconciled itself to the pathos of the Stone Age or of archaic degeneration. It needs punctual and domesticated employees, not primitive Teutons with Cockaigne in their dealings or with a gleam of blood in their after-sales service. Hence the excitement of the beginning and of the preparatory stage, the barbarian swindle, has to be able to disappear for the Saxons without forests as well, to disappear even in the slogans of Nazi art. It is perhaps exaggerated to say that art was the last ideological hiding-place of a 'second revolution'. But it is not exaggeratedly consistent to conclude that in the Munich speech on art a last swell of 30 June 1934,[84] that is of its suppression, died down on the remotest shore. This at least is certain: the motto of calm, fealty and order is given even to the art possible amongst the Nazis (and the slogans coined or preserved here). The SA of the irrational has played itself out on the canvas, and in particular every recollection of genuine Expressionism leads to the knacker's yard of 'degenerate art'. The wilderness is now always to have its sofa-newbuilding within it and above it, its obedient petit-bourgeois kitsch. The fact that the criticism of Franz Marc comes easy to the former picture-postcard designer Hitler is obvious anyway.

Something good is not lacking in all this evil. After his speech the Führer drove to a performance of Tristan and became engrossed in the scarcely Greek Wagner there. Wagner admittedly also has some Nazism of his own, ballyhoo, histrionics, decadent barbarism: Tristan does not deserve the sympathy in question all the same, Hans Sachs[85] even less so. But how dangerously blurring it would be perhaps for intellectuals who are nothing but this, though at least this, yet have now been perturbed by Hitler the artist, if the Nazi heart had the cheek or the hypocrisy even to beat for Franz Marc or, in another field, for Bartók

82 Tribal land owned and inherited by the ancient Nordic race.
83 Pseudo-pagan amphitheatres for Nazi ceremonies.
84 The date of the so-called Röhm putsch. Ernst Röhm, head of the SA, had publicly demanded a 'second revolution' before Hitler brutally suppressed this threat to his supremacy.
85 Hans Sachs, 1494–1576, cobbler-poet of Nuremberg and character in Die Meistersinger.

with the aim of a particular disguise. The confusion would be great; the fact that it is unfortunately not wholly impossible is demonstrated in some respects by the example of Mussolini, beneath whose rotten sceptre progressive architecture, painting and music worth discussing remain unmolested. The good element so to speak is thus that Nazi Germany arose totally of a piece; like master, like man,[86] filled with this temple art. A homogeneous system has entered into things, even art is sent to the torture chamber, the burning of books preceded the burning of people anyway, in name and kind alike. And the false messiah satiates the 'nation' with a well-paid mixture of dance on the alpine pasture over the sofa and blood and soil in the abyss.

86 German saying, literally 'Like master, like his pots and pans'.

FROM THE HISTORY OF THE GREAT WASTE (1934)

There is no talk of money here. But rather of the love which lands falsely. Great feelings have got hold of the wrong person in other cases too. Were mistaken for long enough, until even shame came too late.

Young people are easily seducible with themselves. For there is the most hope in them, and this is, apart from shuddering, the best part of us.[87] But a whole nation has also been reliant on hope from time immemorial, the Jews. They sought the Promised Land, and when they had it the wish for it did not come to an end. The Book of Isaiah is full of promise of the 'servant of God' who will be the future saviour. When the nation came under new servitude, under that of the Syrians, then under that of the Romans, then especially under the western servitude of the diaspora, the idea of the Messiah grew more and more relentlessly, with no reduction, totally fused the earthly and the heavenly Jerusalem. It was precisely for this reason that they had abandoned Jesus to the Gentiles, because he did not seem to fulfil the burning image of the Messiah, because he did not actually turn the world upside down. They remained true to the dream of the King of Jerusalem and waited for the Paraclete without appeasing their hunger on the way, without a pre-liminary stage. Even the poorest Jewish thief could not be persuaded, not even before and in the pogrom, to acknowledge the Messiah Jesus, who would at least have saved him here, through baptism. But in the year 1648, the Thirty Years War was over, only not for the Jews, the silent waiting acknowledgement changed, and the expectation seemed just as suddenly fulfilled as it had previously been restrained and strictly reserved. For in Asia Minor a prophet had arisen, by the name of Sabbatai Zewi, who claimed to be the Son of God and the promised Messiah. He was actually a mediocre man, who had fallen into blas-phemy without any gifts of his own, driven more by the possessed

---

87 Cf. Goethe, *Faust*, Part II, 6272: 'To shudder is the best part of mankind.'

young people around him than by any plan of his own. But his ambitious fame spread more and more fierily among the Jews, kindled an ecstatic movement in the west as well, among the Jews of Italy, France and above all Germany, with St Vitus's dance, visions, jubilant followers, and intoxication by the saviour; all the more inexorably the closer the 'apocalyptic year' 1666 approached. The Jews, who regarded Jesus as the most despicable criminal because he had called himself the Messiah, the Son of God, the Lord's Anointed, fell for the most part without reservation to a Sabbatai Zewi, who not only claimed the same thing of himself, but who reached even higher up into the power of Jehovah and signed himself: 'I the Lord, your God Sabbatai Zewi, who led you out of Egypt'. The possessed deceiver revealed his true nature soon after his peaks, he kept none of his promises and performed none of the miracles, he even staged a Jesus–Pilate scene in the interrogation before the grand vizier, then went over to Islam and died as a hired doorkeeper. So it was for this that the Jews had suffered sixteen hundred years of deprivation, persecution, and death, for this that Jesus had been rejected and the expectation of the Messiah had been kept intransigent, to be discharged in the flash of such paltriness. The dream of the kingdom had been thrown away on a confidence trickster, who did not even possess sufficient stature to know what he promised and posited. The Jewish renewal was squandered, everyday life, after so much wasted intoxication, all the more bitter.

In those days the Jews had to bear, to their detriment, even more than derision. But the other nations, above all the Germans, later deceived and spent themselves in much the same way. The credulous power of the investment, the false goal did not lie so high, but the process repeated itself. Even in increasing phases, from 1813 to the First World War and the thoroughly baroque present day. In 1813 the nation rises in arms, the storm breaks, and undoubtedly a genuine storm, blown up by the awakening bourgeois consciousness. However the wars of freedom became so-called wars of liberation, namely from the soldier of the French Revolution, and the bad old times were afterwards more firmly entrenched than ever. The democratic youths themselves had put their rulers back in place again, without the sort of freedom I mean, unless in the shroud with it. In 1832 came the Hambacher Fest;[88] in 1848 the storm finally broke under other banners than those of the king, the skies of an unknown freedom stood totally in the German heart. Young people perceived their peculiar, frenetic character, the abstractness, yet also the 'universality' of their enthusiasm, when the great men of the people called out to them at the Hambacher Fest, Wienbarg or Wirth or

88   Hambacher Fest: an assembly of the Democratic Republican movement of Southern Germany in Schloss Hambach, leading to total suppression of the freedom of the press and assembly.

Siebenpfeiffer or the ardent Mazzini,[89] the dreamers on democratic splendour. Protest flared up against all unnaturalness and arbitrariness. 'Things must change', shouted Wienbarg, the preacher of young Germany, 'we ourselves are called to see to this, in a thousandfold echo of feeling. How many withered leaves must we tear out of the garland of our life to achieve this, how much ugliness we must shed, how much vulgar prose we must sink forever in the sludge and silt of stale time, which new opinions of science, of art, of poetry, of religion, of the state, of life we must form and make the property of our hearts, all this must occupy us often and fervently, and friendliness must combine with friendliness in order to produce a mutual exchange and to reinforce itself.' But behind all these surging and genuine feelings, behind the intoxication and the subjectivity of this false consciousness there actually stood nothing other than the interest of the bourgeoisie, which had gained strength even in Germany. Precisely this bourgeoisie became 'vulgar prose' to a high degree, and one which only used the enthusiasm of the young citoyens and their revolution to sink them well and truly in 'sludge and silt', but into that of wasted poetry. If this did not yet succeed in 1848, then it did in the silent compromises later with Junkers, the throne, the army, and Bismarck's empire. As a new fervour there came the World War of 1914, to which social-democratic idealists marched off 'in order to have seen the foundations', those which were in fact called Hindenburg and Ludendorff. Almost already with an unconscious Hitler was the will to another life, the aversion to a bleak, reified, mechanized existence, the pathos of the national community, deceived at that time, was a false catch-phrase given to these emotions, for surprise attack and big business. And today in particular the dervish himself has leapt into business; for in this excess it is not only the sadists, the shabby idiots, the enthusiastic Saxons, the literary whores, the cold-blooded deceivers who flourish. But quite a few believe with precision, credulous youth succumbs to the dazzling illusion, dances around an apparent Midsummer's Eve bonfire, wants to burn like it, to change like it. The household effects of their forefathers join in the dance, Barbarossa in the Kyffhäuser,[90] the ravens fly, the ravens alight, Frederick the Only[91] is the first National Socialist, Hitler hopefully the last. In a wide arc the age of Sabbatai Zewi has been reached; with the difference that behind the false Messiah there stood nothing but his psychopathy, behind the Third Reich, however, there stands heavy industry.

89 Ludolf Wienbarg, 1802–72, German writer, leading figure of the 'Junges Deutschland' literary movement. Giuseppe Mazzini, 1805–72, Italian republican freedom-fighter. Wirth and Siebenpfeiffer were minor democratic republican figures.
90 See 'Amusement Co., Horror, Third Reich', in n. 33.
91 An ironic reference to Barbarossa.

Where does the jubilation go which has been deceived? Mostly it still sways for a while in the excited heart and then sinks into nothingness. The survivors experience suffering and are slightly paralysed; which does not prevent the same case recurring in the same people, and they have not learnt a thing. Thus only fifteen years lie between the World War and Hitler's victory; the liability to deception, the 'national community', even the 'ideas of 1914' which are supposed to supersede those of 1789 are preserved in a related way in the contemporary scene. This is no wonder in material terms, since late capital since the war, indeed even since the beginning of the century, equally has to disguise itself socially and to remain formidable. The wonder is only the vast credulity with which proletarianized youth and ex-servicemen with burnt fingers shower the same powers with credit and all the surplus of an unspent heart which have proletarianized them and will send them off to a new war. Even the impulse of the Peasant War, the closer one of the red Forty-Eighters and that of the Paris Commune, perished before reaching its goal; yet how illuminating the differences are. The devotion of those days was not one of those who have been seduced to deceivers, but one to their own clear, oppressed cause. Those who were then defeated live on as martyrs, not as the deceived; they were beaten by the superior strength of their enemies, not merely taken in by the same leader for whom they allow themselves to be taken and cut to pieces. In the case of the most active sections, even among those 'idealists' who are not all too precisely connected with the ruling class, the deceived jubilation may perhaps go to the proletariat; perhaps it also totally goes to the wall and shuns the fire. There is still enough youth coming up which has not disgraced itself as gullibly as the brown variety. But whatever is able to disappoint pure devotion, to discredit its good idea, indeed to pervert it into the total opposite, also approaches fascism ipso facto, today and tomorrow, from this side. Enthusiasm and love are of course a powder that will never run dry. It will take the right goal for itself, both in fireworks and in gunshot, first in gunshot, and will preserve the cause, and also keep it unmistakable, until and so that it encounters no fascio any more.

RACIAL THEORY IN THE VORMÄRZ
(1934)

But now good blood is prepared only in the Nordic way. Race always looks the way business needs it. That is why this Nordic element is not merely blond in any case, but loyal, prone to fealty, star-studded and decorated with masters, believing in them. It has looked that way, they say, since time began.

But what if exactly the opposite was true before the meal? The racists go back exclusively to Gobineau,[92] of course, as the ancestor of this nonsense. And the latter did actually teach that Germanic noblemen were high above the cowardly and impudent, and probably even grumbling subhumans. His 'Essai sur l'inégalité des races' typically appeared in 1854, in the period of general reaction, of the incipient alliance between money-bag and sabre. But before Gobineau, shortly beforehand, another book on race had already appeared, the Frenchman used it, but the racists have concealed the fact to this day. For good reasons, as we will see in a moment; for at the time the sons of Teut had very different characteristics from those now popular and tied to blood. The author, Friedrich Klemm; the title, 'A General Cultural History of Mankind'; the content, the first Germanic-pathetic racial theory. An important year of publication, 1845, hence in the midst of the seething vogue for freedom in the Vormärz.[93] Accordingly, Teut still looks particularly freedom-loving, full of reason and science, not to say foreign, enlightened and so liberal he is almost ripe for the concentration camp.

Only the exploitative pride is already the same here, at source. Indeed it seems more modern than in Gobineau; Klemm already recognizes 'active' and 'passive', 'dynamic' and 'static' races. Wherever high

---

92 Joseph Arthur Comte Gobineau, 1816–82, French writer, propagator of Aryan racial theory.
93 The period from 1815 to the March revolution in 1848.

civilizations have arisen, for him they go back to members of the active race. These have 'overlaid all nations with ruling strata and hence brought civilization', a cliché which has been used ever more expansively from Gobineau to Chamberlain[94] to Woltmann to Hitler, but is here found for the first time. Only in fact, the cliché had a content opposite to the modern one, in the still liberal interest of the bourgeoisie. The dexterity of fantasy was of a different order in those days; of which a small instructive extract from the source-book will convince us: 'The first or active half of mankind', says Klemm, 'is by far the less numerous kind. Its physique is slim, mostly tall and strong, with a round skull [!], with a forward-pressing, predominant forehead, protruding nose, large round eyes etc. With regard to the mind, we find predominantly the will, the element of activity, restlessness, the striving towards the wide blue yonder, progress in every way, but then the drive towards research and scrutiny, defiance and doubt. This is clearly expressed in the history of those nations which constitute active mankind, of the Persians, Greeks, Romans, and Teutons, With them there is freedom of constitution, whose element is constant progress; theocracy and tyranny do not prosper; knowledge, research, and thinking take the place of blind faith. Whereas in the case of the passive races we find fear of research, thinking and intellectual progress. The passive nations have . . . psychology, but no philosophy, they have remedies and knowledge of the human body, yet no medicine, in a word, they lack a really living science.' In short, the source-book of Nordic racial theory cultivates the same cheap and abstract antitheses, the same black-and-white presentation as its offspring, only with the opposite content. That which is the worst form of decay or intellectual bestiality today, was for the nobleman before 1848 Germanic inheritance. That which is archaic depths today, was for the proto-Gobineau 'Mongolian', deeply inferior race, 'standing under the influence of shamans', in short, only existing among Hitlerites. Even Hitler's deputy, Hess from Alexandria,[95] who totally consistently plays off quackery against medicine, would have found no mercy from this progenitor. Everything occult was here base, black-haired machination – the nobleman is enlightened per se.

So much for Mr Klemm, and only so much may he be dug up here. It is not as if there were not still cracking places today or as if they had not still given pleasure a short time ago. As in history lessons, precisely in the Greek and Roman ones, among the 'most active' Aryan nations. What jubilation over the birth of the Republic, over the murderers of

94   Houston Stewart Chamberlain, 1855–1927, son of an English admiral, later became a German citizen and writer, married Wagner's daughter, Eva. A champion of the Aryan spirit.
95   Rudolf Hess was born in Alexandria.

tyrants and kings, over Harmodios and Aristogeiton,[96] over Brutus. What embarrassment over the downfall of the Roman Republic, over the prorogation of the wretched Senate, what contempt, what an un-Roman image was supplied by the arsonist Nero. What pathos was expended against the Persian bringing into line,[97] against proskynesis,[98] despotism, the godlike humbug surrounding the rulers. How warm the sympathy with the Macedonians when they hated the aura of the great king with which Alexander surrounded himself. These emotions seemed alien, almost treasonable in the German, and especially the royal Prussian grammar school. They split the nobleman-like element almost schizophrenically in run-of-the-mill senior primary school teachers, the majority of whom were Teutonically monarchical through and through, as soon as Athenian democracy or the Roman Republic were no longer being dealt with. If these evaluations had long since become a cliché, their origin in the revolutionary bourgeoisie was still unmistakable. And even the Nordic pride was always ruffled by Hannibal, who has not yet been made into a Teuton to this day, as far as we can see. This pride is admittedly old, older even than our friend Klemm; a certain Rudbeck,[99] a contemporary of Leibniz, had already transferred not only the tribal homeland of the Teutons but the very origin of all civilization to Scandinavia, and the motto: Lux in tenebris cimmeriis[100] attained great importance at that time in the struggle for the Indo-Germanic homeland, and flourished into competition with that of Ex oriente lux.[101] But paradise itself did not yet lie in Pomerania; so little was this the case that even Schopenhauer presented the laurels to the sun-tanned, black-eyed breed of people. Indeed, this likewise older 'philosopher of race' even abused the breed to which he himself belonged; he called the Nordic race 'albinos' or those deprived of pigment beneath a miserable sun – all with racial pathos, all in contradiction to the modern kind. So double-edged is the knife through which Jewish blood spurts. So variously above all does even the 'active' nonsense reflect the ideology which this bourgeoisie needs at any one time.

96 Harmodios, a noble Athenian who in 514 BC, with his friend Aristogeiton, murdered the tyrant Hipparchos. Both were then put to death.
97 Bloch uses the term 'Gleichschaltung' here, an ironic reference to Hitler's policy of regularizing all aspects of society and opinion to conform with Nazi ideology.
98 Proskynesis: humble genuflection to a ruler or object of ecclesiastical authority.
99 Olof Rudbeck, 1630–1702, Swedish polymath.
100 'Light in Cimmerian darkness'.
101 'Light out of the East'.

MYTH OF GERMANY AND THE
MEDICAL POWERS (1933)

My dear friends, that finer times existed
Than our own – it cannot be resisted!
And a nobler nation flourished once.

Schiller

The soft sort is long past and gone. The new one feels it is of steel, a
blade through and through. It is one to the extent that it readily carves
that which has been made defenceless. But excellently as this type raves,
he can just as easily be called off if it pleases his masters. Always
wonderfully talented at the commanded fight, he finds the fight for
himself or that of rebellion all the harder. The German beast becomes an
ass as soon as it is led back into the stable. Thus the new German can be
much more easily bent than the liberal one of old. Does not even seek a
remnant of individuality like the latter, in which he may seem free. And
how astonishingly the new hard man, whether bent or leading, leaves
out the human face. The tame hero and the wild one, both turn into the
steaming animal. Not just the soft person, but often every person ceases
who previously shone.

The new one comes here on blood, even on his own. He thinks he
can breed himself, like dogs or horses. The *first* place to be German in
this way is thus the *pure* bed. So the fight is directed against those with
hereditary illness, they are not 'nursed', but exterminated. But even
illness of other kinds allegedly stems from innate bad juices, not from
hunger or the hellish life of the worker. The Nazi loves what has grown,
not what has been made; thus he does not need to intervene in what
has been made, namely the capitalist economy. But he intervenes all the
more safely in organic growth, has in 'good blood' the remedy for most
infirmities. Seduces doctors with it, not by making the social life important to them, for example, to which the healthy or the cured kind is

sent. National Socialism does not show that the ill are today being made 'healthy and productive' for a hell; does not show that illnesses are coming back today like wounds in a war. Instead blood care operates up until birth and then no longer; at the same time it combines very well with hatred of the large town. Peasant blood is supposed to create health ab ovo, however exhausted it may be by inbreeding and other damage, in contrast to sporting types of the town for example. Towns are nevertheless regarded, right the way through, as ravagers of national vigour; again not on account of the capitalist economy, but on account of the 'materialistic view of life' (i.e. on account of the proletarian one or that advanced in crisis). Moreover, a totally liberalist fear pervades fascism; the fear of the sinking birth rate. The German rate is indeed particularly low at present, even below the French one; thus here too the cultivation of blood is intended to give a boost. A superstition of large numbers underlies this fear, as if the liberal age still prevailed, the middle capitalist one, when the employer could not utilize enough workers, whether as employees or as a wage-squeezing reserve army. Today the unemployed person is thoroughly sufficient for the formation of this army, indeed is a downright danger for the capitalist economy, or at least a burden. Nevertheless the Nazis, as so often, cultivate a superannuated ideology; they have the 'healthy opinions' of a backward stratum. Whereby the boosting of the reactionary domestic sense is not excluded of course, and certainly not the commissioning as cannon fodder. Hence the large numbers – and once again from the point of birth – are precisely divided up at the same time, namely into the mass of those who are led and into the small stratum of born leaders. Those who have come off badly are to believe even on the evidence of their own body that they are rightly in such a state and must remain so. One is thus born into the caste of the employees more strictly and more inescapably than formerly into the caste of the serfs; what was willed by God at the time of serfdom is willed by nature in fascist terms. Conversely the leading businessmen and politicians rule by virtue of their *master-race* blood; this alone determines the new nobility, the new elite of exploitation. Rule over other people remains eternal; after it threatens to become shaky, 'the whole future legislation is to be founded on racial doctrine'. But the German state fares best because it also has its capitalists as Germans and only as Germans. The German nation is for the Nazis not bad enough to tolerate Marx, but good enough for Stinnes or Thyssen. All kinds of dreams swirl about the Nordic race as well, with features which it never had or which it does not have alone. And the real face of the new nobility, if not its guiding image, is always the facelifted exploiter of today.

Yet blood again, one even finer than the healthy kind, also holds together. The average man, often injured, finds his self in a strong nation again. The *second* place to be German in this way is thus the *aryanized fatherland*. The average citizen, and especially his youth, no longer wants to be anything at all 'particular', but something general so to speak, namely an adequate cog and link in the nation as a whole. Individual advancement, make way for efficiency, successes in free competition are hardly possible any more; so the craving for admiration throws itself into the general national feeling to which it already belongs, and overdoes it. It is wrong to say that here the individual first of all rebelled and fought against stereotyping as a collective fate. The 'soul' of the employee admittedly fights against the business concern; there are certainly also individual tendencies in it from former days, from the age of free competition, but they are no longer as important as many petit-bourgeois intellectuals believe, on the basis of their own individual remnants. Instead, for the main troop of the Nazis the sought-after field lies beyond the individual and the collective (which both appear to be liberal and mechanical to them). What are desired instead are comradely groups, as federations, camps, workforces; these give the business a deceptive consecration, rechristen it organically. If the consciousness of class differences is most idealistically prevented in this way, and lasting exploitation, lasting empty mechanicism most romantically disguised, the doctrine of blood itself seems almost like 'materialism', though in a strange sense. For the 'mind' is by no means primary here; it and its framework are rather 'dismantled to the ground', as if there were 'analysis' here too. Just as the Nazi goes back to the *peasants*, as the most organic caste, so for him the *personal physicians, racial doctors and hygienists* are his *social science* so to speak. They are also important to him in terms of state theory; hence not only the pathos of heredity and selective breeding, but above all the *national pathos of blood*. Thus almost even better than the Protestant state theologians, the German doctors proved themselves able to be brought into line. Precisely the 'Deutsche Ärzteblatt', one of the most distinguished medical organs, highly instructively announces: 'Reverence for our forefathers, for the life- and bloodstream of the Germanic race, must lift our souls again beyond the individualistic and liberalist thinking of the times.' The nation thus becomes, in medical terms as well, a unity filled with blood, a purely organic river basin, from whose past humanity stems, into whose (most traditionally limited) 'future' its children go. Thus 'nationhood' drives time, indeed history out of history: it is space and organic fate, nothing else; it is that 'true collective' whose underground elements are supposed to swallow the uncomfortable class struggle of the present, as totally superficial and ephemeral. 'Nations are units of blood', says the fascist sociologist Freyer; if Marx taught that the mind was a reflection of the economy, the strange idealists of fascism judge it exclusively to be a reflection of blood. The medicine which is digging out this new 'substructure' is – like its blood – made of special stuff,[102]

102   Cf. Goethe, *Faust* Part I, 1741.

of course. It is admittedly still 'Darwinism' to excess (natural selection and the like), but the blood which its 'analysis' emphasizes has become a mystical entity: moreover in the economic service of a new ideology of the fatherland. This new ideology is certainly better understandable from the viewpoint of the economy than from that of 'medicine'; thus Marxism still encircles and fetters those who, in their ignorance, think they have overcome it subjectively. For the pathos of the nation-state is not just a modern one; it stems instead, in its first manifestation, from none other than the – liberal, the French Revolution. As has already been seen in an earlier chapter, the 'Saxons without forests' have only this first beginning of national feeling as a genuine one, one which was genuinely revolutionary: in the French Revolution enfants de la patrie did indeed catch up on their 'hereditary prince' and establish themselves, only themselves as a nation. The child of the fatherland was the bourgeois class in revolt against the hereditary feudal economy; and with the progressive development of the bourgeois forces of production national pathos also marched into Germany, ideologized the German Customs Union[103] (against the individual dynasts), the foundation of the German Reich and ultimately – with an ever more thoroughly capitalized domestic market – the highly capitalistic necessities of imperialism. This German national pathos had always been crossed by medieval and feudal remainders (which no revolution had removed from their political power); as in the Old German or chivalric romanticism, as in the romanticism of the second imperial Reich, the bull's-eye pane or 'German Renaissance', as in the Hohenstaufen dream of pan-German imperialism. But now expansion is blocked for German capital and its most pressing need has become defence against the crisis, with all the consequences: and immediately a *new national ideology* presents itself, precisely the state of blood or the distraction towards Irratio, the bond via an organically common mystical entity. But the new state is even less national than the earlier ones in the genuine, real sense free of ideology; it is at best non-international, namely autarkical or a remnant of the collapsed world economy. And it is also eminently international, in so far as capital in all fascist states must develop the same kind of national feeling and national ideology, namely against class-conscious proletarians. This class struggle from above connects Italy, Germany, and Hungary in the same Roman, Germanic, even Turanian[104] ecstasy and has only economic and political as well as strategic differences, none of real nationality. This does not prevent the revolutionary situation from

---

103 Deutscher Zollverein: customs union of small states under the leadership of Prussia, founded in 1834, which prepared the way for later political union of the Reich in 1871.
104 Turanian: of Turan, the ancient name of the land east of Persia, beyond the Oxus.

compelling even the myth of blood, indeed this very myth, to include 'archaic revivals' whose wildness and Irratio are not necessarily favourable to capitalism, as was to be seen. But their arrogance serves deception for the time being, and their Irratio shows – not merely that it lacks reason – but very little instinct too, neither of the socialist kind nor that of genuine 'nation'. We stress: *of a genuine nation*; for 'nation' is surely a reality and not solely, as always up to now, an ideology. But only genuine socialism will also catch up on genuine nation, as a linguistic or cultural unit; only the international control of the production of goods and distribution of goods will really expose the multiverse of nations; only this Esperanto of the insubstantial will bring substantial human existence, even as a nation, to light free of ideology. Until then workers do not indeed have any fatherland, any more than the increasingly 'proletarianized' do, despite their subjective patriotism; for the nation is split into classes, the majority of the means of production belongs to a small stratum, the fatherland is actually one of the rich. For a long time 'nation' has not been a revolutionary factor in western Europe as it was at the time of the French Revolution, and still is in India, China and all colonial countries; it is imperialistically aggressive instead (in connection with the rivalry of the great capitalist states) or in fact the numbing of revolution through a 'common myth of blood'. The fatherland is born only by removing its profiteers, by the actual abolition of classes, by transferring land and property, and all means of production and cultural assets, to the *ownership of the nation*. The state of blood deceives peasants and petit bourgeois, shoots at proletarians; it is a national unit in appearance and with an ideology in which even the 'archaic' element is only very inauthentic into which it claims to lead back and to melt back. So-called National Socialism is for the same reasons neither national nor socialist, but a deception or mistake in both. Only the International causes the National to seize possession of itself, and makes of meagre and ideological 'national souls' national bodies of nearness. In class society up to now nation has been at best a fragment or the particularly cunning use of a revolutionary motif by the ruling class-ideology. Only in the actual national unit, not in the romantic-deceptive one of 'patriotism', does nation thus become real.

Blood in the end, the very special stuff, is supposed to make its own into believers again. Thus they dance around the fire, youth wants to burn and to transform itself like its age. How much good, dulled sense is often wasted here, how imaginatively and emptily it asks to be abused in every way. What has become important here is the will or at least the spectacle of a dangerous life; with this the Nazi makes the strongest pre-capitalist seduction. The third place to be German in this way is thus *romanticism of heroic paganism*. The soldierly type rules in the federations and imaginary castes; masculine soldierly substance breaks through in an eroticizing fashion, alongside unprecedented brutality and psychopathy. Discharged officers, pugnacious and adventurous figures whom the respectable bourgeoisie had earlier termed desperadoes, and much grotesque mediocrity as well throw on 'the helmet-armoured face of the haughty warrior' and play the anti-bourgeois, in the manner of mercenaries or at least aesthetically. In the face of this undeniable seduction, liberalism (which is no longer useful to capital) naturally fades particularly easily. Its type is totally at the mercy of National Socialism (and the Communism from the other side certainly does not help it); the kinetic class struggle throws away the gentle illusions which the static class rule tolerated for a century. They had remained in Germany for a long time only as the League of Human Rights,[105] as the vegetarian restaurant, as good-naturedness without power, as life-security without cultural fullness, as tolerance without revolutionary alcohol, in short as a mere governess of capitalism or as social democracy. A vacuum had thus arisen here, and that is why (when Severing[106] had cleverly banned the Red Front) the energy of the unemployed post-war broke in all the more seductively here. And became, since its steps were not directed by reason, a Peasant War as imperial parade, counter-revolution as a substitute for a genuine one. This accused the bourgeois and the Communist alike of 'betrayal of the dangerous' which they 'degrade to senselessness' – and merely protected with this dangerous element as such, with the abstraction of the dangerous, the true senselessness, that of the bourgeois. It ignored in revolutionary communism the fact that it stands more genuinely in the dangerous element than the colonial force of the existing order; it misunderstood with the greatest disorientation the fact that the classless society, the socialist state of the future, precisely represents no security, sold out to everybody, no bourgeois republic, totalized, no poppied virtue, but would be the first *controlled* history, the first closing of thighs to treat life in a really commanding way and give it an open field to ride in, both without cares and without lies. But the faith in blood does not want an open field at all; it is satisfied to smash to pieces or to galvanize (with much enthusiasm in both cases, mostly for falsehood). It dances round the fire of Midsummer's Eve, throws in make-up, powder, stop-watch, Emil Ludwig,[107] Karl Marx and Lenin, as if it were all the same thing, 'the symbol of a now perishing society'. Through promptly willing literati à la Benn or Winckler[108] it has even espied 'the hour of genius', with a great deal of war poetry from 1914, with a fortissimo seldom

---

105 The League of Human Rights was originally founded in Paris in 1898 to press for a review of the Dreyfus case; it went international in 1922.
106 Carl Severing, 1875–1952, SPD politician, Reich Minister of the Interior 1928–30.
107 Emil Ludwig, 1881–1948, biographer.
108 Josef Winckler, 1881–1966, writer.

even at the time and sheer solstice celebrations in permanent form. 'Gone', cries Josef Winckler, 'gone is the depravity of sensational asphalt problems, the intellectual indecency of artistic masturbation – the animal-human element is spat out which struck up its own dance with lecherous songs. A civitas Dei of all creative minds must grow with crystal battlements above a purified nation. Call us for this purpose alone, fiery-ancient, often disgracefully lost, again and again gloriously arisen, world-rebellious, world-unfolding sacred-barbarian genius of the Germans!' Very bad German of course, very imitative, Sturm und Drang industry, resentment of the untalented and an Expressionism which has sunk to the level of the local gazette; the hour of real genius sounded different. This does not hinder the enthusiasm of the listeners, however; for them the radio hour of genius came from Goebbels to Benn, they thus travel on blood not only into bed and the Nordic state, but into the land of Germanic dervishes, into the slaughter-house and epigonic satyr-play at one and the same time. Arctic sultriness makes an embarkation for Cythera; but not in fact for a cheerful, cultured, Mediterranean or simply westernist one, as formerly when Teutons advanced into the ancient world. But the Germany of the reduced and the reduced Germany loves the opposite to the old one: where it does not already stand in barbarism, it seeks the *Cythera of barbarism*. National Socialism thus fused this whole irrational system in broad plebeian terms; from George[109] to anthroposophy, to ecstasies which were previously in mere schools of dancing, to the diverse crypto-religions of which an alienated and lacking age was full. And it drew them together precisely in the myth of blood or in the almost mysterious fire which Hitler has bestowed on 'Germany'. As a country hardly on the earth any longer; as a patria in which blood lust, pogrom, primeval forest, Rome, Mazdaznan,[110] dream-world, crazy drawings, dancing rapports, archaic rapture and heavenly Jerusalem chime in a single blasphemy. Only the Jews do not chime with this blasphemy, the same people whose Bible had once nourished and thoroughly christianized the whole of the old Germany; that Germany which extends from Eckhart to – Mahler. And Christ, the Jew, stands so awkwardly and crookedly in relation to the new religion, that characteristic of its species; and yet 'German Christians' place the image of Jesus together with their own just as if he were Hamann[111] and his father were Baal. 'The German faith', says one of these Christians of blood, 'thus denies that there is a further particular

109 Stefan George, 1868–1933, poet and centre of the George-Kreis, a fashionable circle of aesthetes.

110 Mazdaznan: from the Persian divinity Ahura Mazda, a religious salvation movement based on the teachings of Zoroaster, founded by O. Hanisch around 1900.

111 Johann Georg Hamann, 1730–88, philosopher of religion, known as the Magus of the North.

word of God which jointly holds good for all nations, apart from the highest inspirations and intellectual creations of its country.' Hence Christianity is 'purified of its Jewish concepts and ideas' (which is about as meaningful as purifying Homer of his Greek concepts and ideas); hence God becomes the Prime Minister of Germany, German birth a Christian baptism, ritual murder of Jews a Sermon on the Mount, unparalleled natural magic a descent of the Holy Ghost. Murder calls itself the SA of Christ; but even the remaining Church which has been brought into line excludes the Jews, excludes the sacrament of baptism and continues to call itself a Christian church, founded on the Bible (of which not a single author was Aryan), founded on Jesus Christ (whose family tree, with which the New Testament begins for inspection, contains not a single Gentile). This Church, at least serving in Protestant terms, at least making a Concordat[112] in Catholic terms, is based on the Bible, of which after all the new Führer says: 'Judaism was always a nation with certain racial characteristics and *never a religion*; only its progress caused it to seek very *early on* for a means which was able to divert the unpleasant attention directed towards its members' ('Mein Kampf'). So the Jews had no religion (the Greeks no art or philosophy either of course, and the Romans no state); so the prophets and apostles, Jesus Christ, the early Christians and Spinoza are disposed of, their progress clarified – and there remains the church of Hitler, it does not divert the unpleasant attention directed towards its members. There has always been a lot of deception in the religious field, but never so much base lunacy, so much bloody farce as well; the combination of the New Testament with the Ring of the Nibelungen and the Horst Wessel Song is Satanism, and a miserable kind at that. So remote has the Germany of blood become from the ancient Gothic one, indeed even from the romantic one that it still conjures. Non-contemporaneity as a mere after-dream, the 'Christian heroic cult' as a religion of mere blood frenzy, they link up with Gothic images of hell, not with the German All Souls' Day, All Saints' Day which once stood at the heart of the Gothic period. Indeed, the features of the beast from the abyss are sketched out, infernal evil in still inconceivable horror; it was surely this that found its Enabling Act,[113] shabby and fundamentally uncanny at one and the same time. 'A nobler nation flourished once': Schiller meant the Greeks, but no false present bars us from also thinking of the old Germany, of the land of mystically extended inwardness and apocalyptically nourished dreams, of which almost nothing has remained today but an anti-semitic rabble, decadent barbarism and above it the most

---

112 There is a long history of treaties between the papacy and the state, but Bloch undoubtedly has the treaty between Pope Pius XI and Hitler in mind here, concluded between their representatives on 20 July 1933.
113 Nazi Act of 1933 enabling Hitler to supersede the constitution.

hardboiled capitalism in the world. Very different forces from those rampant today would be necessary for the inheritance of this old Germany to become a possessed, a realized one, and then certainly one of the most important observatories of that and solely of that which indeed 'jointly holds good for all nations'. Namely of the human face to be processed out; in Gothic Germany some of its outlines appeared perhaps most powerfully, even if only in the tangled line enforced by mere inwardness. 'Where are the barbarians of the twentieth century?' Nietzsche asks, and means a kind of refined ice age. This cry – in a less refined way, though certainly with an ice age now and then – has kindled disciples, nonsense and susceptibilities today. The myth of blood forgets, however, that barbarians who know and say that they are such are not even barbarians. Only the *unbecome* light, which possibly even lies hidden in archaisms, allows itself to be known and said; though then it becomes light and is not ailing capitalism with competitive myths of the centre or even deceived-deceiving wild revival in its belly. Rather, the alpha of the prehistoric 'gentes'[114] becomes the very much transformed omega of the posthistoric 'commune'. And even now: the contradiction of much young peasant recuperation-seeking blood to these times, the contradiction of genuine non-contemporaneity to the capitalist death machine, rightly understood and grasped, rightly guided in a multilayered-material dialectic, does not necessarily land up, as previously, in the logic and physics of capital.

114   Gentes: patrilineal clans; the concept is particularly associated with the early Romans. In his *Origin of the Family* Engels described how Communism would restore the society of the 'ancient gentes' on a higher level.

SUMMARY TRANSITION: NON-CONTEMPORANEITY AND OBLIGATION TO ITS DIALECTIC (MAY 1932)

A. EARLY CONDITION

Not all people exist in the same Now. They do so only externally, through the fact that they can be seen today. But they are thereby not yet living at the same time with the others.

They rather carry an earlier element with them; this interferes. Depending on where someone stands physically, and above all in terms of class, he has his times. Older times than the modern ones continue to have an effect in older strata; it is easy to make or dream one's way back into older ones here. Of course, a merely awkward man who for this very reason falls short of the demands of his position or little position is simply backward in himself. But what if in addition, through the continuing effect of ancient peasant origin for instance, as a type from earlier times he does not fit into a very modern concern? Various years in general beat in the one which is just being counted and prevails. Nor do they flourish in obscurity as in the past, but contradict the Now; very strangely, crookedly, from behind. The power of this untimely course has appeared, it promised precisely new life, however much it merely hauls up what is old. The masses also streamed towards it, because at least the intolerable Now seems different with Hitler, because he paints good old things for everyone. There is little more unexpected and nothing more dangerous than this power of being at once fiery and meagre, contradictory and non-contemporaneous. The workers are no longer alone with themselves and the employers. Much earlier powers, from a very different bottom, begin between them.

B. NON-CONTEMPORANEITIES, REPORTED

One sort always starts from the front. *Youth* mostly turns away from the day which it has. Which it does not have today, yet its dreams do not merely come from an empty stomach. They are just as corporeally supported by a hollow being-young which is not present. Young people without work can easily be paid and seduced from the right. Young people of bourgeois origin, yet without bourgeois prospects, go to the right in any case, where they are promised some. But it is nevertheless indicative that no youth stands with the fairly present centre; there is no economic party of twenty-year-olds. The condition of twenty-year-olds is rather devoted to a different life from the reified life of today. Naturally there is no youth as such or none which grows up so homogeneously, so independently of the times, the way the same beard grows on young lads at all times. But however much this condition is a different one in different classes and times, however much even the words which describe it are different ones today from yesterday, very early bodies emerge just as clearly here in the Now, send in an element of prehistoric life. If boys recover bow and arrow, young lads easily join movements,[115] and thereby seek friends and above all a father, who was often not their natural one. This proves easier in bourgeois youth than in proletarian youth; though not only because it is bourgeois, but because it is more disintegrated and consequently lets games and enthusiasms through more often. Preoccupied with itself over and over, of the utmost importance to itself, this youth shows, together with its shift to the romantic right, how external its badly present, its factual gesture was. The keen air of youth causes left-wing fire, when it burns, to burn even more strongly; but if there is 'renewal' on the right, then the youth

---

115 Bündisch werden: literally 'become federative', with a further reference to 'Die Bündische Jugend' here, the 'Free Youth Movement', a term used to describe various youth organizations after 1918.

of bourgeois and seduced circles is all the more seducible: the blood-based, the organically young is a good soil for Nazis. Federations of very ancient style spring up on it, blood-based, tangible life in small groups, with a known leader, not with numbers at the top. The taste of this youth is particularly receptive to successful manly qualities, to strength, openness, decency, purity; whereby this 'decent' element belongs to healthy fellows, and does not want to be one of fixed prices. Attitudes have a more powerful effect than doctrines, inspiring words a more precise effect than inquiring ones, traditional costumes a more beautiful effect than cities: thus the economic motive which drives bourgeois youth into past dreams commits itself to organic unrest and early light of one's own. That which previously roared and enthused in an empty fashion is unrestrainedly off to one side in the beautiful old realm, now that the adult life at present has become too unconvincing to react against it by sowing one's wild oats. Youth which is not in step with the barren Now more easily goes back than passes through the today in order to reach the tomorrow. As long as the different time in which it exists does not shift towards tomorrow.

Another sort is from a very long time ago, by being rooted. Still lives almost exactly like its forefathers, does the same as them. It is the *peasantry*: in the country there are faces which for all their youth are so old that the oldest people in the town no longer remember them. If misery or a softer opportunity drives into the factory, there is nevertheless a peasant proverb: work to which you are whistled is no good; precisely the small peasant farmer thinks this, even if previously he had not lived much better than his labourer. The peasant is admittedly excellent at calculating, has given up his traditional costumes, furniture, much ancient style, and by no means merely under compulsion. But even if the peasant reacts to economic questions in a refreshingly sober way, even if the handwoven phrases he now uses are not all rooted in the soil, the sober element is still not of today, and wherever silence and dullness, convention of custom and belief occurs the peasant wears traditional costume. He doggedly defends his economically superannuated place, is harder to displace by the machine than the craftsman a hundred years ago. He is harder to displace if only because he still has the means of production in his hands, and also uses agricultural machines merely as aids in the ancient framework of the farmyard and accompanying fields; no factory owner here introduces against economically weak craftsmen the mechanical loom and corresponding things which only the capitalist could possess. This form of production which has remained communal also makes it so hard to mobilize the great economic differences in the peasantry. There are midget peasant farmers in misery, small peasant farmers, middling peasant farmers, big peasant farmers, and these very different property conditions are certainly an obstacle to taking the peasantry as a uniform 'class'. Yet the midget peasant farmer still has property, even though paltry and totally encumbered in debt, and the big peasant farmer cooperates, plays the active patriarch: the different property conditions as yet generate from within themselves no struggle between exploiters and exploited (only very different propaganda from the proletarian kind takes a grip here). Thus the peasantry feels itself to be, if not a uniform class, then still a 'caste' which has remained relatively uniform. And above all, apart from private ownership of means of production, the peasants have yet another non-contemporaneity, that doggedness in being rooted which comes from the matter they cultivate, which directly sustains and feeds them; they are fixed in the ancient soil and in the cycle of the seasons. Thus not only the agrarian crisis drives peasants to the right, where they think they are sustained by tariffs, where they are promised the precise return of the good times. Their tied existence, the relative ancient form of their conditions of production, of their customs, of their calendar life in the cycle of an unchanged nature, also contradicts urbanization, unites with the reaction which is expert at non-contemporaneity. Even the soberness of the peasants is an anciently mistrustful, not an enlightened one, even their alert sense of ownership (of the soil, of the unmortgaged farm) is even more deeply rooted in things than the capitalist one. Soberness and a sense of ownership and even peasant individualism (ownership as an instrument of freedom, the house as a castle) stem from pre-capitalist times, from conditions of production which had already demanded the sharing out of land when there were as yet no individually managing bourgeois citizens. Thus the farmhouse, despite all capitalist forms, despite all ready-made clothes and urban products, is Gothic in outline and aura even today; the abandoned traditional costumes and furniture could even easily be put back in their old places again without this having a bull's-eye pane effect, as in the town. Remote places here seem particularly instructive, since they show cultural ground water which lies only deeper elsewhere. Chests are still made in Gothic form by the village carpenter for present couples with a modern date of the year, not as a fake, but as if by his father, great-grandfather and the old folk too. Despite the radio and newspapers, couples live in the village for whom Egypt is still the land where the princess dragged the boy Moses out of the river, not the land of the pyramids or the Suez Canal; it continues to be seen from the viewpoint of the Bible and the children of Israel, not from that of the Pharaoh. Konnersreuth again: the sweating of blood by the ecstatic virgin Therese Neumann there, in 1928,[116] against the will of the much more contemporaneous bishop, denotes a different piece of Gothic in Germany. The

116   Konnersreuth (Oberpfalz), birthplace of the visionary Therese Neumann, 1898–1962.

Fichtelgebirge,[117] the related Black Forest, and related Spessart[118] encapsulate this kind of thing; if these mountains are no longer as gloomy and haunted as they still were in Hauff's times,[119] raftsmen, glassblowers, spirits and robbers would be the nearest scenery surrounding such peasant Gothic even today. Economically and ideologically the peasants, in the midst of the nimble capitalist century, have an older position, however much capitalism has also adapted landed property, a pre-capitalist element, for its own ends, however much it has thoroughly capitalized the peasantry and provided it with its products, however much even the last village is connected by radio to the juste milieu. The peasants nonetheless retain a crooked remnant, feel themselves to be co-represented rather by manorial estates than by workers in the suspect city. As long as the time difference between city and country is not effaced in a very much broader tomorrow than the urban one of today.

For some years, as is well-known, the urban sort has also been learning to lose time. An impoverished *middle stratum* seeks to return to the pre-war period when it was better off. It is impoverished, and hence susceptible in revolutionary terms, but its work is far from the action and its memories make it completely alien to the times. The insecurity which produces merely nostalgia for what has been as a revolutionary impetus places figures in the midst of the city which have not been seen for centuries. But even here misery invents nothing or not everything, but simply blabs out, namely non-contemporaneity which long seemed latent or at most one of yesterday, but now refreshes itself beyond the yesterday in an almost mysterious St Vitus's dance. Older sorts of being thus recur precisely in urban terms, an older way of thinking and older images of hate as well, like that of Jewish usury as exploitation per se. The breaking of 'feudal tenancy'[120] is believed in as if the economy were at around the year 1500, superstructures which seemed revolutionized long ago come revolving back again and come to a standstill in today's world as whole medieval townscapes. Here is the Tavern of Nordic Blood, there the castle of the Hitler-duke, there the Church of the German Reich, an earthy Church in which even city folk feel themselves to be a fruit of the German soil and worship the soil as holy, as a Confessio of German heroes and German history. This sort of patriotism, the froth and the eye growing dim with which Germany is conceived in Germany, is not merely a substitute for the lost sense of

117 Fichtelgebirge: a range of mountains in Upper Franconia.
118 Spessart: forest in Lower Franconia.
119 Wilhelm Hauff, 1802–27, a Romantic writer, chiefly known for his fairy-tales.
120 Bloch uses the term 'Zinsknechtschaft' here, a medieval system of holding land in tenancy to a landlord; literally, 'tax-slavery'.

caste-status. 'The country's power and honour' is not merely a dream (a very convenient dream for the armaments industry) which compensates in collective feelings for the actual powerlessness and degradation of the individual petit bourgeois. There is not even simply a transfusion of the 'chosen people' on to the Germanic one, on to the totally idolatrous one here; but rather, the obvious excess is reminiscent of primitively atavistic 'participation mystique', of the attachment of the primitive man to the soil which contains the spirits of his ancestors. More than ever, the petite bourgeoisie is the moist and warm humus for ideology; yet it is evident that the ideology becoming rampant today has long roots and longer ones than the petite bourgeoisie. The peasants occasionally still believe in witches and exorcizers of witches, but not nearly as often and strongly as a large stratum of city-dwellers do in the ghostly Jews and the new Baldur.[121] The peasants occasionally still read the so-called sixth and seventh books of Moses, a colportage against diseases in the stable, and also about the forces and mysteries of nature; but half of the middle classes believe in the Elders of Zion,[122] in Jewish snares and Masonic symbols on all sides, in the galvanic forces of German blood and the German meridian. The employee lashes out wildly and belligerently, still wants to obey, but only as a soldier, fighting, believing. The employee's *desire* not to be proletarian intensifies into an orgiastic desire for subordination, for a magical bureaucratic existence under a duke. The employee's ignorance, which seeks past stages of consciousness, transcendence in the past, intensifies into an orgiastic hatred of reason, into a 'chthonism' in which there are berserkers and crusade images, indeed in which – with a non-contemporaneity which becomes extraterritoriality in places – negro drums rumble and central Africa rises. This means that the middle classes (unlike the proletariat) do not take part in production directly at all, but enter into it only with intermediate activities, with such a distance from social causality that an illogical space can develop, in an increasingly undisturbed way, in which wishes and romanticisms, primeval drives and mythicisms revive. Even the directly economic content of middle-class fascism is non-contemporaneous or has become so, since the freedom of trade and industry has solely been benefiting the large employers and destroying the small ones: parliamentary democracy is thus the hated guarantor of free competition and the political form corresponding to it. In its place, precisely the corporate state seeks to lead the economy back to the stage of the early-capitalist small business again; it commends itself to big business as an instrument against the class struggle, but to the middle

121   The Norse god of light.
122   A reference to the 'Protocols of the Elders of Zion', the forged protocols of a fictitious Jewish gathering, containing a scheme for Jewish world-domination under a king from the house of Zion.

stratum simply as a salvation and a topically romantic expression of its non-contemporaneity. Equally the middle classes find 'rationalization' *ideologically* unbearable and abandon the Ratio all the sooner the more it has appeared to them only hostile, doubly hostile in their world. Namely as mere late-capitalist rationalization and as equally late-capitalist undermining, though interpreted in 'Marxist-Jewish' terms, of the value of traditional contents. The superman, the blond beast, the biographical call for the great man, the scent of witch's kitchen, of a long past time – all these signs of escape arising from relativism and nihilism, which had become a source of cultured discussion in the drawing-room of the upper stratum, became genuine political land in the catastrophe of the middle stratum. Of course, however wild it pretends to be, this land is always inhabited only by employees, its houses are those of the family and of the 'clean' economy, whether of the pre-war period or of a corporate state; and the benefit is reaped by the big-capitalist upper stratum, which employs Gothic dreams against proletarian realities. Certainly obscurities also never had to endure such lively dealings with bourgeois conformists before, so much spitefulness, nastiness and most stubborn provinciality, so much Edda in pokerwork, so many heraldic mottoes in Saxon. But nevertheless, in the rage of millions, in the landscape which has become archaic around them, there are also fields of a different Irratio here. Living and newly revived non-contemporaneities whose content is genuine, whose manifestations bring pagan rawness, Panic nature with them. Rebellions of older strata against civilization have been known in this demonic form only in the Orient up to now, above all in the Mohammedan sector. Their fanaticism now still benefits the White Guards with us too; as long as the revolution does not occupy and rename the living yesterday. With the decline of Hitler the non-contemporaneous will also perhaps seem weaker: yet it remains as the seed and ground of the National Socialist and of every future heterogeneous surprise. National Socialism has shown enough proletarianized people in demonized form; their ridiculously horrible image must not be forgotten, let alone unused.

C. NON-CONTEMPORANEITY AND CONTEMPORANEITY, PHILOSOPHICALLY

Many of these were certainly only losing time in the Now. Only fell behind its procession because they walk too slowly, although in other ways their walk is completely of today. We will not therefore already try to see any older sort where there is merely a backward one. Which is admittedly badly disposed to the today, but belongs to it.

The little man, for instance, has lost money and wants it back again. On this path he can become brutalized and dream, he then also lies intellectually crooked,[123] but precisely in the Now. If the situation improves for him, the wild and dreaming element will cease in any case. If it does not improve, and Hitler, once in power, disappoints, then the proletarians who are fellow-travellers or are giving him a single try will jump off to the left in any case, where they are expected; but at least the petit bourgeois will not believe in ghosts any more. Much is only falsely non-contemporaneous there, would sooner return to the parlour today than tomorrow,[124] has 'sound' sense with rage and clichés, but no St Vitus's dance. Fills itself with beautiful words, loud games, radiant nonsense; and yet, on the basis of this drunkenness, only seeks to be a domestic animal again. If we do not want to underestimate it (which has not been happening to most people only for a short while), we will certainly therefore not make a movement garish at all points either. Believing, obeying, fighting, are these the fascist virtues? Perhaps, but for many people obeying is the best one among them. Order and hierarchy the fascist style of architecture? Perhaps, but many people are

---

123 Bloch is here also playing on the colloquial meaning of 'schiefliegen', 'to be wrong'.

124 'Lieber heute als morgen', 'the sooner the better'; but we have kept the translation literal because of the concept of 'Tomorrow' in this section of the book.

seeking their peace and quiet in this order,[125] a position in this hierarchy. Indeed, National Socialist agitation has been called, hardly unjustly, an appeal to the baser instincts[126] in man: again, no negative remark can be more actual. The images of more quiet inwardness are a different matter; even if many of them were not so cheap, one would still see that they cannot be more than thirty years old and have grown stale in that time. Here the little man simply does not notice where he is, although, in a small and stupefied way, he is thoroughly in the Now. Thus if many of these mists are unexpected and strange, they are not old.

Genuinely non-contemporaneous arrears

But equally not everything here is the little man who deceives himself. Alongside the early morning arising from mustiness, deprivation also brings the genuine one which is to be reckoned with. Today there are galoshes of misery which lead just as much into past times as the galoshes of happiness in the fairytale.[127] If misery affected only contemporaneous people, even though of a different position, origin and consciousness, it could not cause them to march in such different directions, particularly not so far back. They could not so little 'understand' Communist language, which is in fact totally contemporaneous and precisely orientated to the most advanced economy. Contemporaneous people, despite all the mid-position which keeps them economically stupid, despite all the appearance which finds room there, could not for the most part allow themselves to be so archaically degenerated and romanticized. Of course middle-class people also rebel differently from the proletarian against becoming a commodity because they are only indirectly involved in production. And also because the employee, at least until recently, was not yet so annulled, not yet so alienated in his work, not yet so unsecured in his position; moreover, unlike in the case of the proletarian, little individual possibilities of promotion existed. But even if now, after total proletarianization and insecurity, after the decline of the higher standard of life and all prospects of a career, the masses of employees do not join the Communists or at least the Social Democrats, quite the contrary, then there is obviously a reaction of forces which conceal the process of becoming a commodity not just in subjective-ideological terms (which was certainly solely the case with an unradicalized centre until after the war), but also in real terms, namely

125 Bloch is playing on the phrase 'Ruhe und Ordnung' here, the German equivalent of 'law and order'.
126 Bloch uses a colloquial phrase here with the literal meaning of 'inner swine'.
127 A reference to one of the fairytales of Hans Christian Andersen, 1805–75.

out of *real non-contemporaneity*. Impulses and reserves from pre-capitalist times and superstructures are then at work, genuine non-contemporaneities therefore, which a sinking class revives or causes to be revived in its consciousness.

After all, not only peasants and little people, but also superior masters have stayed fresh, namely old here. The road which capital cut through the 'organically' traditional land shows, as a German one at any rate, a particularly large amount of byways and cracking places. Even in the war it had become apparent that Germany is not only big capitalist land and the caste of Junkers not only a sham; this mixed even older causes and contents into the imperialistic war, as the 'rebellion of the forces of production against their nation-state form of exploitation'. (German social democracy had realized this at the time, though without drawing revolutionary conclusions from it, namely a fight primarily against the Junkers at home and automatic militarism; but the value of this non-contemporaneous realization is not cancelled by its unenforced conclusion.) Germany in general, which had managed no bourgeois revolution up to 1918, is – unlike England, and especially France – the classical land of non-contemporaneity, i.e. of unsurmounted remnants of older economic being and consciousness. Ground rent, large landed property and its power, were almost universally integrated into the capitalist economy and its political power in England, and differently in France; whereas in long backward and even longer diverse Germany the victory of the bourgeoisie did not even develop to the same extent economically, let alone politically and ideologically. The 'unequal rate of development', which Marx assigns in the introduction to the 'Critique of Political Economy' to material production compared with the artistic kind for instance, equally existed here for long enough in material terms alone and thus prevented the clearly dominating influence of capitalist thinking, and hence of contemporaneity, in the economic hierarchy of forces. With East Elbian feudalism a whole museum of German interactions was preserved at any rate, an anachronistic superstructure which, however economically superannuated and in need of support it may be, nevertheless prevails; world history was certainly not always urban history in Germany. It is not in question here whether Prussian Junker-dom has not itself exhibited very artificial, even rationalistic features for ages (unlike genuine boyardom[128] rooted in the people): the Prussian support of the Holy Alliance was, if it was the 'most modern', not the weakest at any rate. Today though, Junkerdom is half subdued or dependent on German National 'people's parties', or even on national 'socialism'; yet the Marxist revolution which seeks 'to revolutionize the old world with its own large overall means' does not in turn run up

---

128   Boyar: member of an old Russian aristocratic order, adviser to the princes and tsars.

against big business alone in the capitalist republic. But against new reactions of non-contemporaneity; it runs up against their padded 'contradiction' to capital, their sharpened one to Marxism. Alongside and in much false non-contemporaneity there thus equally stands this certain kind: the nature, and all the more so the spectre of history comes particularly easy to the desperate peasant and bankrupt petit bourgeois in Germany; the economic crisis which releases the spectre is taking place in a country with a particularly large amount of pre-capitalist material. It is very much the question whether Germany, in terms of its *strength*, is even more undeveloped, indeed more volcanic than France for instance; but the capitalist Ratio certainly has not thoroughly formed and balanced it so contemporaneously by a long way. Precisely this relative chaos then also rolled towards National Socialism 'untimely',[129] non-contemporaneous elements from even 'deeper' backwardness, namely from *barbarism*; and it would have needed no Nietzsche in Germany to turn the antitheses of blood against mind, wildness against morality, and intoxication against reason into a conspiracy against civilization. Needs and resources of olden times consequently break through the relativism of the general weariness like magma through a thin crust; indeed, the nihilism of bourgeois life, this process of the whole world becoming a commodity, becoming alienated, here shows preserved non-contemporaneities in a doubly 'natural' way and preserved 'nature' in a doubly magical way. Thus campfires and sacrificial smoke burn in the folkish hall. Trumpet-blasts announce the Führer more powerfully than in just a Wilhelminian fashion, the thin little gardens of ideology which falsify the myth really turn sultry and rise – in the raging middle masses – as a jungle. The pancake craters of nature, which usually steam in the parlour, become genuine volcanoes, that is to say volcanoes of mud, but also those of a darkest primitivization, of a totally non-contemporaneous, indeed disparate insanity. We recall the St Vitus's dancers and latent butchers of children who shout: 'Stop thief!' when they accuse Jews of ritual murder. We recall the tune: 'When Jewish blood spurts from the knife', which drifts over the SA troops as a swastika in music, we feel the dream of preserved insanity, preserved overcompensations from puberty in this kind of National Socialism. We smell the colportage of Indian sects of murderers and Chinese secret societies, the whole creeping forest, whispering forest of early colportage (with the Elders of Zion or the caves of the Freemasons at the heart of the mountain), we find age-old sadism even at funeral ceremonies, in oaths of revenge or in the ceremonial of rage at the 'memorial'. Thus there are uncanny elements enough in the whole 'departure'; it is not just simple 'rejuvenation', nor just competition with bestial means. Be-

129   An allusion to Nietzsche's *Unzeitgemäße Betrachtungen (Untimely Meditations)* (1873–6).

neath the threshold of sunken share values, beneath an intoxication which in the cold light of day often contains nothing other than somewhat disturbed bull's-eye panes, beneath a false non-contemporaneity which only appears in the guise of Papua in so far as it is not up-to-date: beneath all these bad anachronisms there is thus still a genuine one which poses a problem. Its acts are to be logically defined in what follows, though its contents are a wild confusion of unsold history, and also prehistory. The temporal alienation of this contradiction facilitates both the deception and the pathos of 'revolution' and reaction at the same time.

Logical character of non-contemporaneous contradictions

Deprivation lacks food and, in the centre, something higher as well. Which it can no longer find in present life, indeed has missed in the bleakness for a long time. This habitually, and ultimately 'spiritually' missed element thus likewise contradicts the Now, just as powerfully as the lacking food, and not just economically. Furthermore every fomenting contradiction, even its appearance, has two sides: an *internal* one so to speak which does not like something, and an *external* one in which something is wrong. The impoverished centre then, predominantly not of today, contradicts the Now, which lets it fall further and further, inwardly in a *muffled* way and outwardly with remnants which are *alien* to the Now. Thus the contradictory element is here, inwardly or subjectively, a muffled remnant, and it is equally in the times themselves, outwardly or objectively, an alien and surviving, in short, a non-contemporaneous remnant. As a merely muffled non-desire for the Now, this contradictory element is *subjectively* non-contemporaneous, as an existing remnant of earlier times in the present one *objectively* non-contemporaneous. The *subjectively* non-contemporaneous element, after long being merely embittered, appears today as *accumulated rage*. In tranquil times this was the peevishness or contemplativeness of the German petit bourgeois who withdrew with curses and fervour from the life in which he could not keep up. The fallen branches of duty, of education, of the 'caste' of the centre in an age which knows no centre any more are also subjectively non-contemporaneous in a more withered sense, but are firewood in rage. Corresponding to this is the *objectively* non-contemporaneous element as a continuing influence of older circumstances and forms of production, however much they may have been crossed through, as well as of older superstructures. The *objectively* non-contemporaneous element is that which is distant from and alien to the present; it thus embraces *declining remnants* and above all an *unrefurbished past* which is not yet 'resolved' in capitalist terms.

The subjectively non-contemporaneous contradiction activates this objectively non-contemporaneous one, so that both contradictions meet, the rebelliously crooked one of accumulated rage and the objectively alien one of surviving being and consciousness. There are elements of ancient society and its relative order and fulfilment in the present unordered one here, and the subjectively non-contemporaneous contradiction animates these elements in a negatively and positively surprising way. Home, soil and nation are such *objectively* raised contradictions of the traditional to the capitalist Now, in which they have been increasingly destroyed and not replaced. They are contradictions of the traditional to the capitalist Now and elements of ancient society which have not yet died: they were contradictions even in their origin, namely to the past forms which never in fact wholly realized the intended contents of home, soil, and nation. They are thus already contradictions of unfulfilled intentions ab ovo, ruptures with the past itself: not there and then, like the ruptures of contemporaneous contradictions, but throughout the whole of history as it were; so that here concealed contradictions even to history, namely still unrefurbished intentional contents of the past itself, possibly rebel as well. The past is of course embellished by the petite bourgeoisie today, it opposes its unfulfilled element, mixed precisely with the relatively better aspect of the past, to the Now. Thus accumulated rage has its non-contemporaneous contradiction not so much against what is badly traditional as above all against a Now in which even the last element of fulfilment has also disappeared. But the subjectively non-contemporaneous contradiction would never be so sharp, nor the objectively non-contemporaneous one so visible, if an objectively *contemporaneous* one did not exist, namely that posited and growing in and with *modern capitalism* itself. The anachronistic degeneration and memory is released only through the crisis and replies to its objectively revolutionary contradiction with a subjectively and objectively reactionary one, namely non-contemporaneously in fact. Only the non-contemporaneous contradiction, even if it is released by growing impoverishment, disintegration, dehumanization in the womb of late capital, by the intolerable nature of its objectively contemporaneous contradictions, does not become dangerous to capital, in its non-contemporaneous capacity, for the time being. On the contrary, capital uses the non-contemporaneously contrary, if not disparate element to distract from its strictly present contradictions; it uses the antagonism of a still living past as a means of separation and combat against the future dialectically giving birth to itself in the capitalist antagonisms. Throughout the whole of the nineteenth century 'the interests of two classes simultaneously blunted one another' (Marx) in the petite bourgeoisie; this blunting is now joined today by harmonistic images of the past which merely seek to revoke the excess of capitalism or to subordinate it to themselves. They fill nihilism – this eminently contemporaneous contradiction in the wake of late capitalism, this ideological parallel to the process of all people and things becoming a commodity – with mixed structures, like the front-line spirit of 1914, with romantic theories of the state and their feudal anticapitalism, with Prussianness and socialism or other ideologies as rash solutions to social contradictions. The non-contemporaneous contradiction is thus the opposite of a driving, exploding one, it does not stand with the proletariat as the historically decisive class today, nor in the battlefield between proletariat and big business as the space of today's decision. After all, the non-contemporaneous contradiction, and its content, has released itself only in the *vicinity* of capitalist antagonisms and is almost an accidental, or at least warped otherness there; so that between the non-contemporaneous contradiction and capitalism there exists a hiatus, a rift which can be consoled or filled with mist. Above all, the non-contemporaneous contradiction, as that of mere declining, even unrefurbished pasts, produces from its quantity, however large it may be, no sudden change into a new quality. The revolutionary knotted line, in which contradiction finally tangles up at a single point and rapidly presses for the revolutionary unravelling, can accordingly occur only in contemporaneous contradictions which are themselves the growing child Future or differentness, not in non-contemporaneous ones whose greatness is long past, namely a historical one, as are also the adventures of their quality. Even the possible afterripening of the actually unrefurbished element of this past can never veer round of its own accord into a quality which is not already known from the past. This would at most be helped by an alliance which liberates from the *past* the still *possible future* within it only by placing both in the present. In the unequal contradiction, at any rate, there is a reality which – as the terrible example shows – cannot automatically be moved along and included by the contemporaneous one. It has been said, in a Communist resolution, of German fascism that it contains both the offensive of the ruling class and the elements of its disintegration, in short, it reflects the dialectical contradiction of capitalist late development and hence its own destruction. Completely correct, yet this does not also exhaust the non-contemporaneous content which is expressed remotely enough in accumulated rage and surviving ties.

The deprivation born purely of today, that of the workers, has much easier means of defending itself. There is the *contemporaneous contradiction* alone here; in the Today which it wholly has, it is also wholly tangible or the victorious cause itself. Its subjective manifestation, its subjective factor, are not accumulated rage but the class-conscious revolutionary proletarian. Its objective manifestation, its objective factor, are not a declining remnant or even *unrefurbished past*, but *prevented future*. Namely the existence of the proletarian itself, the discrepancy between the forces of production unleashed by capitalism and the capitalist circumstances of production, the crisis. The worker who recognizes himself to be a commodity reveals at the same time the equally frenzied and spooky commodity character of capitalist society, without him – as a new class – being fooled with old stuff, without even the 'person' or the 'life' which he opposes to reification already being historically determined anywhere. The proletarian as the self-dissolution of bourgeois society, indeed of every class society whatsoever, is the subjectively and objectively personified contradiction of contemporaneous society itself, and his revolution – as the fruit of the dialectical *recognition* of contemporaneous contradictions – complains about no figures and memories, nor at first even any contents of the past at all, but activates purely the future society with which the present one is pregnant, towards which the anarchies and nihilisms of the present one seek to effect their sudden change. But this does not of course hinder the fact that the contemporaneous contradiction is partly cultivated by the same substance which the non-contemporaneous one also misses in the Now, which it seeks so crookedly in what is past. The forms and contents of what is past naturally do not stimulate the class-conscious worker at all, or only at a few electively affinitive, revolutionary points, yet the relatively more lively aspect and wholeness of earlier relations between human beings is clearly understood. These relations were still relatively more direct than the capitalist ones, they brought more 'matter' with them than today both in the human beings between whom they prevailed and in the environment which they acted upon. This directness was only apparently more closely defined, only relatively better defined in earlier forms: yet this relative element suffices not merely in reactionary terms to keep what is past partly still genuinely undeceased in the face of what is present. In places it also positively supplies a part of that matter which seeks a life undestroyed by capital again, indeed which revolts in terms of proletarian leadership of course, but also 'generally' as the alienation[130] 'of man', as the laceration 'of life'. We called the non-contemporaneous otherness warped and its rebellion, as a much older matter, one of the vicinity: yet ultimately it appears that precisely one part of the matter of non-contemporaneous contradictions has long been supplementing that of contemporaneous ones. The matter of contemporaneous contradictions is in fact not only that of the very existent, namely unleashed forces of production, but equally only the extreme *negativity*, which 'hence' drives toward sudden change, of the modern condition: the alienated person or proletarian, alienated work or the fetish of the commodity, the instability of nothingness. These negativities admittedly have their dialectically posi-

---

130 'Entäußerung': Bloch is not using the classical Marxist term 'Entfremdung' for 'alienation' in this passage, but a term which has more connotations of the alienation of property than of psychological alienation.

tive element within them, even the highest kind, though of course within the contemporaneous contradiction and its matter only as a rebellious missing: namely of the whole person, of unalienated work, of paradise on earth. In short, in the revolt of proletarian and reified negativity there is ultimately at the same time the matter of a contradiction which rebels out of by no means unleashed 'forces of production', intentional contents *of a still non-contemporaneous kind*. This positivity touches not merely – in the profoundest sense – on the subversive-utopian element 'of man', 'of life', which has not as yet found fulfilment at any time, and which is thus the final goad of every revolution, indeed even the broad shining space of every ideology: the above also touches, beyond this hidden generality, on those positivities which precisely as forms and contents of older matter have been recalled very early on against capitalism. These include not only bourgeois-revolutionary positive elements, like Rousseau's arcadian 'nature', but also those mixed in restorational terms, if not abdications of revolution: like the Middle Ages of Romanticism, like the rebirth of a qualitative-organically graded world from the hollow spaces of the 'thing-in-itself problem' and other deceptive images, picture puzzles, treasure vaults of a not wholly refurbished past. The factors of non-contemporaneous contradiction which are – as we have shown – powerless for sudden change have thus nevertheless, sentimentally or romantically, already recalled that wholeness and liveliness from which Communism draws genuine matter against alienation, from which, alongside Communism, degeneration, attachment to space, and arcadian-Dionysian 'nature' are confusedly rampant again today. As creation which was not satisfied, as portent and witness of spheres which at least make the *problem* of a multi-layered wholeness the duty of the dialectic which is merely associated with capitalism in an all too single-layered way. Marxism is not itself radical like destructive capitalism, not itself omitting like the abstract calculation of the latter; nor is it half enlightening, but wholly departing and surpassing, it is least of all ascetic towards the claims of 'nature', this antiquarium of unsolvedness. There would not be such reverses, and certainly not any problem of the 'inheritance' in process, if its final stage in each case were the only one at which the dialectic has to stand, and the concrete revolution has to occur. The foundation of the non-contemporaneous contradiction is the unfulfilled fairytale of the good old times, the unsolved myth of dark ancient being or of nature; there is here, in places, not merely a past which is not past in class terms, but also a past which is not yet wholly discharged in material terms.

Problem of a multi-layered dialectic

Thus it is a question of making the turbulent Now broader at the same time. We had to distinguish between the falsely and the genuinely non-contemporaneous contradiction, the latter and the contemporaneous one, and again in both the subjective and the objective factor of contradiction. *The subjectively non-contemporaneous contradiction is accumulated rage, the objectively non-contemporaneous one unfinished past; the subjectively contemporaneous one is the free revolutionary action of the proletariat, the objectively contemporaneous one the prevented future contained in the Now, the prevented technological blessing, the prevented new society with which the old one is pregnant in its forces of production.* The basic factor of the objectively contemporaneous contradiction is the conflict between the collective character of the forces of production developed by capitalism and the private character of the aversion to them. The increasing socialization of work no longer gets on with the private capitalist property relations, with the bourgeois form in which industrial work has grown up. This is the objectively contemporaneous contradiction of the times or their exact class contrast: forces of production and property relations are here two essential parts of an equally contemporaneous unity. Thus only this exact contrast is the decisive one of the times in revolutionary terms, yet in fact it is not the only one in them. The other contrast, that between capital and the non-contemporaneously impoverished classes, lives alongside the contemporaneous one, even if only as diffuse. Thus in the 'ahistorical' class of the petite bourgeoisie it generates fear and accumulated rage, no separate, alert class consciousness, let alone one which has been worked through. It therefore makes the impact of the conflict external and blunt, directed only against symptoms, not against the core of exploitation; the content of the conflict itself is romantically, and also so to speak 'archaically' anticapitalist.

It is a question then of seeing a possible force in the contradiction even when it does not go beyond the non-contemporaneous rift. This remains favourable to the Now of capital only so long as the non-contemporaneous lack the leadership, and also seduction,[131] to march into the modern battlefield. The task is to release those elements even of the non-contemporaneous contradiction which are capable of aversion and transformation, namely those hostile to capitalism, homeless in it, and to remount them for functioning in a different connection. There therefore remains the 'Triple Alliance' of the proletariat with the impoverished peasants and the impoverished middle classes, under proletarian hegemony; the genuinely contemporaneous contradiction has the

131 Bloch is here punning on 'Führung' (leadership) and 'Verführung' (seduction).

duty of being concrete and total enough to detach the genuinely non-contemporaneous contradictions from reaction too and to bring them up to the tendency. As such, the older contradictions do not become a problem on the proletarian ontological basis; the revolutionary dialectic still remains exclusively one of the set contradictions of late capital, not of the cracking places which are set free and in which the Hitler movement has its mine. But precisely no proletarian hegemony in the due Triple Alliance will succeed, above all no unfaded, unendangered one, without its also thoroughly 'mastering' the substance of genuine non-contemporaneity and its heterogeneous contradictions. By false consciousness and unfounded romanticism being everywhere expelled of course, but also by an understanding which is no *abstractly* omitting one taking in the subversive and utopian elements, the repressed matter of this not yet Past. It is certainly right to say that it is part of the nature of fascist ideology to incorporate the morbid resources of all cultural phases; but it is wrong to say only the morbid ones, namely as if the healthy ones were not accessible at all to the ideology of decay. Such a summary judgement incorporates, in a totally abstract-negative way, even the specific opposition of non-contemporaneity, because of its cloudiness, into humbug and no other kind of magic.[132] So that in the final analysis fascism is supported; namely the distinction between non-contemporaneous contradiction and fascist deception in it is denied, this time denied and pasted over from the vulgar Marxist side. But for long enough fascism exploited that which stirred in the way of peasant and petit-bourgeois opposition, and of non-contemporaneous opposition in general. There thus arises, in order that the non-contemporaneous element can be mastered, the problem of a multi-layered revolutionary dialectic; for obviously the entirety of earlier development is not yet 'resolved' in capitalism and its dialectic. World history, as the bourgeois revolutionary Börne[133] already said, is a house which has more staircases than rooms; and Marx himself, when he stresses the relatively more tolerable aspect of the pre-capitalist situation, and even describes Greek art and epic poetry 'in certain respects as a norm and unattainable model' (Introduction to the 'Critique of Political Economy'), then in his work this 'social childhood of humanity' is a hardly relaxed stimulus, and capitalism at any rate not the only house of history which is to be dialectically inherited. To have everything that is past without a prevailing voice as it were infinitely many-voiced is merely historicism; to apply typically identical, or at least formally identical 'laws' or 'shapes' to everything that is past is merely sociologism; whereas Marxism pre-

---

132 Bloch is playing here on the phrase 'fauler Zauber' which means 'humbug', but has the literal meaning of 'rotten magic'.
133 Ludwig Börne, 1786–1837, writer and leading figure in the revolutionary 'Junges Deutschland' movement.

cisely does not find its dialectic everywhere just as it appears in capitalism, it varies it concretely according to the individual social conditions,
it seeks above all to preserve for it even in the past continuing to have an
effect in capitalism that *totality* which characterizes the dialectical developmental tendency – not at every stage, but at every mastered stage.
A multi-temporal and multi-spatial dialectic, the polyrhythmics and the
counterpoint of such a dialectic are thus precisely the instrument of the
mastered final stage or totality; naturally not of absolutely every one,
but of the critical, the non-contemplative, the practically intervening
one. This totality must be *critical* in order not to invite into itself stale
modes of being with their doubly false consciousness as a result of this
staleness. That which history has not yet accomplished in this absolutely
past element, namely to make it hopeless and into a mere tomb of
historical memory, is completed by the materialistic analysis of the
residual false consciousness by dissolving its appearance, unmasking its
modern delusions throughout. Thus precisely for the sake of the element in the past which possibly also genuinely continues to have an
effect and is not past, for the sake of the *genuine nebulae* (which still
have to give birth to a star), the totality will not encumber itself with
mere nebulous appearances, indistinct and long since developed star
clusters; even if they seek to look as similar to the nebulae as the cliché
of the soil does to the new earth or the Third Reich to the future state.
The totality must further be *critical* in order not to fall from its legitimate contrast to the capitalist laceration of all life-connections into a
false similarity with the idealistic 'totality' which is a mere one of the
system (of the spinning out from a single idealistic principle and its
uninterrupted, panlogical connection), indeed which is a derivative of
myth (of the belief in the great, unbroken Pan). And in fact the totality
not only has to be critical, but above all *non-contemplative*: only in this
way does it manage not to leave the unbecome, uncorrected element of
the past behind in it; the concealed contradiction to history, the one
which has become open to the present, passes instead into the dialectically practical cogwheel. Hegel's dialectical totality was still a mere one
of remembered knowledge and a monadic one as well, in which admittedly 'no term was not drunk', but in which each one was able to sober
up on the spot as it were, because it was 'endowed with the complete
wealth of mind'. Hegel, of course, equally has the next stage as the
intended higher truth of the preceding one and the totality more and
more precisely in the last term in each case; indeed, as the driving basic
contradiction in all individual contradictions (and even in the individual
reconciliations as well) he has that to the entirety of the entire matter;
dialectic is here not only, as in Schelling, unity of the contradictions, but
unity of the unity and the contradictions. But if the Hegelian truth of
the final stage is to be taken seriously, along with the 'self' which 'has to
penetrate and to digest this whole wealth of its substance', then the

penetration can be only a non-contemplative one or one which possesses the wealth of the substance not in gilded pasts but in the actual inheritance of its end in the Now, in short which gains *additional revolutionary force* precisely from the *incomplete* wealth of the past, when it is less than ever 'resolved' at the final stage. It is only thus that non-past, because never wholly become, and hence lastingly subversive and utopian contents in the relations of human beings to human beings and to nature are of use; these contents are as it were the gold-bearing rubble in the course of the previous work processes and their work-based superstructures. A multi-voiced dialectic as a dialectic of the 'contradictions' collected today more than ever has at any rate even in capitalism enough questions and contents which are not yet 'overtaken by the course of the economic development'. The proletarian voice of the contemporaneous dialectic firmly remains the leading one; yet beneath and above this cantus firmus there run disordered exuberances which are to be referred to the cantus firmus only through the fact that the latter – in critical and non-contemplative totality – refers to them. And a multi-spatial dialectic proves itself above all in the dialecticization of still 'irrational' contents; they are, in accordance with their positive element which remains critical, the 'nebulae' of the non-contemporaneous contradictions.

D. ON THE ORIGINAL HISTORY OF THE THIRD REICH[134]

(*internationale literature*, Moscow, 1937)

Nothing must bar this glance or make it blind itself. In the following there is mention of various old and peculiar elements. There have been crooks at work, and how, but one must keep a close eye not only on the crook's fingers but also on that which he holds in them. Particularly if he has stolen it, if the soiled object was once in better hands. Hence there is no getting out of examining the concepts which the Nazi has both employed and purloined for the purpose of deception, but one to be ended. Führer, and above all Reich thus crop up, and if their meaning originally to be ended is investigated, they crop up in a different, more thoughtful way than has been customary of late. The material is still largely fresh, but that which blindness and crime have done with it is and had to become precisely all the more rotten. The somewhat dreamy essence of the matter was moreover often open to abuse. But even something beautiful and noble shines across from forgotten, unforgotten days, it is important to recall this.

After all, the Nazi did not even invent the song with which he seduces. Nor even the gunpowder with which he makes his fireworks, nor even the firm in whose name he deceives. The very term Third Reich has a long history, a genuinely revolutionary one. The Nazi was creative, so to speak, only in the embezzlement at all prices with which he employed revolutionary slogans to the opposite effect. With which – alongside the shabby nonsense of the backmost tables reserved for

---

134 In this section it must be borne in mind that Reich also has religious and mystical connotations of 'kingdom' and 'realm', as well as the political dynastic sense so familiar from the Nazi collocation 'Third Reich'. The thousand-year 'Reich' that Hitler promised was also semantically the traditional 'millennium' prophesied for Christ's reign on earth in Revelations by St John the Divine, and anticipated by many utopian movements and spiritual leaders in the Middle Ages.

regulars – he used the dark lustre of old phrases and patinated the revolution which he claimed to be making. Such an old phrase is the Third Reich, sonorous through the very triple character alone ('as in a fairytale'), sonorous as the third coronation of Germany (after the medieval Reich and Bismarck's Reich). But in order that the revolutionary appearance did not come off badly, Moeller van den Bruck, the actual reviver of the term, added mystical traditions from very different 'realms'.[135] For in its original form the Third Reich had denoted the *social-revolutionary ideal dream of Christian heresy*: the dream of a Third Gospel and the world corresponding to it. The class struggles arising in the early Middle Ages found their first expression in hatred of the secularization of the Church. The more the situation of the peasants and ordinary urban citizens worsened, and the more visibly on the other hand mercantile capital and territorial princedom succeeded and the purely feudal empire, founded on economic modes of the past, disintegrated, the more powerfully the prophecy of a new, an 'evangelical' age necessarily struck home; in the case of Münzer as a peasant – proletarian – petit-bourgeois battle-cry against increased exploitation, in the case of Luther, of course, as the ideology of the princes against central power and the Church. There were thus opposing interests which met in the mist of heresy; and yet alongside the cloud the left lacked the pillar of fire least of all; it was in the impetus and ideal of the revolutionary cause. The contents of modern socialism, of that in the process of being implemented, are no longer the theological ones, in class terms not even any longer the theologically disguised ones of those days. Nevertheless, socialism may pay respect to the dreams of its youth, it sheds their illusion but it fulfils their promises. Germany still heeds, as has been shown, the old dreams of saviour and Reich, even when they are advanced by deceivers, and it heeded them all the more seducibly when socialist propaganda was in many ways cold, schoolmasterish, and merely economistic. Two shining motifs aroused revolutionary consciousness from the twelfth to the sixteenth century: the motifs of saviour and simply of the Third, finally even of the Thousand-Year Reich, into which the saviour-liberator (mostly conceived as 'emperor of the people') leads the way.

The future liberator

The poor help themselves only slowly and late. The wish for a *Führer* must be the oldest of all. It exists in the relationship between child and father and in the search of the young person if their father was a simpleton. Group animals have the strongest male at their head, hunting

135 'Reichen': see preceding note.

peoples who as yet know no division of labour whatsoever choose a chief. Moses represents the first image of the leader in the humanly splendid sense; he is at once a leader of the oppressed and one into the Promised Land. But even under very different circumstances the glances were directed forward and upward, often embellished what could be seen at the top. Alexander was already supposed to be a saviour, the lord of all-assembling peace. Augustus in particular was fêted as an emperor of peace. as the restorer of the Golden Age prophesied by the sibyl. The passage by Virgil, in the Fourth Eclogue, is well known, about the wonder boy who will shortly appear, who will lead up the happiness of primeval times after all the confusion in society and state. The Aeneid passed on this role of saviour to Augustus; later it was transferred to Trajan, Antoninus and other 'good emperors'. Social expectations of the fluctuating, landless masses of late Rome and the wishes of the upper strata for undisturbed tranquillity were almost indistinguishably muddled up in all this. Besides, the expectation of the wonder boy saviour is also very old and was inserted into dynastic dreams of salvation very early on; it captivated with its touching, gentle manner, moving in general human terms so to speak. The Egypt of the Middle Kingdom first augmented the oriental prophecy of a redeemer-king with the image of smallness, indeed of the crib, with the idea of the divinely miraculous birth of the beneficent child Horus (cf. Eduard Norden, Die Geburt des Kindes (1924), p. 73f.). It was the same legend which was afterwards transferred to Jesus, this time with a distinctly proletarian and by no means patrician expectation of salvation; the image of Christ which was precisely supposed to keep the slaves up to scratch, although intimated in the Sermon on the Mount, was only formed in the Roman Imperial Church. On the whole, Jesus the saviour was merely supposed to redeem inwardly of course, only as the Paraclete, at the end of time, did he serve up his visible kingdom.[136] Thus earthly misery and real disorder were preserved, and thus the expectation of salvation of an earthly kind was also naturally prolonged, the prospect not of a distant Paraclete but of a near incarnate saviour, as invoked by Virgil; and the sibylline imperial legend continued in Byzantium. The more rotten the internal situation was there (burden of debt on the populace, palace revolutions), and the more menacing the external one (Arabs, Bulgars, Turks), the more promising the painted prospects seemed of earthly glad tidings alongside the heavenly ones. Such a book of consolation emerged towards the end of the seventh century in the prophecies of Methodius; at the same time the imperial legend here assumed a strange shape. For a death motif was mixed in with it in secular terms for the first time, and Methodius prophesies: a great powerful emperor will arise, 'like a man awakening from sleep, people

136   Reich: see preceding note.

have looked upon him as a corpse'. Alexander is probably meant here, who is introduced as the grandson of an Ethiopian king and rises from the dead from the direction of Ethiopia; before the end of the world (conceived to be near) he returns as emperor of the Greeks and Romans in power and glory. The ancient motif of the dying god of vegetation who rises from the dead in the spring, which had already been adapted to the death of Jesus, on Good Friday and Ascension Day, sees itself secularized here, is needed once again in this world. This change had a powerful influence on the later Kyffhäuser legend,[137] but besides this Byzantium transmitted another, totally magical saviour motif into the German imagination. It is contained in the legend of the so-called Prester John, and India is the setting, the magic land with its garden of paradise, its miraculous stones, its prophesying trees and the like. In deepest India lives the entranced priestly king (now Daniel, now John the Baptist, the Evangelist, the Divine all in one), the ten lost tribes of Israel are with him awaiting their hour, he possesses miracle-working stones which make him invisible, and other supernatural powers of his own. Undoubtedly the image of a yogi or mahatma is discernible here; but the Novum of the legend is the fact that his magical powers, which are indeed in a remote trance beyond the world, are supposed to stand in the service of Christian justice. Prester John, as a saviour from the East, was later even suspected to be in the army of the Turks by German peasants; as the most secret governor of Christ so to speak, as the messianic emperor abroad. The authentic dream of the leader now became more historical of course, namely referring to people who really existed or had really existed, the *imperial legend of the Middle Ages* which had become dynastic again, the Charlemagne legend of France, the German one about Friedrich II and his return. The Byzantine prophecy of Methodius is recalled (it was circulating in numerous copies) and its strange corpse-motif. It was precisely this which presented itself when the demonic Staufer[138] had died: Friedrich II, the dreamed-of and feared scourge of the Church, the rationalistic-imperialistic originator of the phrase about the 'three deceivers' (Moses, Mohammed, Jesus), the Antichrist towards whom so many apocalyptic thoughts were directed precisely for this reason, Friedrich II was not able or allowed to remain dead, his work was undone, his sign unfulfilled, and only in his name – according to the prophecies of the Methodius-prophets of the time – could it be fulfilled. Such a new (very much higher) Methodius shortly before Friedrich was in fact the abbot Joachim of Fiore: his school as well as other widespread prophecies saw in the emperor the sign of social-chiliastic change. The emperor was not

137 See 'Amusement Co., horror, Third Reich', n. 33.
138 Member of the Hohenstaufen dynasty, named after the family seat at Hohenstaufen castle.

allowed to remain dead for the excited imagination, he admittedly had not gone to heaven, certainly not, but no more had he gone to hell, to no (transcendental) place whatsoever from where there is no return. But the legend transported the emperor into a mountain, first into Etna (perhaps Sicilian memories of the Empedocles legend continued to have a haunting effect here), then, proceeding northwards, into the Kyffhäuser. Ancient, chthonic images were associated with this figurative grave: in pre-Christian times a mountain cult was at home on the Kyffhäuser, and the mountain god was a subterranean one, lived in the caves of the interior among mysterious treasures. Friedrich II took his place and only much later did the heretical emperor change places with Friedrich I Barbarossa, the pious, insignificant ruler, the romantic epitome of banal imperial glory in the style of Wilhelm 'the Great'[139] (whose monument now stands there). Meanwhile even the perverted legend has preserved its original social-chiliastic trend in the fact that the emperor always only appears to simple people of the populace. Just as it is associated with the old motif that the messianic emperor, when he has humbled the powers of social and religious deprivation, humbles himself, abdicates, marches to Golgotha and lays down his crown, sceptre and sword there (cf. Kampers, Die deutsche Kaiseridee in Prophetie und Sage (1895), p. 104). Like Friedrich II, the Emperor Charlemagne is also dreaming, in the Untersberg;[140] indeed wherever the work of a supposed saviour appears not to be done or not to be completely done, popular belief has made of the dead saviour a merely vanished one, one of the Seven Sleepers[141] who is waiting for his day. Even today the motif of disappointment itself is so little extinct that the death of no vitality is willingly believed which has gripped the imagination. The content of the old sibylline saying, 'vivit, non vivit', is revived afresh again and again in folklore. Even the death of such modern figures as Napoleon and also Ludwig II has not been willingly admitted by an unsatiated Fama:[142] for Fama, Napoleon lived on in the mask of a Turkish general around 1822 who attacked the English with amazing success, and a Bavarian peasant legend claims that Ludwig II fled to America and will return with a beautiful woman when his Bavarian nation is worst off. The motif of the Seven Sleepers is admittedly replaced in the case of Napoleon by the enlightened ruse of an apparent death and an escape, the Kyffhäuser has become St Helena (as previously, with more justification, it had become Elba), but the pathos of return is not lacking and in the case of Ludwig

139 Bloch is alluding here to Kaiser Wilhelm I.
140 Untersberg: a mountain in the Berchtesgaden Alps near Salzburg. Hitler of course also built a retreat, Berghof, in these mountains.
141 Seven legendary Christians of Ephesus, who slept for two centuries after being incarcerated by a Roman Emperor.
142 'Fama': an allusion to the allegorical figure of Fame or Rumour.

II not even the pathos of the pupated saviour. All this indicates how extraordinarily firmly rooted the prototype of a saviour is, a revival of radiant figures of the past, or at least a revival of radiant times of the past by a new restorer. Here we also find those mounted messengers of the king who in the Threepenny Opera[143] are made to appear at the last moment and to change everything; whereby it by no means merely satirizes the cheap solutions of the old opera or of colportage. The fact that the mounted messengers very seldom arrive and the deus ex machina even more seldom, such a failure, as the Hitler effect in particular has just proved, does not cancel out the old outlook. Indeed even the actual archaic myth of resurrection lives on, even though in a very weakened, analogous, historically misrepresentative form. None other than Napoleon decorated himself as a returned Charlemagne, while Hitler (if it is at all possible to mention him in the same breath) marches to the grave of Henry the Lion[144] and thereby awakens associations for a future 'incarnation'. There is no doubt at least that in the case of the Nazi it was intended from the beginning to replace the embarrassed title of Führer with the title of emperor of the people on a tolerably triumphant occasion; though such an occasion will not arise any more. But the old vision of the saviour, which had gone to the dogs, was nevertheless a great help to the Nazi, and even more so the decisive vision in whose service it stood: precisely that of the *Third Reich*.

The gospel of this world

People have mostly seen happiness in the place where they are not. Eating, living, loving are the simplest places, this is little changed. Since classes arose, two different kinds of people, this happiness has atrophied or even disappeared for the exploited kind. Where much is lacking, there are many wishes, there is much intoxication in wishful images, particularly in religious ones. But here there is intoxication in a double form: one consoling over the misery, one all the more roused against it. Thus we find defusing religions, which console with the other world or even with the flight into inwardness; Christianity has accomplished much with both. But if the other world seeks to plunge to earth and inwardness into outwardness, instead of opium an unparalleled explosive then of course arises in the subjective factor, a will towards heaven on earth. This volition also existed in Christianity, existed in the medieval prophecies of the above-mentioned abbot Joachim of Fiore, who pro-

143 Brecht's *Dreigroschenoper*, 1928.
144 Heinrich der Löwe, 1142–80, Duke of Saxony and Bavaria, early champion of German expansion and founder of the cities of Lübeck and Munich.

claimed a third Testament or the due cash payment of the second one towards the end of the twelfth century. The point does not need to be laboured here that the thus produced revolutionary intoxication was abstract and mythological; that it had no eye to reality and was incapable of doing so; that it set in motion merely the subjective will to change the world, but not any concrete method for this change. However, the will itself was thorough enough, the dream of the Third Reich ardent and stimulating right down to the Hussite movement, right down to the Peasant Wars. It is not unimportant to descend into the cellar of this so infernally abused term; it is, after all, originally anything but a torture chamber (it contains rather too many charges of love than too few). In fact the foundations of this dream stretch down to *Origen*, to his doctrine of the three possible ways of interpreting the Christian records; a physical one, a mental one, a spiritual one. The physical interpretation is the literal one, the mental interpretation the moral-allegorical one, but the spiritual interpretation reveals from the veils of the Scriptures the 'eternal gospel' intended within them. In purely contemplative form the doctrine of the three cognitive levels recurs in the twelfth century with *Richard and Hugh of St Victor*, the contemporaries of Joachim, the great psychologists of inner meaning. Here the carnal interpretation appears as cogitatio or grasping of the bodily world, the mental one as meditatio or grasping of inwardness, the spiritual one as contemplatio or elevation to the visio beatifica Dei, indeed to the deification of man. The Victorines thus provided a salvation-based view of history through and through, a mystical novel of development[145] of stages and realms – it could almost be said, a first Phenomenology of Mind;[146] but the sequence of stages remained one of the mere individual. And the final stage did not lie ahead, for instance, the final realm was not in the process of utopian birth, but was present at all times in finished form together with its object. *Joachim of Fiore* himself probably knew the Victorines and used both them and Origen as his starting-point; but he splendidly abandoned the mere inwardness of both. He was the first to transform the trinity of standpoints from an individual-pedagogical sequence into one of progressive, unfinished humanity. What was in mysticism a graduated development of the soul, a coherent passing from one mental condition into the other, is projected by Joachim on to the whole process of humanity; there thus appears a graduated development of *history* through the degrees of spiritual perfection; and these degrees are not attainable by individual human beings, but only by whole ages in each case (cf. Grundmann, Studien über Joachim von Floris (1927), p. 131f.). Joachim was the first

---

145 'Entwicklungsroman': Bloch uses a German literary term here, a reference to a genre of novels tracing one person's central spiritual development.
146 Bloch has Hegel's famous work in mind here.

to voice this assertion, although later supporters of his doctrine also cite as a witness one of his contemporaries, the great pantheistic materialist Amalrich of Bena (c.1200). Amalrich too is supposed to have specified the degrees of illumination not as individually attainable, but as historical: the Father became man through Abraham, and revealed himself in the Old Testament, the Son became man through Christ, and revealed himself through the New Testament, but now the age of the spirit was imminent, and the Christian sacrament had to disappear just as the Jewish law had disappeared. But whether Amalrich really taught this historical sequence cannot be determined from the surviving sources. The doctrine does not tally with Amalrich's anti-Christian pathos either, which must have seen in law and sacrament no preliminary stages of itself, but only lies. Thus the doctrine of deadlines authentically emanates only from Joachim, and with his name, above all from his work, it has influenced the future.

Hence the light glows up three times, and it burns ever more precisely. Whereby Joachim's doctrine of the third status, the third kingdom is this: the first age was that of the servitude of the law, that of the Father and his Old Testament, of the laity and the married. The second age is an intermediate condition between flesh and spirit, it is initiated by the Son and his New Testament, is governed by the Church and its clerics. But the third age, which precedes the end of the world, is now in the process of being born; it is inhabited by monks, that is, by the viri spirituales, by the 'freedom of the spirit'. The letter of the gospel of Christ with its Church and its clerics will pass away, the early Christian community descends from heaven to earth, a communist brotherhood and realm of peace begin. The first age was that of 'fear and narration', the second that of 'research and wisdom', but the third will be that of 'love and illumination', of the total Pentecost, of the 'pouring out of the Holy Spirit'. The first age lay in the night of the stars, the second in the red dawn, the third will be the full daylight, with the Holy Spirit not from the viewpoint of God the Father but that of the Son of Man (Joachim, Concordia 5, chapter 77). Strange as these categories may sound to the modern revolutionary (even more surprising than the recollected imperial birthday celebrations of the previous section), we equally must not allow ourselves to be thereby deterred from noticing and honouring the hunger for happiness and freedom, the images of freedom on the part of people deprived of their rights, in these dreams. Socialism has a fantastically splendid tradition; if at such early stages, as goes without saying, it lacks any kind of economic view, it certainly does not lack one of its other essential features: humaneness and the Advent view connected with it. The sentence, 'They deck the altars, and the poor man walks in bitter hunger', is Joachite; the rejection of the 'fear of the Lord' is Joachite. Even the coming 'age of the monks' is conceived less as an ascetic one than as a propertyless and brotherly one, as general monastic and consumer communism. Indeed, the monastic prophecies were so tinged with the this-worldly lustre of a 'Thousand-Year Kingdom' in Joachim's school (he had founded an order of his own) that precisely the spiritual strictness became one of the zest for life and seized the whole body. In this spirit Telesphorus of Cosenza proclaimed at the end of the fourteenth century that God had become man so that the whole man should become happy in himself, and not just the inner one, but 'all the eyes, ears, mouths, hands, feet, livers, kidneys', in short the age of perfection was also to give birth to all earthly happiness along with the sacred kind. The Joachite hymn in Telesphorus thus sounds much more earthly than the Franciscan prayer to brother sun: 'O vita vitalis, dulcis et amabilis, semper memorabilis', 'O lively life, sweet and lovable, always memorable'. If this song prophetically graced the cradle[147] of the Joachite movement only latently so to speak, then at least the nearness to a new earthly-sacred intertwining and career of happiness is already completely manifest in Joachim: the path from the servitus legis to the libertas amicorum occurs in this world. This is the actual boldness of Joachim: he directed the glances fixed on the other world towards a future period on earth, and expected his ideal not in heaven but on earth. He proclaimed the freedom of the new viri spirituales not as freedom from the world but for a new world, and if he placed the earth under strict Christlike demands, if he broke through the lax two-worlds doctrine of an even more lax Catholicism, if he did not know religious-indifferent culture in the Third Kingdom and already did not acknowledge it in the second, then it was only so that the other world should be consumed and the word of love should already become flesh here below: the kingdom of Christ is of this world, *as soon as this world has become a new one*. This is the continuingly influential boldness of Joachim, continuingly influential in revolutionary terms down to the Peasant Wars, and the substance of his world of ideas. Whereby it should be mentioned that Joachim satisfied even the highest poetic judge of his age: Dante promotes him, the 'prophetic spirit', to the solar sphere of paradise, to join the saints of knowledge (Paradiso, xii, 140f.). But Joachim restructured not only the mystical graduated doctrine of knowledge but also its final content in such a way that the latter is stored in an immanent image of history with a this-worldly, or at least descending heaven, instead of in the relationship between this world and the other world. The 'spiritualism' deriving from Joachim had just as revolutionizing an effect in its day, i.e. the interpretation of the Bible (of the letter) in accordance with the 'inwardly driving spirit'. Nemo audit verbum nisi spiritu intus docente[148] – this orthodox principle was already so overdone by the Joachites, as the first 'enthusiasts', that the

---

147 Bloch is using the phrase 'an der Wiege gesungen', 'sung at the cradle', literally and figuratively here. Its figurative meaning is 'foreseen of somebody or something'.

148 'Nobody hears the word unless with an inwardly teaching spirit.'

Scriptures, indeed everything outward and traditional in general, were consigned to the interpretative arbitrariness of the 'inner word'. Whereas the arbitrariness of the inner word was in reality no such thing at all, but the spirit which illuminated, just like the spirit which drove, was *exclusively orientated towards the impetus and the wishful content of revolution* for the spiritualists of the time. Just as the viri spirituales were conceived as citizens of a communist age, so the inner word was 'David's key' to unlock 'the revelation of the freedom of the children of God' in the Bible and to bar all hindrances to this revelation. After all, from an economic standpoint, Christianity differs from all other religions in the fact that it began as an ideology of the oppressed; this rebellious beginning, despite its immediate deflection (into the inner world), and despite its later concealment and inversion by the Church, never completely vanished from the world. So that even Joachim's idea of the third age and realm lived on unperverted among the heretics, indeed could even be cited by *Lessing* with direct recollection of the enthusiasts of the thirteenth century. Lessing's 'Education of the Human Race' introduced precisely the Joachite doctrine of stages into the Enlightenment and its tolerance; the study of the 'primer' of Christianity begins to be complete, a kind of meta-religion composed of reason begins. 'Beware', Lessing thus warns, 'you more capable individual stamping and glowing over the last page of this primer, beware of allowing your weaker schoolfellows to notice what you can scent or are already beginning to see ... It will certainly come, the age of a new eternal gospel, which is promised to us even in the primers of the New Testament. Perhaps even certain enthusiasts of the thirteenth and fourteenth century had caught a ray of this new eternal gospel and were only mistaken in the fact that they proclaimed its outbreak to be so near. Perhaps their three ages of the world was not such an empty whim, and certainly they had no bad intentions when they taught that the New Testament would have to become just as antiquated as the Old one had become ... It was only that they ... were over-hasty, it was only that they thought they could make their contemporaries, who had still hardly outgrown their childhood, without enlightenment, without preparation, at once into men who would be worthy of their third age.' We can see from these astonishing words that even the German Enlightenment, in its boldest and clearest mind, knew how to use the old threefold division, the 'resolution' of Christianity in an almost Hegelian double meaning of the word: as a destruction and preservation at one and the same time. The patriarchal age was the caterpillar, the ecclesiastical age the chrysalis of reason, and now the bourgeois revolution hails itself as the butterfly. The graduated division of history in accordance with the Old and New Testament is certainly itself the most antiquated, it is the remotest one from the real historical sequence, as one of class societies; but the end itself, the third age, proposed the same humane condition in the mist and in generality, towards which the socialist revolution seeks to steer in sunshine and precision. Hence it is not surprising that the idea of the Third Kingdom – still so powerful in Lessing – expires with the victory of the bourgeoisie or usually occurs only sporadically and without being understood. As in the case of *Schelling* in his late work, the often reactionary lectures on the 'Philosophy of Revelation'; the Joachite tradition, still alive in Lessing, was here already so threadbare that merely the pattern but not the content of the sequence remains in the memory. Solely epochs of ecclesiastical history (and further of 'potencies in God'), but not of overall human history, are divided into the three realms by Schelling. St Peter or Catholicism are regarded as the realm of the Father, St Paul or Protestantism as the subsequent realm of the Son, and St John wrote his gospel for the spiritual church of the future (Schelling himself maintains in the lectures that he discovered the 'harmony' of this purely theological, indeed gnostically interpreted sequence with Joachim of Fiore only later). It is thus amazing that the Third Reich appears in *Ibsen* again, in the youthful drama 'Emperor and Galilean', though this time connected afresh with a kind of humaneness, with a premonitory echo of the late-bourgeois 'emancipation' in the Art Nouveau period. The symbolism of the 'three cornerstones of necessity' is enacted here palely and yet whisperingly: the first is admittedly classical antiquity rather than the Old Testament, the second Christianity, the third the synthesis of both, the fusion of 'beauty and truth'. Emperor Julian is to bring it about, the Third Kingdom of 'joyful noblemen' is to appear – a particularly troubling hope in view of contemporary Germany. In view of Streicher, the nobleman, Hitler, Göring, Goebbels or the synthesis of truth and beauty. But it should not be forgotten that the Nazis also received the term Third Reich from literature; not from Ibsen, but rather from Dostoevsky. Or rather from the racy masculine perfume which Moeller van den Bruck, the editor of the German Dostoevsky, bottled from the latter in a half tsarist, half prophetic way. Moeller calls his book simply 'The Third Reich', it became a 'major work' of Nazism and gripped the 'elite of the movement' much more powerfully than Hitler's stylistic exercise and Rosenberg's compilation did. 'Africa is darkening up' – this is Moeller's alleged fear; he plays off Prussia-Germany against this, and also the well-known 'socialism in the Prussian style'. The peculiar connection which Dostoevsky had established between his neo-Byzantine speculations and the 'presence of the Holy Spirit' (both united in the 'God-bearing Russian people'), – this unparalleled anti-Voltaire world was transferred by Moeller to Germany, to the Germany of monopoly capitalism, of incipient crisis, of impending revolution. So the 'Third Reich' came in time anew, but what a different one from that of Joachim and Lessing; blazing darkness fell on the land, a night full of blood and nothing but Satan. So this is what has become of the 'reality' of the old dreams of love and spirit; Lessing's 'rational gospel' on the one hand, Hitler's 'Mein Kampf' on the other. Nazism has uniquely mobilized for itself both economic ignorance and the still active image of hope, chiliastic image in earlier revolutions. *Chiliasm* of course, this is the last catchword to be dealt with; the doctrine of the *Thousand-Year Reich* was, as Luther said, 'the conjurer's hat of all troop-leaders'. In Luther's time, of course, chiliasm was a battle song of the rebellious peasants, in the 'Third Reich' which has arrived today it stupefies or stupefied – in totally polluted, perverted, betrayed form – the victims of reaction.

Chiliasm or the earth as paradise

The wish for happiness was never painted into an empty and completely new future. A better past was always to be restored too, though not a recent past, but that of a dreamed-after, more beautiful earlier age. And this golden age was not only to be renewed but also surpassed by an as yet nameless happiness. It seems reasonable to discern in these dreams of the golden age memories of the early commune, especially when remnants of it (like common land) or that which had not yet been lost for too long (like freedom of hunting and fishing) supported the revolutionary praise of primeval times. This was clearly the case during the Peasant Wars: the demand for the return of the old 'communal freedom' counteracted the wishes of some groups to parcel out the land, and strengthened Münzer's slogan, Omnia sint communia. The image of the golden age naturally does not reproduce any real beginning of history, any prehistoric reality at all; if only because the early commune, with its undeveloped forces of production, cannot have been that paradisal. But hope had its first portent, and also content, in the freedom, equality and fraternity of the original gentes. It overdid this with a backward-looking utopia, but it caused it to approach again from the future all the more, from the future of the restored paradise. It is precisely here that the myth of the *Thousand-Year Reich* begins, of a happy final age towards which history is striving, or rather: which history has in store for the 'just'. The myth itself stems from the interaction between economic and political misery and shining memories from a past which in fact – with utopian, and not merely romantic longing for happiness – was bent over into a final age that lay as near as possible. The ideas of prophetic Judaism based on an eschatology of salvation, before and particularly after the period of exile, must have first given birth to these historical utopias; from the Orient they travelled, long before the victory of Christianity, to imperial Rome and spread the hope of the returning golden aeon. As far as the more specific case of the Thousand-Year Reich is concerned, this *ancient background* of the Third one, its entire content stems from the prophecy of Isaiah, chapters 30, 55 and 60, its chronology from the Book of Daniel, chapter 7, and the battle between night and light at its inception from the Revelation of St John, chapters 20 and 21. Wild Persian dualisms let off steam in the description of the last days: the dragon, the old snake, is bound for a thousand years and sealed in the abyss, but the just will return from the dead and rule with Christ for a thousand years; this is the first resurrection. But when a thousand years are completed, Satan is unbound again, he lures the pagans, the peoples of Gog and Magog into the final dispute, a time of final suffering and confusion reigns until the fire of God falls from heaven on his enemies, Doomsday and the Last Judgement begin, hell is prepared for sinners and a new heaven and a new earth for the chosen; this is the second resurrection. The furious pedantry of these prophecies preoccupied all the revolutionary movements of Christendom, right up until the Enlightenment; even today it still circulates among the so-called Jehovah's Witnesses, among those banned by Hitler. If such nightmares of salvation are essentially noteworthy only in historical terms, this is not the case with the *content* of the final realm, particularly in the form imagined for it by Isaiah. For this content surprises, for all its extravagance, not only by its rational purity, but even more by its hedonism, not to say by its humane materialism. Compare the following sentences from the cited chapters of *Isaiah*, concerning the happy last days: 'Then shall he give the rain of thy seed, that thou shalt sow the ground withal; and bread of the increase of the earth, and it shall be fat and plenteous: in that day shall thy cattle feed in large pastures (30,23)... Ho, every one that thirsteth, come ye to the waters, and he that hath no money; come ye, buy, and eat; yea, come, *buy wine and milk without money and without price* (55,1)... For brass I will bring gold, and for iron I will bring silver, and for wood brass, and for stones iron: I will also *make thy officers peace, and thine exactors righteousness* (60,17)... A little one shall become a thousand, and a small one a strong nation' (60,22). Thus far Isaiah, thus far the primitive-socialist content of the imagined covenant between God, man, beast and all existence. All later depictions of the millennium[149] in sectarian theology follow Isaiah. Long life is prophesied, sin and death are weakened, the body attains undreamt-of strength, the soil bears thousand-fold fruit, the desert is transformed into orchards, the whole of nature into a human house, godlike existence begins in innocence, peace and pervasive joy. Thus though the empty promises and passive fantasies are conspicuous here, the class-hostile heresy is also just as conspicuous in these constructs, or rather the standard it caused to be applied to the Christian Church, and even to the Christian state. Consequently the chiliastic hopes in this

149 'Des tausendjährigen Reiches': 'Millennium' and 'Thousand-Year Reich' are the same in German. In certain, specifically non-Nazi contexts as here, we have chosen to translate it with the more usual 'millennium'.

world were soon rejected by the official doctrine of the Church, most vigorously by *Augustine*: the fire was deadened, the standard desocialized. For according to Augustine the millennium already begins with Jesus; if a person professes faith in his Redeemer, this is already the first resurrection. The kingdom in which the just who have been resurrected reign with Christ is solely the ecclesiastical community of the faithful, the earthly City of God, the civitas Dei terrena. The second resurrection and the Last Judgement accordingly have no significance for the history of humanity, but only for the individual soul – the kingdom of God on earth is and remains the expanding Church. Augustine certainly put the state itself on trial, both as a Church thinker and as a philosopher of Christian inwardness; in the historical state structures, including Rome, Augustine perceives only a community of the damned, one divided by discord. Here alone is world history (namely gradually increasing separation between the realm of sinners and that of grace). Salvation history is not world history, however, but merely that of individuals, just as the future is solely the individual other world. Augustine had every reason for this dismissal of the millennium, for chiliasm certainly had not expired in the early Church. Even in the second century AD a 'prophet' had appeared against the 'secularized Church', the dervish *Montanus* had founded an early Christian community which, secluded from the world, was to prepare itself for the descent of the higher Jerusalem. In the third century restlessly strict Montanism began a triumphal march through the world; only towards the end of the fourth century was chiliasm ruled out; from then on it was universally regarded as heresy.

But precisely for this reason the dream banned by the Church particularly appealed to the rabble-rousers. It lured forward with double affinity, and the rejection by the masters attested it. But the fact that the fantasies of the millennium on earth, of the new Jerusalem, could not be eradicated despite the victory of the Church, and that they continually had an inflammatory effect in league with social deprivation, was proved much later, in social revolutionary epochs, by the Münster of the Anabaptists, and above all the Tabor of the Hussites. The Hussite movement marks the first heroic age of a communist (communist-spirited) revolution; at its ideological centre, however, stood chiliasm itself, as the teacher of a possible this-worldly character of the other world. Its Taborite preachers proclaimed, wholly in the style of Isaiah, the Zionist kingdom of freedom and equality for the 'just', for those returning to the paradisal state of innocence. Only in this hope was Tabor founded – a New Jerusalem in which the Christian communism of love of the early Christian community was to be renewed: no castes, no domination, no private property, no taxes; a democratic community under God as the mystical king. The fact that the sectarian politics of these times brought absolutely no paradisal innocence but intergrated itself into manufacture, indeed supplied the ideology for the purest forms of capitalism (England, America), is well known. The materialistic logic of the forces of production at the time was stronger than the early Christian moral will and the apocalyptic-revolutionary melting-point in false consciousness. Nevertheless, the Hussite and Baptist movement would not have got off the ground at all if chiliasm had not kindled it ideologically; if it had not added to the revolution the apparently objective certainty on top of the subjective one. Chiliasm (as incidentally also the astrological prophecies at the end of the Middle Ages of a 'necessary' change of times) represented at that time the science of revolution so to speak, namely its objectivity and inevitability; the times were experienced as not just subjectively but also objectively ripe for revolution, the revolution stood 'at the hearing', the heavenly court-clock seemed to be striking its hour. It is impossible to overestimate the fostering of the will to rebellion by such reflections and anchorings of it, and this too is certain: it was not chiliasm which prevented the economic consciousness, and the concrete control of reality at that time. It certainly did not stand in the way of this consciousness (as a quack stands in the way of a doctor, for instance, and prevents his timely intervention), but rather, no economic consciousness existed at the time purely for economic reasons, and if chiliasm had not existed, no revolutionary consciousness would have existed either, and therefore no revolution whatsoever. And it was not because of chiliasm that this revolution perished or expired in the period of manufacture, and especially in Puritan capitalism. But just the reverse: up to the French Revolution, if not longer, chiliasm – in rationalized form – incited broad masses not to put up with their current 'fate', and to commit revolutionary acts for the 'breakthrough of the kingdom'. The slim or wholly lacking correspondence of these acts, and even goal-definitions, to reality is obvious of course, indeed it occasionally gives late chiliasms like those of Weitling,[150] and especially Fourier,[151] a curious aspect from the Marxist standpoint. Precisely because, in times for which economic consciousness had become possible, they treated both the present and the near future as blank areas or undiscovered tracts of land; because, instead of the lions with which the old cartographers had decorated their blank areas, they sketched in exuberant palm leaves or other abstractions of mere wishful imagination. Nevertheless, fantasy must not be allowed to conceal either the power of ancient dreams or the explosive force which – both for evil and for good – is still inherent in them. The explosive force existed wherever the promise did not have a quiescent effect, did not seem like internal-spiritual tinsel or even like contemplative fibbing, but provocative like a withheld good and illuminating like the Land of Cockaigne. Until, of

150 Wilhelm Weitling, 1808–71, early German socialist.
151 Charles Fourier, 1772–1837, French utopian socialist.

course, a Pied Piper[152] appeared here as well, 'at the twelfth hour', and is leading towards just as glorious times as his predecessor did, namely towards war. No swords are beaten by Hitler into pruning-hooks, no spears into ploughshares;[153] rather the reverse; instead, the new Thousand-Year Reich will last several hundred thousand years from the outset, allegedly without a Last Judgement. An enormous mouth, a mouth like a bowl of blood, drains the container of the entire future. Thus the Thousand-Year Reich is also realized in Germany just as splendidly as the messianic emperor, and the Third Reich. There is German socialism, practised by viri spirituales beyond compare; there are Reichsbank bills of exchange drawn on the third gospel, payable in the currency of the Kingdom of God.[154] 'I will also make thy officers peace, and thine exactors righteousness' – but these words do not yet seem to have been completely fulfilled by the German super-race. And in other respects as well, Hitler's Third Reich has about as much similarity with that imagined by Joachim of Fiore as his socialism has with the realm of freedom.

Result for a part of concrete-utopian practice

Everything flows, but the river comes from a source every time. It takes matter with it from the regions through which it has run, this colours its waters for a long time. Equally for that new form there are remnants of an older one, there is no absolute cut between today and yesterday. There is no totally new work, least of all the revolutionary kind; the old work is merely continued more clearly, brought to success. The older paths and forms are not neglected with impunity, as has been shown. Dreams in particular, even the most wakeful ones, have a past history, and they carry it with them. Among backward strata these remnants are particularly strong and often totally musty, but even the revolutionary class honours its precursors and still heeds them. The old forms partly help, if correctly deployed, with the New.

The fact that they are extremely effective has been better noted by the enemy than by our friends. Some old material is due to be made our own again, the needs of the moment insist upon it. The soft arrogance with which a Kautsky[155] smiled and did nothing but smile at 'heroes' or 'little samples of apocalyptic mysticism' is at an end in theoretical and

152 'Rattenfänger', literally 'rat-catcher', can also mean 'rabble-rouser' in a figurative sense. Both meanings are implied here.
153 Cf. Isaiah 2,4: 'And they shall beat their swords into ploughshares, and their spears into pruning-hooks.'
154 Bloch is punning here on the political and religious connotations of 'Reichsbank' and 'Reich Gottes'.
155 Karl Kautsky, 1854–1938, socialist politician and theorist.

NON-CONTEMPORANEITY AND INTOXICATION

practical terms. Even such an apparently absurd and undemocratic structure as the old dream of the Führer (leaving the 'revolutionary' imperial dream out of account) does not appear in practice – mutatis mutandis – to be quite so stupid. The revolutionary class and quite certainly those who are still undecided in revolutionary terms wish for a face at the top which will captivate them. A helmsman they trust and whose course they trust; the work on board ship is then made easier. The voyage is safer if everyone does not find it necessary to check the direction all the time. All this has been proved in practice, with the best democratic conscience; there must be a vanguard and a spearhead on the march. As long as the march is still theoretical, this does not become so apparent, but as soon as it is realized it does so at once. The Communist Manifesto still contains no mention of leaders, or only between the lines, in the given existence of its authors as it were, of those who issued it. But as soon as the Manifesto began to be realized, the name of Lenin flashed up alongside the founding fathers of Marxism, and the appearance of Dimitrov[156] in Leipzig was of greater help to the revolution than a thousand blatherers or speakers at meetings. Such human matters as revolution can hardly be implemented without visible human beings, without the image of real individuals (not idols). In the classless society this may and will be superfluous, indeed totally different.

The further dreams of olden times, those that are still misty, are not also the safest ones. After all, precisely the total opposite has set in in their name, the opposite not of the mist, but of the dream. But must the seed therefore be sacrificed with the husk, or is it not the case that even the seed of the dream, properly extricated, refutes the monstrous forgery which the Nazis have perpetrated by means of the misty husk? The question is practical and it arrives in time precisely under the banner of the incipient German popular front or, more specifically, of Christian anti-fascism within the popular front. Shortly before Hitler, a public discussion took place in Berlin, between the half- and high-class Nazi Hielscher, the Jesuit father Przywara,[157] and the Protestant theologian Dehn,[158] on the topic 'Reich and Cross'. Dehn (already persecuted by the Nazis at that time) declared on the basis of his Christian premises that the imperialist Nazi Reich 'nowhere took into account the ideas of peace and justice'; indeed he played off the Communist doctrine against

---

156 Georgi Dimitrov, 1882–1949, Bulgarian Communist, acquitted on the charge of arson (burning of the Reichstag in Berlin) in Leipzig in 1933; 1933–43, General Secretary of the Comintern in Moscow; 1946–9 Bulgarian Prime Minister.

157 Erich Przywara, 1889–1972, philosopher of religion, sought a synthesis of Thomism and modern philosophy.

158 Günther Karl Dehn, 1882–1970, Protestant theologian and early critic of the Nazis, and consequently relieved of his chair at Halle university in 1933.

the barrenness of this concept of the Reich, in so far as in the former
there were at least still echoes of expectations derived from salvation
history. But the Nazi Reich was devoid of any human content, it came
from the darkness of mere drives, from the cunning of mere capitalist
interests which were making use of these drives, and would return into
the darkness. Unlike the Communist idea of the Reich, it could not be
substantiated by the 'idea' of the classless society, which involved not
least a topical transformation of early Christian and theologically heretical specifications. Thus far Dehn; thus far the neutralization, indeed
possible sympathy of these men for Communism. However his 'early
Christian definition' may be corrected and reprimanded, this is the most
important point of contact between Christian and Communist anti-
fascism. It is the function of Communist propaganda (or more precisely,
of the traditional revolutionary company which it has to carry along
with it) to look after things at this point and to correct the superstitious
fear among the devout of the 'movement of the godless'. Without the
problems of atheism even having to be touched upon, without the
slightest embarrassment, let alone dishonesty, such propaganda has a
place among members of the Confessional Church and humane Catho-
lics. Many precursors of socialism were so from the standpoint of
Christianity; this unites both, this is a common stretch of road at this
time. And later times, in which previous religion will be stale, will more
easily do justice to the source of power which flowed in the 'freedom of
the children of God' alongside all empty promises and ideologies of
exploitation.

We have already touched on the question whether precisely the mist
did not make the old dreams so useful to the Brownshirts. Economic
ignorance has undoubtedly made their deception easier for the Nazis,
and they have undoubtedly exploited the old dark words in a highly
demagogic way. But much more important is the question whether this
use, this abuse, did not succeed so easily precisely because the genuine
revolutionaries did not keep a look-out here. Economic vagueness,
petit-bourgeois mustiness and mystical mist certainly go splendidly
together; one assists the other. But economic clarity and the critique of
metaphysical appearance do not yet therefore need to disavow a priori
the entire extent and content of the constituents described as irrational.
This had a revolutionary point in Voltaire's times, but today, as the
German effect has shown, it almost exclusively serves the forces of
counter-revolution. There is also no realism at all in this mechanism
of refusal; on the contrary, large strata of social, and indeed physical,
reality are cordoned off by such mechanical banality. The times of this
narrow-mindedness are over, the understanding and the application of
Marxism are attaining ever more complete objectivity, ever greater
width and depth. At the same time, however – and it is important to

stress this here, on the very threshold – at the same time, however, the attained width and depth directs irrational overblownness much more thoroughly and knowledgeably than the pseudo-Enlightenment was ever able to do. Indeed, in the improbable event that mysticism should make up further ground as a result of this anti-banality, then the very knowledge of width and depth itself, as such, will move to the head of the opposition, the opposition against mysticism. For mystical banality is not a hair's breadth better, but rather a whole kitschy mane more objectionable, than the rationalist kind; mysticism is the ignorant caricature of depth, just as the pseudo-Enlightenment was the quarter-educated caricature of clarity. Reason is and remains the instrument of reality, though concrete-materialist reason of course, which *does justice to the whole of reality; consequently also to its complicated and imaginative components.* Accordingly the right-minded therefore know that the difficult voyage of the world, that the many unresolved features of its past, that the horizons of its future which have not yet appeared – that all these constituent factors towards dialectical-real tendency represent no objectives of secondary modern school enlightenment any more than they do those of Martin Buber or Keyserling[159] mysticism. Thorough philosophical, i.e. truly Marxist, reason directs and corrects itself in the same act as its opposite: irresponsible windbaggery, mysticism. The Nazis thrived on the latter, but they were only able to deceive with it so undisturbed precisely because an all too abstract (namely backward) left undernourished the imagination of the masses. Because it almost surrendered the world of imagination, without regard to its highly different characters, methods and objects or, more pointedly, without proper differentiation between the mystic Eckhart and the 'mystic' Hanussen[160] or Weissenberg.[161] But there is a lasting distinction between prophecy from tea-leaves and that other prophecy of Meister Eckhart, in the 'Sermon on Birth', about the hidden glory of man: 'I become aware of something in myself which shines in my reason; I certainly feel that it is something, but what it is I cannot grasp; only this much strikes me: if I could grasp it, I would know all of the truth.' This is the same *human feeling of glory* which subsequently made Thomas Münzer, the disciple of Eckhart, Tauler[162] and Suso,[163] into the ideologist of the Peasant Wars; which, beyond hunger and scurvy, aroused protest against the conditions in which man, in Marx's words, had

---

159 Hermann Graf Keyserling, 1880–1946, mystical philosopher.
160 Jan Erik Hanussen, 1889–1933, notorious clairvoyant and charlatan in the twenties, whose prophecies were later exploited by the Nazis.
161 Joseph Weissenberg, 1855–1941, occultist and mystic healer, founder of various minor religious sects.
162 Johann Tauler, c.1300–61, Dominican monk and mystic.
163 Heinrich Suso, 1295–1366, mystic, pupil of Meister Eckhart.

become an oppressed, contemptible, lost being.[164] German mysticism of the Middle Ages, with its lay preaching, its practical Christianity, its thirst for the 'revelation of the freedom of the children of God', stems from early revolutionary movements of the bourgeoisie. And the existing mist was not one of the *entire content*; this rather comprised goal-setting light, the same light which caused Münzer to state quite reciprocally, with a mutual functional harmony of his rebellion and his Christianity, in his 'Highly Provoked Rebellion': 'Just as Christendom has to be put straight in a quite different way, the profiteering villains must be removed.' Thus the mist is certainly not everything in the old dreams (whether they be the political-chiliastic ones, or whether they be the only seemingly individual ones of mystical slave-smashing, Son-becoming, of charging with immanent glory). Hence, paradoxical as it may sound, a large part of revolutionary pride came into the world only through German mysticism, and Christian-humane utopia acted it out before it.

We must repeatedly distinguish between mist and light, of course, and the light also corrects itself. This is particularly true of the further sequence of utopian dreams, of the narrowing they underwent in the so-called fairytales of an ideal state of modern times. They extend from Thomas More to Weitling, only to expire seriously after Marx; science superseded them. Over half of this constructive form of utopia was subjective intellectual arrogance, undialectical postulation, mythological transference of an unconscious class-interest into the 'last days' or into a 'distant land' in general. But the impetus and the background of these constructs is here likewise something different from the husk in which they are cloaked. Hence as certainly as the defects of this abstract system exist, and as economically as socialism has progressed from this kind of utopia into a science, just as little must the core be confused with the husk here either, and just as little is it destroyed with it. Lenin even extricated a good core in the concept of *ideology*, a core without mist and deception, and he emphasized it when he called socialism the ideology of the working class. The rescue of the good core of *utopia* is equally overdue (as a concept which at the most lay in mist, never in deception); the *concrete-dialectical utopia of Marxism, that grasped and alive in real tendency*, is such a rescue. The undialectically attached dreaming was the mist of the matter, and in the mist lay – although with distinctions – all the wishful times and wishful spaces of the old utopia. The phantasmagorias which the longing for a better world projected into future times or distant islands or inaccessible valleys also mainly contained only the respective class-contents of the respectively oppressed class (even though transparent for classless premonitions in general).

164 An allusion to a favourite quotation of Bloch's from Marx's *Einleitung zur Kritik der Hegelschen Rechtsphilosophie*.

Most old utopias also stagnated in the reality given to them, they condensed only the torpor out of it as it were and distilled out the spirit, they recognized no *process* and no *totality* of renewal. The *concrete utopia of Marxism*, on the other hand, runs with the process of the forces of production towards the classless society per se in tendency. Thus Marxism, on most careful mediation with the material tendency, ventures forward into the not yet arrived, not yet realized. Even the happiness which has its career in Marxist terms is not that of an already existing and simply more plentifully allocated kind: like the 'bliss' in the religious utopias, like the boredom of a permanent Sunday in the bourgeois ones. On the contrary, the Marxist hope is so productive even here that it does not embark on mere mythological transpositions of something already given, although something relatively better given. Marxism teaches that all previous happiness stands in the mere prehistory, or at best in the suggestion of the right thing; it keeps its this-world, its corporeal this-world, as one which is both open and still unfathomed. But precisely this is genuine utopia, and only this extracts lasting velleity and humane imagination from the fairytales of an ideal state, and particularly from the dreams of the Reich. Stands in the closest connection with everything which was contained in the old utopia in the way of genuineness, in the way of dreams which continue to fire with enthusiasm. Stands beyond the subjective postulate, beyond the mythological distant transposition of finished wishful contents. But the sphere itself is not absolutely different from that of Joachim of Fiore, nor is it absolutely deserted. In other words, the Marxist-directed work criticizes the *ideology* of uncomprehended *necessity* by comprehending and *destroying* it, but the *utopias* of uncomprehended *freedom* by comprehending and *fulfilling* them. The socialist revolution is distinguished from its predecessors by its scientific character and concreteness, by its proletarian mandate and classless goal, yet it is just as fundamentally connected with them through the fire and the humane content of the revolutionary impetus and intended realm of freedom. The so little realized dreams of this realm still intervene in the present so that they are concretely corrected and fulfilled.

E. NOT HADES, BUT HEAVEN ON EARTH

Every Now is already differently there tomorrow. It is even possible that misery subsides a little. Then a lot of ordinary people stop running with the pack. They return to that centre which can be one for them anew. The mere shallow yesterday which they are and have intended begins again.

But this calm, if it comes, hardly lasts for a long time. The recuperation is likely to be short, and certainly no longer as unquestionable as the earlier ones. A sting is left behind, both of insecurity and of former baiting and degeneration. What is now already clearly changing is also less the misery than the trust in Hitler. His enormous credit is slowly crumbling away, creditors and the credulous are grumbling, the payday has been missed too often. Perhaps 'disillusioned' SA proletarians and also younger sections of a proletarianized and utopianized petite bourgeoisie are becoming ripe for Communism. But the non-contemporaneous contents of this stratum, which have been indicated here, have thereby not yet become inoperative themselves, of course.

Against these the red remedy is only halfway effective, or mostly not at all as yet. Nazis speak deceitfully, but to people, the Communists quite truly, but only of things. The Communists often also flog slogans to death, but many from which the alcohol has long since disappeared and which are merely schematic. Or they bring their most correct figures, examinations and registered entries to those who are stultified with nothing but figures, registered entries, office and dry work all day long, and are thus subjectively weary of the entire 'business world'. Here linguistic and propagandist reform are the needs of the moment: *of the head which must not be allowed to become stuffed with nonsense or fossilized, of the limbs by means of which the revolt also progresses among employees and the non-contemporaneous.* Even an expectable turning towards Communism will long be a negative one, a mere disillusionment with Hitler; this alone does not yet secure the new loyalty.

For will slogans which were *too weak* to penetrate the National Socialist front be *sufficient to embrace* the *deserters?* In the country there are as yet no grain factories, in the town the middle classes are admittedly proletarianized but far from being proletarian. They are proletarian neither in their economic being nor even in their consciousness, do not speak the language of the proletarians, have non-contemporaneous memories or seek them, and not totally empty ones. But freethinking vulgar Marxism seems to lie under a curse of virtually confirming the hatred of reason among those who are proletarianized (as if all reason resembled the halved capitalist kind of today). In a time and a country where capitalism, with its poor rationalization, has also discredited the Ratio for 'broad circles', the separate emotional values of Communism are hardly sufficiently stressed, and nobody points towards the genuine and full, the concrete Ratio; as the liberation from the economic system, as the means precisely towards the humanization and totalization of existence. Dialectical materialism is not separated comprehensibly enough from the miserable 'materialism' of the industrialists; the fact is hardly sufficiently stressed that Communist materialism is not an attitude but a doctrine, that it is not a total economy over again, but precisely the lever to place the controlled economy at the periphery and human beings at the centre for the first time. Instead, much vulgar Marxism almost supports the caricature which irrational minds have drawn of 'mechanical' reason. But the times are so strange that the revolution cannot directly intervene in impoverishment, but – among the proletarianized – only in emotional and irrational contents, not just in claptrap and ignorance but also in intoxications and 'ideals' which contradict misery in a non-contemporaneous way. If some of these contents have already been meddled with in an imitative fashion (which, with regard to nationalism for instance, Hitler the original can do better), the next step is none other than dialectical mobilization, as a grasping of the dialectical hook which all these ambiguously contradictory resources contain. There will be no successful attack on the irrational front without dialectical intervention, no rationalization and conquest of these areas without its own 'theology', adjusted to the always still irrational revolutionary content. It is necessary that Marxism should no longer be misunderstood as the other side of 'empty mechanics', that it should irradiate those depths of revolutionary content within it which it abandons to its enemies for deception, to non-contemporaneous elements for exploitation, although it has its origin in them itself and alone. This situation even has its 'Teutonic' parallel or, in the face of the Nazis, the following comparison: when the Teutons once migrated south and west, the Slavs streamed into the vacated, originally German regions; laboriously, say the Nazis, knights of various orders reconquered East Elbia. When scientific socialism incorporated France and England, i.e. the French Enlightenment, the English economy, but vulgar Marxism had forgotten the inheritance of the German Peasant Wars and of German philosophy, the Nazis streamed into the vacated, originally Münzerian regions; laboriously, peasant propaganda and deepened theory are reconquering the profusion. Expelling all mist, all 'irratio' of merely false consciousness, all mythology; but the peasant is alive, even the pauperized petit bourgeois of today is to be taken very seriously, and most seriously of all the voice of the human What For (still beyond the next step). Marx writes at one point in 'The Eighteenth Brumaire': 'Through the discontented peasants starving to death on their parcel of land the proletarian revolution receives the chorus without which its solo in all peasant nations becomes a song of death'; this statement is of decisive importance even among petit-bourgeois nations, especially among 'irrationally' accustomed, 'irrationally' starved ones. The primacy of the proletariat or of controlled contemporaneous contradictions also proves to be a critical-dialectical handling of non-contemporaneous ones.

Enlightenment and dialectical wisdom together

The dust of what is old does not settle differently. It is repeatedly blown up where the New does not have the whole person. It therefore will not do to speak only ironically with often very cheap understanding where the dearest kind should at least be ready to be surprised. It will not do to write thick books about National Socialism, if after reading them the question as to what it is that is thus influencing many millions of people is even more obscure than before. The problem becomes all the greater the *more simply* the water-bright author has managed the water-clear solution; namely for his vulgar Marxist needs, which simplify everything for him just as their stupid enthusiasm does for the National Socialists. Even a critique which solely notes 'barren clichés' in the 'self-integration into the ancestral peasant blood kinship', in the 'fanatical religious bond with the soil', abstractly cordons off dangerous depths of older ideology instead of dialectically analysing and practically grasping them. The creative form of Communism is instead, precisely with regard to such inequalities, *wisdom*, that dialectical wisdom which Russia displays in many respects. Which not without reason provokes such precise questions of larger dialectics as this: can the house which has become musty be dismantled in order to be used in a socially new way in individual components, that of the mother for instance? Or can the bond with the soil which has become mouldy be converted from an element of family egoism into solidarity and thereby into a new mainstay of the village commune? In order to lead contents through the great crisis to which circumstances have subjected them, their previous vehicles, applications and manifestations must of course have become alien; but what then appears is no Not-only-but-also of the social-democratic type (which almost consists of nothing but Not-only), but rather that centre of which Brecht says that it belongs to Communism, because it is the middle course: 'Communism is not radical, it is capitalism that is radical.' It is above all that centre which abandons convictions in the face of wisdom, in short, which recognizes no abstract principles when new contents press forward, but which recognizes only one *content* as the sole 'principle' itself, namely the production of conditions for the victory of the proletariat, for bringing about the classless society. But until then the unrest cannot be observed separately enough which both causes to darken and itself darkens today. The 'diversion' had only fished in shining troubled waters, but the 'intoxication' fishes in chaotic ones, which are much more ambiguous and more charged at the same time. Or as far as the dust is concerned, Lützow's[165] hunt disturbs it all the more, but not in fact as the sparkling, interrupting dust of diversion, but as veiling and excessive outburst at the same time, as *dust to the power of three* as it were. But at the same time that kind of enlightenment is thereby called into question anew which once had its revolutionary locus, whereas today, with its principles, it misses the new locus. In the second half of the nineteenth century mechanical materialism, at least in Germany, still had a certain revolutionary role against the nobility, against the Church allied with it, and even against the great bourgeois and his ledger 'with God'; thus Marx could leave the broad 'metaphysical' legacies of the dialectical method – not that they were lacking – *implicit*. Whereas today, when precisely the main upper middle-class opponents of revolution are 'materialistic', when no financial backer of the National Socialists can be surpassed in any way in cynical freethinking or even fears it as a weapon, it is precisely the 'irrational' which not least grounds their contradiction for susceptible peasants and petit bourgeois – and ideologically prevents their contact with Marxism. The proletarian-Marxist avant-garde has a 'faith' which was never more real, but the petit bourgeois, however impoverished he is, does not heed it. Instead, just as they have stolen the red flag, the first of May, and finally even the hammer and sickle, stolen and perverted them for the purpose of forgery, the Nazis have also particularly known how to make use of the less manifest symbols of revolution for their own ends. It is not as if philosophy 'missed' something in socialism or wished to 'improve' it with contents which did not grow in the soil of the historically decisive class; as a Marburgizing[166] of the irrational so to speak. But rather this is the basic question recurring from all sides: whether the less manifest symbols and contents of revolution with which the Nazi goes crabbing

165 See 'Rough night in town and country', n. 28.
166 A reference to the neo-Kantian school of philosophy in Marburg in the late nineteenth century.

among the petite bourgeoisie were not simply able to serve to deceive so easily because they were still too little highlighted by propaganda, because the *well-exposed* backgrounds of Marxism have been still too little *developed* and made into prints. It thus becomes a concrete task to *show* the *mediated* transcending (repeat: transcending) in Marxism urbi et orbi as well; it becomes a duty also to make public and explicit its ultraviolet, the future-'transcendence', mediated in dialectical materialism, which Marxism implicitly contains, for the purpose of occupying and rationalizing the irrational movements and contents. For the Marxist world in which it is possible to think and act concretely is least of all mechanistic, in the sense of bourgeois bigotry, least of all fact- and law-based in the sense of mechanical materialism. But rather it is a movement in which human work can be deposited, and then a process of helpful contradictions, towards a dawning, arch-human goal: it is working, dialectical, hoping, inheriting per se. To forget nothing, to transform everything, both powers fall due here. Charon, of course, does not ferry whole figures but merely *shades* across the river; but it is Charon. *Socialism does not want Hades, however, but heaven on earth*; it thus ferries across the entire substance of history, in its both corrected and transfigured body. All the bourgeois-feudal share in ideologies is unmasked by *dialectical* materialism, but the undischarged and 'cultural' remnant, as substance with reluctance, is inherited by it.

Examples of transformation

If we look back, three trends[167] ran crosswise in the Now. They bear *early*, or at least earlier banners and symbols, those which contradict. *Youth* longs for discipline and a leader, the *peasantry* takes root in soil and homeland more strongly than ever, and the impoverished *urban centre* seeks to spare itself the class struggle through the corporate state, installs Germany – a blood-based, aryanized one, not the present one – as a gospel. These three discontented groups bear all the non-contemporaneous contents of today; and they bear them towards the right. For capital, of course, it is ultimately extrinsic whether parliaments or generals 'rule', whether the Republic or the Third Reich provides the backdrop of true power. There is no doubt here that from a contemporaneous-material viewpoint there is nothing in National 'Socialism' but 'anti-capitalist' demagogy of total mendacity and insubstantiality; the sole *contemporaneous* content of Hitlerism is control of big business through increased pressure and romantic illusions. But the *seducibility* through these very illusions, the *material* of this seducibility still lies in a different region; here class contents of non-contemporane-

167 'Zug' also has the sense of 'procession' here.

ous impoverishment are in mere service and predominant abuse by big business. It is thus only partly correct when Lukács writes: 'Fascism as the collective ideology of the bourgeoisie of the post-war period inherits all tendencies of the imperialistic epoch in so far as decadent-parasitic features are expressed in them; yet all mock-revolutionary and sham opposition elements also belong here. Admittedly this inheriting is a re-structuring, a rebuilding at the same time: that which was merely shaky or confused in earlier imperialistic ideologies is transformed into the openly reactionary. But whoever gives his little finger to the devil of imperialistic parasitism – and everyone does this who falls in with the pseudo-critical, abstractly distorting, mythicizing character of the im-perialistic sham oppositions – will find he takes his whole hand' ('Great-ness and Decline of Expressionism', 1934[!]). This turning away, this a priori ready-made analysis of an otherwise so significant thinker admit-tedly has the advantage of decidedly circling above its subjects and not proffering the littlest finger to them, but it brings nothing home either; it does not blur the difference between petit-bourgeois romantic and proletarian concrete opposition by means of any gangplank, but it does not construct any boarding-plank either. A *non-contemporaneously re-volutionary* opposition nevertheless exists, that genuine stock of 'irra-tional' contents as well, which, if it currently hinders contact with the revolution, indeed will remain a restorational danger zone for a long time to come, may still equally remain unfavourable to capitalism in the long run. Much ignorance will disappear when the fascist deception has come to light cash down; many class-based and more genuine non-contemporaneities will balance themselves out in the *process* of revolu-tion. And just as it is not up to theory to make demands instead of seeing the concrete possibilities of the tendency, it would be foolish to set an invariably idealistic programme in extenso for the dialecticization of non-contemporaneous contradictions. In this respect even the entire orientation attempted here had to appear 'abstract', so to speak, precise-ly because it is not so, because it avoided rashly concretizing from abstractions. However, it would be just as wrong to prevent the existing possibilities of the 'auxiliary troop' artificially; even more wrong to find merely blind alleys in the 'Irratio', instead of those explosive aspects of hope which were never alien to the economic revolutionary impetus and ought not to be artificially strangulated. How differently young student fraternity members[168] embarked on their early enthusiasm, how similar-ly others push forward to poor peasants and their ancient language. How differently Lenin's Russia already fitted in *homeland* and *folklore* (the early communist gentes shine through); not just in bourgeois conformist or affixed terms, the organic forces of the *family* and the

168 Reference to the progressive political dimension of original German stu-
     dent fraternities in the early nineteenth century.

organic-historically remaining ones of the *nation* appear here refunctioned and placed in the service of a *national community*, but a genuine
one. How concretely even the fight against 'religion' wrenches from the
latter its *longings* and *symbolic powers*, not just, as the Russians still have
to agitate, 'in order to abolish heaven' (capitalism managed this both
here and there), but in order finally to 'establish it as the truth of this
world'. The path of inheritance continues, for there are – as not only
fascism shows – many ruins of Rome which are or remain none. After
all, the geometry of the non-contemporaneous is so strange that even
the Third Reich of the National Socialists is equally smaller and larger
than itself; by both and only by both together, by the analysis of
deception and by the extrication of the appearance of substance, it will
be destroyed in the long run, without new masks, without pseudo-
morphoses. History is not merely spectres and a rubbish heap, nor
merely chaff, and all the corn is already removed at the last stage, on the
last threshing floor in each case: but precisely because so much of the
past has not yet come to an end, the latter also clatters through the early
dawnings of newness. The German Walpurgis Night will disappear and
come in no new year only when the first of May makes it completely
light; and 'Museums of the religious past' will really arise only when the
genuine relics are removed from them. When they have to serve 'heaven
on earth' and keep alive the will towards it. In another space than that of
opium fumes and not in no religion, but in a religion without lies.

REMINDER: HITLER'S FORCE

(April 1924, *Das Tage-Buch*, no. 15)

At first we coldly ignored it. Shrugged our shoulders at the malicious pack which crawled forth. At the red posters with the drivelling sentences, but the knuckledusters behind them. That which roughly stepped to the bedside early in the morning to demand our papers, stuck itself up as a party here. Jews are forbidden to enter the hall.

All this was able to sink back again. It was still too alien and had not penetrated deep enough, the old Munich was still alive. The animosity towards the war had matured earliest here, for a long time foreign beauty had been brought into the cityscape and flourished with it, became acclimatized. The grim recollection of 1919, of Eisner's[169] death and the entry of the White Guard could at least still fade and the brutality withdraw into its shell, as if it had never been. The successful Kapp putsch,[170] and the banishment of the socialist ministers, admittedly indicated ruffled air again. But even this could still be understood as the reaction of a peasant province, a peasant city against very clumsy Communist dilettantisms. To Hitler this act seemed like a swan song; the further the soviet republic was left behind purely in temporal terms, the more certainly Bavaria seemed to assume its old aspect again.

Instead, as we know, the province became more embittered from day to day. The peasants, the urban peasants, still exist here as a rabble, primitive, suggestible, dangerous, unpredictable. The same people who had blackened the streets at Eisner's funeral in countless processions hounded the leaders of yesterday to their death. From one day to the next the flag shops exchanged the soviet star for the swastika; from one day to the next the people's court, created by Eisner, put Leviné[171] up

---

169 Kurt Eisner, 1867–1919, assassinated prime minister of the short-lived Munich Räterepublik (soviet republic).
170 Right-wing coup in March 1920 under W. Kapp.
171 Eugen Leviné, 1883–1919, prominent Communist leader who took part in the Munich Soviet Republic in 1919 and was condemned to death for his participation in it.

against the wall. The faithless rabble vacillates here which all rulers have despised and used, and it does not merely vacillate, but certainly the hunting of animals and human beings proved itself to be its most characteristic nature. These were not only impoverished petit bourgeois, who grab at now this and now that means of assistance, nor was this any organized proletariat, not even a relatively organizable lumpenproletariat which could be kept up to scratch, but definitely mere riffraff, the vindictive, crucifying creatures of all ages. They are dazzled by the sham, by students in regalia, by the magic of processions, parades and ringing spectacle; but Bavaria does not paint votive pictures any more. And the beaters are as ambiguous, unambiguous as the rabble, often even more contemptible than the latter. Baptized Hungarian Jews became spies for Hitler, bribed 'democrats' from the stock of Balkan journalists[172] filled the ranks. The genuine Thersites[172] and Vansens[173] did not want to be left out, gave the rabble its homogeneous head.

Nevertheless, he who no longer knows what to do knows nothing as yet of the whole. The case lies deeper, disgust and wit are now no longer the correct response alone. For separate from the hideous gawpers and accomplices, new youth glows at the core, a very vigorous generation. Seventeen-year-olds are burning to respond to Hitler. Beery students of old, dreary, revelling in the happiness of the crease in their trousers, are no longer recognizable, their hearts are pounding. The old student fraternity member is arising again, Schill's[174] officers reborn, they find their brother in Schlageter,[175] heroic associations with all the signs of irrational conspiracy are gathering under a secret light. Hitler, their leader, did not deserve the indulgence of his judges and this farcical trial; but even with the wit of Berlin lawyers there is no getting at him, and even Ludendorff, this brutally limited masculine symbol, does not live on the same level with him. Hitler the tribune is undoubtedly a highly suggestive type, unfortunately a great deal more vehement than the genuine revolutionaries who cited Germany 1918. He gave the exhausted ideology of the fatherland an almost mysterious fire and has made a new aggressive sect, the germ of a strongly religious army, into a troop with a myth. Nor is the lasting power of Hitler's programme explained by the fact that liberation from Jews, the stock market, the feudal tenancy of international capital, from the international Marxism hostile to the fatherland, is promised here along with similar confused music for the ears of the undiscriminating petite bourgeoisie. But if the

---

172 Thersites: the ugliest, most scurrilous man in the Greek army at Troy.
173 Vansen: A dissipated clerk and public agitator in Goethe's *Egmont*.
174 Ferdinand von Schill, 1776–1809, Prussian officer who fought with his hussars against Napoleonic occupation.
175 Albert Leo Schlageter, 1894–1923, officer who actively resisted the occupation of the Ruhr. He was shot by the French.

economy here moves to the periphery and the state ethos back to the centre, the music of the old unbourgeois discipline thereby rings out again at the same time, the secularized ethics of the chivalric orders.

Thus the extent to which Hitler has young people on his side should not be underrated. We should not underestimate our opponent but realize what is a psychological force for so many and inspires them. From this standpoint various connections certainly also appear with left-wing radicalism, that of a demagogic, formal kind, if not with regard to content. Through this affinity (mostly only a draught-excluding copy of socialism, tuned to primitive instincts) changing banners was made all the easier for the Bavarian rabble. Among the Communists as among the National Socialists an appeal is made to able-bodied youth; in both cases the capitalist-parliamentary state is negated, in both cases a dictatorship is demanded, the form of obedience and command, the virtue of decision instead of the cowardly acts of the bourgeoisie, this eternally discussing class. It is above all the type of Hitler and of those who follow his example, characterological and in formal terms strongly revolutionary. The *goals and contents* of this gang are also of course all the more recognizably, despite all confusion, only the totally counter-revolutionary expression of the will of sinking strata and of their youth. The twenty thousand dollars of the industry of Nuremberg already indicate the way in which the bourgeoisie does not feel at all threatened here, how it faces the new state mysticism, apparently hostile to capital, without fear. Engels called anti-semitism the socialism of the stupid mugs, whereby non-Jewish financial capital and above all original capital superbly prosper. The socialism of the cavalier, patriarchal-reactionary anti-capitalism, is an even greater misconception or rather an open deception, in order to conceal by means of the mere contrast to financial capital the very much greater contrast to socialism. Folkish instead of international, romantic-reactionary state mysticism instead of the socialist will towards the atrophy of the state, faith in authority instead of the ultimate anarchy latent in all genuine socialism – these are incompatible contrasts of positive volition, stronger than the apparent affinities of form and of the common negation of the present state. Othmar Spann,[176] the Austrian sociologist, a small imitator of the Austrian state theologians of the Vormärz, sought in this way to create a definition for National Socialism; and what emerged was as different from socialism as was the Romantic idolization of the state from this sentence of the young Engels: 'The essence of the state and of religion is humanity's fear of itself.' The underling races around, whom the feudal pressure lasting for centuries has produced and left behind, and longs as a formal predator to return to the strict stable. Churns up messianic dreams and

176 Othmar Spann, 1878–1950, Austrian economist and philosopher who demanded a Christian corporate state.

perverts them with feudal ones, radicalizes the dull centre in order to make them into ascetic rebels, and adopts the ideology of 'rebellion' by the grace of Metternich,[177] from the author of the Karlsbad decrees and guardian of the Holy Alliance.[178]

So to what lengths has this unrest yet to drive? It divides into three elements, to be considered separately, and indeed also already treated with a very different tone of voice. *Below* drives the petit-bourgeois pack, which deserted from Red to White and is willingly open to malicious and mindless agitation. *Above it* stand the shock troops of Hitler and his officers, good vigorous youth, raw and infected by the hideous background of the camp followers, but on the whole with pure intentions. Nauseated by the stock market age, the depression of the lost war, the lack of ideals in this dull Republic. Hitler himself here ignited or at least fanned a thoroughly unbourgeois movement in bourgeois youth, and shaped a certain ascetic energy which at least differs by several degrees from the mindlessness of the first German enthusiasm for war, and also from the senior primary school teacher pathos of the former fatherland party. But *thirdly*, though, the National Socialist *ideology* and *practice* is very treacherous. It seeks to oust the bourgeois by the knight and attains no more than that the bourgeois feels all the more protected and preserved by the young knights. And even the knight himself – he is admittedly more human than the bourgeois, but at the moment even more unreal than the latter, even more abstractly and even more unclearly preventing the breakthrough into reality. Hitler, Hitlerism, fascism is the ecstasy of bourgeois youth: this contradiction between strength and bourgeoisie, between ecstasy and the most lifeless nationalism makes the movement into a spectre. It does not become any more real through the feudal ghosts it carries with it, through the alliance of powerfully present enthusiasm with long-sunken chivalric dreams or Old Germanic folk royalty from the tenth century. All the same, the Hitler Youth sustains the only 'revolutionary' movement in Germany at the moment, after the proletariat has been robbed by the majority socialist leaders of its own, of the solely valid, consistent revolution. One part of fascism in Germany is as it were the crooked governor of the revolution, an expression of the fact that the social situation is by no means static. But the genuine tribunes of the people are lacking or prove by themselves the shrewd saying of Babel:[179] Banality is the counter-revolution.

---

177   Clemens Fürst von Metternich, 1773–1859, Austrian statesman; the Karlsbad decrees were issued under his influence in 1819 by the German governments against the National and Liberal movement.
178   Alliance between Tsar Alexander I, the Emperor of Austria and the King of Prussia, 1815.
179   Isaac Babel, 1894–1941, Russian writer.

FINAL FORM:
ROMANTIC HOOK-FORMATION

That which becomes stale easily goes over. We do not only mean the people of whom the Nazis are unsure anyway. Distrustful peasants, captured workers, in short, fascist foreign bodies in any case. These groups are already directly susceptible, only not quite so awoken as they shout out.[180] If they will not become red of their own accord, then they will not remain brown, on a hungry stomach, either.

But even that which dreams in them is two-sided. Indicates cracks, jumping-off points in the 'mind' of the Nazis itself. Some of these contradictions have already appeared: as those of the 'Third Reich' in the bourgeoisie, as those of genuine 'non-contemporaneity' per se. The *following sections*, then, aim to show certain hooks in several differently conventional premiums of the romantic disposition, from the fairytale to colportage, indeed from various kinds of 'occultism' to the myth of life; hooks of unclarified contradictions to the existing world, not just of the bond with the latter. There are imaginative modes of the 'puerile' and of the 'mythicistical' here which apparently combine easily with National Socialism and nevertheless seem suspicious to mustiness, ambiguous to domestic wildness.

For the flame which burns in this hearth likewise looks around, with long necks, on all sides. Even when it had not yet been discovered that the Jew is always nomadic and the German always a root, journeymen sought out distant climes in order to be at home only later. Even the rover, such a cheap being today,[181] was once best youth and not as firmly established as the old folk; he followed in the wake of the old folk songs which he sang, and was part of their unrest, before he became the earphone hairstyle. If singing unemployed people (who are forced to

180 A reference to popular chants and marching songs with the central Nazi theme of national awakening. See 'Rough night in town and country', n. 30.
181 Bloch is here referring to the Wandervogel youth movement of the day (1896–1933).

be romantic) are bringing the rootless hit-song back to the German folk song again today, precisely this folk song was in fact roving and raving like no other, and so loyal to its homeland that nothing at home had yet become homeland enough for it. Thus the German journeyman followed the German fairytale, which seeks out the *wide* world, the *rebelliously* unknown, the *liberation* from pressure, in order to find happiness. Childlike escape has one hook, as does youthful colportage, curious occultism has another, and the so-called philosophy of life has a particularly dialectical one. All these are not favourable to the mouldy-autarkical aim of such 'folksiness' or 'irrationality'. Even if the hook-formations do not intrude on the mire and leave it absolutely to itself, they still land many a fish which does not belong in the fascist brackish water, and also many a pirate chest which only reason opens and inherits. Benjamin[182] has already given pointers to this; and 'Traces'[183] has also taught the significance of incidental material, of all kinds of little stories, fairytales and further instances of wonders of the pond. The intoxication occurs only for the sake of the lie; yet the fair in it, the colportage of happiness, the passage to the 'beginnings of life', and particularly the forest murmur, sea murmur of Pan bear, unintentionally, rebellious signs. The fairytale seeks to escape from the folkish legend to which it is banished and spellbound; utopia of the first 'beginning' seeks to escape from the archaic realm of mere 'primeval times'. Which is either irretrievably past and lost or conversely an encapsulation of uncompleted, unbecome contents. And the lasting significance of these romantically described contents does not reveal itself romantically, but only from the intention of the Unbecome, Not-Yet-Become, in short, not from the retained past, but from the maintained path of the future.

182 Walter Benjamin, 1892–1940, German essayist and critic, and a close friend of Bloch's.
183 A reference to Bloch's own earlier work, *Spuren* (1930).

THE COLOURFUL ESCAPE

Even when breathing we go in and out. In the first case we stay here, in the other there is already a passage. We draw in the air, floating, while we rest, thrust it from us as soon as we shoot forward. All this runs in both draughts to and fro.

It begins with sucking of course. Plantlike, a child still sticks wholly in the house. But when he gets older and apparently has no choice, he seeks it, in dreamed distant lands. And when most children cry, it is over their parents, over the place where they are. Its nearness is only rarely their own, and beautiful expanse lures early.

What is nearest still lives in this expanse and drags away with it. As soon as the apparently so domestic child looks around, he is already elsewhere. The floor is sliding sand on which he crawls. The gap between the boards, the crack between floor and wall is promising in a way which no rock cave is later. A hidden Easter egg intensifies the countless hiding-places of which the parental home consists and to where the child escapes, at least with his eyes. But at the same time searching drives on the hunting dog in the child and one which does not bring back the prey. Nor is collecting that of the narrow self or of miserliness in love with itself, but precisely accompanies the escape and supports it. Alleys, marbles, stamps are fetched here because they fetch to themselves; transfers display their unexpected, very expected other side and are loved for this reason. Only through a thin film of water are the distant lands separate here, is the donkey cart at the front and behind it the fir tree with the bird, or the family at supper and behind them the volcano. The sea has been murmuring from shells from time immemorial, silver paper shines from its coast, and the child thinks he is no longer seen at home if he shuts his eyes. If these distant lands are old ones and if they lie in primitiveness, like the child himself, they are nevertheless in the same breath expansive ones. The playing child not only travels around in that world which is long past for the adult and which he attains again only in sleep, under the protective cover of sleep, but the terror and magic of this world are equally kidnapping, exotic, indeed full of hope. Even the sinking digging beneath the here and now flies into the far expanse or contains this flight. Admittedly in bourgeois children the fear is always nursed of that which could 'steal' them; a song lulls them to sleep for instance, a curious song of the little dog that has bitten the man and torn the beggar's coat. But the beggar whom they fear or are supposed to fear, whose torn coat lulls them into a sense of security, is not at all the poor man at the door for them. He is inside them, as the adult in one or several individuals against whom the child defends himself even when he loves him. Now the child no longer 'belongs' to his parents, is among his own kind and their dream. This has many faces, good and evil ones, and precisely the hesitant one is not among the good ones.

ON FAIRYTALE, COLPORTAGE AND LEGEND

Tom Thumb

That which a child hears lives as a part of himself. His sucking becomes different when it is done on the book. Defiance is released and only that felt or loved which shows it on the way. The more colourfully it emerges and puts everything right, the more the child says yes to everything. Addiction always moves up in order to save itself as well.

The listeners travel with it, find what is theirs in dreaming. Read fairytales, full of little and colourful people like them. These had often come from a good home, more often everything was so poor and wretched that one came to terms with it when the way back was lost. Hansel takes Gretel, Gretel takes Hansel in the fairytale, and not only in the fairytale, by the hand. If they find a new house of course, the witch lives in it, locks up again and burns. Other witches order the girl who stays with them to spin. To spin yarn in one night that could not be managed in years. The fear with no way out is contained and intended in this image in fairytale form; thus even in foreign parts the house appears as a prison, indeed as the totally erupted power of the spell. But strangely enough, precisely in the fairytale the force of the way out begins to work again, weak and cunning, strong through cunning which knows how to deceive the forces of evil, and has the right to do so. Hansel pokes a little piece of wood at the witch through the bars, so that she thinks it is his skinny finger. Or the poor soldier bores a hole in the boot which the devil is to fill with gold and places it over a pit: so the Evil One has to pour gold until cockcrow, without the boot becoming full; but the soldier bags it, and the devil departs without his soul. Thus these fairytales are the revolt of the little man against the mythical powers, they are the good sense of Tom Thumb against the giant. First roving being here makes space for a different life from that into which one was born or, spellbound, had stumbled. Instead of fate a fable begins,

Cinderella becomes a princess, the brave little tailor wins the king's daughter. Where this occurs is uncertain, it is suspended just like the time in which the triumph will occur. If they have not died, they are still alive today;[184] since no child understands death (for them being dead means having disappeared, having departed), the happy characters in the fairytale go on living after they have become *happy*. Once upon a time: this is in fact very near at hand, but near to children, and thus it is both intoxicating and foreign.

Winnetou's Silver Rifle
(Literature section of the *Frankfurter Zeitung*, 31 March 1929)

Even that which lads like reading is good for them. Rotten stuff, contrived stuff, lying sentiments have no place there. If they appear in smaller amounts, they are not perceived. If they appear in larger ones, the class does not go on reading the book. Although Karl May never did what he relates of himself, was never at the place where he professes to know every bush, every boy still finds him correct. So there must be something in the lie, namely the genuine wish for distant lands which it fulfils.

The green volumes did not always circulate in such an unhindered fashion. Admittedly motor cars could not do anything to harm the noble horses, Rih, the Wind, Hatatitla, the Lightning. Alongside tanks and the aeroplane the Bear-killer[185] stands unmoved, so heavy that only Old Shatterhand can lift it; the Henry carbine remains a marvel, with twenty-five shots, because it is a dream gun. But the truth cannot be concealed: when dreams were at a discount, thirty years ago, Karl May came under fire. Armed as he was; and the cannon stood in the 'Frankfurter Zeitung'. Old Shatterhand was blown sky high, his fairytale biography was replaced by the police report. Karl May: a proletarian without an educational background, a liar who never encountered Red Indians and Arabs, a criminal who even as a fourteen-year-old came into conflict with the rules of the fire brigade. A released convict, a Protestant who has Catholic business dealings, with the crucifix in the pool of blood. The provincial press reprinted this, parents were seized by cultivated horror, the adventures disappeared from beneath the Christmas tree, the world became narrow, the Puritans of the newspaper had conquered the Shakespeare of the boys. Although the verdict is all over and done with, its categories are still running in the world. Karl May is regarded as a disreputable case, or at most as a funny act without

184 Traditional ending to a German fairytale, equivalent to 'and they all lived happily ever after'.
185 A weapon.

literary value. In the final arguments over smut and trash it turned out that Rudolf Herzog[186] remains outlawed, Karl May does not.

Injustice was done years ago here, coyly and ignorantly. In Karl May crimes are often redressed at the place where they occurred. Thus it is stated here in the same newspaper, in an elevated position, in a changed time: Karl May is one of the best German story-tellers, and perhaps he would be the best, pure and simple, if he had not been a poor, confused proletarian. The shot which the well-meaning fired at that time is backfiring, on society itself. It is unprecedented how this convict became a writer; even in his cell he began to write: 'Geographical Sermons' – adventure and the will to reform, with such a light and fresh hand. Karl May is of the same lineage as Wilhelm Hauff;[187] only with more action, he writes no flowery dreams, but wild dreams, rapacious fairytales as it were.

Lads easily read beyond what is bad in his work because the suspense helps. The hero has just been tied to a tree, the leader of his enemies gives the order 'Fire!' – and we skip pages ahead to see if Karl May is actually still alive, the same I that must once have written all this. What is written disappears, so superbly and purely near are the foreign parts. Or the suspense in the first volume, quite purely from the world of dreams: Kara ben Nemsi is crawling through a passage to rescue the kidnapped girl from the palace. The passage turns into a canal, swimming, wading, foul water which is already up to the eyes, finally a way out into the courtyard, Kara ben Nemsi surfaces – and bangs his head on a grille which shuts off the well. When the hero now smashes the grille, comes up with his head in the water and half choked, a bullet whistles past his head – the action is like a nightmare from which we can find no way out, or like an escape which we do not tire of hearing about a hundred times. Genuine colportage can be read over and over again, because we forget it like dreams and because it has the same suspense. But even in technological terms there is much that is excellent (without 'waking up', without turning from colportage into adult literature). The house of the blacksmith in 'Ravines of the Balkans': in the dark everything is tangible, right down into the cellar, where the smith and his wife lie tied up beneath lumps of coal. The exposition of 'Rio de La Plata': with the streets of Montevideo, the pursuer, the old organ-player, the tea-gatherers, the pact to go into the primeval forest and the eerie sudden change which turns friends into enemies, turns the whole exposition round. The ravine-like or alley-like eeriness and bazaar atmosphere in general is something new which Karl May introduced into the Red Indian story; or rather, he bore all the charms of the Red Indian story into the Orient, where not merely the *adventure* of foreign

186   Rudolf Herzog, 1869–1943, popular German novelist and story-teller.
187   See 'Non-contemporaneities reported', n. 119.

parts, but also their *mystery* is. Winnetou has only the free prairie to himself, everything free and open, creeping only through grass, forest, seldom the city or attacks on the express which the city brings out there; simple language, in jargon of the late Cooper:[188] 'Midnight is long past and before the morning dawns the Yumas must be surrounded.' Yet the Orient books are sprinkled with the characteristics of the urban mystery of distance, in short with the deeper dream elements of colportage, beyond its first characteristic: the thirst for adventure and freedom of movement. Thirst for adventure and dream anxiety on the one hand, dream lustre on the other, are the elements of colportage of the nineteenth century; very unlike the settled calendar stories with which those who had not grown up or who had been shut out had previously whiled away the time. Nowhere are the tensions of this very dynamic literary genre more powerfully to be found than in Karl May, and seldom more completely. (Except for the erotic, which the man of the west does not need, and the traveller in the Orient does not want to have, in the celibacy of his courage.) And as for 'Christianity', an intelligent reader notices nothing of the kind, at least not in the Orient volumes, where he prefers Islam. Or Christianity is a stylistic device which lets the criminal go again and again as soon as one has him, and hence as soon as the action would have to be at an end; its harmony is the dissonance which drives the dream material.

Everything is fabulously healthy, long journeys and open air. A yearning bourgeois conformist who was himself a boy pierced the mustiness of the age. His colportage was not that of the romantic ideals of the bourgeoisie (elegant people, drawing-room lustre), nor of the chivalric tales from the Biedermeier period. But his colportage was again that of the Red Indian novel from the age of Cooper, of revolutionary ideals (when the savages were still better people). This was joined by the tinsel of the fair, the genuine fair-booth Orient which belongs to colportage, so that the freedom of movement is not exhausted in crude nature but changes colour and is reflected in dream layers. Almost everything is an externalized dream of oppressed creation which seeks to have large life. Only in the later books did Karl May become eccentric and private, his naivety was over and he symbolized. The dream rose from illness, whose world was no longer in common with that of youth. The thirst for adventure no longer spun fables out of the four walls, but feelings of inferiority, indeed feelings of guilt overcompensated for themselves. Karl May evidently became psychotic, basted with meanings composed of cheap fat, even the horses had to put up with being symbolic. Halef Hadschi Omar was deepened into an 'incarnate soul', Old Shatterhand (who was at worst simply a harmless Wilhelm II) into a 'self of humanity'. The beautiful smithy where slave-hunters and kidnappers of girls

188   James Fenimore Cooper, 1789–1851, American novelist.

used to stop became a 'ghost smithy' between 'Ardistan and Dschinnis-
tan', between this world and the other world. Friends visited Karl May
shortly before his death; both in order to see Winnetou's silver rifle
(which really exists) and in order to meet Karl May on the old trails, the
prairie, the dream Stamboul. In vain, Karl May was an ill man, he
regarded his travel stories as an 'aerostat', which allegorically 'had to
circle around the Dschebel[189] Mara Durimeh and Mount Winnetou'; but
Mara Durimeh was an old Nestorian[190] woman who bores every boy
even in Kurdistan. Thus the last books are failures, roughly from the
'Realm of the Silver Lion' on; the others remain all the clearer: travel
stories of concrete imagination which cross every Baedeker guide. They
are exactly the youthful dream of distant lands, a transposed fair, the
Orient as the *landscape* of the fair, of the wild and mysterious booths.
The Orient stories are better than the Red Indian ones, which are more
well-known in return. Both could be abridged only where Kara ben
Nemsi on the one hand, Old Shatterhand on the other, is *not* asleep,
where he tumbles out of his dream. Karl May is intoxication of the
dream, like all colportage, an intoxication certainly of blood, but equally
of distant lands: whereby the ambiguous river appears here too, the
dialectical river which also flows through the lake of colportage. It was
not in order to preach it that Karl May pierced the homebound mustiness of his age; and the heroic reading matter, which has become so
widespread in the meantime again, been toughened up, and interpreted
in 'Aryan' terms, is as double-edged as a Malayan kris.[191] Even if Old
Shatterhand is not the 'self of humanity' to which Karl May had finally
elevated him, he is certainly not autarky, and Winnetou, his red brother,
is not racial hatred. Only reluctantly can colportage be deflected towards home, in order to awake, from the dream of distance which it is,
to Germany, namely to a Germany of mouldiness all by itself. The black
horse Rih is not a military horse, but a gift from the Arabian sheik
Mohammed Emin, and he rides into the East, not to Saxony.

Dream appearance, fair and colportage

That which did not grow around them tastes all the better to lads
everywhere. Each of them dreams the deeds of his colourful heroes
while he is reading them, and forgets them some time after waking

---

189   Dschebel: 'dschabal' is Arabic for mountain, so the word is clearly
      synonymous with 'Mount' here.
190   Nestorian: follower of the doctrine, ascribed to Nestorius (d. 451), pat-
      riarch of Constantinople, that the divine and human aspects of Christ
      remained separate.
191   Kris: Malay or Indonesian dagger with a serpentine blade.

up. And yet the reader of colportage can even lack the awareness that he is reading, just as the dreamer can that he is dreaming. Such a book can be read several times and is forgotten again and again. That is to say, unconsciously married again and again and as new in the daytime to the person in suspense as an image which once frightened him or conversely goes on shining in a ship's wake that is long past. We do not see any real people, after all, but their wished adventures, openly narrated.

An equally open plot, which belongs precisely here, is the fair even today. Distorted by technological kitsch, lovely chimes are still popular. It too brings the south with it for youth and 'populace', oriental colour as well, and is a replica of colportage. To which every memory testifies, every renewed walk through the childlike, age-old, medical, criminal, exotic world of intoxication. Does it not begin immediately spiced, for nose, ear and eye at the same time? The waffles smell sweet, sticks of rock lie many-coloured in their trays, tough sweet snakes hang down into them. Slices of coconut lie on the plate, red and green lemonade can be sucked from coloured little bottles, as if it were forbidden. Sugared American corn bread is being cooked in a little wire frame which swings to and fro over the spirit flame; Tyrolese Alpine bread towers up, brown, cubic, lightly worm-eaten and porous. The little monkey on the stick shoulders his sword or shoots; tired and peaceful, silent on his rescued boat, sits the old one-armed miner beside his black-lined cabinet, and as he turns the handle, the tiny puppets in the coalmine move, the bell rings, the mine cage rises, the tiny wagons roll up and the mystery of the dangerous depths lies revealed. Friendly pretzel men split up the crowd with their baskets; cold morose pedlars stand around fixedly, around their necks the case full of blue eye-glasses, whoopee cushions and inflatable pigs, Red Indians dancing up and down, tickling peacock feathers for grown-ups, wooden scissor handles which, when shut together, propel diagonal pieces of wood into the air, with quivering butterflies on the end. Between balloons the great idolater still strides along, the bagpipes like a corpse in front of him, in which there is humming, on his back the giant drum with triangle, which he operates simultaneously from his elbow and his heel, but on his head there sits a restlessly shaken tree of bells: the south wind, the South Seas, which rings in a hundred bells. The gypsy woman is collecting, and the Italian women hold cages with budgerigars in their arms which draw letters of fortune, the Bolognese devil dances up and down in his glass, and he too knows the future in advance, at an inconspicuous table next to him hang little tubes which you can put in your ears, the whole thing looks half like shoelaces, half like an octopus, then the barrel rotates and you hear, infinitely far away, the mounting of the castle guard in Berlin. Yet again and again the real McCoy vehemently yells out in between, on high boards not far from Lauck's waffle booth and the well-hidden Punch and Judy show in the Dock Road; but at the feet of the real McCoy are spread out, are piled high, the batches of Egyptian cotton shirts and underpants, the handkerchiefs, bundles of pencils, notebooks, braces, oilcloth covers and stain-remover, the tombac[192] chains sparkle with a little pendant to be attached. He recites old obscure rhymes about Cain and Abel, but on the oilcloth cover Adam and Eve are to be seen together with the whole of paradise, and spicy images steal into the hearts of the women, peasants, sailors, the sooty Hemshöfer, the men in caps from the Rhine valley and the Gräfenau. All this is only the forecourt or row of pylons of the booth-town, indeed of the ship-town which has dropped anchor and is unloading exotic a priori goods (to which nothing any longer or nothing as yet corresponds). But inside live the 'Terrors of the Orinoco', with howling shells and mermaids in the hull, and next to them 'Rare people and their art': not only cowboys and knife-throwing at the lady from her head to her feet, but also hermaphrodites and Egyptian golden women, living aquaria, last Aztecs and men who immerse themselves in their colossal memory. Madame Lenormant murmurs motionless as a doll behind glass, but a step further and Schichtl's magic theatre follows her, Doctor Faust is not forgotten, the 'doings of old Brahmans and Egyptians in their temples and special halls'. White in his cloak stands Doctor Faust (and also Dr Archimedes for many a year), conjures flowers out of ostrich eggs, charms snakes back into the rattling chests which travel through the air. Samiel[193] hovers as a red face through the jet-black room: the music is just giving the last signal and Magneta appears, the escaped Indian harem princess as queen of the air. It is abducting magic without compare, twice a year the secret Middle Ages threw back its cloak; this life pushed forward with the air of a host who knows all about kitsch and horror, the shock of anatomy and lecherousness of appearance, or at least all about super-fluity. So is the fair, so does its cheap, its overflowing *dream ship* moor on the dusty squares. The peculiar beauty of shooting gallery ladies still stands before the evening temples (with make-up which claims to be such, and eyes that seem enamelled); the beauty of the Martian girl Adruide, you have to see it unveiled as the picture shows it out here, Adruide is wild and hot-tempered, is therefore brought in in chains, Adruide is the most original living reproduction of the century. The dream and curtain idol walks barbarically over the square; orchestrions whirl the shreds together, and the equator runs through your own body. The trumpets though, which musicians are blowing in front of many booths, shirt-sleeved, with open waistcoats, their stiff hats on their cheek-filled heads, have remained a village phenomenon, music of village beer. And yet it is instructive, in changed times, in the times of

192 Tombac: alloy mainly of copper and zinc used for cheap jewellery and
     gilding.
193 Samiel: a devil or evil spirit in German and Jewish legend.

diminishing, indeed of disappearing peasant folklore, that the more
proletarians a city actually has, the less this popular magic has disappeared, the more gaudy its fairground squares look, the more vividly
ancient folklore is converted *precisely into a new one*. For a long time
now the orchestrion has augmented, not lost, the barrel-organ, and
precisely because of its exoticism, because of the primitiveness in this
exoticism, jazz is closer to the country waltz[194] than the National
Socialists think (who know the country waltz only as a parlour piece);
even electricity has not harmed the roundabouts, but rather fired them
on a very different mass basis. Here in fact, from the very beginning,
that ambiguity of folklore was at work which tolerates local customs
together with magic spectacle pushed off in an urban way; the village
fair was the peasant city (even the exotic one), the urban fair produces
city peasants. And the nineteenth century added its own bombast as
well, apart from mechanics: it brought its braids and glass beads, ornament as brutality and roaring, music as colportage, the laughing gas of
the Oriental Maze, the paradoxes of a steam roundabout in baroque
style (which simply are not such here, in fact); in short, all the dream
montage of the enigmatic century came home to rest here long before
surrealism. A 'Blue Rider'[195] with the index big city instead of Bavarian
glass pictures would have 'expressiveness' once again in this world; it
would have local South Seas even here, wax figures and the sustained
wax figures of mechanical music. Both fair and colportage thus preserve decisive categories in a distorted form which the bourgeois-
cultured system lost long ago; they preserve above all the desire to be
like the missing life, like colourful happiness. Seldom is 'barbarism' so
little favourable to the juste milieu (which National Socialism in fact
seeks to restore on the basis of it). But *colportage*, to which every street
of the fair returns, is as reading matter that which the magic of the fair
partly was in optical terms. It is, in its suspenses and solutions, an
oriental maze, an escaped Indian harem princess at one and the same
time.

Even for the reader of such things it is thus only important to dream
himself away. He hardly perceives the language in which thrilling events
first have to be told. Just as the street directly plunges into the fair, the
written booths are also there for passers-by. That which is so essential
to 'good' books, to be shaped, not to present any material which has not
been formed, is automatically eliminated in the case of colportage. That
which characterizes the idiot, or at least the layman, in the face of 'good'
books, not to perceive the language and structure, this very immediacy
constitutes the connoisseur in the face of colportage. The lack of literary
education of most of the German petite bourgeoisie (though they read

194 Ländler: peasant music usually played by a small band, including a zither.
195 See 'Rough night in town and country', n. 14.

as much and as long as they like) is thus not to be confused with the freshness which youth and 'populace' bring to colportage. Only when the latter *awakes*, when instead of narrated suspenses and wishful fantasies it seeks to write real life at a reduced price, does squandered language arise instead of no language at all, the cliché of the same situations instead of an arabesque of the same motifs, petit-bourgeois morality instead of the path of happiness through night to light; only then do 'inner' human beings composed of paper arise instead of the here solely legitimate ones composed of furious action. Even when trash predominates in one of these books, it is peripheral; whereas it is substantially at home precisely in petit-bourgeois guardian literature, in the reading matter of those who, out of just as much class interest as bad taste, combat colportage with laws on filth and trash. If there is no really good book of adventures, there is certainly no really bad one; this treasure immediately cleanses itself on the power of dreams from which it more or less directly stems, on certain 'primordial' wishful fantasies which are the narration itself. Yet not only the immediacy of the suspense, but also its content itself feeds on the dream, moreover in a double form. First there is the creatural will in it which *screams*, and then the reflection of this will in an early *wishful world*, which shines through the modern world of things everywhere in the dream. For both characteristics of the dream, the creatural primal suspense and the arabesques of veiling, cloaking and stormily discharging, colportage is the nearest and truest locus. In this way it becomes the popular reflection of primal motifs of fear, of return, of courage, of expectation, disappointment, rescue and other shocks to the life of the will *in the mirror of dangerous distant lands or lustre beset with pitfalls*. This has neither psychology nor given reality; it merely shows the fermenting colourful storm of creation and outside the changeable pictorial mist of an ante-real dream world. Thus the interlacings of the will are in colportage always those of the dream-arabesque, though not those of the totally free-floating kind, in which the 'imagination' (we should remember the introduction which Hauff gives to his fairytales) would be without will and creation; it is rather that arabesque which flows, rides, travels in *adventures*, and which therefore itself dynamically possesses its endlessly possible interlacings. All the more so at the end; for through and by means of all these arabesques the tonic of solution operates again and again, *the primal will of rescue and happiness*. Colportage has in its interlacings no Muse of contemplation above it, but wishful fantasies of fulfilment within it; and it posits the lustre of this wishful imagination not just for distraction or intoxication, but for *provocation* and for *invasion*. That is precisely why colportage is persecuted by the bourgeoisie as dangerous, namely as filth and trash per se; that is above all why colportage is not a quiet calendar story any more, nor a mere romantic novel of chivalry for ordinary people. But it is the wishful dream towards Last Judgement for the wicked, towards glory for the good; so that at the end of these books a realm of 'justice' is always established, and furthermore a justice of the lowly who were granted their avenger and happiness. Having first arisen in freedom of movement, indeed analogously only made possible through it, colportage has thus been advancing upward for a hundred years; it has overrun the *settled* calendars, the droll tales of the *undemanding* populace; it seizes on the original topics of the old epics of chivalry, persecution and rescue, if at all, then not romantically, but in a self-referring and revolutionary way. Freedom appears here as its own circenses, with villains who prevent it, with noble avengers who bring it to light. Colportage has poison, dagger, violation, the blazing air of India and as a star in it the only rescued white woman, the angel of Delhi: but by contrasting itself so wildly and primitively, it occurs as an armed fairytale, as highly activated 'entertainment' directed against mythical powers, and above all as their overthrow.

The purpose is also just as different here for which the rushing topics can be used. The well-abducted girl is rare in real life, of course, making way for the lucky man merely distracts its readers. It pretends there is still a life of freedom of movement; as if ordinary people were not all slave labour without advancement again (provided they are not so free as to be made redundant). It is admittedly humanly correct, and also in the end factually in order, to say, 'Let the poor devil enjoy himself who rides with Kara ben Nemsi of Baghdad to Stamboul over his evening's pig's brawn.' But certainly in political terms a reverse side of colportage cannot be overlooked, especially today; it is at once so insistently rough and feeble, as the other side is fiery and uncomfortable. For images of happiness can also appease, and intoxicate in an unreal way; in addition to this, in the actually National Socialist aim and application, Old Shatterhand wears a very German beard, and his fist smashes down imperialistically. So that an application toughened up in Hitlerian fashion does not seem far away (and Hitler in fact also loves this kind of Karl May and fulfils it for the 'nation'). As far as such a National Socialist effect of colportage is concerned, a passage from Schlichter's[196] account of his youth, 'The Stubborn Flesh', may be cited here; this is the most typical piece of Hitler puberty ante rem. The painter Schlichter describes his wretched youth, its inferiority and oppressive sultriness, its failures in terms of friends, socially and erotically; he describes the fruitless courting of a girl and continues: 'The whole way I now tried to initiate her into my world of ideas, I raved on about the French Revolution to her, depicted the dastardliness of wealth, enlightened her about sects of Indian murderers and Chinese secret societies, told her about

196   Rudolf Schlichter, 1890–1955, German painter who sought a synthesis of *Neue Sachlichkeit* and surrealism.

the heroic deeds of Karl May and that the great day would come for me too one day, when at the head of countless armies or riders I would *smash to pieces the depraved world of a civilization alienated from God.'* The subjective seriousness of these clichés is just as obvious as the unmistakable influence, specifically cited by Schlichter, of colportage, namely of its wild and confused Irratio of freedom, interpreted in petit-bourgeois moral terms into the bargain, on a milieu which cannot be more favourable to National Socialism as it then came. Doubtless Schlichter's account is typical of many influences of colportage on puberty, indeed even on unemployed youngsters; concerning both the inimitable Spiegelberg[197] tone of voice and the over-compensation which National Socialist fantasy and 'idealisms' exhibit. Not even the terrible secret society is lacking in the colportage system of German fascism: it is that of the Schut or the Mahdi[198] that has come to be at home, it is the 'conspiracy' of Freemasonry and above all the so-called Elders of Zion; millions of Germans believe in a Jewish 'prince of exile' and his 'orders to all Jews to establish the domination of Israel by all possible means'. All this is believed, indeed realized colportage through and through; it also certainly has such features and effects too, today more than ever, features in which it (and the wild, confused Irratio of freedom, the desire for escape, desire to march, desire for the campfire, of which it is the expressive part) ideologically contributes to the impression of today. Yet, in fact, there is certainly the other side of colportage, that which absolutely lacks, ab ovo, traditional autarky, but not recollection of the French Revolution, as well as a certain ex oriente lux. The grim fantasy of the Nazis has only become possible at all, this *counter-colportage* of theirs has only become possible, because the lastingly revolutionary tensions and contents of the genuine kind (in the most extensive sense) have not been supplied to the proletariat, or rather have not been newly developed from its new revolutionary tension and world. Where this has happened, as in a few Russian films, above all in 'Potemkin',[199] and far removed from this also in 'Storm over Asia',[200] it is immediately apparent that Leatherstocking's sun[201] shines only here, not in the family saga which has become insane. Colportage in the nineteenth century was precisely escape from it; it painted – however indistinctly and class-unconsciously – unfulfilled youth into the world. Readers here sought story-tellers who cannot do without the primeval forest; who had unloading spaces or the dream bazaar out there for everything which had not arisen in Europe. It is conspicuous, yet not

197 Spiegelberg: the most malicious robber in Schiller's early play *Die Räuber*.
198 Mahdi: the expected messiah in Moslem tradition. Schut (Persian: 'The Yellow One'): leader of a gang of bandits in a novel by Karl May.
199 Film by Eisenstein (1925).
200 Film by Pudovkin (1928).
201 Leatherstocking: the hero in Cooper's Indian stories.

conspicuous, that there are no books for young people today which are at least less individualistic. Which depend less on a 'hero', less drag along with them the individualistic pioneering land of America. Which go more in the direction of national-revolutionary popular uprisings, in which Boxers[202] or Mahdis have fanaticized oppressed nations; this explosive has detonated no colportage as yet, has not yet overhauled and augmented Leatherstocking with Storm over Asia. And the region in which colportage has its truly literary enclaves is not the petit-bourgeois guardian literature in which it becomes trash, but definitely the region of Poe (from the angle of its shock), the region of Sealsfield, Conrad and Stevenson (from the angle of its departure and adventure). Whereby even these grand masters lack that which solely the literature of the disinherited (on the march) can have: namely rescue style, indeed, to recall the greatest example of colportage, Fidelio style. Thus if colportage always dreams, it nevertheless ultimately dreams revolution and lustre behind it; and this is, if not actual reality, then the most real thing in the world.

The giants' toy as legend

If things were different at home, then children would not want to read such garish stuff. But as it is they need fairytales, wild men, liberating and shining ones as well. The latter, however, occasionally present a much harsher aspect than the fairytale one in the book of liberation, than the rescuing one. This is so wherever other German pages open, legendary ones, telling of lords, not of little or poor heroes who have evaded them. Lads do not run away here, but rather former fear, former pressure, the commanded stable grows beautiful, once it is in the house of the lord who later eats or spares them, as the case may be. This wild element also belongs here, it is at first a totally different one from the power of escaping from it.

Not only Hansel takes Gretel off with him, greater figures seduce her too. They make faces which press against the window pane, or shining ones, always staring down from *above*. These are the faces of *legend*; for this too grows in the old country, indeed fairytale and legend are so plainly and simply side by side, it is as if they did not present a very different time. As if they did not denote a very different world: the *fairytale*, shining into colportage, denotes revolt, the *legend*, deriving from myth, endured destiny. If there is rebellion of the little one in the fairytale and if it intends an enlightenment of the spell before such a thing existed, the *legend* quietly informs of the irrevocable. People

202   Boxers: members of a Chinese society that sought to drive foreigners out of China in 1900 in the Boxer rebellion.

accept what happens to them here, and obey; whereupon they are at best 'rewarded'. If the ferryman ferries the dwarves across he is granted splendid alms; if not, he grows infirm. If the miner throws his axe into the gold-laden gallery into which the mountain troll has strutted, the gallery remains open; if he has not followed the rule, then there is a blank rock-face again. Bridegrooms are turned into rocks in legend on account of their 'high spirits', babbling princesses, because they have broken the rule of silence, into brooks. Even the good spirits are equivocal, as water-nymphs, and especially goblins, or capriciously despotic, and dealings with them are subject to an etiquette which, even where it is rescuing and disenchanting, is dictated by the spirits. But the other participants are most of all frightened peasants, evil counts and countesses, who terrify them even in death. Even where poor people are given help, one's own cunning or the Ratio of the found escape route are not effective in legends, but ancestral lords give their blessing from above, redeemed knights issue rewards in the arms of breathtakingly beautiful ladies. Thus an instructive example of the pure lordly peace, lordly benefit which the legend produces in contrast to the always rebellious fairytale, is the Alsatian one about the giants' toy: the peasant in the apron, he must suffer his destiny pure and simple on the table, wholly without cunning, and the giants are not stupid as in the fairytale, but playing young noblewomen and serious knights as fathers, who arrange for the peasant to be carried back again; for 'if the peasant does not till his field, then we giants have nothing to live on in our mountain lair.' And typical of the mythical peace, of the peace with ancient myth, is the path which was even taken by the 'christianization' of legends. Here the ancient demons, and also gods, are not removed from their ground or even presided over by the baptized human being, but they remain as devilish former lords (of whom one now has to be doubly afraid). Or they are even, apparently, newly formed and lend a new background to the mythical punishing demonic nature, even in Christianity. Thus not only does Princess Ilse become the babbling brooklet in the Harz Mountains (whose nymph she was in former times), but also the bread-defiling Frau Hütt is petrified into the Tyrolese Mountain (as whose goddess she had ruled and spellbound in former times). Only the accent of the spell is shifted in the 'christianized' legend, not the spell itself; thus even Gotthelf's[203] half-mythical hailstorm on Uli, the wrongdoing servant, stems from the heights of the petrified Frau Hütt, whereas the gardens of the *fairytale* are certainly nowhere affected by this. For in fact: the fairytale is, as we have seen, the cunning of Hansel, the cunning of the poor soldier against the mythical powers, even against those which are morally tinged; whereas the legend most of all only represents diminished mythology and not its opposite. The fairy-

203   See 'Rough night in town and country', n. 19.

tale, we said, *is suspended*[204] like the time in which its triumph occurred; and where it occurred is uncertain. The legend, however, has thoroughly *settled down* both in temporal and local terms, it is moral like oppression, stationary like a chronicle, and passive exactly like the ceremonial of its contents. For the fairytale (as for the Punch and Judy show related to it) not even policemen are considered to be human beings, everything is permitted against them. Whereas for the legend human beings are the same thing in mythical terms that they were in political terms in the age of the Brothers Grimm, in the age of reaction: namely objects to whom nothing is permitted. The fairytale is just as much the first enlightenment as, in its nearness to humanity, nearness to happiness, it forms the model of the final one; it is always a childlike story of the war of cunning and light against the mythical powers, it ends as a fairytale of human happiness, as reflected being and happiness. Whereas the legend narrates a mythical spell, gives its heteronomous charms, is a ghost story of an older order, is the only field from which reaction can fetch its images, mixing them with the fairytale in false 'folklore'. The world of the fairytale lives in children and the a priori of revolution; the world of legend outlives itself, from its gloomily panic-stricken side, in dreams and lunatics, from its heroically panic-stricken side in reaction. Even the *heroes* of legend are in fact mostly no human ones, no Promethean ones with tense relations to the on high, no heroes of tragedy; they are rather nature demons who fight for domination with other natural demons, for domination in the unchanged realm of nature. Thus even every folklore which, as is customary today, coordinates fairytale and myth (because both seem so near, so uniformly near to 'nature') touches in folklore only that which was its spell, not that which was its will to freedom. Wagner of course, with his fascist instincts, saw only 'diminished myth' even in the fairytale (and his son Siegfried followed him, Humperdinck[205] composed Hansel and Gretel with the means of the Nibelungen orchestra); Klages[206] though, the portentous reactionary, sees in the fairytale only the 'childlike offshoot of the visionary life'. But precisely the 'folksiness' of legend is absolutely nothing but one constructed in reactionary terms and beyond that a mere mirror of terrifying lords and demonic natures; whereas the real folksiness of fairytales still blossoms in children and in human happiness today. Just as colportage does not continue romances of chivalry, but at most introduces their adventures, in a transformed state, into the grand fairytale or coarse fairytale of liberation: so in undistracted 'folk romanticism' in general there are only Peasant Wars, no knights' castles, only fairytales of elapsion, no superstition. The Enlightenment did not bring down the

204 See 'Tom Thumb'.
205 Engelbert Humperdinck, 1854–1921, composer.
206 See 'Rough night in town and country', n. 23.

other world so that the forces of reaction should make this world panic-stricken again.

Indeed, even here the listeners sought something better than the lords intended. Heroes who plunge into the forest and release those who are spellbound, even though far too graciously. There are even *living* transitions between the weak figures of the fairytale and the powerful figures of the legend, who thereby emerge from it. The 'noble robber' above all epitomizes this transition; long before the French Revolution the poor folk honoured the Fra Diavolos,[207] speaking of them half in a fairytale tone, half in a legendary fashion. And Hauff, in the most beautiful realm of new-old fairytales and fresh colportage, paints with related colours both little Muck, as a genuine fairytale figure, and the robber Orbasan, as the mighty lord of the desert. The drifting longing of little Muck, who picks up every fragment in which the sun glitters, as if it were a diamond, and the lustre of the noble robber Orbasan, his warlike decency which Zaleukos 'dreaded' anyway, appear related. Such great lords are then *representative* of the wishes for revenge or happiness on the part of the lowliest people and lead them to victory. This is even intensified in many ghost legends; that which peasants wish for, for which they are too cowardly or too weak, is fulfilled, as Sternberger[208] demonstrated by means of a 'Vogelsberg[209] ghost', by demons or powerful spirits of the place; though the one lot are irregular, and the other lot illegal. A further hybrid between fairytale and legend is *inauthentically mythical matter* within the latter, mythical matter which seems thoroughly spellbinding and static and yet not beyond the human beings. Thus 'mythical' in legend are the *Tao-like* figures, above all very old ones, the couple Philemon and Baucis[210] for instance: elapsed in a fairytale way, although resting in a natural way. And certainly there is also such a relationship in the much less prominent Tao of Gotthelf; in places it deprives legend of the locality of the spell, rescues the flame of life, the humanly distinctive flame of life quietly burning indoors and outdoors. The recognition of the legend as a predominant worship of power and gilding of spells thereby undergoes no correction; on the contrary: the mythological nature-demonizing of the legend is illuminated all the more by such invasions, whether of colportage, or of fairytale mysticism. But even in the legend there is occasionally human war and a victory over lords which makes plundering possible. Even in

---

207 Fra Diavolo (Italian: 'Brother Devil'): the Neapolitan robber-chief Michele Pezza, 1771–1806.
208 Dolf Sternberger, 1907–1989, essayist and journalist.
209 Vogelsberg: a mountain in Hesse.
210 Philemon and Baucis: a faithful old couple from Greek legend who gave shelter to Zeus and Hermes. In *Faust*, Part II, Faust attempts to evict them as part of his land reclamation scheme, and Mephisto contrives to burn down their cottage.

the legend the jinxed shot occasionally, against all the rules of the beginning, hits the marksman who terrifies. Even the legend has the Pied Piper of Hamelin, whom precisely children understand so well; and the children, according to one version of this strange story, are also supposed to have been led happily out of the mountain again, in *the distant future*. Perhaps 'colportage', properly applied, will be so strong once again that it too will loosen up the myth where it is at its thickest. Only from reactionary romanticism and ultimately in fact from Wagner stems the dull uniform notion that the myth is an extended fairytale, and the fairytale a diminished myth; and the National Socialists altogether blur the border between fairytale and legend which Grimm had still decisively set, altogether. 'For me', says Nestroy,[211] 'for me the prodigal son was always contemptible; but not because he was a swineherd, but because he returned home' – precisely the dynamite of this recognition is to be found in the spirit of the 'Kinder- und Hausmärchen',[212] is to be found in the speckled intoxication of the anti-legend or colportage. The proletarian revolution is mostly hostile to 'fantastic' literature; yet in fairytale and colportage tensions and colourfulness have their serviceable refuge, from here they can become troops.

211 Johann Nestroy, 1801–62, Austrian dramatist.
212 By the Brothers Grimm (1812–22).

OCCULT FANTASTICALITY AND PAGANISM

The day of most people is bleaker than ever. For a long time now no better letter has arrived, there has been no post. Instead there is trouble enough at home, the existence of the youngsters does not get going, that of the middle-aged early turns to dust. Seldom was bourgeois coldness so oppressive, never was the door so firmly closed.

All the more vehement the will to break through at least covertly. The pessimists of the last bourgeois generation were contented, ultimately just hypocritically mourning bourgeois conformists. They still felt proud of being 'enlightened' in their sense, not only praised, quite rightly, the science which destroys illusions, but the fixed void as well. Their formula was not only the disenchanting 'nothing but', but also the new magic of mechanism, the cold enchantment which posited pressure and thrust, the fight for existence, and a senseless world as 'eternal'. Only the pessimists of the current bourgeois generation feel the horror of this nothingness as one which has been made ahistorical and complete; and the substitute faith in 'art and science' which had satisfied the cultural philistine no longer acts as a consolation. For in the original faith there was neither art nor science, but a separate need, closely intertwined with sexuality and intoxication; but the objects through which the religious primal need had composed and appeased itself were not in conformity with the objects of the later natural sciences. It is admittedly astonishing that the mechanical natural sciences were able to break down this primal need at all (since no sexual enlightenment and gynaecology has ever disenchanted the libido, let alone destroyed it), but it is inconceivable that the same science which destroyed could close the void that had arisen, especially with mechanism. It is all the less capable of doing this as this science has undermined itself together with its bourgeoisie. The quantitative calculation has shattered: thus it no longer maintains mechanism as the amen of the world. From here too fantasticality breaks into the house, in this case in a *totally occult* fashion.

At first only bad or suspicious dreams are visible in it. Escape from one nothingness into the other, grotesque faces in which one does not even believe. Which is why they also appear scientific, so to speak; for one *knows* even the superstitious element here more than one believes it. Thus obscurities are fetched from all over the world, particularly from one's own dim and distant past. One adopts masks by means of which the wearer chloroforms himself; often also merely incense which smokes up the minds of the small, and smokescreens the great. Old women of both sexes, the nobility and the petite bourgeoisie, in short sinking classes particularly populate Steiner's[213] world; it is the most widespread and the most unclean. Obviously only the powerful interest of other countries in the anthroposophical movement prevents it from unanimously going over to Hitler. Not only the social dilettantisms ('tripartite structure') made it suitable for this, but also the 'essence of Michael' at its centre. To which Steiner consigns the domination of the next period of time; despite its Hebrew origin, it could be all the more easily combined with the plain honest German[214] as the latter has not as yet been mythicized by the Nazis. All this negativity is true, but it is also true that the customers of this inverted world do not automatically become more suitable for the crooked one at home. The 'occult' of today has two faces, and the fascist one which has been preparing itself here too for thirty years does not give the whole profusion of its catastrophic and superstitious expressions. There is certainly fascist reaction in the entire advance of the spirit of obscurity, indeed a total about-turn by the 'liberal' bourgeoisie against its former enemy, the obscurantist, occultist. This reaction was just as much to be found in the intoxication of the liberal press over the 'Miracles of Konnersreuth'[215] as it already exists in the various kinds of metaphysical joys of the individual sciences since 1900: in neo-vitalism, in constitutional theory, in the various blends of Virchow[216] and Paracelsus at one and the same time. Thus even the economic content of this directly fascist spirit of obscurity is not itself hidden; and it seems characteristic of the negative character of it that the Anti-Marx Institute in Italy is called the 'Academy for Fascist Mysticism'. For analytical materialism had to become ever more alien to a bourgeoisie the more it distanced itself from its revolutionary days, and above all the more forcefully the proletariat applied reason and analysis to the bourgeois world itself. Yet in fact neither the entire social content nor especially the objective, the nature-related content, as it were, of this neo-occultism is thereby exhausted. Not the *social* one, because the archaic Irratio of those things

213   Rudolf Steiner, 1861–1925, founder of anthroposophy.
214   Bloch is playing on the popular phrase 'der deutsche Michel' (literally 'the German Mike') here.
215   See 'Non-contemporaneities, reported', n. 116.
216   Rudolf Virchow, 1821–1902, doctor, founded cellular pathology.

missed equally represents a vast admission of the bourgeois void or of the weakness that has arisen of the bourgeois world-picture. Here too the space of cracking mechanics fills with pre-bourgeois memories, with rubble of a varied superstition, rubble which is at least alien to 'tidy' calculation and 'systematic coherence'. There is here, taken indirectly, a separate enzyme of late-capitalist contradiction, despite all the fascist usefulness of the moment; the intoxication of pre-capitalist ways of thinking, above all the cracked world of the 'miracle' and the fact that it is possible among finished 'facts' and 'laws', is an anomaly to the mechanically closed calculation of capitalism. But the *nature-related* content as it were of this anomaly is just as little exhausted in fascist terms; for the hollow space which it indicates in the world is exactly that of the 'thing-in-itself problem', hence the *mechanistically unpenetrated* matter and that abyss from which for a Schelling mythologems still came, and for a late bourgeoisie anti-mechanism rises. In short, viewed directly, the occult spookiness is certainly merely fascistization of the bourgeoisie, the transition of its liberalism which has become useless into the authoritarian and irrational camp. But taken indirectly, there is no less a piece of contradiction here which the late bourgeoisie itself has produced against its ideology; even if this contradiction is immediately eased with superstition, nonsense and archaisms, it still reluctantly discloses a segment of mythologically denoted (merely denoted) contents which are at least alien to the mechanical segment, indeed partly perhaps *lie beneath every previous horizon of vision.* A class without future, like the bourgeois one, admittedly creates no new ideas on reality, let alone on the genuinely hidden 'horizon problems' of reality (to use Lukács's expression). Yet the bourgeoisie, in all its stop-gap eclecticism, is certainly still capable of selling out ancient, archaic, perhaps repressed, perhaps also unfinished contents. It is no pleasure to go into this negative dimension of highly different 'colportage', of a colportage of myths as it were; nevertheless, it is its healthy, its paradoxical swan song. It contains undermined myths and elements of fermentation, and thereby releases meanings in places which did not exist in the old system of myths, in the *spell type* of myths. In this respect it is not merely a mirror for fools, and certainly not *simple* reaction, but rises from shaking ground. Occultism in its most widespread manifestation is *reaction, mitigated by weeds*; it does not lack colportage composed of mythology, fantasy confuses the certainty, and the objects of fantasticality are more than the latter itself.

Learnt creepiness

Little fear often takes itself very lightly. The cards turn it up, the table knocks to it. It is the inner unrest which cheers itself up, gives tongue to itself so shabbily. The superstitious man likes to rouse his own inner forces, the woman prefers to ask what will happen to her. The more fortuitous and unfathomed a life is, the more it seems wrapped up in a blanket whose corner is to be lifted privately. This occurs with suffering and only with an oblique glance into that which is inevitably coming. Just as pupils, during break, secretly learn their progress from the notebook in the teacher's coat pocket. Years ago Meyrink[217] already displayed in literary form the consequences of such broken discipline. Originally a joker, he learnt creepiness; it flourished into mercenary spookiness and solemn kitsch. Entertaining will-o'-the-wisps here danced on the social swamp. People set out in the evening, without even seeing where to.

Science drolatique

But the courageous man forces himself on the darkness. Instead of heeding cards and the sayings surrounding them, the superstitious will itself intervenes in superstition. Not merely in the sober manner of Coué,[218] which confines itself to very barren intentions, but in the massive manner of Christian Science. This is faith in the power of the will and at the same time exaggerates the idea. While the right one continually pervades a person, the harmful consequences of the wrong idea, of the mere 'assumption', are abolished. For this assumption is only appearance, and appearance is nothingness; every disease is thus assumed, non-existing appearance, both physical disease and that of the (capitalist) social body. Whereas faith in 'health' or prayer is a transmission belt which connects the tiring individual with the original dynamo of God again. Women make more of a medical, men more of a mercantile use of such 'Christianity'. In practice these widespread articles of faith commend themselves not only naively, on one's own body, but sentimentally[219] even more so, namely socially. The poor man has himself to blame for being one, his false assumption is the same thing as his laziness or vice used to be. It is a very practical religious hysteria with an extremely healthy Jesus and a purely capitalist content of this health of his; it produces no stigmata out of faith, but takes them away, namely the stigmata of a lacking prosperity. But more unchristian spirits also intervene, intervene as magic will; these fetch their tools from the gaps in science, so to speak. Did not national patriots with A levels and all the accessories, precisely these people, believe in the alchemist

217 Gustav Meyrink, 1868–1932, writer, author of *Der Golem*.
218 Emile Coué, 1857–1926, French psychologist and healer.
219 Bloch is echoing the senses in Schiller's distinction between 'naive' and 'sentimental' poetry here.

Tausend,[220] as in a kind of scientific Hitler? American sects line up their beds with the meridian in order to profit from the magnetism of the earth; but Tausend displayed the 'long-oscillating hand of the master', he taught that lead differed from gold only in its frequency of oscillation and could thus be modulated into it. The golden tree at the centre of the earth burgeoned out in thought again, indeed the moon regained its influence on the growth of silver, and the sun its higher influence on the growth of gold. Other fields of half-learning were cultivated in more ideal terms, yet cosmic wheat also had to flourish here, and dark storms stood above it. The most wildly romantic kind is probably manifested by Hörbiger's[221] so-called world-ice theory: there hail becomes a messenger from the universe, the world consists of ice, three moons have already shone on the earth and in between there was a moonless period. Allegorical interpretation of legends is in full swing anew, yet not in order to think these out religiously but in order to read into them petit-bourgeois visions on a very large scale and then, for lack of real proof, to use the legend 'scientifically'. The Revelation of St John, for instance, is 'ten million years old' and not a vision of the future, it rather describes 'the crashing down of the tertiary moon on to the earth', as Hörbiger says, an 'equally terrible and exciting spectacle'. Every geological epoch is thus concluded by a moon crash, every new one initiated by a happy, a moonless period: until a new satellite is captured, until Luna too, the 'quaternary moon', has descended on the unfortunate and the capture of Mars is imminent. These are the 'world turning-points' for the half-educated or the reflex of apocalyptic moods in the petite bourgeoisie – a fantasy rigged up in a bourgeois conformist fashion which would not of course be possible if the understanding of bourgeois science had not also increased by three moons. For what is strange about world-ice when, according to Dacqué,[222] – dinosaur people existed who remember the tertiary moon? A fellow of the guild, precisely the respected researcher into primeval times Dacqué, thus submits the conclusion that microbe and fish people existed, proselenes or people older than the moon, indeed Siegfried the invulnerable was a dinosaur, he probably swam from Xanten to Worms. The sciences, as Jean Paul foresaw, have reached such a high peak that they are dizzy. The will from Christian Science, the musical chemistry of the alchemist, the sober fantasticality derived from legends of the primeval world – all this is useful to fascism as 'atmosphere', not as bourgeois order. The humbug, and also the active magic, blossoms crazily over the fence and spell which it is mythically renewing.

220 Franz Tausend: cf. Bloch's *The Principle of Hope*, vol. 2, pp. 633–4.
221 Hanns Hörbiger, 1860–1931, Austrian engineer, best known for his world-ice theory.
222 Edgar Dacqué, 1878–1945, palaeontologist and philosopher.

Mystery-mongering as a large-scale enterprise

Even more crazily where the courageous glance seems to strike totally far off. Then Steiner reigns, gossipy and quarter-educated, has secrets to send out. We learn of the not very dense body of earlier human beings, and that the modern cartilages of the child are the remnant of this. A sequence of seven times seven lower races within the seven root races encloses the whole of historical development, whereby the world is a school and its way works off a curriculum. But the teachers are the so-called spiritual beings, from those times onwards when the earth was still moistly internal, to the distant goal where it too is angelified, namely into vapour of the soul. All parapsychological phenomena are exploited in this synopsis, whether it be prophetic dreams or yogis who float up to the ceiling, or mediums frothing at the mouth. As if horror were a religious condition and the ghost a chief witness of the real ground and background. Precisely so-called 'Christianity' is here totally immersed in spookified nature, and at the same time (for this occult science is modern) has also become a kind of gnostic stopgap of Haeckel's[223] world riddles. This solar being of Christ, when it immerses itself in the earth and tinges it with briefly buried sunshine, prepared a nature god for northern fascism long before the neo-pagans or 'German Christians': hence the adaptation of Jesus to Siegfried, of the Bible to North Germanic 'initiations'. Even the so-called 'Christian community' of occultists seeks religious renewal through the experience of the 'cosmic Christ' as a 'solar force', as the 'revival of the dying earthly existence'. The divine service of the Christian community, which is also called 'act of human consecration', takes place with a view to this 'thoroughly invigorating centre of life'; Steiner's mysteries are at every point atavistic spookiness, trivialized astral myth, travestied 'natural science'. Yet even their lair is very varied: painting, the theory of colours, the art of dancing, the 'Demeter movement' in agriculture, dramaturgy, botany, physics, geology, astrology, medicine of humours, medicine of spirits, metallurgy, social policy, Aristotle, prehistory, astrophysics – in short, all the branches of the intellect and witches' brooms are uprooted here, with a truly encyclopaedic confusion, and tied into a bunch. Are refreshed with Lucifer gnosis, contrasted with Ahriman materialism, enjoyed by a spiritual eye which already knew the earth when it was Saturn and will recognize it again when it has become 'Vulcan', the next 'spiritual stage'. An atavistic-international large-scale enterprise is operating here which beats all competition in its courage for superstition, in its general display of undermined myths, whether

223   Ernst Haeckel, 1834–1919, natural scientist.

that competition is called Cagliostro[224] or Eliphas Levi.[225] Naturally this enterprise also stocks, long before the Tausends, Hörbigers, Dacqués, certain crooked residual images of a historical kind, as is inevitable with so much atavism and its sell-out. For only through the statements of atavistic, even though little 'clairvoyants' may obscure customs of former ages, belief in witches and magic, be capable of being experienced in retrospect; even such high obscurities as sacrificial drinks, burial chambers of the pyramids, star signs, the zodiac, the Tao of the cross or the INRI (Igne Natura Renovatur Integra) have a (nowadays) parapsychological root. There is no longer any historian of religion, nor any theologian, who despite all Babylonian or astral scientifically paralleliz-ing research comprehends the religious symbols or even the events in the mystery cults (which were more than pictorial introductory courses in mathematical geography). Atavisms of this kind were re-generated in Madame Blavatsky[226] and other Steiner Druses[227] of the 'Unveiled Isis', they flourish in ever more distinguished obscurantists up to the Parapsychological Society or even the Chemical Rose (if you look into the dark, says Yeats, there is always something there). And amazing things also occasionally drift in Steiner's boundless 'cycles'; there is many a bizarre recollection of the mythical Pentecost, for example, or of the interrupted sleep of nature, ancient earth-rites and lost cult sites. This kind of recollection, despite all the good spirits, despite Rama, Krishna, Orpheus or even Swedenborg, certainly does not denote any inheritance, but rather an indication that theosophy, by burrowing in the mud and in formerly religious rubble, possibly also cuts through temple passageways which honest excavation failed to see, and raises figures which the historian of religion, and even the philosopher of religion, did not recognize and was not able to recognize as such. Today all these possible finds are tainted with such disgust on account of their unfortunate mode of appearance that hardly a clear interest can recog-nize them clearly, that though the philosophical drive towards evidence admittedly sees, it does not really attack, despite many a dubious strangeness, despite an indubitable, foolishly enormous decay of myth in the Steiner world. But once the time has come to see in the space of an unsuspicious social world that which still remained of the great obscurity and the atavistic secret paths, then perhaps even on grotesques like theosophy or anthroposophy a light will be cast from the real

224 Alessandro Cagliostro (actually Giuseppe Balsamo), 1743–95, Italian adventurer connected with magic potions and alchemy.
225 Eliphas Levi: pseudonym of the nineteenth–century French occultist Alforse Louis constant.
226 Helena Blavatsky, 1831–91, co-founder of the Theosophical Society in 1875.
227 Druse: member of a religious sect of Muslim origin.

'organic world-nature' which these grotesques ultimately seek to denote; and not merely a light from stupidity, psychiatry, sinking life, sinking class or all four together. Out of the most widespread mirror of fools, indeed even in it another will then possibly rise, one from the abysses of omitted or unknown 'nature', 'supernature'. Thus although not a single one of Steiner's designations, let alone 'correlations', and hardly one of his images (from the atavistic note-world) ought to remain, an advanced consciousness which is well-disposed to colportage and montage will surely not be able to pass even this ramshackle construct of fantasy – despite its wretchedness and 'modernity' – without a divining rod and attempted panning for gold. 'Lightning as the aura of the thought of an archangel' – this proposition of Steiner's completely surpasses Dacqué's Siegfried, Siegfried as a dinosaur; and it poses a problem not only for psychiatry but also for the image of nature in the age of declining mechanics. Archangels admittedly do not befit such a mouth; yet in so far as they are none at all, but myths, played on a comb, and also snapped-off branches of myths grafted topsy-turvy, a fragment of gnosis hangs in the void and makes it all the more ludicrous.

Hidden quality

It is good to go into the troubled waters of others and to fish in them yourself. For darkness is not only useful to criminals, lovers also know what to do with it. That is why a glance is important which, while it wants and knows progress, also knows it in concealed form or in loops. Many Marxists perhaps turn their backs all too a limine on occult or archaic phenomena, just as if with the enlightenment of 1880 the world were at an end. The often so bold, perceptive Engels sees in myths (if not in religion and theology as a whole) only 'a prehistoric stock, found and adopted by the historical period, of that which we call nonsense today'. And he continues: 'These various false conceptions of nature, of the character of human beings themselves, of spirits, magic powers, etc. are mostly based solely on negative economic factors: the low economic development of the prehistoric period has as its complement, but also here and there as its condition and even cause, the false conceptions of nature.' An enlightened statement and all too much perhaps a child of its age, of the bourgeois age, which saw at all stages of history a *single* economy, namely its own, the capitalist one, simply as incomplete; and *equally therefore a single* nature, namely its own, the mechanical one, simply as metaphysically distorted. The statement is surprising in Engels in so far as its 'dialectic of nature' opens up mechanical nature on many sides and drives in qualitative history, not just added developmental history. Above all, is it not concretely presumable that, just as the social relationship at least in the gentes was more concrete than in later periods, even though undeveloped and in 'childish form' (Marx) – that equally the relationship to nature of the primitive world, and hence the prelogical mode of thought and experience, hit upon a different reality in nature, perhaps more reality, than becomes apparent from the viewpoint of the climax magic-metaphysics-positivism? After all, the history of the problem of the thing-in-itself arouses distrust of all too simple progress even later on: the line of Descartes–Kant–Hegel is in fact, as far as concreteness is concerned, rather a line of (mechanical) positivism – (historical) metaphysics than vice versa. It is unlikely that the quality of all mythologies and occultisms – from both their spellbinding and undermined side – were *solely* hypostatizations of unfathomed economy and not also the participation of unfathomed, in itself still unfathomed nature. The Nothing – not just of the mythological designations, but of that which is designated itself – the quantitative Nothing as content of the whole world is at any rate only the opposite extreme of an All[228] consisting of nothing but mythological qualities. That the world is totally empty mechanism, this assertion has already revealed itself as capitalist dogma today, it was ideologically important for the unleashing of the mechanical forces of production, but by no means binds the concept of nature of the following society. Whether merely archaic grimaces appear in the varied spookiness which the mechanical hollow space now throws up, or whether certain determinations from the mechanistically omitted, no longer to be omitted part of the world report back in it, in places and in archaic disguise, this question can be treated concretely only when a no longer capitalist relationship of human beings to nature has exploded both bourgeois mechanism and late-bourgeois mysticism. But we could at least learn from the enemy not to keep the world-segment narrowed and walled up in bourgeois terms any longer than it does itself. Equally, it is not just the change in the relationship to nature that is instructive, which announces itself in late-bourgeois painting – from the Expressionists to the Surrealists; the other 'pictures' are also certainly to be taken notice of, perfectly malicious notice of, which a Klages, for instance, stuffs into the dying bourgeois world, into the now flagrant contradiction of the mechanical world to the living, whole human being. 'Are you ready and ripe to enter the shrine where Pallas Athene preserves the suspicious treasure?' – so Schiller wrote in the album of a young friend when the latter devoted himself to worldly wisdom. The treasure was suspicious to that very Schiller who sought world-fullness, that fullness which the bourgeois understanding felt even then that it had lost. The goddess of the concept is of course by no means suspicious to the Marxist, and her treasure least of all; yet precisely dialectical materialist reason makes loops, and its victory is all the more concrete the more surely he also

228 'All' also carries the sense of 'universe'.

hunts down and – inherits from the ambiguous gods of life. We will insinuate into this none of Steiner's drivel, not even Dacqué, but rather the premonition that even in the concept of nature it is not yet the inorganic evening to end all days.[229] It contains more than pressure and thrust, more than mechanical clods of earth which oscillate around cauldrons of fire; it also contains hidden qualities and those to be mediated, which parapsychologically oppose the automatism of the bourgeois understanding: horror for instance, panic fear, panic happiness, 'natural beauty' and what this, still not understood, announces.

229 Bloch is playing here on the common German expression, 'es ist noch nicht aller Tage Abend', 'it's early days yet'.

SONGS OF REMOTENESS

The literary glance met with a very friendly response in the centre for a long time. This desired high-class product which displays its appearance to it in a well-made way. Well-read education compensated for certain external shortcomings, a not sufficiently high economic or social position. But above all, the middling bourgeois needed constructs which portray his faded life for him at least fictitiously, his questions in playful form, his ideals as if they were still worth mentioning. All this was bestowed on him in the juste milieu by writers of equally domestic and peaceful appearance. Experts like Wassermann[230] or Thomas Mann opened, in the breadth of the novel, a whole gallery of discursive apparent life with all its questions, apart from one: where this life and this questionableness actually came from, and hence what it was really like. In short, despite the powerful concern of the one, despite the even more powerful irony of the other, beautifully curved, beautifully closed constructions prospered here, in which everything is right apart from the world which they apparently so realistically portray. The questions remained on the symptomatic surface on which they are fabricated; the portrayed life of these doctors, public prosecutors, pages, time-wasters is not as real as their eloquence, as the pleasant acidity of their inner-bourgeois doubts. But then the black-red-and-gold public passed away as both readers and subject matter, even the reading centre has gone wild and partly turns against the authors of its juste milieu. A special case among them was only furnished, occasionally, by Gerhart Hauptmann, moreover negatively, because he was the first to bend naturalism into blond curly-haired dreams and submerged bells,[231] more positively on account of the ancient region in which many of his figures dwell.

---

230 Jakob Wassermann, 1873–1934, novelist.
231 A reference to Hauptmann's fairytale play in verse *Die Versunkene Glocke*, 1896.

Soft and treacherous as a social democrat, this author nevertheless occasionally had exactly the half-light which befitted a still genuinely non-contemporaneous world, namely that of Silesia. A world crammed with wooden tables, forest folk, storms, evening, fading snowy light, with Pippa's inn in the red water valley,[232] with sparks from glass-furnaces and the gloomily filled Owl-Glass[233] of a ghostly Germany. With Hannele,[234] who has found her happiness in death, with poor beasts and the greed of confusedly unhappy gods of cold, with slender sparks of longing and sunshine. In this respect Hauptmann introduced an element of 'red water valley' into literature which because of its humanity is not really suitable for fascist use, although it equivocally provides backward folklore, and also mystery for non-liberal education. But the barbarized centre finds no mirror even here, it turns the phrase 'civilized man of letters', which Thomas Mann once invented before he could see the consequences, against the entire liberal race, together with its 'well-depths' or protruberances; it demands less minced appearance. That is why even the airy-fairiness of the newest Thomas Mann (as mythologist) finds little mercy; although all the cerebral questions of The Magic Mountain have become highly 'irrational' archetypes in the Joseph books, although even the problem of time in The Magic Mountain has turned into a veritable myth of time (of the age-old, of the ever again). But if a space like that of the Joseph novels is also a sign of the times, the latter, as fascist ones, lack access all the same; partly because of the cultured-involved, learned-parabolic elements of Mann's 'primeval times', partly because of the irony which liberalism cannot help employing even as 'Goldwana continent' ('not without reasonable applause does one hear the doctrine' – this remains its attitude even to the 'Descent into Hell').

Instead sheer intoxication seeks that which gives it appearance immediately, which permits the sight of blood, steaming. First of all, in a unique mixture, richly Wilhelminian main speakers and poorly renewed 'Expressionists' dwell jumbled up together here, a 'barbarism' beyond compare. Their one locus is the chest of the Lord Mayor or the following main speech on the laying of the foundation stone of a Wagner monument is Leipzig: 'Yet a second bowl will steep the impression of this monumental block in the atmosphere of fully sacrificial consecration.' Their other locus is the depths of German primeval night, isolation and non-humanity; thus the National Socialist dramatist Dietzenschmidt gives his desk the following topography: 'Only this abandonment and

---

232   A reference to Hauptmann's symbolist fairytale *Und Pippa Tanzt*, 1906.
233   Bloch is here playing on the literal meaning of the surname of Till Eulenspiegel, the traditional German clowning rogue, on whom Hauptmann based a late work and Strauss composed a tone poem.
234   A reference to Hauptmann's dream-play *Hanneles Himmelfahrt*, 1893.

loneliness, our feet in nothingness, our brow in the cold of eternal stars, only from this is unwarped creative power to be found.' But night even goes high above these underlings, it abandons cerebral art in order to form printed runes. It replaces the appearance of cultured abstractness with the grimly ancient one of barbarism, recognizes no 'writers' any longer, only 'poets'. The fascist Benn, for instance, has long been per-fuming the void with word-aromas, brews out of them a kind of lax speaking in tongues, beats chthonic night-salt and a small sun-egg into the hollow spaces of the times, does cloud-pushing like Zeus, indeed even more than this: mysticism-pushing. Has that Graeco-Roman terti-ary period, that (as Benn's poetry says) 'thalassic regression' which is no less an authority on regression and fascism than on the Thalatta[235] of a foaming aquarium or antiquarian bookshop. But the mask has long since been growing heroic in the George circle,[236] not at all tertiary, but Graeco-Roman from the start. There is no attitude here and no topic of signifiability which the bourgeois age does not profess to set straight, which it does not equally prepare and pre-rescue for a heroic Eleusis (scilicet: for Hitler). Thus apparent primal experiences shine statuesque-ly: action and friendship, figures of youth, knighthood and the star-bearers of their destiny, the dark solar man, the pantheon of a heroic solar circle. It is vertical remoteness per se, and one whose Pan seeks to be harsh South, nature perfected in Graeco-Roman terms, not the romantic or unhammered-out one of pure barbarism. There is morality of genius above the afflictions of mass existence here, the poet, in the midst of the most wretched civilization, feels himself to be the last of a noble line here; indeed, time in general is illusion, the poet is not tangent to its favour or disfavour as regards subject matter in the slightest, but responds to primal sounds and encloses them with a stern wall. That is why only lyric poetry, epic poetry, and drama are sup-posed to be literature, not so the novel of 'writers'; for only the gardens and forests of lyric poetry hold ancient water, only epic rocks, dramatic flashes of lightning from days of old are supposed to be above it. Apparently against the times and yet so totally with them, with the‧ pathos of intoxication, go songs of *remoteness*; namely of escape which is itself romantic. Of escape into 'archetypes' which were already ap-propriate to the 'shining appearance of blood' when none at all flowed as yet, in reality, which showed its fascism even then, formidable capital, the golden void, the blocked future. Even today a 'basic poet' like Benn announces nothing else and sees directly nothing but the question: 'What do we experience then in these intoxications, what rises then in

235 'Thalatta' (Greek, 'the sea'): according to Xenophon, a joyful cry of the Greeks on seeing the Black Sea after their long march northwards from Babylon.
236 See 'Myth of Germany and the medical powers', n. 109.

this creative joy, what develops in its hour, what does it see, what sphinx does its extended face gaze at? And the answer cannot be otherwise, it sees even here at bottom only what is streaming to and fro, an ambivalence between forming and deforming, gods of the hour who dissolve and shape, it sees something blind, nature, sees nothingness.' This is, in learned academic speech, like Klages and Heidegger read together, like the streaming panmixia[237] of the one, like the nothingness of the other: but only in order to attain this nothingness (from the 'frigidization' of modern existence), is it for this that their All begins with such consolation for poor fascists, is it for this that the 'advance of the old, still substantial strata' is needed, for this a 'splendid, hallucinatory-constructive [!] style in which the origin-like element, the early element of creation turns into consciousness once again'? Is it for this that language almost speaks like utopia – and is nevertheless only one of escape, of self-enjoyed frenzy, of polemically ruffled, of purely antithetical, and hence insubstantial demonism? With nothing behind it, nothing in the way of object and 'perspective' but perpetual 'differentiation between forms and nothingness', as South Sea quotations without a South Sea world. And the George circle, the 'equestrian science', the beautiful gesture-mysticism which satisfies itself with closed appearance almost no matter what appears: whether greased wrestlers and anointed pages, whether Morituri, with lightly chivalrous bearing, or the god Augustus, crimsonly alive on a golden chariot – this cult of figures then and superannuated royal stables, this imitatio of Dante, Goethe and the sun-idol Elagabalus[238] as well: has even this cavalcade of aesthetic pensioner-knights dismounted anywhere other than in nothingness and the feudal animal kingdom, indeed does it not pay homage to the king of the bourgeois conformists as its lionheart of the matter,[239] does it not reveal the emptiness of its decorative rigour, has it not been singing the praises from time immemorial, via Rome and Magna Graecia, despite all 'contemporary criticism', of the ruling clan, as if it were the secret Germany, does it not regard formidable capital, more than ever, as the taboo of all 'contemporary criticism', the paying bank of all appearance, the foundation of all 'hierarchy'? With a hefty clash of cymbals this phenomenon posited the Irratio of a poetic lordly realm, posited the supposed posture of the Horseman of Bamberg;[240] but no George pathos is genuine enough to recognize that the 'idea' of the Horseman of Bamberg would be riding east today, precisely not as an enemy, but

---

237   Random mating within a breeding population.
238   Elagabalus, Heliogabalos: local divinity of the Syrian town Emesa.
239   Bloch is here playing on the German phrase: 'das ist des Pudels Kern', 'that's the gist of the matter', substituting 'lion' for 'poodle'.
240   A medieval sculpture in Bamberg Cathedral. It is not known who carved it nor whom it represented.

in order to fight among the knights of an entire nation and to toss the same dragon which the George clan are decorating with Roman medals at home. Even 'Dionysus', in the George circle and the exploded mythology of intoxication surrounding it, is an 'early god' only as foam at an antiquarian mouth, as a 'cry which roars through a golden harp',[241] through the same harp which is carried behind the god Augustus, crimson on a golden chariot. The other figure of the 'early god' is thereby most usefully submerged, the torch of life, the storming against pressure and spell. What else may be contained in the 'archai' as a legacy, and even in the way of 'eternity', is another story: the sold poets of fascism will see it yet, though not read it any more. Intoxication is a more intuitive bourgeois angel than irony; it does not live on the magic mountain of the present world, but at its propaganda point, occasionally also – with sublime heroic gaze, the gaze of a receiver of stolen goods – at the cracking place. And the intoxicated state arising from it is now Pythianizing[242] this world just as it is making thalassic dreams, compulsory oracles.

241   A line from Stefan George.
242   From Latin Pythius, 'of Delphi'. Pytho was the former name of Delphi. Or from the Greek priestess Pythia in Pytho.

SHAM WITH POISON

The desire for new things is here and pushes itself back. More restricted strata have joined the employee, as was shown. The peasant, and then the older centre: artisans, retailers, so-called free professions. This centre still partly has the plough and soil, the plane and workshop, or even simply the rented office. As, being pauperized, yet with backward or non-contemporaneous ties, it advanced, the earlier pleasure in diversion changed on all sides, even among employees. The parlour returned, thoughtfulness, the moral discipline of our fathers, and finally – below and above the parlour – vindictive brutality and archaic intoxication. The brutality was led by unemployed sadists and discharged officers; the intoxication was poured in above by the German Rasputin. The peasants and petite bourgeoisie were not only distracted towards Jews, the competitive struggle of the centre not only mitigated by the most transparent anti-semitism; more non-transparent elements also had their place in the deception, the community, the 'soul', the 'leader', 'destiny'. Thus the fascist state prospered, the wolf-state (which intervenes 'in mediation' between wolves and sheep, capitalists and their victims); thus social democracy was exchanged for a new sham, social autocracy. 'The shock which runs through the world today is the revenge of nature against the intellectual attempt to break through its laws'; if the feudal order was 'God-given', then the capitalist one arises from 'nature'. The middle classes intoxicatedly think they find their own 'nature' in it, they intoxicatedly see its processions in the uniformed streets, they faithfully believe in the burning of Rome started by the Communists, in the promises of the People's Chancellor. The whole thing is as complicated as book-forgery (with runes of daily blood) and as simple as the truth when it comes to light. A declining centre, non-contemporaneous and hence blunt contradictions on the one hand; deceivers, criminals, monumental crooked prophets on the other, who deform these contradictions and place them in the service of big business; decline of a capitalism itself which makes itself formidable: these are the three elements of German fascism, and for the time being the third is the dominant one among them. But even if bestiality and myth race into blind alleys, the palaces still hardly feel at ease when the intoxication does an about-turn in the recognized blind alley. Hunger does not die even in the case of economic ignorance, the lustre of intoxication satiates and soothes less than ever, quite the contrary; both make people desirous of the Third Reich for so long, until only the Fourth and Last remains. The dust which the explosion of the non-contemporaneous whirls up is more dialectical than that of diversion; it is itself explosible. Socialist application and the art of making the irrational – safe, indeed helpful: this is the farewell to non-contemporaneous matters; it is a concrete one, with controlled future even in the portents of this past.

PART III

UPPER MIDDLE CLASSES, OBJECTIVITY AND MONTAGE

THE JOLT

We are beside ourselves. The glance wavers, with it, what it held. External things are no longer usual, displace themselves. Something has become too light here, goes to and fro.

NEW CORNER WINDOW

This one is hardly a place for relaxation. The eye does not watch, it travels along. The big window does not just shed light on the quiet table, but also on the lives of those without one. Who are happy, as it were, still to have work.

The ground outside shifts, as if it were none. At the rear a view of the harbour; the quay is differently decorated from hour to hour. Ships from far away cover the water; a gently domed sundeck, smoking galley, sometimes a dark blue man can be seen, usually a Pomeranian dog. Cranes travel down the landing-stage, turn their levers and start grabbing. With empty cheeks into corn, wheat, cork, sulphur, with chains around stones and iron bars. The dealers are far away, and the dog who deserves the bone does not get it.

The glance becomes all the more animated on the other side. Carts, cars, electric trams, people and danger in between. In the harbour there was always some moon, so to speak, gliding; the image of the ugly street is, in contrast, garish, more bitter, clear everyday and mess. Early in the morning, late at night workers, business people during the day, a superannuated steam railway creeps through as an open wound. Twice a week a vegetable market in the square, with flowers and oranges, too, which clash with the soot and sing what does not belong here. The square is only genuine again when the poles are taken down at midday; a loudspeaker plays marches, a man tells where to get beds on hire purchase, sometimes you see red flags, sometimes the Salvation Army plays. The street and the square behind are thoroughly true of today, without false light, and there is smoke in the thronging of their tuff.[1] Differently to where gentlemen and ladies stroll, where there are parks so you no longer even know where you are. Here you know and have no silk to spin. The air comes fresh, definitely not pure, but it does not cause rust.

---

1 Bloch is using a volcanic image here. Tuff or tufa is a type of volcanic rock.

LUDWIGSHAFEN – MANNHEIM (1928)

Otherwise the oil smokes more to itself. Or the shavings only lie where there is planing.[2] The planers live in rented holes, the streets are cheerless. Far away, however, the masters live with the money that has been earned by others. Had houses like knick-knacks, dressed in the old-fashioned style. No sound of hard daily work penetrated them.

Thus the quarters were previously already divided where the work and the devouring is done. But of course technology sprang up even in older refined parts of town, destroyed the picture. The approach road from the station had usually become a different one to that from the country road, shifted the old axis. But even so the traditional urban culture did not die completely; the rampart, the ring was planted with trees or even became a residential area. The new water-tower was embarrassed to be one in the eighties, was built like a tankard. Socially, too, the bourgeoisie moved into courtly pleasure, had its good concerts, chatted in the boxes.

But new cities came off badly here with nothing to guide their steps. Particularly if they lie next to an old cultural city, like Ludwigshafen next to Mannheim, on either side of the Rhine. If the river did not divide them enough already, the Bavarian – Baden border made sure any equality was prevented. Ludwigshafen was consequently obliged to become a town in its own right, not just a suburb into which the sewage of industry flows. At its foundation seventy-five years ago it was definitely intended as competition against Mannheim; so it continued to manage on its own resources in a highly current way. Here is a place therefore, thoroughly typical of the capitalist Now, where the planers live in the town itself, where no beautiful houses far away, and certainly no pre-

2   Bloch is alluding to the German proverb here: 'wo gehobelt wird, da fallen Späne', 'where there is planing, shavings will fall'. The English equivalent would be, 'you can't make an omelette without breaking eggs.'

vious urban cultures lie giddily above the Now. The Baden Aniline and
Soda Factory, the nucleus of IG Farben[3] (moved here so that the smoke
and proletariat did not drift over Mannheim), became the literal true
emblem of the town. Over there lay the chessboard of the old royal
Residence, a cheerful and friendly building, as if in the time of Hermann
and Dorothea;[4] had instead of the biggest factory the biggest château in
Germany, perhaps less of a true emblem, in the nineteenth century, but
still a beautiful ornament which gave the bourgeoisie standing. When-
ever it was time for coffee and cigars and higher things. Ludwigshafen,
on the other hand, remained the factory dirt which had been compelled
to become a city: random and helpless, cut in two by the arc of the
embankment, a Zwickau without inhibitions, after the false dawn of the
Biedermeier period which occurred at the time of its foundation, an
extremely wet day. The initial attempts at 'Art and Science' proved
ridiculous, were all intercepted by Mannheim; today there is still no
theatre in the numerically long since perfect big city. In the marketplace
stands a 'Monumental Fountain' (that is what it is called); it is grey,
yellow, white, red, because it is supposed to contain all the various
kinds of Rhineland Palatinate sandstone. Men's heads, heraldic mottoes,
columns, niches, urns, wreaths, little ships, crowns, bronze, basin, obel-
isk, all on the puniest scale – the whole thing is perhaps the most
beautiful Renaissance monument of the nineteenth century. A thousand
parlours look down on us from these stones; here is 1896 in a nutshell
and in the provinces. And from the embankment a weeping willow
waves across to the 'Jubilee Fountain' (again that is what it is called);
over there cast iron stands on tuff, the goddess Bavaria presents the
goddess Ludwigshaferia with the city crown, below at an angle Father
Rhine leans grotto-like, pours a trickle of water from his cornucopia. At
the station there is a bust of Schiller, and the big dipper sings the words
to it, the brandy bars are called 'The Parisian Hour' and the theatre club
are performing 'The Executioner of Augsburg': such is or was until
recently this petit-bourgeois Wild West on the Rhine. On the most
solemn river in Germany halfway between Speyer and Worms, in the
midst of the Nibelungenlied[5] as it were, right next to the Jesuit church,
the rococo library, Schiller's Court and National Theatre in Mannheim.[6]
Seldom did one have the realities and the ideals of the industrial age so
close together, the dirt and the royally built-in money.

Why are we writing about it with such a long preamble? Precisely
because something turned around here, because where the age is mar-

---

3   Major German chemical group split into Bayer, Hoechst and BASF in 1945.
    During the Nazi period it exploited cheap labour at Auschwitz.
4   In *Hermann und Dorothea*, his epic poem in hexameters of 1797, Goethe says
    that the Mannheim Residenz is a 'cheerful and friendly building'.
5   The early thirteenth-century heroic German epic.
6   Schiller worked there as a young man.

ching emerges here. Because Ludwigshafen, which stands for various things, has suddenly become more important, in the new air, than Mannheim. There lies, no, there now *sails* the ugly city, but it kicks up such a crude row, money circulates and IG Farben steams. Something there has become Front which brings everything to light and is no longer educatedly embarrassed. Now even the city goddess Ludwigshafenia and even Father Rhine have had nooses put around their necks, at the Jubilee Fountain, and have been pulled down, which is at least as symbolic as master builder Solness.[7] And they are going to put an amusement machine in the romantic place, and a theatre as well with visiting groups who are currently prominent; in short, all the mixing noise which the bourgeoisie now allows and which is at any rate more concrete than Schiller and Ibsen played by a stock of people entitled to a pension. The boys of Ludwigshafen have cranes in front of their eyes, fair and Karl May, the middle class reads its Rudolf Herzog[8] even here of course, but without believing it, most read nothing at all, but their world looks like Sinclair,[9] sometimes even like Jack London.[10] Wassermann and Thomas Mann, elegant bourgeois problems of an older stratum, have no place in this. Here there is only the stage for factories and what goes with them, there is rawness and stench but without stuffy air. IG Farben, which founded the city to begin with, now gives it more than ever the pure, raw-cold, fantastic face of late capitalism.

Cities of this kind should therefore be especially weighed up. There are many such places in the Ruhr area, though without such sharp contrast so near. They still have enough reactionary mustiness, stupidity of lasting petit bourgeois, a dreadful provincial press. Yet Ludwigshafen has a more honest face when compared with the Mannheim type; its industry did not first destroy natural, cultural connections, but is alien to them ab ovo. Here there is the most genuine hollow space of capitalism: this dirt, this raw and dead-tired proletariat, craftily paid, craftily placed on the conveyor belt, this project-making of ice-cold masters, this profit-business without remnants of legends and clichés, this shoddy-bold cinema glamour in the sad streets. This is what it now looks like in the German soul, a proletarian–capitalist mixed reality without a mask. And round about Ludwigshafen the hazy plain with swamp-holes and ponds, a kind of prairie which knows no little estates and no idylls, to which factory walls and fiery chimneys are significantly suited; the telegraph pole sings along. This is a good standpoint from which to see current reality, to grasp even better the tendency which it is and which it will resolve. Older, more comfortable cities, plush cities

7 Solness: the hero of Ibsen's play *The Master Builder* (1892).
8 See 'Winnetou's silver rifle', n. 186.
9 Upton Sinclair, 1878–1968, American socialist writer.
10 Jack London, 1876–1916, American novelist, author of *Call of The Wild*.

as it were, also have this tendency, but not in such a traditionless vacuum. In fifty years a real swine of a city could stand on the crude earth which has not even cleaned up its swine,[11] but is the most direct growth from ship-building, silos, elevators, factory buildings. The coming age has more to topple here, but less to ignite than in the old culture, which gives more to plunder in return.

In the current dirt hardly anything still blooms worth talking about. Nothing but miserable dross from Berlin, at best, here and there, reaches the most advanced places. In return, however, there are bursting places which Berlin does not yet have, and in which improvisations can nest which no 'cultural will' anticipates. Places like Ludwigshafen are the first sea-ports on the land, fluctuating, loosened up, on the sea of an unstatic future. The cosy Rhineland Palatinate vineyards, half an hour away, Court and National Theatre, the nearby cathedrals of Worms and Speyer, move into the distance for the time being. The international station-boundness fuses everything together, has neither the earlier muse nor can content itself with the receptive enjoyment of handed-down pictures. The zero which screams, the chaos that displaces itself coldly and currently, is probably closer to the origin which created the cultural pictures than the merely 'educated'[12] bourgeoisie which hangs them up in the dining room. Even plundering the old, creating a new montage from it, succeeds best from the standpoint of such cities. They are themselves a knotting place;[13] workers and entrepreneurs tie the knot clearly, contemporaneously, objectively, between themselves and what is coming in the future.

11   Bloch is playing on the German phrase 'es hat sich gewaschen', 'it was a real swine' (but literally, 'it has washed itself'). The idea is that the industrial cities will become increasingly polluted both figuratively and literally.
12   'Gebildet': Bloch is playing on the idea of 'Bild' here, which means 'image' or 'picture'.
13   'Knotenpunkt': the usual meaning of this is railway or road junction.

TRANSITION: BERLIN, FUNCTIONS IN HOLLOW SPACE

This place first drew in fresh air again. Worked with borrowed money, filled its patched pocket. Berlin won the war in Germany, the city is right *in front* in late-bourgeois terms. It has few non-contemporaneous features, in the sense we have come to know; they were only introduced into and foisted upon it at the very last. Berlin seems in fact extraordinarily 'contemporaneous', a constantly new city, built hollow, on which not even the lime becomes or is really set. But no matter how far in front a capitalist city is, of course, it is for the present only 'contemporaneous' in the limited, indeed inauthentic sense, namely that of being merely up to date.[14] Even if the entrepreneur and salesman of such cities feel particularly up to the mark, 'standing at the centre of practical life', completely at par with the 'present', even the relative contemporaneity of Berlin still has the limitation that for the bourgeois, as Marx says, 'skill, knowledge, spiritual insight and intellectual resources do not extend any further than his nose.' He is only in the lead in comparison with older classes and with the provinces, but is himself driven, is himself shackled to a ghostly, thereby reified, movement of goods, to an economy of 'stationary facts and laws'. Simply because 'facts and laws' exist for him at all, namely static or even eternal ones, the bourgeois is not in the genuine present, but only in it as a caput mortuum, namely in the product of its reification. Even the late capitalist who appears in most advanced fashion up to date finds himself that step behind genuine contemporaneity, which separates reification from living *tendency*, mere exploitation of respective 'chances' from real and concrete control of *process*. In other words: contemporaneity is not such if it is not also super-contemporaneous; it is not the capitalist of the uncontrolled, changeable Today who stands at par with the real present but only the knower and controller of the Tomorrow in the Today together, in short,

14 Bloch uses the English expression here.

the active Marxist. So therefore even the contemporaneity of Berlin, despite the tremendous advanced nature and, as it were, unreadiness of its capitalism, *seen directly*, still has no truth. The spirit forms the right chemical compound, says Burckhardt,[15] only with the original source; this is also true in 'contemporaneous' Berlin. Even so, *seen indirectly and from the point of view of genuine contemporaneity*, features of transition (of the Tomorrow against consciousness and will) can be recognized and emphasized particularly actively here. For workers and entrepreneurs are wholly bracketed together in the relative 'contemporaneity' of big business: contradiction of the social forces of production to their private capitalist form of appropriation is in a homogeneous field here. Admittedly we have already seen enough dust, diversion and finally intoxication on behalf of big business; we have already attempted to note all these elements of deception and susceptibility as transitional phenomena. But navigation in the up-to-date sea, even if in one of inauthentic or relative contemporaneity, is of course easier, it is indirectly 'at home' in it. In other words, the Tomorrow in the firm Today absorbs the elements of dust, of diversion, intoxication in a relatively more homogeneous way; they then appear so to speak as *dust to the power of four*, namely in the *momentum* of big business, in its *Objectivity*[16] (which tries in vain to pretend it is a vacuum cleaner) and above all in its *montages*. The culmination of this dust to the power of four occurred at the temporal cracking place between the world of diversion and that of intoxication which superseded the former, i.e. around the years 1927–29. But the perforated 'culture' of the ruling class likewise governs the whole period of time, from the stabilization of the market in 1924 to the stabilization of Hitler in 1933, and it carries on operating beyond this. At this point *higher fascism* (as the stance of big business) overlaps with National Socialism (as recruitment of the proletarianized strata in the service of big business); only *fascism in this sense* is of course the last phase of capitalist economy. Thus wherever there is a boom under way, as appearance or animated by war industry, higher fascism also seeks renewed contact with technology and the most modern 'Ratio' in its wake. This contact in Hitler's Germany is thwarted by bourgeois conformist attitudes which are not 'degenerate' together with narcosis, or appears merely as one element among others in the tension between Goebbels and Rosenberg, flat roof and steep roof, streamline and Defregger-cult; but in Mussolini's Italy precisely the 'most progressive' architecture is effective, and in general a 'cultural life' that is completely functionalist, to the point of snobbery. The more

15   Jacob Burckhardt, Swiss historian, 1818–97.
16   'Sachlichkeit': Bloch is referring here to the *Neue Sachlichkeit* movement in the arts and architecture which he is about to discuss in the following sections. We have capitalized the concept here throughout to distinguish it.

severely disabled fascism-class in Germany does not dance in such modern fashion any more; yet it has of course reached and moved into a different place from that of diversion and intoxication; rather, in the dialectical reflexes of big business these two elements thoroughly *outbid* each other and in their own way. The truly last phase of capitalism contains, in a relatively advanced way, the versatile aspect of diversion and the mixed darkness of intoxication, in short, it contains the relativistic and archaic aspects together. The former, as an element of diversion, is in the naked, apparent, overbright 'Objectivity'; the latter, as an element of intoxication, lives above all in the ruined and mixed figures of the various kinds of 'montage'. Objectivity and montage, however much they serve the deception or make aimless associations, are nevertheless also possessed by the devil. Objectivity does resort, like every rationalization, to other forms of production; and the combinations of manifold montage hold no expired totalities, no fraudulently idolized 'eternal values', but rather interrupted ruins, in new figurations. This is interruption and new instruction in a sense which goes far beyond the replacement of technical parts, indeed beyond photomontage, and yet still obeys this form, as a real 'patchwork'. To this extent montage, not Objectivity, is the actual fruit of 'relativism'; since it *improvises* with the cracked content, it makes out of the elements that have become pure, out of which Objectivity forms rigid façades, variable temptations and attempts in hollow space. This hollow space was in fact created by the collapse of bourgeois culture; and not only the rationalization of another society plays in it, but more visibly a new formation of figures from the particles of the cultural inheritance which has become chaotic. 'Momentum', 'Objectivity', above all 'montage' must now be defined more precisely here and in each case with reference to their two sides, to their *directly* capitalist, to their *indirectly* useful ones. After this there should follow a variable gallery of significant phenomena of the times, which make music out of 'relativism': from 'Ship House' to 'Thinking Surrealisms'. The equally abstract and variable Berlin is nevertheless the most advanced, the most instructive place for these forms, between proletariat and bourgeoisie. Instructive not only in diversion and loosening, but also in the picture puzzles of formed loosening or of experiment in which something *specifically* 'irrational' is not lacking.

The momentum

Thus things have been sailing close to the wind for a long time. The entrepreneur sails with momentum and needs it. This not only squeezes the last ounce out of the crew, goes easy on nothing at all, outstrips. But with momentum late capitalism also pretends that it is active and initiating, instead of being driven along shackled to the circulation of commodities. The emptiness and distance in which the entrepreneur stands to himself and to real things is not of course resolved through over-wound time, but can be better endured. As the city injects more and more pace, the substance seems to form from this which is otherwise missing everywhere else. This holds on to pure motion, in fact, recovers by it, no matter where it sails to. But in contrast also to the peasant, manual worker, Junker: nothing can insist on itself and its own *less* than the entrepreneur. Nothing has more visibly been like this only for a short time and made, nothing less grown, less of a naturally intended state; although the entrepreneur speaks of such things. This movement, when it looks back on its grandfather, at least cannot say that man does not change.

Objectivity, direct

With so much wind the air became really thin. To be objective means here to make life and its things as cool as they are light. To begin with, nothing is expressed in this except *emptiness*, and this exhausts itself in omission. And directly above this *deception* shows itself, provided that the emptiness is so nickel-plated that it gleams and captivates. The despiritualization of life, the process of human beings and things becoming commodities, is polished up as if it was in order, indeed order itself. Here New Objectivity is the highest, also the most unrecognizable form of diversion; it is so as distraction through 'honest' form. It is, however, only the honesty of the foreground, and it provides no holds, not the slightest flourish for further examination; a smooth face guards crooked paths. Just like that peasant who, on receiving a sum of money which he was supposed to check, counted only to sixty and then stopped, because the sum had been correct up to then and would certainly go on being correct, so too should the proletarian and employee deal with Objectivity; which is correct at the front as long as one does not continue counting into the background. Its light, its cheerfulness, its clarity mark the part as the whole, the shop-window as the shop. This explains the obtrusive cheerfulness (in a thoroughly barren life), the obtrusive clarity and sobriety (against a thoroughly ambiguous background); this also explains the obtrusive firmness of form (in a thoroughly critical and frail existence). Even the captivating aspect of the hardening of form still corresponds to the recovery of capital, which happened around the same time; form and capital concurred in making things firm in the post-war period. Only then did the false firmness appear from the bottom up to the top, up to the pictures which were hanging or which were perhaps no longer hanging on the walls (so that not even the most modest imagination could disturb). Instead of the Expressionist dreams, 'concentrations', but also storms, a 'realism' without parallel stabilized itself, namely one of the world settled down again, of peace with bourgeois existence. Only after Noske[17] did painted reifications, air- and gravity-less spectres in pictures à la Schrimpf[18] pretend to be classical reality. The consequence in fact led to a hatred of imagination, as if Noske had been Cromwell and the revolutionary-Expressionist period – before the recovery of capital – had been a Catholic one. So with this hatred of imagination a *further* motive was added to deception, namely the *servility* of the New Objectivity, its puritanical streak in the midst of the jauntiest appearance. A repeat of classicist calm and stringency ran through the world, through that existence full of noble simplicity, quiet greatness,[19] in which the capitalists live. Just as simple deception was effected through cheerfulness, so too this deeper, classicist kind flaunts itself through stringency, lack of ornamentation, downright puritanism; such Objectivity makes an ornament out of having none. It has not been pure functional form for a long time, but is rather covered in technoid decorations. Its mechanical model has long since become an end in itself, serves as an ornament substitute and once again for no other purpose than that of strengthening the façade. It is finally served by the *last* motive of Objectivity, namely *rationality* taken to extremes and yet disjointed, i.e. remaining *abstract*; at the same time this corresponds, in its abstractness, to the big business style of thinking. It corresponds to the 'capitalist planned economy' and similar anomalies with which capitalism reaches for the forms of tomorrow in order to keep those of yesterday alive. This kind of Objectivity, of course, achieves, in the economy and in the architecture as well as in ideology, nothing but sheer façade; behind the in-built rationalities the total anarchy of the profit economy remains. Under cover, of course, many things are stirring even here; the implements become simple and standardized, the machine produces in series, the steely rooms become absolutely practical, and if they were not so expensive, they would seem almost classless. Planned economy, standardized technology, collectives, foundations of cities and the like are objective contradictions to the class society and must, as rationalization without Ratio, bring it to a crisis. But precisely this Ratio, a concrete one, is missing here; Objectivity therefore remains necessarily – seen and held at a capitalist stage – abstract, without content, remains 'exact' façade ante rem. An intellectual expression of this new 'exactness' is thus still the so-called 'empirical philosophy' (as

17 Gustav Noske, 1868–1946, Defence Minister under Friedrich Ebert (President of Germany, 1919–25), instrumental in the suppression of revolutionary movements in various German cities, including Berlin, after the First World War.
18 Georg Schrimpf, 1889–1938, painter who developed from Cubism to New Objectivity.
19 A quotation from Johann Joachim Winckelmann, 1717–68, archaeologist and art historian, greatly admired by Goethe.

lucus a non lucendo), i.e. the philosophy of the neo-Machists which i
totally abstract, yet precisely because of this seems to itself 'exact'
Mach[20] already taught and knew no other knowledge than that of the
more or less adapted 'model' which signifies nothing real. Objectivity o
today, merely of today, thus causes only façade to arise in all fields
façade created out of undernourished or disjointed reason.

Objectivity, indirect

Still nothing leads into the particulars of the pieces that are serviceable
here. What works for the bourgeois economy cannot be used for any
thing else even indirectly. And certainly the deception which Objectivity serves largely prevents it from being disruptive in the capitalis
economy. But the only things that are, in the strict sense, indirectly
useful are those which can already be recognized as suspicious or contradictory in the capitalist locus itself; hic falsum index veri. If one
observes this principle, then without doubt *certain* parts of Objectivity
separate themselves; namely the *Ratio* separates itself from apparently
clear deception, also from classicist solidification. In contrast to appa
rent clarity, Ratio in anarchistic profit economy is an active contradic
tion, even if this contradiction has been throttled or is leading a life
under cover. Though since the Ratio occurs in capitalist Objectivity
only as a disjointed and abstract one, i.e. limited to a private economy
since it ultimately in fact, in Roosevelt's America, serves the planned
destruction of the forces of production in the interest of the capitalis
system, in short, the 'stabilization' of the crisis, it also in no way already
appears as the full index of what is true or as one which only needs to be
continued to the end, to be made completely 'reasonable' in order to
become one. The basic condition for the concrete use of the many
'systematically arranged things' of today is rather the completed revolu
tion; without this, in fact, Ratio is only the familiar – rationalization
Hence then also the so-called stirrings under cover, namely the many
technical-collective 'beginnings' in late capitalism can nowhere already
directly be greeted as 'socialist'. Along the lines of social-democratic
'modernity' à la Giedion,[21] even along the lines of an architect's confide
nce which has definitely not grown out of politics, but out of tech
noidally progressive expertise and out of the desire for its application

20   Ernst Mach, 1838–1916, empiricist philosopher. He saw the ideal of scienc
     as the extinction of all metaphysical ingredients, and the correct philo
     sophical method as simplified description of the material world. This doc
     trine was also attacked by Lenin.
21   Sigfried Giedion, 1888–1968, champion of the new architecture in the 1920
     and author of influential works on modern architecture, and mechanization

but which likewise propounds, even if in other words, a kind of 'peace-ful growth of capitalism into socialism', at least at this juncture. But this seems a false indirectness, namely none at all; if it already sees in every sliding window a piece of future state, then it obviously overrates the technical-neutral, underrates the class-biased element. It overrates the neutral cleanliness, comfort of the new architecture, the origin in the factory, in technical expediency and standardized machine-commodity. It underrates the fact that this 'uniform hygienic living' is still in no way orientated nor can be orientated even only potentially towards a class-less society, but rather towards the young, modern-feeling, tastefully clever middle classes, towards their very specific, in no way classless, let alone eternal needs. It underrates the termite character which New Objectivity sets up and underscores wherever – as in workers' and employees' estates – there is not enough money for the Babbitt environ-ment; it underrates the representation which conversely modern big business produces out of its 'functionalism'. False indirectness also underrates the bad decoration which is promoted with unadornedness, as well as the façade-character and the dreadful emptiness which char-acterizes these constructions; this is the price that the late-bourgeoisie pays for demythologization in these areas and for the renunciation of the bombast of the nineteenth century. In any case there is no inheri-tance that is direct here, but definitely only one of indirectness; even the enjoyment of this architecture is aware of its misgivings, is ready to make its enthusiasm sensitive to the bourgeois poison which is after all more copiously contained in the steel buildings of Mussolini than in the – columned monstrosity of the Soviet Palace. This sensitivity is all the more important, the more the old society seems a thing of the past in the new architecture; the more capitals, portals, central risaltos[22] and the other reflections of feudal superiority seem to disappear, the more openly flexible equality determines the image of the room and the façade. Even if Russia itself has taken over elements most closely related to Objectivity, not only technology therefore, but also 'interdenomina-tional schools', 'collective town-plans' and more besides, it has never-theless already so decisively changed the so-called cover and the frame, above all the *matter of responsibility*, that even the forms of this Ratio are not or cannot remain the same, let alone its content. Here it should be said that the most recent Russian architecture, if representation is in fact necessary, sets less store by engineer *art* than by 'native classicism'; one senses bourgeois poison in Objectivity at least as clearly as possible future. Yet if active revolution has happened or is even only under way, then the concrete-rational contradictory bodies, future bodies in capital-ism inevitably enter into mediation; they free themselves from their suspectness and disjointedness, they definitely free themselves from

---

22 'Mittelrisalit': a central vertical protuberance from a building.

their abstract barrenness, from the content-free monotony of their architecture. Of course, Communist Objectivity is not only the late-capitalist kind minus exploitation; rather, when the exploitation is omit-ted, the unimaginable difference removes profit and anarchy from the background which abstract Objectivity had only covered up or avoided, it changes even the lifeless functional forms into socially animated ones and the chalk-white tenement blocks in which a lesser variety of work-ing animals resides today acquire colour and a completely different geometry, namely of a true collective. Which does not like today make disappearing privacy into a misery nor like today make the social form of life into mechanics or into prison. And in the hollow space left by the lack of ideology there is fresh air here instead of cynicism, instead of nihilism the nothing in terms of appearance from which a universe[23] can first develop. Even the 'thought-models' with which the functionalism, relativism of new-objective Ratio toys in front of its rigid anarchy, have become dialectical pieces of theory, belonging concretely to a tendency which is itself dialectical. But in no way are these elements under the so-called capitalist cover already present, certainly not in a developed form; otherwise New Objectivity would not be so façade-based and reflexive. Thus there is no inheritance to claim here for reformists, but the indirectness of the glance and the use is the revolution. At any rate, even now the parts which have become naked feign only more façade, not more correlation of culture, theatre and plush. And the Ratio is so flatly disjointed and perverted by capitalist Objectivity because it is or is becoming so dangerous to it, so forward-driving, so very much consistency among compromises.

Montage, direct

For the first time the wind is definitely here, it blows from everywhere. Parts no longer fit together, have become soluble, can be mounted in a new way. To begin with, only the snipped, newly *stuck* photograph 'mounted' was comprehensible for many; the word is of course much older for those handling machines. Even in the human body skin, internal organs are transplanted; but at best the transplanted organ performs in its new place only what is appropriate to that place, nothing else. In *technical* and *cultural* montage, however, the context of the old surface is decomposed, a new one is formed. It can be formed as a new one because the old context increasingly reveals itself as illusory, brittle, as one of surface. If Objectivity distracted with shining veneer, much montage makes the confusion behind it attractive or boldly intertwined.

23   'All' means 'universe' in German, but of course also carries the sense of 'all'.

Objectivity served as the highest form of diversion, montage appears culturally as the highest form of eerie intermittence above diversion, indeed possibly as a *contemporaneous* form of intoxication and irrationality. In this respect montage shows less façade and more background of the times than Objectivity; equally it has the showpieces of Objectivity only as ruins. It does not pretend any stability which wishes to harden the foreground; its form was instead – already in stability – jazz, revue, mosaic made up of scraps, rags and loosening. Jazz mixed machine and sentimentality together; but just as the beat of the machines let in the African drum (and once again doubly: as excitement and spell), sentimentality also knew the ironic quotation, drove Chopin, even the Pilgrims' Chorus into the cheekiness of improvisation. Even more astonishingly than in jazz, the revue touches on more concrete intentions of loosening: the revue became not merely decay of the decay, as represented by the mere vulgarity of late operetta, instead it also resolved – in the strength of perfect nonsense – the unity of characters, the last coherence of architecture; the stage seemed made of so-called dreams or a kaleidoscope of haphazard wishes. Of course, the result showed in jazz and in revue that the material was not concretely changed anywhere here yet through montage, but big business was distracting both again (without a change of material taking place) into the small forms of the Irratio – in the first case the military drum, in the second the Hitler parade. Thus even montage can *directly* always end only as a way of filling in hollow space; if Objectivity was façade of the foreground, then *montage of this kind* ends as castle-restoration of the background. If the fashion of neo-Machism corresponded to reflexive Objectivity, then montage likewise lives off 'models' (which it adapts and varies), then it patches up above all, as bourgeois empty montage, the abyss of the 'existere' with the so-called ontic experiences (in the wake of the Husserl School, in Heidegger and, against his will already transitionally, in Jaspers). These latter montages, more kaleidoscopes, will be considered later in their proper place; the spirit of Joyce is almost beginning to spook in here, in a philosophy of professors which knows nothing at all of that kind. Without the interfusion of states and things there would likewise hardly be understanding for the metamorphoses-mythology of the revived Klages, however much this is separated – by will-less dream and archaisms – from the nolens-*volens* of 'montage'. *Directly* of course, in their own bourgeois truth, all these crossed emotions or hieroglyphs are only equally crossed and obstructed background. Composed of ruins which cannot find the courage to phosphoresce, composed of parts of the old world which are only refunctioned time and again for use in the old world. Thus at least ordinary montage is directly only a sealed bottle: shaken, or a finished remnant: mixed in. Despite an age which seemed to be making many transitions to the avant-garde with 'revue' and its consequences.

Montage once again: of a higher order

But not only easy form presses to get under way here. It was already frothing when brush and pen aimed very high, namely Expressionistically. At that time all artists, being 'inward' ones, wanted to play a musical game, as it were, a mobile game full of intersection. This loosening, this pouring of forms into the melting pot, was one of the Expressionist offices; shortly before, in and shortly after the war. Since form in the work of the fellow-travellers of that time lost all content with the external one, i.e. came to say nothing in contrast to the intended fullness of expression, its interfusion, confusion also very often became rigid mannerism, of course. Abstract rebelling then let off steam, without finding a different ground from that of the existing society, only as a negated one; boundless motion per se lived in this appearance, boundless scream against war in general, for man in general. Abstractly exploded form restored itself precisely in the self-sufficient, in the artistically fixated decay, because it remained without an object, i.e. because it found no contact with real, class-based sinking and rising, with other objects than the abstractly rejected ones of the capitalist thing-world. The musical kaleidoscope congealed in this *inauthentic* Expressionism in an arty-crafty way, almost into wallpaper, indeed resulted directly in its opposite, namely in so-called cubism, that is, in self-sufficient enjoyment of engineer art, in the reification of geometric construction per se. Even if paths led very quickly from cubism into New Objectivity, Noske's campaigns[24] also ended *authentic Expressionism* of course, this first and most genuine form of non-representational, differently representational dream-montage in our times. This montage was not the literal one in the arts and crafts sphere (clock-wheels or lumps of wood on many oil paintings), not even the quite random title of the Münchhausens (seven hat-boxes piled on top of one another representing the birth of Christ): rather, Expressionism *in its original form* was image-explosion, was torn-up surface even starting with the original, namely with the subject which violently tore up and cross-connected. Thus this subject of bourgeois–aesthetic opposition (against coherences of the surface, pictorial and stable ones) did not stay, like the fellow-travellers, with that painting which still proudly called itself 'abstract'; not with cubism and wallpaper. Instead it definitely sought contact with the world, admittedly with a different one than with the subject–object of indistinct fermentation and fantastic crystals. Genuine Expressionism (the Folkwang Museum in Essen preserves from it a collection of true volcanic eruptions) did not only instil subjectivistic intentions into a denied

---

24 Defence minister Noske co-ordinated the campaigns of the reactionary Freikorps to suppress socialist revolutions in Berlin (1918), Munich (1919) and elsewhere in Germany.

matter, but covered the world with war, mounted its fragments into grotesque caricatures, mounted into the hollow spaces above all excesses and hopes of a substantial kind, archaic and utopian images. Even this Expressionism, although it wanted to explode the reification (instead of abstractly ignoring it), still had no considered or comprehended contact with the concrescence, namely with the revolutionary process of the subject–object mediation. Nevertheless it had, in the avant-garde of its time, enough 'tendency' in the background; which is why the 'Blue Rider' of Expressionism was especially repressed when the social-democratic revolution entered the 'factual ground'. But even today there is no great talent without Expressionist origin, at least without the highly speckled, highly stormy after-effect of the latter. The so-called surrealists provided the last 'Expressionism'; only a small group, but again avant-garde is to be found in them, and surrealism is most certainly – montage. In *Joyce*, as the monument of the 'surrealists', montage is directly the key to all strangeness, it is the description of the confusion of experienced reality with collapsed spheres and caesuras. The language here attains nothing but beginnings, wild beginnings of tinkling sound and combined again within it; the plot runs between inner dialogue (which says everything that is going through the character's mind), underworld, crossworld and overworld (which again stand in the closest bodily contact). The space and theme of the plot in 'Ulysses' is a day of insignificant characters (which however seeks to be more than a thousand and one days, in fact an Omnia ubique in the nut). Dirty joke, chronicle, claptrap, scholasticism, magazine, slang, Freud, Bergson, Egypt, tree, man, economy, cloud pass in and out in this flow of images, mingle, permeate each other in a disorder that is of course seeking its model in Proteus, in the confusion of fermenting nature, no longer in Prometheus, in the expressively fermenting subject. As final book-magic Proteus himself is even tinged with his opposite, namely with asserted symmetry, indeed thorough correspondence of all parts; in such a way that not only leitmotifs wind their way through, but every chapter – in the *cathedral* of relativism – attempts to correspond to parts of the body, colours, minerals and the like, with restlessly concealed concordance. The dissected violin of Picasso has thus, in inscrutable broad imposture,[25] become verbal kinetics; relations – not exactly to Dante, but rather to the Romantics – give this kind of montage the moonlight in which it flourishes. Today this is all just picture-puzzles of burst consciousness; with a 'totality' which has its universe in scraps, scraps of conversation, cross-galleries of undirected experienced reality. But a world whose most curious literature rings out the end of bourgeois education in this way is nevertheless capable, if it does not practise

---

25 'Breitstapelei': Bloch is playing on 'Hochstapelei' (imposture), substituting 'broad' (Breit) for 'high' (Hoch) here.

dialectics, of having this practised on it. The constitutive montage *takes the best pieces for itself, builds other coherences out of them*, and the owner of the previous coherence is pleased by the new one, if this does not remain patchwork and artistic myth, no longer.

Montage, indirect

Even here still nothing leads into the particulars of the pieces that are serviceable. Not so much deception through new distraction as that of a *static* intertwining prevents even montage from being contradictory on the spot. We characterized, in indirect Objectivity, as being indirectly usable only that which can already be identified as suspicious or full of contradiction in the capitalist location itself. This is also the criterion for serviceable heirlooms here: they must be, in the late capitalism that forms them, as imperfect and prevented as they are suspect. They must be the irregular, i.e. a contradiction developed in the capitalist womb, composed of genuine Today, of both Today and concrete Tomorrow. This is certainly often the case with phenomena of montage; otherwise restored capitalism would not have stopped the manifold Expressionist rousings and shakings. Otherwise montage would appear only in Joyce or in other 'interesting' figures of decay and not also in Brecht, who directly uses it as a force of production. Namely as interruption of the dramatic flow and instructive displacement of its parts, in short, as directorially based politics. But what we said about indirect Objectivity also holds true here: only in and after the revolution can particulars themselves be raised out in montage. Particulars of the gigantic improvisational and mixed system which characterizes the structures of this time, like no other, in its flow, in the *ornaments* of its relativism, its 'revue-culture'. One may just as little reject every inheritance from capitalist contemporaneity, except 'the respective latest machine', as conversely note every antinomially damaged aspect as already life under cover. And just as little, without doubt, can transitions be constructed from a mere 'idea' of montage, merely because the burst consciousness of late capitalism poses picture-puzzles here. Picture-puzzles and vexing pictures which are in fact partly irregular to capitalism, yet still serve to put a sheen on it, precisely the 'interesting' sheen of an intellectual production which in regular terms would not be possible at all here any more. In and after the revolution, of course, the usefulness of this particular aspect, and especially of the whole disposition, will also stress itself, and without poison; only in this direction can 'montage-structures' now already be recalled so that they are in the frame, namely in that of a curiously swirling culture-past, *which even under socialism can have this form for a long time.* Thus as far as *montage, indirect* is concerned, it lacks in its concrete responsibility every joke of empty combination, every deception of the kaleidoscope (to make the chaos of the background mysterious in a bad way). Even montage without exploitation takes its parts from the surface chopped to pieces, but does not put them into new closed unities, rather makes them into particles of a different language, into different information, into different On-the-Way form of broken-up reality. In Brecht, for example, unobjectionable usages of neo-Machist models exist, along these lines; however, if every separate form, not to mention every material content, is remounted, then no 'adapted' kaleidoscope appears which seeks to change nothing, neither is any attempt made at artistic chaos. Instead, the montage of the fragment out of its old existence is the experiment of its refunctioning into a new one here. Mechanical, dramaturgical, even philosophical montage is certainly not exhausted by more or less rapid refunctioning, i.e. by the use of short and disposable models. It is evident in the philosophical cross-drillings of Benjamin, for example, that montage takes its material from much improvisation which would have previously been random, from much emphasized interruption which would have previously merely remained unemphasized disturbance; it takes intervening means from despised or suspicious forms and from forms which were formerly second-hand. Also from the ruin-meanings of decaying great works and from the jungle of material that is no longer smoothly arranged. Montage is inclined towards the interim, towards new 'passage-forming' through things and towards the display of what has previously been extremely remote; in other places, for example in many remarkable experiments by the surrealists, from Max Ernst[26] to Aragon,[27] it is a kind of crystallization on the chaos that has come, attempting to mirror in a bizarre way the coming order. Everywhere here there is not much more than programme, fleeting, lonely and often temporary; and yet the attraction of this programme or disjointed participation in its consequences is in most of what the twenties have produced in the way of significant art and perception. Even the pervasion and interchangeability of the parts, which appears in the self-collapse of the bourgeoisie, is superior to the closed unity of its previous 'world-picture'. Indeed this is still relatively advanced consciousness compared with that kind of vulgar Marxist slickness which knows everything in its place, strictly according to the division of labour, and everything really abstractly in the frame. Relativism which announces the crack in the closed surface, montage above all, which is at home with the uncanny, experimental shape of these ruins – this is how the late bourgeoisie still hands down 'culture' or causes it to be handed down. Nothing succeeds on this territory any more from a single cast,[28] it

26   Max Ernst, 1891–1976, surrealist painter.
27   Louis Aragon, 1897–1983, surrealist French writer.
28   'Aus einem Guß' has the figurative meaning 'as a unified whole', 'of a piece'.

succeeds only on the next or on the spits of land which the next sends out into chaos. But the cast is inclined to absorb a lot of bankrupt's estate into itself, above all in fact picture-puzzles of a burst consciousness which means 'man' in such a strange and new way. This type has all the negative aspects of the void, but it also has, indirectly, as a possibly positive aspect, the fact that it shifts ruins into a different space – against the usual context. Montage in the late bourgeoisie is the hollow space of the latter's world, filled with sparks and intersections of a 'history of appearance', which is not the right one, yet possibly a mixing place for the right one. One form, too, of making sure of the old culture: perceived from the perspective of travel and consternation, no longer of learning.

THE VOID

But no one gets used to living here. The further forward in the New, the bleaker it gets. The wall in the room looks grey or yellowish like the street, and the floor is it. The chairs move smoothly, nothing is fixed.

It is hardly possible or necessary to live the right way any more. The empty ego forms no shell any more to hide the one inside who is not at home anyway. The furniture vanishes, dissolves into its mere purpose, goes to the wall. Like light on the wall, the hand on the switch will soon turn on a table, the load-bearing area of the top, and turn it off again when it is no longer needed. The new streets are completely lifeless in themselves; if an old installation is pulled down and a fresh one put there, a hole still remains. Nothing is deposited, the space remains open for what is missing. Very arid way of not getting old, it moves elsewhere.

THE SHIP-HOUSE

From this too we learn to freeze. Inside and out the wall is bare. But in return we see the inside open, the outside breaks through. The thick fabrics have fallen, a penetrating will departs. All this wants to be somewhere other than where it stands so hollow.

Even this house no longer pretends to take root here. Straps run round the ledges, made of blue steel, shining at night. The emphasized breadth is no longer such, it reminds us rather of the hunger queues which stood in front of the shops and which have now shot upwards or piled on top of one another. Deprivation forces people into large blocks, but the open age blows on the die and changes its shape. Low doors no longer lead into the safe house, but on board. Curves form a ship's bow, the queues pull bands around the hull, even the flat roof that looks so southern is not so much copied from the south or in broad repose, but more like a sundeck. Steps on the outside, riveted circular windows strengthen the travelling impression: the whole house becomes a ship. Here no ghosts of dead styles affix themselves and go on haunting afterwards; something new haunts ahead, which is and is not. Jazz sounds superb with steel, and Weill's[29] tunes show that the steel is not in tune. The house as ship denies the space in which it stands; since ships would like to vanish. The order revealing where they are bound is not opened as long as we are still cruising; only later. But one or two parts of it (a ragged or squally wind is whistling through) are already known now.

29 Kurt Weill, 1900–50, composer of the *Threepenny Opera*.

ON THE THREEPENNY OPERA

This made a particularly amusing impression on very many people. They had a proper lark, took it home with them. Hits too, sweet and bitter ones, remarkably sharpened ones, but not attacking. This non-dangerous element appears especially where the bourgeois laughs. The hits appear the same which he dances elsewhere, only better arranged. And the beggars appear happy with a situation which causes them to go on singing and acting so cheerfully. Many things dance along to the fresh tone which do not need to.

All correct, but once again the fresh tone is not up to much. Rather, Weill succeeded, in a very lively way, in baling out the foul waters, precisely those of the hit. 'It suits no one, it suits no one to stay at home, they need fun': the false tones, transposed rhythms of this fun are composed out and unmasked. In this way the drive-satisfaction which the public usually finds in hits is betrayed and treacherously turned over; namely the *commodity* as hit ceases, and the latter appears as a would-be substitute for a *good*. Weill reached in light, indeed vulgar, mask many people to whom advanced music did not get through. Even if only a very few of these many are proletarians, Weill nevertheless does not create out of the better class-mix which is listening 'nation' to be sung, but rather decomposition which gets to the bottom of light music. Weill is not radically monotonous, and exactly like Eisler,[30] definitely not 'musicianly', i.e. falsely direct, like the social-democratic primitive soul Hindemith;[31] he incorporates even less the hit into song-form, as if it was a new folk-song. After all, it has long been an industrial product; precisely the new hit, composed of poor negroes and more elegant primal feelings, has become particularly standardized and withdrawn, particularly anonymous and objectless in its satisfaction of

---

30 Hanns Eisler, 1898–1962, composer.
31 Paul Hindemith, 1895–1963, composer.

drives. But equally there is a bit on the side in the hit, a bit of whore's alley and peep-show alongside the magnificent boulevard; even though the hit, as rhythm, melody and lyrics, totally follows the standardized trend of the times, it still has a wry face underneath, a colportage face that removes its make-up of surfaces with the greatest superficiality. The shoddy aspect of the hit does not only mean that it remains longer in the memory than the mediocrity of its age (even quite early hits like 'You Little Fishergirl', 'The Timber Sale in the Greenwood', 'Male, Male, is my Male still Alive', 'Rixdorfer', hang in the related subconscious). The Threepenny Opera was also able, thanks to the fermenting times, to latch on to this shoddy aspect in a particularly exact way: its beggars and rogues are no longer those of the opera buffa, let alone of the ragged ball, or of charity, but of decomposed society in person. Hence, O false friends, these tones, hence Brecht's scornful sweetness, sharpened lightness once again, hence the tunes of 'Mack the Knife' and this 'Tiger-Brown'. Hence the voice of Lotte Lenya, sweet, high, light, dangerous, cool, with the light of the crescent moon; hence Pirate Jenny and the demonic ballad for which she finally gets her breath. Without the decay made bold in Stravinsky's Soldier's Tale, the Threepenny Opera would not exist; but most definitely not without the common decay, without the hits since 1880. There is no longer any better music beyond the 'tingling' element and schmaltz except that in which they are quoted; the breaking beauty of the trumpet melody when Polly leaves the Robber becomes the quotation of a life that still has no place. The experiment of the Threepenny Opera has put the worst music in the service of the most advanced music today; and it proves to be dangerous. The whore walking the streets for the bourgeoisie was turned into an anarchistic smuggler, at least an anarchistic one.

Various features mingle, rub together. The angular tone and the bad atmosphere, the closed number and the rebellious content. The simplified means of expression and the extremely many-voiced dream of Pirate Jenny, the happy melodies and the blossoming desperation; finally a chorale that explodes. The song does not act, but reports on the situation, like the old aria; but without exception it reports a cursed situation (and the 'damned Can-you-feel-my-heart-beating-text'). Here an old cellar settles as a house, sometimes a new roof even settles directly on the ground; from a cross-section of both, the future of a society cannot yet of course be predicted, let alone pursued. The very pleasure which such music brings with it stands, if not in the way of the transformation of the society, then not always on the way there; its tone only has its sword from time to time. Artistic limits in general are drawn here, to even stronger things than the experiment of the Threepenny Opera and its liberated hit-weapons. The nail which even the politically most directed music and poetry hit on the head is only very indirectly a nail in the coffin of given reality. But even if music cannot change society, it can nevertheless, as Wiesengrund[32] rightly says, indicate its change in advance, by 'absorbing' and speaking aloud what is dissolving and forming under the surface. Above all it illuminates the impetuses of those who march into the future even without music, but more easily with it. Weill's music is the only one that has socially-polemical strike-power today; and the wind whistles through, the honest wind, which exists where no buildings stop it, where round about the times are still no reality. Weill has spoiled the enthralling concept for the 'musicianly' singers, in their own 'nation'. The cannon-song showed that soldiers also live on the left, but the right sort of soldiers. And for moments Pirate Jenny came as close to the heart of the nation as Queen Luise previously did. Nothing shows more clearly what hits and the pleasure of mixing improvisation are now capable of.

32 Wiesengrund: original patronymic of Theodor W. Adorno, 1903–69, philo-sopher and writer on the theory of music.

TIME-ECHO STRAVINSKY

Things that are hollow are good for piping on.[33] That is also the way Stravinsky likes it to be with himself and what is his, he has already attempted a lot. Void drums beguilingly on itself, clothes itself too, puts old things on, becomes mask-like and sounds like this. The sound was first sweet and glittering, then melting and cheerfully confused, until a *rift* occurred. It occurred in 1918 in 'The Soldier's Tale'; nowhere else was this year notated in such a decayed, such a lonely and significantly crazy way. But Stravinsky is the mask which can always be something else. Nothing is coherent in his playing; a faithless music, but also honest precisely because of this today. The sound is different every time and, while his piece is still being played, already no longer quite belonging to him.

The Soldier's Tale: this chops a man to pieces until he lies in shreds. A conscious lark, which soon becomes unconscious, and in which there is horror. The soldier Joseph has fourteen days' leave, gives the devil his fiddle, takes a book in exchange that goes on ahead. 'Exchange rates', he reads (a precise intersection between fairytale and devilishness here), rates that do not yet exist; he is a guest at the devil's table for three days, but they are three weeks, his girl at home is lost, no one at home knows the man they thought dead and he reads the hellish book, wretched, soulless, without music, it rains titles, notes, gold. And then, totally out of the whimpering, false, shredded score, out of the ingenious falseness of its stakes, the winnings: victory of the soldier over the devil and evil under the table. The stage becomes bright, the whole theatre, even the chandelier flares up, at half power, a chorale comes to the orchestra so to speak, ragged and carious, but true and pious as 'God be Praised' in breathtaking colportage, when rescue nears, the friend, armed man, light. But even this luck does not hold, nor the princess he has won,

33 This also has the colloquial connotation 'are easy not to give a damn about'.

least of all his home village; accompanied by music of sheer death throes, under the old spell and in complete darkness the insatiable creature gropes its way after its devil into nothingness. And what a scene of schizophrenia! the flies all around, an open hollow space, the pitiful little theatre in the middle of it, the narrator in triple montage: reporting on the soldier, often as the soldier himself, as a friend of the soldier and assistant in the scene which does not know from one moment to the next where the master is driving it out of the door to. Clouds of foul-smelling tobacco and insanity rise in the court theatre, rough dream-images drift in its smoke, the curtain of the little theatre goes up and down, shows the canvases of a street ballad, then people motionless, then acting, then wax dolls that have come to life in mime. This whole topsy-turvy creation, however, this strange poem of the strange poet Ramuz[34] has condensed music in images, ugly as the dream of a lunatic, bloody, incoherent, bright with subterranean light in the sky and then pocketed again, as the paid bill of the deep night. Perforated rhythm everywhere, an orgy of wrong notes; impression and montage in a confused mixture of rags and march royal, a hunger-dream which drifts out of bygone folk-dances and market-magic on to a country road, where only the ghosts of past music-parades still walk. In Stravinsky's 'Petrushka' there was still the blossoming sound of the fair, the ballerina still looked like a boy imagines a woman to be, there was the peculiar sweetness of the barrel-organ melody, this overstrongly coloured aspect singing out mellifluously to the last. But in 'The Soldier's Tale' folklore itself spends the night, and the music of what is evilly sleeping appears, the world of what has been driven and is sleeping into death. In its images, in the ghostly squalls from the night-dream which whip up and scatter the creaturely images, Stravinsky has set a kind of ragged Faust to music, namely the hungry man without world. Stravinsky, the unreliable, wears the most reliable mask here, namely that of death; and his music is the dying dream of an inwardness for which hardly even lunacy, the lark of lunacy, is a ground which stops the fall.

Oedipus Rex: all the more astonishing here the new tone, steely, sure, refined. Instead of rags stiff robes, instead of the frenzy continually white repose. Every trace of flickering and confusion, but also of storm and human unrest is extinguished. The sound sharply broken off in succession; fusion, not to mention sultriness, totally avoided; no motion between the people. Closed movements, the minute detail and the whole structure incredibly precise, rammed home hard; a music which does not flow romantically, does not fragment either, as in 'The Soldier's Tale', but *beats*. Always only beats there and then, of course; this is true of melody and rhythm as well as of the scene which totally rests on itself. Rigidly seated chorus, in the darkness of the sheer mass; Oedipus

---

34   Charles Ferdinand Ramuz, 1878–1947, French-Swiss writer.

and Jocasta in musical block unity, archaic stance; characters around whom their fate inescapably winds up and unwinds. This mechanical character is even in the music, in its deterministic substance which, not without reason, is fixed by itself. If Stravinsky already had mechanical tendencies early on, and if he only found his 'Concertino' played correctly when, as he said, it 'ran like a sewing-machine', then this ultramodern exactitude is committed here to the exactitude of a fate-play which is equally inescapable. Music affirms in both instances the conveyor belt of necessity, ennobles assembly-line work without breaks, fate without light. Oedipus Rex, with 'psychology' neither before nor behind it, thus itself runs as a musical fate-machine, screwed into concrete. Or walled up in marble: this is admittedly richly veined, by Italian phrases (in the song of Jocasta), by Old Russian vocalises (in the song of Oedipus and Tiresias), but the rigidity remains even in the curving; the mechanical-archaic element releases no uncontrollable blossoming. This rigidity is the tribute of the later Stravinsky to Paris reaction, indeed to the capitalist stabilization of the world; from this also stems what is called the 'objectivism' of this music. It is emphatic alienation from all psychology, but also from everything human; it is an aesthetic alienation which is striving to make music and thereby clear conscience out of the real and intolerable alienation of the factory, out of inevitability. Not without Cocteau's[35] Latin text adding further quite different, indeed almost mysterious elements of fascism, and these elements at the same time interspersed with an arch-French, and yet fantastic, memory. In a time when so much repressed material rises up again, not only 'Pelasgic' images circulate in the country, but also in the city to a certain extent 'Attic' ones; very much more weakly, also more in France than in Germany and even in the former merely in literature, though in sensitive and harshly reactionary literature. It is a strange recourse of bourgeois civilization to the antique world from which it derives; thus the cool world of vase-images multiplies, which now and then resounds through Objectivity, living-machines, hollow spaces, around a kind of revenant music from Hades. Another play of Cocteau's (Orpheus and Eurydice), cold music would of course be alien to him, not only walls up modern necessity in antique, but conversely mounts antique material into the brightest Now. It casts Eurydice platinum-blonde and in pyjamas, Orpheus in horn-rimmed spectacles and polo-shirt, and in fact in a French country-house in 1928: but Greek figures blend in with precisely the modern backdrop quite naturally. Madame la Mort wears Paris evening dress with an antique gold-mask without incongruity; the ancient myth echoes in the life of such elegantly-morbid 'present', as if it were a piece of prognosis. Picasso, Stravinsky, Cocteau – they have, in approaching antique form, become a triad and the last seduction to

35   Jean Cocteau, 1889–1963, French dramatist and film maker.

'proportion' that the upper stratum of the bourgeoisie, at the eleventh hour, has produced. No longer against or beyond machines as in the 'antique world' of Strauss – Hofmannsthal,[36] but with them. The hollow space is filled with demonic masks and echo-reflexes, with a petrified montage of mechanical, antique, Byzantine, white-archaic 'order'. Oedipus Rex, in steel tone and Latin language, signifies the most cryptic façade which New Objectivity has achieved with montage.

Such is the amazing effect of resounding void and the Now with which it echoes. It is a precisely upper middle-class void, every thrust or idea from below is lacking. Since his 'Histoire du soldat' Stravinsky has nothing more in common with drums which are not those of fate, his place is that of alienation, mythologizing divestiture. Yet even in this he is unreliable, the game of alienation constantly stands on a gloomy background, can switch into laughter and quite obvious desperation. Thus this most exact contemporary and most fashionable musician of theirs is still suspicious for the bourgeoisie; because he nevertheless has the genuine false consciousness of the age. Located at the exact peak of the upper middle-class world, despite all objectivism he is not musically and not positive; Stravinsky plays in the hardest upper middle-class contradictions, without attempting a positive ideology, a musical 'Weltanschauung'. Although he has added machine-music, indeed musical inhumanity to New Objectivity, Stravinsky appears to the bourgeoisie as suspect as he does up-to-date: the 'fascist' acts as 'cultural Bolshevik'. This became clear when Klemperer brought Oedipus Rex to Berlin, in the memorable winters of the Kroll opera.[37] Instructive seen together with 'The Soldier's Tale', together with Klemperer's other deeds of purity, exactness and new birth. Under the conductor of precision, of fiery and clean background, the most recent Stravinsky also sounded, regardless of its reaction, like demonic contemporaneity and became it. The bourgeoisie still finds luxury in Stravinsky, even its highest luxury, but not one that inspires confidence; instead systemlessness is its name, the hardness one in masks and the steel sheen one above the spookiness of the void. Before Oedipus Stravinsky had already ironized its classicalness in 'Pulcinella'; after Oedipus came the Symphony of Psalms, a temporary structure of overblown and sluggish feelings. The randomness of stance and theme which had characterized a Richard Strauss even in his heyday has become steely unreliability and thereby precision in Stravinsky: namely that of a late culture exploding in a thousand and

---

36   Richard Strauss, 1864–1949, composer. Hugo von Hofmannsthal, 1874– 1929, Austrian writer. Bloch is principally thinking here of Strauss's opera *Electra* which took its libretto from a verse tragedy by Hofmannsthal.
37   Otto Klemperer, 1885–1973, conductor. He was music director in Berlin from 1927–1933, first at the Kroll Opera and subsequently at the Staatsoper.

none subjects. Stravinsky, so far removed from revolution, indeed even from any concrete experiment, has nevertheless become the most precise musical player with a late-bourgeois age, with an abstract, much broken space rich in reflexes.

A further word on what continues to circulate as more or less steely. All voices now stand firm, precise and hard which have something to sing, above all to say. Even Weill's music goes back to the firm number, does not want to intoxicate in this, but, as precisely and plainly as possible, to underline. But the 'dramaturgical utilization of closed form' is here in no way itself closed; it became instead revolutionary march or aria of cursed conditions or the protest precisely against reification and human emptiness. In Weill's 'Surety' for example, not a faultless work and one with musicianly-objectivistic appearance, melancholy and mist break into the closedness: Jewishly darkened south in the mother's lament for her daughter, music of the misty order in the robbers' cries at the bridge which lead astray like voices of nature, like *drifting* voices of nature from an Irish ghost-story; even mist on the river becomes the cantata of that distance which people are from themselves, which equally still separates them from sound order and proper tone. Thus Weill's music, standing against reification, does indeed have agitatory hardness, anti-romantic form, definitely certainty of goal, yet definitely not Stravinsky's abstractly (i.e. precisely as reification) continuous steel. Musicians, on the other hand, who stand extraterritorially to reification anyhow, like Alban *Berg*,[38] make objectivism (without object) more difficult through a subject which has remained expressive and its certainty of a peculiar kind. As far as Berg's 'Wozzeck' is concerned, the theme of its music is neither the automatic hardness of a fate, nor even the sublime one of a cathedral, but poor, suffering man, the abyss precisely of the defenceless *weather* in and outside of him. Wind in the street, the gigantically striking up anxiety of the evening sky over the city, the dim moon become the extension of man or the mirage of the terribly *imminent* in the sky; weather, only this, is dramatis et musicae persona in 'Wozzeck'. Hence the espressivo is here likewise not pathetic, but realistic, namely as the most intensive characterization of man existing in suffering; Berg's music of Wozzeck-man is the weather-music of his loneliness, his uncertainty and sorrow. Thus Berg's music admittedly has definitely got realistic hardness and precision, namely at the abyss of defenceless weatherliness or of the poor people; but on account of this *concrete* contrast to all abstractly continuous steel Stravinsky's abstract, demonic or premature steel-tone is downright lacking, rightly so. Berg's music strikes the abstract steel-tone of objectivism precisely in *reality*; it strikes the collective without human beings which objectivism posits, with human beings without collective, as the most real condition at that

38   Alban Berg, 1885–1935, composer.

time. And hardness itself? It is a strange spectacle that in fact the masked figure Stravinsky possesses it, whereas the strictest of all, most constructive of all composers, the twelve-tone musician *Schönberg*,[39] does not get off so lightly. In fact a restless ego speaks in his work, underground, compulsive, journeying, remote, even technically there is no tonic keynote to refer to, the governing key disappears, the new strictness becomes one of the path and of the unfulfilled movement which goes along it. Schönberg's enemies therefore misunderstand the innovator as a last Romantic, if not as a kind of desensualized Chopin; the strictness, though, with which the atonal is controlled, appears idealistic to them, namely abstract and smugly closed. Schönberg's cognoscenti, on the other hand, see here precisely the expressive music of the private bourgeois individual, simply following its own consequences, brought to its resolution; in the overintensification which 'subjectivism' and 'idealistic systematics' experience simultaneously here, that dialectic is at work which legitimately conquers both heritages from Romanticism. Precisely the perfect expression comes to an end, provided the whole musical material is subject to its power; precisely the most strictly de-reified counterpoint becomes on the other hand, as Haba[40] said, the musical style of freedom, i.e. as Wiesengrund said, perfect construction throughout which first lays bare no longer mechanical man. Thus Schönberg's programme and the difficult manner of its expressivo is admittedly without proper connection with the age, but still a ferment of the future; even if Schönberg's music is only its armament and reconnaissance, not yet real invasion or 'Beethoven'. This higher rank of Schönberg's, sub specie saeculi, must of course be maintained, in contrast to the more interesting Stravinsky, to the shifting mosaic of his hardness, to the phosphorus of his time-art in archaic mask and archaisms. Neither the virtuosity of Stravinsky therefore, nor the statics of the atmosphere-free steel-tone (even if moderated by unreliability) come to the experiment of man, as the object of every concretely experimental music. The neurasthenic steel of Stravinsky builds out only the perfect void, shifting void certainly and one appearing in ever new gestures, void into which shattering music resounds, screams of the like never heard before, when trumpets announce the deadly fate of Jocasta, when incessant triple beats of the kettledrums, as if in darkness without end, accompany blind, penitent Oedipus on his way, and yet void whose catchable echo ultimately remains only fate, desperation about it or its spellbound celebration, not man. Stravinsky has every material, even the steel of his music in the fashions and latest forms of his time, in the spell-type as well, in Byzantine religious longing and complete disbelief; real process is lacking, and most definitely the material of the coming

39   Arnold Schönberg, 1874–1951, composer.
40   Alois Haba, 1893–1973, Czech composer.

house. But how currently too, i.e. how very much at the peak of the bourgeoisie, with what faithless art of echo and twistings this important musician makes his way. Cold, gracefully bold, sinuous ultimately as a meander and equally continuous; stuffed full of masks like a masked ball and yet equally turbulent and unreliable, equally improvisational, uncanny and mixing. Stravinsky shows what folk song, march royal, archaic destinies have beaten out in the machine age, what they have to say to this. And the rift which 'The Soldier's Tale' made in a cosy tonal art has not, through the music of automatic spell which followed it, exactly become easier to close.

NOVELS OF STRANGENESS AND
THEATRE OF MONTAGE

A head that dreams finds it particularly difficult to exist here in front. Even more difficult to build itself up with material, nothing composes itself in the void. Young people with the so-called higher gift often do not really know today where to head. If the inside is any good, if it brings in a real poetic plus, then it can only express itself crookedly in the materials which are available today in upper middle-class terms. Only indirectly above all; writers then react by cutting through, exaggerating and in any case interrupting these. The form can be particularly simple, in order not to let in the confusion here at least. It can also be particularly open, in order not to lose a single word of the confusion. This is no longer decisive in any case, the matter represented remains bent in both media. The sharper a glance is, the more surely it will see the bars cracked.[41]

This above all at the crosswise place which remains in upper middle-class terms for the writer. There is now, as prevailing or still lasting, no other existence except that of the crack, of dislocation. What would have been Expressionist in 1918, boards in the post-war period a ghost train which travels around coolly, dreamily and gruesomely in the ruins, intersections and hollow spaces. Here are Chirico's[42] Turin squares in which nothing but razor-sharp shadows stand, and drawing rooms the parquet floors of which run out to the left into the surf, but to the right wall, fireplace, mantelpiece clock stand in the primeval forest; here are Aragon's Paysans de Paris, causing the meanings of a still nameless future to be sung out of 'the unburied corpse of our parents' (as Benjamin says). Surrealism had popular sources in the silent film, which was in fact itself often the stuff of dreams; but the echo is esoteric which

41 'Die Stäbe gebrochen sehen' contains the colloquial expression 'den Stab über jemanden brechen', 'to condemn someone'.
42 Giorgio de Chirico, 1888–1978, Italian painter.

is thrown back to its Freudianisms from today's hollow space, and in which it principally finds its objects. Most definitely esoteric are symbols which no longer cross over into an overworld, but which incorporate archaic-utopian presentiments merged together into the porosities of the upper middle-class world. Quite close to this symbolic probation, also this-worldliness stands the silent, great phenomenon of *Kafka*; here a submerged or other world up till now found in the life in this world its uncanny return. A submerged world: it reflects old prohibitions, laws and order-demons in the ground water of pre-Israelite sins and dreams, as this water advances again in the decay. An other world up till now: it orbits in Kafka's novels, in 'The Castle', in 'The Trial', as existing mythology of unmastered dependencies, 'of far foreign missions into which one never gained insight'. Seldom have anxiety and matters of piety been drawn closer together, seldom has house security been more ransacked, more complicated. The surrealists themselves to begin with had as unifying purpose only this: to put rotting substances, dream substances into the gaps in the world; this surrealism, an aesthetically isolated dynamite, is no doubt finished. But even writers who consciously do not stand close to this direction at all, or only partly, still show that every bold foray, rebus sic stantibus, touches on 'surrealism'. 'Grotesquely' dream-building grows into the hollow space; not to mention gloomy dream-building, the remembering kind from the expanded hour of death (which, in Proust, a life became), the montaging kind from the fusion of present ruins (in Joyce). Here there is continuous intersection of the collapsed Before, After, Below, Above, and behind this a darkness.

The writers who seem so strange became particularly evident in German. They are in fact French ones and one Irish one living in France, hence in the relatively most preserved society. Also they are in no way connected with one another, the contemporary space between them has itself burst; but they act seismographically, as witnesses of an *object-dream* which one notices especially in Germany; Green,[43] Proust, Joyce – sheer fracture-lines of poetic balance. *Green*: an ego which dreams tormentingly, and never ends itself, tackles anxiety. These people are dull as animals, mostly from small towns, there is a smell of falling leaves. Of studies out of which the occupants never seem to emerge any more, in whose circle they are spellbound as if in graves, inlaid with plush and trim. The action takes place only through, almost in individuals, but these become as large as frescos, indeed as landscapes; since each of them stands for a passion. Nothing more than these lonely addictions is in this space, nothing but the creeping, spellbinding fate of this addiction; no cooperation, no way out. The spell is heavy and immobile in a bourgeois way, it sucks people dry and bumps them off

43   Julien Green, 1900– , French novelist.

before it gets light. It exhausts them heavily, to death, all things and events become heralds of this pressure. *Proust*: an ego which sees its own and external life melting away, grasps what is lost too sharply, writes the dying gleam upwards. The excess of this writer is the finesse and micrology of his porcelain gaze, which is the same as a memory that collects everything. It penetrates to the intensively enormous aspect of the little incidental details as well as to the after-ripening of an age which, while it was lived, was already past; this is how the kaleidoscope of these great gentlemen and ladies operates, of these deceivers, adventurers, heroes of the deluge, of this palely glowing late world in which everything appears real and everything has gaps in which the metaphors nest. The metaphors from collapsed spheres, the planets from restaurant tables, the sun as king's mummy on the unwrapped day, social etiquette as liturgy. Proust divides his own personality into countless egos which know nothing of each other and whose worlds intersect; Proust not only collects the things of lost time, with details which their empirical context had never shown, he equally *turns* past time, precisely as such, via his fading ego into a dome; this only spreads out its images post festum. The Faubourg St-Germain of a declining world has remembered and pervaded itself in this, has condensed into the no longer Euclidean mosaics of Proust's and its own hour of death. Even actions which inspire no other feeling except curiosity, even miscellanies, apparently only become visible from out of the collapse, apparently only petrified in the mosaic of memory, render account to a no longer existent judge. Finally *Joyce*: a mouth without ego is in the middle of the flowing drive here, indeed beneath it, drinking it, babbling it, pouring it out. The language totally emulates this decay, it is not finished and already shaped, let alone articulated, but open and confused. What otherwise speaks, misspeaks, puns at times of tiredness, in pauses in the conversation or in dreamy, also nervous people: here it has gone wild. The words have become redundant, sacked from their sense-relationship, sometimes the language moves like a chopped-up worm, sometimes it comes together like an animated cartoon, sometimes it hangs down like flies into the action. Thus in 'Ulysses' there is already 'work in progress', both workshop and literature, but a workshop which equally suffers, gets dusty, decays, levels itself to the undergrowth. The language barely follows grammatical rules, hardly ever logical ones (of today); its source is supposed to be primary sound-pictorial relationship, its sense the unleashing and grasping of subconscious life; through this it is woken to life again, the words are given back their prelogical value. Irrelevant for the symptom and symbol of the work whether Joyce succeeds, whether his wildness ever passes over into the sweet madness of the poem; whether he is a serious author at all and not, for example, the broad impostor of an inconceivable non-idea, the association of a bourgeois earth-memory after the destruction of the earth, after a cosmic catastrophe; whether Ulysses, even if it does not shine ahead with transparent conduct, does at least still prove the logic of an opaque, collapsed one. The style of Ulysses corresponds in any case to a world without supervision throughout; it is frement-absorption of the decay, firstly of the ego (in the internal soliloquy), then of the bourgeois context of the subjects. The mere 'monologue' of previous time had left the character still recognizable in its continuous ego-state, still intact, still full of conscious surface connections and moral coverings; the 'inner dialogue' in Joyce, on the other hand, does not even have the ego as witness, even the body of the speaker almost falls away which encloses the language, and an anonymous flash-flood is loosed. So naked and shameless, so unembellished and unclosed that all previous naturalisms become court ceremonial in contrast and Döblin's[44] novels, which had sometimes already lain in the orbits of such a ci-devant planet, reservations of reduced wilderness. Bubbles of steam from the unconscious rise up too; they create the crazy word-structures, fill the deep spaces, the masterless treasure-chambers, the abyss beneath the claptrap of these run-of-the-mill people, compose themselves at best in the architecture of that Romanticism in which for the first time multi-storey ways of speaking were in a single one. Again therefore hidden orchestra lives in the simultaneous with a quite different scene, whispering of leitmotifs lives at a crooked angle to the surface of the text; admittedly the verbal kinetics of Ulysses is a purely musical one and actually not one of the southern *tone-frieze*, rather of the Wagnerian *tone-abyss* beneath the text. As in many programme symphonies in the manner of Wagner, here too motifs of its later shape hurry on ahead prophetically, others conversely attempt to venture out of a former interior of the earth and to bring news from it belatedly, news from graves, from erudition and labouring memory, from pornographies and mythology. Pulverized glass from church-windows lies around the banality of every step, cocktails rise in mythology and Rameses from whores, the most artificial montage transforms itself into a mass-migration of the objects themselves, at least into the spectre of an artistic metamorphosis. All this through emphatically few and indifferent people, yet through fully-rounded ones, about whom nothing is left out, who talk without comma to eternity, digress without knowledge into the most remote areas. The Odyssey which is bestowed on man takes place here, if not at every moment then still made wildly topical in twenty-four hours: here are the suitors, namely of Mrs Bloom; here is the Nausicaa scene, namely Mr Bloom's encounter with three girls on the beach; here is the Cyclops scene in the cave of the twelfth chapter, in the gloomy pub, with the gabbler Bloom and the 'one-eyed' nationalist who throws him out. This world in fact im-

44   Alfred Döblin, 1878–1957, doctor and writer.

mediately goes crazily downwards just as it throws itself crossways and upwards; it goes downwards in that the three girls on the beach speak the boarding-house language of 1900, the marmalade style by the ocean, in that Bloom himself, the advertising Odysseus, is a hulking great Irish loud-mouth; crossways and upwards, however, extends the boundless association of the flattest experienced reality – as far as the god Ptah in the teacup, the water-gleaming palaces of Old India in the break in the conversation. The cross-relation of 'correspondence' which attempts as it were to break through the people, mountains and islands, after they have moved from their places, indeed which is keen to make even the individual book-chapters into 'ruling jewels and planets', into 'concordances' of utter chaos post rem: this astrological system still does not fix the cracked world, mixed world. Instead astrology between the shreds of experienced reality, scholasticism in a Last-Book-Judgement show the anarchic subject only all the more clearly, the concrete endlessness of all the intervening subjects (and their marriage) only all the more helplessly. Proteus, the confusion of fermenting nature, appears as patron even of this end; and a single day, the stream of a single day, becomes the bed again for the nature-god, in such a way that even the six-thousand-year-old world of history, with caves, Irish-Syrian brothel whores, intestines made of stone, Jesus of filth, sceptres, adverts and serpents, returns to the space of this single, in fact average day. A dead loss and the most incredible sell-out at the same time; a randomness of mere scrunched-up slips of paper, ape-chatter, eel-knots, fragments of nothing, and at the same time the attempt to ground scholasticism in chaos; a dies irae randomly torn from the middle, without judgement, without God, without end, filled with dream-decoction, with the decoction of a sunken consciousness, with fermentingly new dream-essence at the same time. This is the most hollow and the most overcrowded, the most unrestrained and the most productive grotesque, grotesque-montage of the late bourgeoisie; high, broad, deep, cross imposture from lost homeland; without paths, with nothing but paths, without goals, with nothing but goals. Montage can now do a lot, previously only thoughts lived easily alongside each other, now things do too, at least in the flood area, in the fantastic primeval forest of the void.

A dreaming head remains one even where it wants to disappear in a completely cold manner. Where it has no desire to contemplate, like so many of the previous kind, does not choose beautiful words, especially 'peculiar' ones. But actively intervenes instead, stimulates with the well-trained phrase, rehearses in advance real actions in scenes; like *Brecht*. Consequently literature with epithets still remains, overhanging, not totally covered, not totally factual; since the border-space between the upper middle-class and the coming world, in which such writers act, is also still hollow, brewingly hollow. The literary signature in fact becomes all the more individual, the more it believes it is capable of losing itself in factual features, even collective features. Brecht is also an example of such *involuntary literature*: in so far as he does not want to be a personality, but rather an arrangement, a powerfully effective, factually instructive arranger of sheer objective Outside. But the dreaming surplus pours precisely out of all 'words' here: hence the perversely simple language, this complex plainness, this tropical sunshine on proletarian questions, this hymn of indifferent disbelief. And positively: whereas a proletarian sense often only seems forced upon the adventurous romanticism, the 'primary' aspect of Brecht, the action- and dream-plus is genuine here in the cunning with which Objectivity and montage are used as means for the production of a subject which is quite different from the upper middle-class and still so cracked one. In this way adventurous and distant romanticism move into a cooled and experimental object; the distant scene of the action turns into a future one, anarchy (the best part of every exoticism) turns into a kind of laboratory, an open experimental space. The subject, however, which Brecht tests out in advance in the laboratory of the stage by means of Objectivity and montage, is the revolutionary birth of the future society and world in the current one. On this subject the wildly cold, mythically disdainful direction of Brecht's talent balances itself out; much dries up on it, much becomes newly experiencing, even practising logic, wisely experiencing, with the will towards ever more precise responsibility. The 'Objectivity' provides him with the relativistic models; but from façade-like methods for working something out they become recipes here for demonstrating something to oneself. The montage likewise creates no artistic kaleidoscope, but processes fragments of the old society, even freed possibilities in it ('Man is Man'); it refunctions them firstly into Communist teaching-machines, experimental machines. The theatre thus transforms itself into a political issue; more precisely, Brecht's direction strives for Leninism in situations and in the problems which they raise. Leninism in the sense that the theatre becomes a studio for each respective 'theory' on each respective 'practice'; its action-play thus becomes a pre-rehearsal of political stances and theories in set and changing situations in the locus minoris resistentiae of the stage. Thus to his 'Man Who Says Yes' Brecht added a possible 'Man Who Says No', thus the four firm decisions of his experimental play 'The Measure Taken' likewise found soon afterwards their reworked, elastic, unconcluded correction; thus Brecht confronts in 'St Joan of the Stockyards' a well-meaning idea with the very different reality which it has helped to bring about. St Joan – a bit of Schiller, a bit of Indra's[45] daughter in Chicago and above all a nature-Christian: but what she preaches from purest sympathy and desire to help locks out the workers and makes the

45   Indra: ancient Indian god of war and heroes.

Meat-king even richer. On balance the capitalists canonize Joan thus: 'We want to launch her in a big way because she has helped us get over difficult weeks by her benevolent work in the stockyards, her plea for the poor, even by her speeches against us.' Likewise: heart without knowledge is good for nothing, theory per se is neither good nor bad, not even the truth is true, but each respective socialist practice (from which it must come, to which it must lead) decides on this. The audience does not become intoxicated with these 'experiments', but should give an opinion; it finds no culinary pleasure, but rather an anatomy, no evening at the theatre which draws nicely to an end in uninterrupted action, but often interrupted, non-idealistic, real action, concrete situation-logic, pure practice-theatre. A Leninist on the stage thus carries out the experiment of objectively reporting and self-correcting, 'epic' drama; in contrast to the dynamic kind, understood as the self-intoxication of an 'idealism' which rebounds off nothing external, which rises in an irresistibly closed way and storms its own enjoyment. What is meant here is the contrast between the dynamics of the bourgeois revolution and the concrete experiment of the proletarian one which time and again has its bones of contention, and has these outside the idealistically closed action, outside of the admittedly idealistically 'included', but realistically unconquered 'fate'. This epic programme is also a useful approach of Communist anti-liberalism to pre-liberal forms, to ballad-ages, whose 'customs' first posit the stance and then the given case, indeed to static lands, whose 'classic authors' lend theory to experience and seem to have their Confucius as wisest practical man. Of course, however far over the mountains Brecht searches for 'medicine and instruction', they are always meant for the next bad valley. Even the American utopia play 'Mahagonny' which is all too strongly prosecuted with illusion and disillusion, even this anarchic ensemble ('here there is fresh meat-salad and no management') has its 'procession of the men' very close by, has its 'Here-you-can-tavern', the cantus firmus which one can hold on to, has the primeval-human, ultra modern song of Jonny's on something that is missing.[46] Foreign adventures, age-old symbols are so little foreign to Brecht country that even demons are not lacking: only they are sitting in modern directors' offices, and the little bells of the Magic Flute, the disenchanting, favourably enchanting ones, are mounted into Lindbergh's machine.[47] This ultimately still makes his theatre into a refunctioning, into an experimentally mounted one; echo and intersection of symbols connect Brecht as much with Cocteau,

46   The song of 'something that is missing' is actually Paul Ackermann's in *The Rise and Fall of the City of Mahagonny*, quoted correctly later by Bloch. See 'A Leninist of the stage'.
47   Charles Lindbergh, 1902–74, the American airman who was the first to fly solo across the Atlantic in 1927.

Kafka, even Joyce, as aimed practice separates him from the kaleido-scope and experiment from literary reflex.

Thus important writers no longer directly find accommodation in their material, without merely smashing it to pieces. The prevailing world no longer radiates any portrayable appearance to them which could be turned into fiction, but only void, with mixable breaks in it. The great strangeness and most definitely the conscious mixing of the parts (for an already different purpose) lack the idealistic life-appearance of the middle-bourgeois writers; there is an equal lack of the speaking in tongues of barbarism which rides on the fascist wave. The hollow space is perfect for the avant-garde; in contrast to earlier times when the bourgeois world was still revolutionary or had conversely developed the note-world of a both shapable and shape-like 'balance'. The path there was still that from the Sturm und Drang period to Wilhelm Meister,[48] as the bourgeois novel of education[49] through the 'world'; the imagined balance culminated, even if no longer directly, as Hegel's 'reconciliation of the subject with necessity'. In the sense of an imagined 'logos' of the existing society, indeed in emulation of even more filled ages, namely of that medieval one when the innermost sun seemed to stand precisely at the outermost zenith and, as in the world of Giotto,[50] the most sacred objects settled down quite firmly into existence. After Goethe, however, there followed, instead of further novels of education, the French one of disillusion; and today in fact, in the perfect non-world, anti-world or even ruin-world of the upper middle-class hollow space, 'reconciliation' is neither a danger nor possible for concrete writers. No other attitude here except a dialectical one: either as material for dialectical montage or as its experiment. Even the world of Odysseus turned in artistic Joyce into the strolling-gallery of the all-exploding, all-shattered Today in the smallest circle and cross-walk, because human beings lack something, namely the main thing: their face and the world which contains it. Thus above all Brecht's responsible drama becomes one of interruption and practical montage, with 'heroes' in the stalls, 'catastrophes' in practice, possible 'reconciliation' only in another society. The drama becomes healing again, indeed philosophical; in such a way that it offers a new kind of 'catharsis': not with feelings, but through plans, not with great gentlemen, but through exponents, not with actions that have already been, but through ones that have been prepared.

48 Goethe's major novel cycle comprising *Wilhelm Meisters Theatralische Sen-dung, Wilhelm Meisters Lehrjahre* and *Wilhelm Meriters Wanderjahre.*
49 'Erziehungsroman': a novel that describes the gradual education of a young man in the world, a genre of German fiction that flourished in the late eighteenth and the nineteenth century.
50 Giotto di Bondone, *c.*1267–1337, Italian painter.

A LENINIST OF THE STAGE (1938)

Whatever we do, it could be different. The painting of a picture is never finished, the writing of a book is never completed. The conclusion of what we have just printed out could still be changed. And if it came to that, then the effort would start from the beginning.

Difficult to distinguish what is vain or else conscientious about this. Very often this conduct is only nervous and concerns nobody except the author. In *Brecht's* work, however – and he is a matador of change, of the rewriting of something soi-disant concluded – the case is different. Structures like 'The Threepenny Opera', 'Mahagonny', even 'Man is Man' were really written too early, i.e. not yet properly adequate for the material and its problems. Thus when Brecht, as conscientious and cohesive author, patrols the front of his creations, certain burlesque, sometimes anarchistic, sometimes again all too collectivist features (particularly in 'Man is Man') fall out of line. Yet more important is another unfinished aspect, one to be valued extremely positively, and this does not concern only the author. Brecht wants to change the audience itself through his products, so the changed audience (and Brecht now belongs to it himself) also has a retroactive effect on the products. Seldom have there been less withdrawn works than those of Brecht; they are none at all in the reified sense of this word, but – according to an earlier expression of the author – 'experiments'. Consequently in Brecht's Collected Works (volumes 1 and 2, published by Malik, London) the collected as well as the work aspect is to be understood in a particular sense. The *collected aspect* represents no harvest which is contentedly brought in to the barn. Instead, sowing, reaping, binding, threshing, these continuing tasks are still all recognizable. The play 'Man is Man,' for example, could be misunderstood in a 'textbook' sense as collectivist propaganda. Now Brecht instructs us in an appended note that the anti-individualist parable of the play could 'without great difficulty . . . take place in Germany instead of India'. Here there are not just cracking places which are subsequently worked on further or even just reinterpreted, here time has taught something, and it teaches again back into the play. Therefore, apart from the collected aspect, the *work aspect* does not draw a line under completed endeavours either; instead these structures form the correct conduct in the social struggle for liberation, and they always form it afresh. *They are stance-experiments in the laboratory of the stage, not still lifes dopo lavoro.*

The will to change is the first priority here, it comes out well time and again. In it there are of course various features, they do not combine so simply as intended. One-sidedness rouses for a purpose; but this one-sidedness is like all light, made up of several colours. Of the colour of a thoroughly original person; of a writer who turns to good account even the most contemptible or hackneyed expression. Of a young man who drifts through India with his Kipling, but does not spurn Baker Street either, with Sherlock Holmes at the fireside and Dr Watson, sunk in Afghan memories. Of an old man who loves his classics and to teach from them in many voices like an actor, intolerant as a priest. Most vividly effective are two different keys from the age, one inherently dubious (only Brecht could get away with it) and that splendid, political-revolutionary one which determines all Brecht's writings. The dubious tribute is characterized by a certain approach to the bare, dry fashion of yesterday. Brecht has nothing in common with the bourgeois 'New Objectivity', with that narrowing and reduction which understood truth as drought and reality as lack of imagination; but rather with the kind intended in non-bourgeois terms, which appeared as 'liquidation'. Yet Brecht knew how to animate even this ephemeral phenomenon, at least to use it creatively; Brecht has, as he says of himself, 'the cool of the great forests' in which his mother carried him. It is evidently a different coolness to that of 'liquidation'; Brecht wants 'sparing language, choosing the words cleanly', but in fact he wants with this an exact imagination which calls a spade a spade and cannot be diminished. Brecht's simplicity therefore has nothing in common especially with abstract 'liquidation'; rather, political acidity and fullness make their presence felt. Their mode of expression now looks precisely as variable as the nature of its objects, it sounds disdainful ('You could learn something from this, Brown'), then complicated ('Life is the greatest, nothing else is standing by'), then formulatory ('The question of the meat that is missing in the kitchen is not decided in the kitchen'). And where the nature of the object itself shows no simplicity, sublimely rich expression develops. For example in the duet of the cranes (from 'Mahagonny'), poetry of extraordinary value and not unworthy of late Goethe ('So under sun and moon's little differing discs/They fly out, totally devoted to each other'). It is the old man in Brecht who uses or breaks his simplicity; the old man with Luther's German and realism from Shakespeare; the revenant from the Peasant Wars, then again the

level-headed man from Old China who reveres moderation in the revolution and speaks of it as a legend. This curiously antiquarian tone
runs through the whole of Brecht's work, mixes strangely with tropical
sun and sauciness, significantly with action-direction and Marxism. Very
often Brecht consists of Swabian late Gothic, which suits his disposition,
a form which seems to stand in stark contrast to the content; as in the
poem-title 'Devotions for the Home',[51] in the 'chorale' at the end of the
'Threepenny Opera' and in other hymns of disbelief. But content,
however enlightened, in Brecht seldom has a reassuring effect, something is in the air, and one can see how much is hidden in atheism when
it is no longer grasped in a bourgeois way, as mere denial which has
become comfortable. In this way the colours mingle, more than one
single process gets under way at the same time; one could almost say, in
Brecht's writing there is an element of very old German bolshevism.
   To push forward the new, different, overdue kind, this is what is
being rehearsed from case to case here. In serious cases a stage-case is
underlaid; by means of this the correct choice of action should be
investigated and tested in a model way. This then is Brecht's genuine
tribute to the age, namely to that age which is pregnant with the new
society. And the tribute does not only come from the revolutionary
solidarity of the author, but also from his specific talent: from that of
the concrete director. It is thoroughly associated with the didactic drive
in this writer, with the desire to transform the stage from a 'place of
entertainment' into an 'organ of publication'. Thus Brecht opposes the
'Aristotelian drama of empathy', which allows the audience to work off
their feelings with enjoyment, instead of influencing them by intervention. This intervention in the social conduct of the audience derives
according to Brecht solely from the 'parable-drama' and its epic, objectively observable style based on gesture. One of its methods, indeed the
principal one, is montage, which means in Brecht, the removal of a
person from their previous situation and their refunctioning into a new
one or the testing out of a rule of conduct stemming from another set of
circumstances in a changed relationship. The experiment by means of
montage is not abstract, no 'subversive' intervention into a supposedly
coherent reality in closed form; rather, reality is itself full of interruption. It is intermittent in its continuously dialectical coherence and
precisely because of it, i.e. full of leaps and full of not yet decided
changes posited as finished. And from this perspective precisely the
attempted Leninism of Brecht becomes apparent, the elastic stance- and
action-experiment through situations which are produced on the stage in
a manoeuvre-like way. 'Didactic plays' of this kind are above all 'The
Man Who Says Yes', 'The Measure Taken', 'St Joan' and the dramatic

51 'Hauspostille': an old-fashioned collection of instructional reading for the
   family, the title of Brecht's first collection of poems (1927).

adaptation of Gorky's 'The Mother';[52] common to them all is (dialectical) refunctioning of one element. In 'The Man Who Says Yes' the element is old custom, in 'The Measure Taken' a fourfold morality, in 'St Joan' the sermon of abstract humanity, in 'The Mother' it is motherliness. It is shown by her that she has a reactionary effect in the family, yet in the party, when she has changed her place to there, a progressive, propagandist, conspiratorial effect. Undoubtedly this didactic play style (through displacement of the situations, through damming the dramatic wave, through the production of what was greeted in the previous century with the cry 'Tableau!') is one of the most fruitful renewals. Vividness is essential here, vividness not only of the situations, but above all precisely of the element which is to be rehearsed through, of the maxim which is to be concretely modified. When of course the maxim remains identical and – as a result of its all too obvious simplicity – already stands the same at the beginning as it does at the end, in that case no dialectical didactic play is performed, but rather an example on a model; as in one of the last dramas of Brecht, 'The Rifles of Frau Carrar'. This is also useful, only here nothing is investigated, tested out, varied, but a maxim that was unfounded to begin with is reduced to absurdity. In all other didactic plays, however, the theme has experienced something during its implementation, and this constitutes the characteristic aspect of Brecht dramas; they are *theory-practice-manoeuvres on the stage*.

Once the classless goal has been achieved, there will no longer be so much to learn from plays of this kind. But there remain the valuable treasures, even oddities, which go on and on being relevant to us, as the best writing. To these belong the already mentioned song of the cranes, above all also remarkably deep conclusions, unsettlingly sharp images, forming as they do almost everywhere in Brecht's writing. 'Under our cities there are drains. In them there is nothing and above them there is smoke' – can the capitalist void be described more graphically? 'But the whole of this Mahagonny/Only exists because everything is so bad/Because no calm prevails/And no harmony/And because there is nothing/One can hold on to' – can one find a more demagogic, a more human advertisement for utopia? To read also in 'Mahagonny' scene viii ('All true seekers are disappointed') is to meet one of the most lasting human statements there is. Paul Ackermann repeats there at all possible stages of happiness his unstatic refrain: 'But something is missing.' This is a central phrase, nothing already available now makes it already superfluous, meaningless. But Paul has said all he can, unfortunately comes back with the others to Mahagonny. And as far as the song of Pirate Jenny in 'The Threepenny Opera' is concerned, one has to go back to the Gnostics and the Fathers of the Church to encounter such a phan-

52 Maxim Gorky, 1868–1936, Russian writer.

tasmagoria of incognito, revenge and resurrection. The world-judge, whom the poor hussy in the dive is circling round, is a pirate: 'And the ship with eight sails/And with fifty cannon/Will vanish with me.' Likewise, the work of Brecht packs a punch, it is suitable and effective largely for what is slowly changing and continuing to be relevant. It is true of this work what a poster from Mahagonny promises: 'They were only asking after you yesterday there'. And the darknesses reply, with irritation, those friendly to capital who were not asked, with stupidity, the schematic ones on the left who do not understand it.

Epitaph, 14 August 1956

The blow dealt to us by Brecht's death is cushioned by Brecht himself. The poet has done justice to life and to death with soberly-deep, resonantly-precise wisdom. Another West-östlicher Divan,[53] completely new and equally ancient, Eighteenth Brumaire[54] confronting Lao-Tzu, the one reading and proving through the other. The cloud, 'very white and enormously above', of which Brecht's 'In Memory of Marie A.' speaks, will never disperse. It has become he himself, high and close, pure light and completely human.

53 A cycle of later Goethe poems (1814).
54 Marx, The Eighteenth Brumaire of Louis Bonaparte (1852).

EXPRESSIONISM, SEEN NOW (1937)

It still presumably expresses[55] something. The degenerate[56] pictures were seen by four times as many people as the true-to-type ones. Entrance into the chamber of horrors is of course free, that too must be taken into account, so that the result is not overestimated. Nevertheless it is probable that Marc is a bigger draw than Ziegler,[57] the latest reversal of good and bad has not succeeded. The German learns here to be ashamed of his masters, not only to suffer from them.

But even beyond this an injustice is redressed. How many people still knew further details about the curious Expressionist period and its works? Since 1922 Expressionism had been slandered. Noske's campaigns,[58] the wish for law and order, the pleasure in the given opportunities for earning money and in the stable façade finished it off. This pleasure was called 'New Objectivity'; it admittedly led from all too extravagant dreams back to the world again from time to time, but it concealed the maggot in this world, it became literally the painting of whitewashed graves. Hausenstein[59] and other art-prattlers were quick, in the wake of the 'stabilization', to make the public suspicious of what they had only just been worshipping; most German painters followed the changed economic situation. Klee almost alone, the wondrous dreamer, remained true to himself and to his unrefuted visions, he nailed the Expressionist colours to the mast, and it is not his fault that they

55 'Ausdrücken': in this section 'Ausdruck' is translated 'expression', 'Express-ion' as 'Expression', and 'Expressionismus' as 'Expressionism'.
56 Bloch is referring to the Nazis' exhibition of 'entartete Kunst', see Trans-lators' Introduction.
57 Adolf Ziegler, president of the Reich Chamber of Art who organized the exhibition of 'entartete Kunst'. A close friend of Hitler and himself a mediocre painter.
58 See 'Montage again: of a higher order', n. 24.
59 Wilhelm Hausenstein, author of *Lux perpetua* (1947).

were no longer regarded as a flag, but as a mere handkerchief with a monogram. Also dubious remnants of Expression were left over, like Benn, whose great will towards expression has for too long come up with the primeval slime[60] of today, without a 'balance of perspectives', except the nihilistic one. So Expressionism in Germany perished, in the same country which previously possessed it as the most German expression, as music in painting. Surrealism (to which in France and Czechoslovakia many Expressionist natures have fled) found little reverberation in Germany. The strife-torn environment and the phosphorescing at the edges – all this uncanny reality officially found no expression. Or the expression, when it partially appeared, for example in 'The Threepenny Opera', was conveniently misunderstood, in other cases laughed at. Even Marxists (so that this shall not be concealed) like Lukács have stuck a less than knowledgeable label on Expressionism lock, stock and barrel. They denounce it as 'expression of petit-bourgeois opposition', in fact even, totally schematically, as 'imperialistic superstructure'. But Marc, Klee, Chagall, Kandinsky are hardly accommodated in the cliché 'petite bourgeoisie', and least of all when this cliché is supposed to designate bourgeois conformism, at best of a grouching kind. And even if there were nothing but petit-bourgeois opposition here (one would like to get to know the petit bourgeois whose expression is Marc's 'Tower of the Blue Horses'), is there anything better at the disposal of the petit bourgeois than at best – opposition (and indeed this sort)? But the fact that the Nazi afterwards on occasion, at the beginning, turned Expressionist literary remnants to his own account (Benn) or made a Thingspiel-industry[61] out of them (Euringer),[62] is not to be blamed on Marc's 'imperialism', but on Goebbels's appreciation of effective forgeries (almost regardless what they are based on). And in fact Hitler's latest attack proves that even the so-called 'petit-bourgeois opposition' may not always be so contemptible. It definitely proves that Expressionist art – first demolished by Hausenstein, then much more splendidly by Hitler – contained no justification of the enemy, no ideology of his imperialism and his order. The 'agreement' of a few Moscow intellectuals of schematic type with Hitler is consequently not pleasant. Least of all when even in these times red fanfares are still being trumpeted against Expressionism. From the direction of classicism; but Hitler possesses this too, he has become the ideal of the amateurs and the senior primary school teachers. And Roman eagles, triumphal columns and the rest of the 'noble simplicity, silent

60 Gottfried Benn (see 'Jugglers' fair beneath the gallows', n. 81) often wrote about man returning to a 'healthy' primeval consciousness.
61 *Thingspiel*: theatrical spectacle designed to propagate Nazi ideology, performed in amphitheatres called *Thingstätten*.
62 Richard Euringer: a major Nazi director of *Thingspiele*.

greatness'[63] of today are also certainly just as imperialistic as –
Becher's[64] lyric poetry around 1918 or even Klee's drawing Angelus
Novus.

Thus it is more important than ever to be clear in our minds about the
so bloodily hated pictures. What was intended in 1912–22, why does
that concern us again to some extent, why does the art of these years
seem so 'unhealthy' to Hitler? The conclusion is of course not valid
everywhere that what Hitler is fighting against is the right thing. Since
much, if not most, of what is contained in Nazi judgements is so wrong
that not even its opposite is true. But in the case of 'degenerate art' we
may let the enemy dictate the route of the march, at least his attack
means that the attacked object moves into our vicinity and can demand
faithful examination. Both its bad, empty, stale features and the meanings of *real* Expression have become surveyable and striking today. And
it is chiefly a question of the latter, i.e. of the previous original work
against which even Hitler is taking steps on principle. And here it is
most evident, not only on the surface, but essentially: instead of the
'imperialism' which has been constructed on to it, it definitely contained
anti-capitalism, subjectively unequivocal, objectively still unclear. It
contained objectively archaic shadows, revolutionary lights all mixed up,
dark sides from a subjectivistically unmastered underworld, light sides
from the future, wealth and undistractedness of human expression. An
art which was neither in agreement with the traditional forms nor above
all with the given around it, turned the world into a war at that time.
This war had of course no other weapons except paint-brush and tube,
except direct scream, and its battlefield was the canvas or artistically
printed paper. And the warring power consisted of the pure subject, of
the emotional deprivation and wilderness of the subject, which projected
itself with its magic lantern into an apparently objectless world. The
pictures themselves were in fact fetched, hauled up with a mixture which
is possible only in Germany, in the Germany of Ossian,[65] of Romanticism and ultimately also of the swamp-flowering, freedom-dreaming Art
Nouveau, from archaic and utopian material simultaneously, without
one being able to say precisely where the primeval dream stopped, the
light of the future began. And the world which had apparently been
made objectless, on to which the self-discharging applied itself, gave the
'compositions' or 'constructions' no contact with the real world; even
from this perspective Expressionism was partly 'abstract art', and indeed
in the *bad* sense of this word. Gottfried Keller in 'Der Grüne

63 Winckelmann: see 'Objectivity, direct', n. 19.
64 Johannes R. Becher, 1891–1958, Expressionist writer. He emigrated to
    Russia for the duration of the Nazi regime and was appointed Minister of
    Culture in the GDR in 1954.
65 The verses of Ossian, a legendary warrior, were forgeries composed by
    James Macpherson, 1736–96. They were influential in the Romantic period.
    Both Goethe and Herder were convinced of their authenticity.

Heinrich'[66] long since bestowed a criticism on the *negative aspect* of this abstraction, which anticipates all legitimate criticisms, although the object of the criticism still lay three generations away below the horizon. Grüner Heinrich too, 'in order to seek a refuge', had resorted in 'deep diversion' to the objectless system, had immersed himself for days and weeks on end in the painting of a kind of spider's web, which definitely demonstrated 'certain tangles in the mazes of his soul' and no doubt also caught certain contents of the unconscious, deeply hidden, until his friend, likewise a failed painter, derided the product cleverly, in words which almost remind one of the panegyric with which even bad Expressionism had once been lauded, lauded to the objectless nonsense-skies. In order to distance ourselves from bad Expressionism, but to protect the significant kind all the more emphatically from rejection lock, stock and barrel, from jubilation lock, stock and barrel, nothing is more advisable than to repeat by way of distinction the prophetic words from 'Der Grüne Heinrich', chapter 3, 'Moodiness': 'With this important work, Grüner Heinrich, you have entered and begun a new phase to solve a problem which can be of the greatest influence on the development of German art. It had indeed been unbearable for a long time always to hear people speaking and grumbling about the free world of the beautiful, which exists for itself and which may not be marred by any reality, by any tendency, whereas with the coarsest inconsistency they always still gave expression to people, animals, sky, stars, forest, field and meadow and nothing but such trivially real things ... Well now! You've decided without further ado to throw out everything objective, despicably full of content! These industrious hatchings are hatchings per se, suspended in the perfect freedom of the beautiful: this is industry, efficacy, clarity per se in the most charming abstraction! And these tangles, are they not the triumphant proof of how logic and artistic skill celebrate their finest victories only in the insubstantial, give birth to passions and darkenings in nothingness and brilliantly conquer them?'

Thus Keller, and who doubts that salt could be stupid too? Indeed the *caricature* of Expressionism shows through here, the insubstantial element in which impostors have established themselves, who have painted six hat-boxes, one on top of the other, and, for the sake of external 'objectlessness', were able to pass it off as 'The Birth of Christ'. Less naively than Grüner Heinrich hollow subjectivities, private sphinxes without riddles, were thus also rife at that time, which made a lark out of the void of their late-bourgeois world, meaningless hieroglyphs out of abstractness. Almost uncannily the scorn of a precise, great, arch-objective writer strikes home here; and it is precisely this reverse side of abstractness (whether it is a cubist or symbolist one) which could be rejected as 'formalism' for example. But the *great feats of Expressionism*

66 Keller's major novel (1854–5).

have a completely different status, their signs have a completely different effect – as real signs and as signs of something (humanly) 'real' – on us. Here there is no decay for its own sake, but storm through this world, in order to make room for the images of a more genuine one. Here the will towards change is not confined to canvas and paper, that is to say, to artistic material that contents itself with shocking artistically. Here there is most definitely no prevalence of the archaic, brooding, no intentionally lightless and forged diluvial elements as so often in Benn's work, but integration of the No-Longer-Conscious into the Not-Yet-Conscious, of the long past into the definitely not yet appeared, of the archaically encapsulated into a utopian uncovering which finally does the former justice. Montage, in addition, of transplanted, rearranged parts of the face and world which betray more through this than they could in their old place, this was begun a long time ago in Picasso's work. The pictures of Chagall and Marc contain not irrational material per se, but also a rationalism of the irrational, a philanthropy of the irrational which takes pity on the latter and incorporates it into the person who bends over it. Like guilt which he has forgotten, all this brooding material is confronted with the Expressio and with the light which falls from high above and yet fraternally into the soft or roaring silence of creation, into the untranslated testimony of the primitive, of child-, captive- and lunatic-art, into the stammering letters of mountain, valley and starry sky. There was no objectlessness per se in the work of Klee, Chagall, Marc either; the object (dream-fishes, calves in the mother's womb, animals in the forest) was de-reified instead, brought into our fable. And nowhere here was there progress with the head thrown back, progress into nothingness or into anti-human, anti-cultural primeval sleep (at best with the disturbance of the jungle), but the avant-garde of that time intended man even in the wilderness, concealed or dawning man admittedly; in short, it cultivated the mysteries of humanity. It expanded the world in man, and man in the world, far beyond the previously familiar expression; it sought the scream which did not first roar through a golden harp, i.e. through the harp of the ruling classes and its dishonest, decimating melodious sound. This alone was genuine Expressionism, certainly still an inner-bourgeois revolt, an inner-mythological conquering of mythology, but one which wanted to get out of the night into the light and was not afraid to choose to distil the light from the night of the oppressed rather than from the previously ruling day.

The movement was therefore not by chance, just as little has it already achieved its purpose. The Nazis have profited by its remnants, admittedly only by those that have become stale and been halved. By the dark without dawn, by the archaic without utopia, by the fraudulent or confused scream without human content. And here as everywhere even this partial profit would not have arisen if we had not allowed the irrational to become boggy, instead of exploring it and concretely doing justice to it. Expressionism, it has been said, is as old as artistic expression itself; it is to be found wherever unregulated 'emotion' (no matter which) outweighs 'reason'. This is undoubtedly a too broad, an itself unregulated and above all contentless formulation; not only the form (let alone mere formlessness), but also the specifically human content makes valid Expression. The humanly subject-based aspect indeed forms precisely the positive element in the undeniable (and dubious) subjectivity of Expressionism; an undistractedly human element became known Expressionistically. As escape, protest and confusion, as new form and creation simultaneously, the movement was already inherent in such illustrious names as Gauguin, van Gogh, Rimbaud; and undischarged, as a stream which least of all runs dry in the subterranean, it runs on in surrealism. More clearly than surrealism, however (with its montage, its threateningly cited fragments from the nineteenth century, its phosphorescing into the unknown) – more clearly Expressionism was centred around the humane. We enlisted Keller above against the caricatures; as testimony of the originally Expressionistic impulse let us here mention the contemplation of a philosophical work which originated in the final heyday of Expressionism and which reflected the production of its ornament. The passage runs thus (Geist der Utopie (1918), pp. 50f.):[67] 'We are searching for the magic creator who will cause things to approach ourselves, us to meet ourselves. The new gaze kneads around unrecognizably and moves like a swimmer, like a cyclone through the given. All those should keep this in view who need to ask with every Expressionist picture what it represents, i.e. by what means to their eye, which is like a mere photographic plate, a hell can now once more shrink back into a street-corner. Because already since van Gogh it has clearly become different: we are suddenly in the middle of it all, and precisely this is painted; it is indeed still visible crowd, still railings, bridge, iron girders, brick wall, but it intersects suddenly in a strange way, the discarded cornerstone all at once strikes sparks, and what is signed in all appearances, what is incomprehensibly related to us, lost to us, the near, distant, Sais-like[68] aspect of the world, comes to light in van Gogh's pictures. And then it goes further, to confront itself, further in burning around, grass is no longer grass, the diversity disappears and the visionary triumphs. The thing becomes a mask, a concept, the totally deformed, denaturalized formula of secret goal-excitations, the human inside and the inside of the world move closer together. Even if van Gogh still pointed out of ourselves, if things still speak in his work, no matter how violently they speak, seemingly only

---

67 Bloch's own early work.
68 Sais: ancient Egyptian city in the Nile delta, renowned for a mysterious veiled image.

of themselves and not as an echo of man, then we suddenly resound back from them, then in the new Expressionism man is a Kaspar Hauser nature[69] which uses objects solely as memory-signs of its hidden origin or as written signs for the retention and preservation of its progressive re-remembering. Here sculptures, strangely familiar, can appear to us like earth-mirrors in which we glimpse our future, like the disguised ornaments of our innermost form. This is the same as the longing finally to see the face of man, and thus even for magic sculpture there can be no other dream-roads any longer except those on which the experience of riding towards oneself can happen, and no other relationship to objects except one which reflects the secret outline of the face of man all over the world and thus combines the most abstract organics with the longing for our heart, for the fullness of appearance to oneself.' Thus far the interpretation at that time, not unrelated to Expression, and undoubtedly it refers to problems of unexhausted, of utopian humanity. Undoubtedly these problems are and remain the most stirring in the course of the whole revolutionary mobilization, including that in painting. Humanity distinguishes socialism from fascism; reason enough to remember with honour an art which the philistine spits on, an art in which human stars – however insufficient, however strange – have burned or wanted to burn.

One other factor makes this review new and inevitable. Before us stands the problem of cultural inheritance; but why has it become a fresh problem, a thoroughly bold one? Simply because the Expressionist epoch so completely tore to shreds the casual routine, the conventional associations from the past. The people with 'the works of our fathers' in the previous century were not heirs, but epigones; Goethe's words weighed heavily on them: 'Alas, you are a grandchild.' Youth, however, which is renewing itself in our century, renewing itself time and again, has the great past not as curse, but as testimony. Since it has itself experienced what expression is in its genuineness and glow, and that it is something other than the petrified objet d'art that can only be eternally copied. This too obliges us to thank 'degenerate art'; the epigone, of course, finds in the past only a 'wealth of forms', the Nazi though only the kitsch that he is himself. But the Expressionists dug out fresh water and fire, wells and wild light, at least the will towards light. Not through this alone, but in the wake of this renewal the view of the artistic past has also been refreshed, it shines in new, and thus currently burst-open, contemporaneous depth.

69   Kaspar Hauser, 1812–33, the mysterious foundling who suddenly appeared in Nuremberg in 1828.

DISCUSSIONS OF EXPRESSIONISM
(1938)

Excellent that conflicts are beginning again here. A short time ago this seemed unthinkable, the 'Blue Rider' was dead. Now not only voices are raised which remember it with respect. Almost more important is the fact that others are getting so acutely angry about a past movement, as if it were a contemporary one and stood in their path. It is certainly not so contemporary, but has it not yet had its day?

One commentator presented this as if it continued to spook around only in a few elderly hearts. Previously these were moved by youth, now they are professing faith in the classical inheritance, but still suffer from certain remnants. Ziegler[70] (in 'Das Wort', Moscow (1937), no. 9) sees an Expressionist who seems especially concise – Benn – ending in fascism and concludes from this: 'This end is part of a logical pattern.' The other Expressionists were just not consistent enough to find it; today it can clearly be seen which spirit Expressionism was the child of, and where this spirit, followed to its conclusion, leads: into fascism. According to this view the newly awakened anger with the Expressionists is thus not only private, but politico-cultural, anti-fascist: the 'dawning of mankind'[71] of that time was a – premise of Hitler. Only here the misfortune befell Ziegler (his name in reality is Alfred Kurella and he continued to be known by it) that a few weeks before Ziegler's genealogy was published Hitler in his Munich speech and exhibition did not in the least recognize the premise. On the contrary, as is well-known, a false derivation, a hastily negative value-judgement, has seldom been more quickly and manifestly reduced to absurdity.

Was it also fundamentally reduced to absurdity, i.e. in a way adequate for us? The agreement in which Ziegler, to his horror, found himself with Hitler, is certainly fatal, but the deceiver in Munich could have had

---

70 Bernhard Ziegler, pseudonym of Alfred Kurella. He held the view that Expressionism led directly to fascism.
71 The title of Kurt Pinthus's famous anthology of Expressionist verse (1919).

a reason (though it is difficult to see what it could be) for covering over the tracks of fascism. In order to clarify the fundamental question therefore, it is appropriate not to single out the chronological accident of the Ziegler article, nor even the article itself, but to pick up that 'groundwork' of the whole which Leschnitzer[72] has already pointed out in his lyrical contribution to the discussion. We mean therefore the four-year-old essay by Lukács: 'Greatness and Decline of Expressionism' (Internationale Literatur (1934), no. 1, reprinted in 'Schicksalswende' (Aufbau-Verlag, 1948), pp. 180–235); it contains the draft for the latest funeral oration on Expressionism. We refer in the following essentially to this essay, since it underlies intellectually the contributions of Ziegler and also Leschnitzer. Lukács is in fact considerably more cautious in formulating his conclusions, he emphasizes that the conscious tendencies of Expressionism were not fascist ones, that it could ultimately 'be incorporated into the fascist "synthesis" only as a subordinate factor'. But the conclusion nevertheless remarks that 'the fascists – with a certain justification – see in Expressionism a useful inheritance for themselves'. Goebbels finds 'healthy beginnings' here for his interests, since 'Expressionism as literary form of expression of developed imperialism [!] rests on an irrationalistic-mythological basis; its creative method moves in the direction of the pathetic-empty, declamatory manifesto, of the proclamation of a pseudo-activism ... The Expressionists undoubtedly wanted anything but a retrogression. However, since they could not divorce themselves ideologically from the ground of imperialistic parasitism, since they were complicit with the ideological decline of the imperialistic bourgeoisie without criticism and without resistance, indeed were temporarily its engineers, their creative method does not have to be distorted when it is pressed into the service of fascist demagogy, of the unity of decline and retrogression.' It is evident: the interpretation that Expressionism and fascism are children of the same spirit has its fundamental starting-point here. The antithesis, Expressionism and – let us say – classical inheritance, is also just as rigid in Lukács as in Ziegler, only it consists less of feuilleton zeal, is conceptually well-grounded.

Though not factually as well, with regard to the material; here much is in a bad way. Anyone who picks up Lukács's essay (which is very advisable, the original is always most instructive) will notice immediately that not one line mentions any Expressionist painters. Marc, Klee, Kokoschka, Nolde, Kandinsky, Grosz, Dix, Chagall are not present (not to mention musical parallels, the Schönberg of that time). This is all the more surprising since not only the connections between painting and literature were the closest at that time, but also the Expressionist pic-

---

72 Franz Leschnitzer was one of the figures involved in the Expressionism debate from Moscow along with Kurella.

tures are much more characteristic of the movement than the literature. Moreover painting would have provided a desirable impediment to the scathing judgement, since a few of these pictures remain lastingly important and great. But even the literary creations are considered neither in a quantitatively nor qualitatively sufficient way; the critic contents himself with a very small, barely characteristic 'selection'. Trakl,[73] Heym,[74] Else Lasker-Schüler[75] are completely missing: early Werfel[76] is taken note of only in view of the pacifist tenor of a few lines of verse, likewise Ehrenstein[77] and Hasenclever.[78] Whereas of the early, often significant poems of Johannes R. Becher it is affirmed only that the author has succeeded in 'gradually getting rid of' the Expressionist method, would-be poets like Ludwig Rubiner[79] are quoted thoroughly, yet once again only for the purpose of corroborating from them what – abstract pacifism is. Here characteristically a quotation from René Schickele[80] also appears, although Schickele was never an Expressionist, but in fact only an abstract pacifist (like many worthy writers and men at that time, Hermann Hesse,[81] Stefan Zweig[82] among them). But what is then the material from which Lukács makes an interpretation of Expressionism clear? It is forewords or afterwords to anthologies, 'introductions' by Pinthus, newspaper articles by Leonhardt,[83] Rubiner, Hiller[84] and others of that ilk. It is thus not the matter itself, with its concrete impression there and then, with its reality to be re-experienced, but the material is already itself indirect, is literature about Expressionism, which is literarized, theorized and criticized a second time. Certainly for the purpose of making clear 'the social basis of this movement and the ideological assumptions arising from it', but with the methodological limitation that a concept is given from concepts, an essay on essays and

73 Georg Trakl, 1887–1914, early Expressionist Austrian poet.
74 Georg Heym, 1887–1912, early Expressionist poet in Berlin.
75 Else Lasker-Schüler, 1869–1945, Expressionist poetess.
76 Franz Werfel, 1890–1945, Prague poet who introduced the 'O Mankind' type of Expressionist poetry. Later became a novelist.
77 Albert Ehrenstein, 1886–1950, Expressionist poet and prose-writer.
78 Walter Hasenclever, 1890–1940, Expressionist dramatist and poet. His best-known play, *Der Sohn*, appeared in 1914.
79 Ludwig Rubiner, 1881–1920, writer and translator. An exponent of political activism, he wrote manifestos as well as literary works.
80 René Schickele, 1883–1940, poet, writer and editor of the *Weisse Blätter* (1914–20). Developed poetically from Art Nouveau through Expressionism to New Objectivity.
81 Hermann Hesse, 1877–1962, the celebrated neo-Romantic writer, author of *Steppenwolf*.
82 Stefan Zweig, 1881–1942, Austrian writer and poet with neo-Romantic leanings during this period.
83 Rudolf Leonhard, 1889–1953, socialist and pacifist writer and poet.
84 Kurt Hiller, 1885–1973, writer and publicist, leading activist expressionist in the post-war period.

lesser material. Thence also the almost exclusive criticism of mere Expressionist tendencies and programmes (mostly those which the littérateurs of the movement first formulated, if not brought in with them). Very many correct and fine statements are to be found in this context; Lukács characterizes abstract pacifism, the bohemian concept of 'bourgeoisness', the 'escape-character', the 'escape-ideology', then again the merely subjective revolt in Expressionism, also the abstract mystification of the 'essence' of Expressionistically represented things. But even the subjective revolt of this movement is hardly sufficiently grasped, when Lukács – on the strength of the 'forewords' – chalks up simply the 'fanfare-like arrogance', the 'tinny monomentality'. When in terms of content he simply finds 'petit-bourgeois helplessness and forlornness in the hurly-burly of capitalism', 'the impotent rebellion of the petit bourgeois against his being worn down and crushed by capitalism'. Even if nothing else had appeared, even if the Expressionists really had had nothing else to report during the World War except peace and the end of tyranny, this would still be no reason to characterize their struggle, as Lukács does, as mere sham struggle, indeed to certify that it represented a mere 'pseudo-critical, abstractly-distorting, mythicizing nature of the *imperialistic* [my italics, E.B.] mock-oppositions'. It is true, Werfel and others of his kind transformed their abstract pacifism *after* the end of the war into a toy trumpet; the watchword 'non-violence', in the face of the new situation, of the revolution, thus turned into an objectively counter-revolutionary one. But this does not alter the fact that, *during the war itself* and before its possible conversion into civil war, this watchword was a thoroughly revolutionary, even objectively-revolutionary one, that it was also understood as such by the politicians determined to hold out. Incidentally, many Expressionists also had a word or two to say about 'armed kindness', about the scourge of Christ driving the money-lenders out of the temple; this love of humanity was not so totally clueless. Even the statement that Expressionism did not leave the 'common ideological ground of German imperialism', that it was consequently even useful to imperialism through mere 'apologetic criticism', is not only one-sided and distorted, but gives an inflatedly distorted classic example of the banal sociologism and schematism opposed by Lukács himself. But, as we have said, that almost solely quoted by Lukács did not belong at all to *shaping* Expressionism, as it solely interests us as a phenomenon anyway. It belongs essentially to the 'Goal-Yearbook' and similar quite rightfully forgotten diatribes, (even if these, under the leadership of Heinrich Mann, in no way imperialized). But in the still mysterious subject-outbursts in the archaic-utopian hypostases of the art of that time we also encounter, as need not be first affirmed, considerably more than the 'USP ideology'[85]

85   See 'A victory of the magazine', n. 20.

to which Lukács moreover would like to reduce Expressionism. Subject-outbursts into the merely objectless are in fact undoubtedly even more dubious than they are mysterious; their material, however, is hardly sufficiently paraphrased by mere 'petit-bourgeois helplessness and forlornness'. It is a different material, partly composed of archaic images, but partly also composed of revolutionary imagination, of a critical and frequently concrete kind. Anyone who had ears to hear would have been able to perceive in these outbursts a productive aspect in revolutionary terms, even if it was irregular and without supervision. Even if it still 'undermined' so much 'classical inheritance', i.e. at that time, classical casual routine. Lasting neo-classicism or the belief that everything produced after Homer and Goethe is unrespectable unless it is made in accordance with their model, or rather the abstraction from it, this is of course no standpoint from which to judge the art of the penultimate avant-garde and to see that everything is right within it.

With such a position, is there anything at all in the way of recent artistic experiments which is not given a dressing-down? They are summarily assigned to capitalist decadence and not only, as goes without saying, to a certain extent, but a hundred per cent, lock, stock and barrel. Then there is no avant-garde within late capitalist society, anticipatory movements in the superstructure are not supposed to be true. This is like a black-and-white drawing, which scarcely does justice to the real circumstances, and even less so to the propagandistic ones. It ascribes almost all oppositions to the ruling class which are not Communist from the outset to the ruling class. It ascribes them to it even when the opposition, as Lukács inconsistently admits in the case of Expressionism, was subjectively benevolent and felt opposed to the tendencies of the later fascism, and painted and wrote against them. In the age of the popular front a continuation of this black-and-white technique seems less appropriate than ever; it is mechanical, not dialectical. Underlying the whole dressing-down and purely negativistic criticism is the theory that since the ending of the path Hegel-Feuerbach-Marx there is absolutely nothing more to learn from the bourgeoisie, except technology and possibly science; everything else is at best 'sociologically' interesting. Thus even such peculiar and previously unheard-of phenomena like Expressionism are condemned from the outset as pseudo-revolutionary. Thus the Expressionists are granted, indeed driven to the Nazis as forerunners, Streicher's genealogical tree sees itself improved in a totally improbable, highly confusing way. Ziegler in fact made a climax out of names which are chasms apart, but he separates them only by commas and puts one after the other, as brothers of the same 'gnawing' spirit: 'Bachofen, Rohde, Burckhardt, Nietzsche, Chamberlain, Bäumler, Rosenberg'. Lukács now even doubts Cézanne's substance as a painter for the reasons given above, and speaks of the great Impressionists as a whole (i.e. not only of the Expressionists) as if of the decline of the West. He leaves nothing of them in his essay except 'the emptiness of content . . . which becomes apparent artistically in the accumulation of insubstantial, merely subjectively significant superficial features'. Against this, classicism looms large, in Ziegler even Winckelmann's antiquity, the noble simplicity, silent greatness, the culture of the undecayed bourgeoisie, the world of a hundred and even more years ago; it alone is the inheritance. Against such simplification it may perhaps be remembered that the age of classicism was not only the age of the rising German bourgeoisie, but also of the Holy Alliance; that column-classicism, the 'strict' manor house style have this reaction in mind; that even Winckelmann's antiquity is in no way without feudal composure. It is true that the laudatores temporis acti do not exclusively stop with Homer and Goethe. Lukács reveres Balzac most highly, identifies Heine as a national poet, and is on occasion so far removed from classicism that in his Heine essay he called Mörike,[86] who is regarded by all lovers of earlier literature as one of the most genuine German lyric poets, a 'cute little dwarf'. Everywhere else, however, the Classical is the healthy here, the Romantic the sick,[87] Expressionism the sickest thing of all, and this not only on account of the chronological decrescendo of these creations, but admittedly also – as Lukács emphasizes with downright Romantic invocation of closed ages – on account of the beautifully sweeping element and elegant proportions, on account of the *undecayed objective realism* which characterizes classicism. It is not the place to go into this point here; it would require the most thorough treatment precisely on account of its importance, but in addition all the problems of dialectical-materialistic image-theory would have to be voiced. Here let us only say this much: Lukács presupposes everywhere a closed coherent reality, and one in which the subjective factor of idealism admittedly has no place, but instead the uninterrupted 'totality' which has flourished best in idealistic systems, and thus also in those of classical German philosophy. Whether this is Reality is open to question; if it is, then of course the Expressionist experiments with fragmentation and interpolation, as well as the recent experiments with intermission and montage, are empty games. But perhaps Lukács's Reality, that of the endlessly mediated totality-coherence, is not so – objective at all; perhaps Lukács's concept of Reality itself still contains classical-systematic features; perhaps genuine reality is also – interruption. Because Lukács has an objectivistically-closed concept of Reality, he therefore opposes, apropos of Expressionism, every artistic attempt to chop to pieces a world-picture (even if the world-picture is that of capitalism). He therefore sees in an art which

---

86   Eduard Mörike, 1804–1875, Romantic poet and novelist, author of *Maler Nolten*.

87   A dictum of Goethe's.

utilizes *real* underminings of the surface-coherence and attempts to discover something new in the hollow spaces, only subjectivistic undermining itself; he therefore equates the experiment of chopping to pieces with the condition of decline.

At this point, finally, even astuteness wanes. Undoubtedly, the Expressionists used late-bourgeois decline and even continued it. Lukács holds it against them that 'they were complicit with the ideological decline of the imperialistic bourgeoisie without criticism and without resistance, indeed were temporarily its engineers'. But in the first place this is very little true as far as the flat sense of 'complicity' is concerned; Lukács himself recognizes Expressionism as an 'ideologically not insubstantial component of the German anti-war movement'. But then, as far as 'complicity' in the productive sense is concerned, the actual continuation of *cultural* decline: is there no dialectical relationship between decline and ascent? Does even the confused, immature and incomprehensible material automatically belong, in all cases, to bourgeois decadence? Can it not also – contrary to this simplistic, surely not revolutionary opinion – belong to the transition from the old world into the new? At least to the struggle for this transition; whereby simply immanent-concrete criticism but not one on the basis of all-knowing pre-judgements can help further. The Expressionists were 'engineers' of the decay: would it have been better if they had wanted to be doctors at the sick-bed of capitalism? If they had patched up the surface-coherence again (for example in the sense New Objectivity or neo-classicism did), instead of tearing it open even further? Ziegler even accuses the Expressionists of 'undermining the undermining', i.e. a double minus, without considering in his hatred that out of this generally comes a plus; for the decline of classicism he has no appreciation at all. Definitely none for the strangest contents which became visible precisely in the collapse of the surface-world, and for the problem of montage. For him this is all 'pitifully glued junk', and junk that he holds against the fascists, although they do not want it at all and are quite of his opinion. Expressionism had significance precisely in that for which Ziegler condemns it: it undermined the casual routine and academicism into which 'works of art' had degenerated. Instead of the eternal 'analysis of form' on the objet d'art, it referred to man and his content pressing for the most genuine expression possible. There is no doubt that swindlers seized hold of precisely this unsecured and easily imitable directness, that the all too subjectivist breakthrough- and premonition-contents were not always, in fact seldom, canonical. But a just and factual evaluation must stick to the real Expressionists and not, for the sake of easier criticism, to distorted pictures or even just to distorted pictures from one's own memory. Expressionism was a previously unheard-of phenomenon, but it did not feel itself to be without tradition by any means; on the contrary, it definitely sought, as the 'Blue Rider' proves, its witnesses in the past, it believed it found correspondences in Grünewald,[88] in primitive art, even in the Baroque, it stressed rather too many correspondences than too few. It saw literary forerunners in the Sturm und Drang, highly-revered models in the visionary creations of the young and the very old Goethe, in 'Wanderers Sturmlied', in 'Harzreise im Winter', in 'Pandora' and in the late Faust. Expressionism had no anti-popular arrogance at all either; again on the contrary, the 'Blue Rider' depicted Murnau glass-pictures, it first opened up the view of this moving and uncanny peasant art, of the drawings of children and of prisoners, of the shattering documents of the mentally ill, of the art of the primitives. It emphasized Nordic ornamentation, i.e. the wildly entwined carving which was preserved on peasant chairs and peasant chests until well into the eighteenth century, as the first 'organic-psychic style'. It emphasized this phenomenon as secret Gothic and set it against the humanless, crystalline lordly-style of Egypt and even of classicism. That the art-historical specialist term 'Nordic ornamentation', indeed even the solemnity with which this phenomenon was greeted by the Expressionists has nothing in common with Rosenberg's Nordic swindle and does not represent its 'beginnings' hardly needs to be affirmed. All the less so, as Nordic carving is full of oriental influences; the carpet, the 'linear creation' of ornamentation in general, was another contribution to Expressionism. And indeed one more factor, the most important: Expressionism, for all its pleasure in 'barbaric art', was directed towards the humane, it orbited almost exclusively human material and the form of expression of its incognito. Quite apart from pacifism, even the Expressionist caricatures and industrializations testify to this; the word 'man' was just as frequently used at that time as its opposite is today by the Nazis: the beautiful beast. It was also misused, then there was 'resolute humanity' everywhere, the anthologies were called 'Dawning of Humanity' or 'Comrades of Humanity' – purely overblown categories, but reliably not pre-fascist ones. The genuine revolutionary, materialistically clear humanism has every reason to reject these overblown categories, no one is demanding either that it takes Expressionism as its model or from its point of view as its 'forerunner'. But there is just as little cause to attract attention to a neo-classicist interest through superannuated struggle with devalued Expressionism. Something that is not a forerunner can nevertheless for this reason – in its will towards expression and its interim-existence – be closer to young artists than a trebly epigonic classicism which also calls itself 'socialist realism' and is administered as such. This is foisted upon the painting, architecture and writing of the revolution in a suffocating way, and there is no Greek vase-painting here, but later Becher as red Wildenbruch[89] and Zieglers-

88   Matthias Grünewald, c.1480–1528, German painter.
89   Ernst Wildenbruch, 1845–1909, patriotic writer.

tic stuff as the true, the good, the beautiful. As unreally as possible a declining world composed of interwoven fragments, a rising world composed of tendency and experiment is 'depicted' with the false formal yardstick of yesterday. Even more genuine classicism is of course culture, but culture that has become duplicated, abstractly formed; it is culture, seen through no temperament.

Nevertheless the previous glow still excites, even as such. Is Expressionism therefore not yet superannuated, has it not yet had its day? With this question we would have come back, almost involuntarily, to the beginning of our contemplations. The voices raised in anger certainly do not yet suffice to affirm it, even Ziegler's three other problems at the end of his article shed no light on this. For the purpose of an anti-Expressionist self-examination Ziegler asks firstly: 'The ancient world: "Noble simplicity and silent greatness" – do we see it as such?' Secondly: 'Formalism: main enemy of a literature which is really striving for great heights – do we agree with this?' Thirdly: 'Folk-closeness and folksiness: the basic criteria of all truly great art – do we unconditionally affirm this?' It is clear that even the person who answers no to these questions, not to mention the one who sees them as being posed incorrectly, must therefore not yet harbour any 'remnants of Expressionism' within himself. Hitler – this reminder is unfortunately unavoidable with such summarily posed questions – Hitler has in fact already unreservedly answered yes to the first and third question and is still not our man even so. But let us leave the 'noble simplicity and silent greatness', a purely historical-contemplative question and a contemplative stance to the historical. Let us remain with the questions of 'formalism' and 'folk-closeness', however fuzzily these problems may have been posed in the present context. We know for sure, however, that formalism was the least mistake of Expressionist art (which we must not confuse with Cubism). It suffered rather from too little forming, from a rawly or wildly or confusedly hurled-out fullness of expression; the unshaped element was its stigma. But so of course was folk-closeness, folklore: in complete contradiction therefore to Ziegler's view, who imagined Winckelmann's ancient world and the academicism which was drawn from it as a kind of Natural Right in art. Kitsch is also folksy in the bad sense, of course; the peasant of the nineteenth century exchanged his decorated cupboard for a factory Vertiko,[90] the ancient stained glass-pictures for an oleograph, and thought he had arrived. But one would hardly wish to call these most poisonous fruits of capitalization folksy; they have demonstrably grown in different soil and will disappear with it. Neo-classicism is not so certainly an antidote to the kitsch and an element of real folk-closeness; instead it is itself far too much the 'higher' aspect,

90 Vertiko: a cupboard with removable top, named after the Berlin carpenter who first patented it.

that which has been falsely set on top. Whereas the Expressionists of course, as already noted, definitely went back to folk art, loved and respected folklore, indeed first discovered it for painting. Particularly painters from peoples of recent independence, Czechoslovakian, Latvian, Yugoslavian painters found around 1918 in Expressionism a mode of expression which was significantly closer to their native folklore than most previous artistic styles (to say nothing of academicism). And if in many cases (not in all, when we think of Grosz or Dix or even of the young Brecht) Expressionist art remained incomprehensible to the observer, that can mean that what was striven for was not attained, but it can also mean that the observer is showing neither the mental grasp of unspoilt folk nor the open-mindedness which is indispensable for the understanding of any new art. If the will of the artist is decisive for Ziegler, then Expressionism was really a breakthrough to folk-closeness. If the attained achievement is decisive, then understanding cannot be required for every individual stage of the process: Picasso was the first to paint 'glued junk', to the horror even of the educated people; or very much further down: Heartfield's[91] satirical photo-collages were so close to the folk that many educated people do not want to have anything to do with montage. And if Expressionism still gives cause for agitation today, at any rate has not become unworthy of discussion, then the 'USP ideology', which is undoubtedly without foundation today, does not seem to have been the only one in Expressionism either. Its problems remain worthy of consideration for as long as it takes until they are resolved by better solutions than the Expressionist ones were. An abstraction, however, which would like to skip the last decades of our cultural history, in so far as it is not a purely proletarian one, hardly provides these better solutions. The inheritance of Expressionism is not yet at an end, because it has not yet been started on at all.

91 John Heartfield, 1891–1968, German painter, designer and journalist, best known for his memorable political photomontages.

THE PROBLEM OF EXPRESSIONISM ONCE AGAIN (1940)

The thus affected glance has stopped being direct. It is essentially mediated, in the same strain as its objects are. But now such an essential
relationship occurs in various form according to the times in which it
opens up objectively: as *abruptly mediated* or as *broadly mediated*. In
one case precisely what has been overlooked or what has decayed
becomes meaningful, in the other case the whole and essential material
opens only in the breadth of the context.

Abruptly mediated, it can certainly also proceed in disorderly fashion.
It is then threatened by the direct aspect of a merely subjective experience. But the very situation of the times, in which the abrupt, often
fragmenting glances towards concealed and peculiar things become significant, shows that a real matter – and in fact of a strange kind – is
interfering. An essential relationship behaves in an abruptly mediated
way above all in those times when as a consequence of unsecured
conditions holes and hollow spaces open up in the previously smooth
context; about this and about that which appears in them the – one
might say – irregular artists give information in their own way.
Openings-up of this kind have appeared time and again since the end of
the Middle Ages, i.e. in the hollow spaces which arise as a consequence
of the long-lasting collapse of an old society, but above all as a result of
the excavation of a newly rising one, just as in the early twilight night
and morning are mixed together. Of course only the shapes of the
predominating, in fact ruling morning glance are important, despite all
the peculiarity which indeed characterizes these still unordered crack-
creations. Thus in painting a mixed, but nevertheless not unrelated series
extends from Baldung Grien,[92] from the mock-humorously-gruesome
Hieronymus Bosch to the indignantly-real grotesques of Goya, to
dismantlingly-shocking strangenesses of Franz Marc, Chagall, Picasso.

92 Hans Baldung Grien, 1484/5–1545, German painter.

In poetry a series, however itself interrupted, extends from François Villon, this medieval beginning of all 'irregular authors', to the 'wild Apollo' in revolutionary Sturm und Drang, to the early works of Bertolt Brecht. Whereby evidently it is not the random authors who are themselves decayed, those being or remaining decadents who are primarily remarkable (although even they may have fostered comical or Stygian objects which are now to be held up to the light). Important are rather the masters of *true mediation through abruptness*: smashing into the incidental dimension and the homelessnesses of the hollow space (although these too had to pay in many cases some of the production costs of their works to the decadence of the others, indeed occasionally stood with one foot still inside it). The whole phenomenon culminated correspondingly during rapid collapses of the bourgeois house, during the final crisis of capitalism. And since evening red and morning red can intersect with each other dialectically in the crisis, Expressionism, and then, as Ernst Fischer[93] rightly emphasizes, Surrealism were occasionally in the position of possibly providing a by no means merely subjectivist, let alone formalistic, montage. This kind of thing appears in the opus of the Communist Picasso very remote from the mere art of decadence, in all those late-early birth-allegories composed of chopping to pieces, indeed of decay. It is thus in no way as if such abrupt mediation were not – mediation at all, that is without relation to the strife-torn reality itself, rebus sic non stantibus. Or as if there were here, as Lukács maintains, only distortion, reversal of an inherently balanced, so to speak always formally perfect reality-context. On the contrary: even the world of Goya, and especially the 'Guernica'-world of Picasso definitely did not first wait for strife-torn modes of experience to be full of hollow spaces, torture-chambers, tension-figures. Independently of mere subjectivisms *reality in times of crisis* is itself a largely split one, *in no way attainable only with broad-calm mediation*. The crisis is the divergence of the ever more independent moments, and if the crisis, according to this great Marx definition, also equally 'manifests the unity of the moments rendered independent against each other', then in no way as previous bourgeois classicism and its reproducibility, indeed exemplariness, just as if in time and content nothing had happened. The Marx quotation points to the fact that the dialectic as *unity* of the unity and the contradictions can never be mocked, but this of course does not mean to say that the crisis is a paragon of order and uniformity. The latter is rather – and thus the transition from the abruptly to the *broadly-mediated aspect* is produced – only representable in relatively calm peak-times of a social stabilization or else – most concretely – only in a society after successful social revolution, without crises, but also without great difficulties of social construction. *Broad mediation* there-

93 Ernst Fischer, 1899–1972, Austrian Marxist writer on aesthetics.

fore, this happier mode of essential relation, it is certainly not threatened by disorderly material and by the direct aspect of a merely subjective experience like the abruptly mediated material. But rather this mode is threatened in all *ages of transition* by *all too ordered material*, i.e. by *epigonic classicism* which passes off its merely idealistically-formal totality falsely as realistic. Broad mediation in the really concrete and then of course in fact most concrete sense is possible only where a world which has become socialist is no longer full of crises, or else, in the previous prehistory of humanity, where the glance goes out from a great work of art in a very far-seeing way, i.e. at the attained peak of a progressive culture. This happened in Giotto and Dante, philosophically in Thomas Aquinas, it happened – already mixed in with a wealth of 'irregular authors' – in the great novel of modern times, in Shakespeare's world-drama – with a relative Totum of the social context, with a utopian-entelechetical Totum of the characters, situations, actions at the same time. But of course trenchantly interrupting instances are not lacking here either; since in fact reality is never unbroken context even in times and great works of broadly possible mediation, but always still – interruption and always still fragment.

RELATIVISMS AND EMPTY MONTAGE

The fresh draught changes up here. Youth lies confusedly and maliciously way back. Its teachers have also been going downhill, but into the bad old ways. Without exception, the student now bears the home from which he comes with him, mostly the narrow one. Adopts the wishes, the vindictiveness, the unaired opinions of the sinking centre. He avoids thinking because he would have to recognize how desperate the situation of the class is which he wants to maintain, in which he wants to prosper. Now many students at the universities are seeking a kind of father (mostly because they have not had an adequate one at home); they are seeking him more urgently than they are a lover. But the teachers who serve this purpose stem, as younger ones, mostly from the same centre as the students, a sinking, irritated, mistaken one; as older ones, and also upper middle-class ones, they only chum up to youth or live in magnificent imperial sunshine anyway. Their attitude towards the national-'revolutionary' students is the same as that of heavy industry to the SA troops: they are ideological viceroys of heavy industry in the academic storm.[94] It is clear that under such rusty circumstances, allied with such withered consciousness, studies do not flourish. The place in general where the nationalist students take counsel does not lie within the university any more, at any rate contradicts its previous rational-humanist tradition. The maxim 'One does not die for a programme one has understood, one dies for a programme one loves', this fundamental National Socialist maxim, a creed not just of dull youths and unconscious squanderers of conviction, but of the fieriest 'academics' of today, leads into dervish-like encampments, not into lecture halls. Thus the 'reason' of German colleges is at best still in their technologically purposeful subjects, and the 'systematic' educational

94 Bloch has the Nazi SA ('Sturmabteilung', stormtroopers) in mind again here.

ideal (from the age of Humboldt)[95] is long past. Indeed, even viewed in socialist terms there could be little worth retaining and certainly nothing worth repairing in the 'educational ideals', in the remnants and egghead contortions of the philosophical university, where it still exists, with a German National[96] tradition. For socialism, almost only the technologically rational subjects remain as a *direct* inheritance, at any rate they have more future than an educational ideal which, not without reason, has burst, relativistically on the one hand, irrationally on the other. Even the young church has not occupied the temples but the basilicas. At any rate the humanistic-ideal superstructure which the Sprangers[97] or Rickerts[98] were still providing up till then was lost toto coelo to the 'universitas litterarum'. Epigonism was not able to maintain it against the economic-political reality, nor even against the mythical superstructure which now conceals what is real better than the humanistic-ideal one. It is instructive, however, beyond the egghead contortions and the 'educational ideal', to examine *indirectly* the nevertheless most advanced forms of decay of bourgeois philosophy; they hang in the basilica like articles from a bankrupt's estate, also like a non-Euclidean, non-mechanical forget-me-not, and also like tributes of virtue to vice. Modern 'empiricists' must automatically subvert the bourgeois Ratio and they make it mobile, namely with models. But even modern idealists have reached a zero point of bourgeois Ratio, namely so-called 'existing'; they fill its abstract abyss partly with emotional 'ontology' (from late-bourgeois moods), partly with 'ciphers' from collapsed orders. Under the appearance of a beginning a bourgeois end to thinking sells itself here, with a false gesture or 'a questioning, uncovered withstanding amidst the uncertainty of That-Which-Is in the whole' (Heidegger), with insubstantial solutions. But over the drive-organization and the activities of a dying political clique there are very colourful death throes; a logic and metaphysics so to speak of questioning death throes. A glance which is at home with hollow spaces will therefore, occasionally, sense problems here which stand on edge, and death-material which is not always wholly remote from that of – Joyce. It is a sell-out of *relativism* and *empty montage*, amidst the decline of

---

95 Wilhelm von Humboldt, 1767–1835, scholar and statesman who influenced the Prussian educational system and created the University of Berlin.
96 Deutschnational: See 'Amusement Co., horror, Third Reich', n. 43. on 'Deutschnationale Volkspartei', 1918–33, the monarchist and conservative party.
97 Eduard Spranger, 1882–1963, philosopher and educationalist who specialized in the psychology of youth.
98 Heinrich Rickert, 1863–1936, philosopher and co-founder of the SW German school of neo-Kantianism.

the bourgeois pride in knowledge. Relativists are trumps, their cognition is writ small, they do not after all write it at all any more in the end. Namely as soon as sphinxes (which nevertheless, given such a choice, are somewhat better than an omniscient 'It is achieved') have taken their seats.

THE EYE

Again and again one now begins from one's own viewpoint. Clears away until there is nothing at all outside any more. In piecemeal, barren work bourgeois thinking became weak anyway, modest. Its material no longer went into concepts; these became fluctuating, the material itself disintegrated into what was merely seen or completely receded. Thus *Ziehen*[99] claimed to know from the very structure of the eye that man does not perceive things as they really are. That also every cognitive statement about them is words and nothing more. The way things are is gladly left out and open. It is all the easier to make variable statements about them, tomorrow differently from today.

99 Theodor Ziehen, 1862–1950, German psychiatrist, philosopher and psychologist.

THE FICTITIOUS ONES

Others already doubt from the start, only not themselves. Dry mud from yesterday comes into fashion again, becomes funny and general. Mach[100] lives, his theory of the conformity of ideas to facts is even gaining ground very organically. A *Vaihinger,*[101] with the theory of the As If, came home only after forty years, is at home again. Meets an age which takes its concepts in a totally fluctuating fashion, namely as merely fictitious, and gets itself a certificate of this, however belatedly. Cognition becomes mere fictitious assumption; nothing and not even assuredly nothing corresponds to it in real terms. Just as an illness has phases, so too does bourgeois conceptual decay, and it is conceived more and more easily, more and more comfortably. The mere As If commends itself even if only because it permits all bourgeois principles to be cleared away. It transforms scientific concepts, and even ideal convictions, most usefully into share certificates which fluctuate according to the given situation. Moreover, the fictionalizing entity clears away the truth for itself, to establish it nowhere better either before or afterwards. It makes the doubt about the Being graspable today into one about anything and everything. It thus runs through large parts of modern thinking, easy, comfortable, faithless. Boards all precisely practicable trains of the concept, to travel to the end with none of them.

100 Ernst Mach, see 'Objectivity, direct', n. 20.
101 Hans Vaihinger, 1852–1933, philosopher, author of *Die Philosophie des Als-Ob.*

THE EMPIRICISTS

Cool people emerge from doubt by completely going along with it. Pure thinking is empty for them, the remaining internals merely mawkish, and that which it adds 'cognitively', made up. Only two ways of thinking are regarded here as really appropriate ones: the new logic, in Russell's[102] mathematical sense, and the method of individual scientific, empirical research. Plain and clear – the old cry from the beginning of bourgeois thinking, the cry of abstract calculation thus returns; though as far as the power of calculation to recognize what is real from within itself is concerned, with a very diminished, very defeated claim. For the circle of 'scientific' philosophers there are no synthetic judgements a priori; thinking beyond experience reaches into nothing, into fantasies, into totally unfounded remnants of mythical thinking. There are only analytical judgements a priori; these constitute the new logic, as a contentless framework of tautologies which are admittedly unconditionally correct but state nothing about that 'which is the case' (Wittgenstein). Content-filled cognition is furnished solely by the empirical sciences, the synthetic judgements a posteriori, which can be traced back to the given and can thereby alone be determined to be true or false. The philosopher is simply responsible for logically thinking through the 'form' of the individual scientific questions and judgements with the utmost clarity; for scientific theorems are only clarified by philosophy, but they are verified by experience. Philosophy thus becomes a pure ordering control of the individual sciences; its 'semantic research' is one of form, by no means of content. Clear as this entire system is, the relation it has to the older critical empiricism, namely to Mach, is admittedly just as unreflected. The circle around *Schlick*[103] and

102 Bertrand Russell, 1872–1970, English empirical philosopher and mathematician.
103 Moritz Schlick, 1882–1936, philosopher, advocate of neo-positivism.

Dubislav[104] is connected with Mach (the second ancestor, after Russell) by its rejection of all 'humanizing' thinking, its tendency to remove synthetic judgements a priori (hence subjective-mythical ones) even in the formal basic concepts, above all from causality. It seems unclear, however, how the empiricists deal with the *model idea* of Machism, that is with the conformity of ideas to facts by means of a thought model. This lack of clarity is all the more strange as the model idea would be the only thing which revealed the idealistic hangover even in the individual sciences, not merely in that which is here called metaphysical venturing beyond. Yet precisely the critical dissolution of the individual sciences themselves still seems to be en enfant among the empiricists; likewise the insight into the dubiousness of those reifications which in terms of the individual sciences are still called 'facts'. Just as the very temporal subject is here suppressed to which all the given is after all first 'given', so the given experience itself remains badly direct, unhistorical and unchangeable. A different logic from that of equations is unknown; nothing had as yet been heard here of dialectics, which cannot even enter the same river once (and hence with the best will in the world is not tautological). The greater the modesty in the face of bourgeois science, and the more meagre the hold which doubt believes it has found logically and 'scientifically', the more ignorant is the 'arrogance' in the face of all thinkers of the past, in the face of all 'musical examples' which have expressed more than a = a. The closeness of this abstract rigour to New Objectivity is obvious; it has the same human emptiness, the same clarity of a merely external understanding, the same refusal to penetrate into the 'cryptic background' of experience (even movement is a background). Nevertheless, many Marxists show respectful mercy to this thinking, because it seems so contemporaneous; indeed, even the remaining thinkers of 'conformity' are welcomed by them as being technologically advanced. Like the so-called behaviourists (Watson),[105] because they wholly manage without internals and deny consciousness or incorporate it into the rest of the organic attitude to the environment. Like the Pragmatists (Schiller,[106] James),[107] because they define truth only as biological, altogether as practical usefulness and take an 'interest' in it only in this respect; finally like the neo-empiricists because of their thinking free from metaphysics. Hence many Marxists, despite Lenin's warning, accept an inheritance here; the crystal-clear system seems to them to correspond to 'the ripest capitalist development'. This philo-

104 Walter Dubislav, 1895–1937, philosopher of nature.
105 John Broadus Watson, 1878–1958, American psychologist, founder of Behaviourism.
106 Ferdinand C. S. Schiller, 1864–1937, British pragmatist philosopher.
107 William James, 1842–1910, American pragmatical philosopher and psychologist.

sophical 'objectivity' is indeed a piece of England and the USA, but it is so philosophically too, and thus not in the best way; but then its origin is fairly mossy, namely Mach and the not very American Vienna. As far as pragmatists are concerned, their claimed closeness to the Marxist relationship between thought and practice is only an apparent one. For something is not true for Marxism because it is useful, but the practical basic question is here equally a theoretical one: namely whether a theory tallies with the real tendency; only in so far as it tallies with the latter is it also true, and only in so far as it is true in such a way is it also useful. Particularly as far as the freedom from metaphysics of the logicians and neo-empiricists is concerned, this does not set Hegel on his feet, which would be solely Marxist, but throws him out, says a = a and for the rest trusts bourgeois science, as if it were pure 'experience'. Fluctuatingly, yet irrefutably Mach himself haunts all this understanding; just as fluctuatingly, yet of course – qua research of today – just as irrefutably the model idea, elastic relativism. The latter seems crooked and explicit only in certain social-scientific reflections, fruitful in modern physics.

LAX, SOCIAL AND PHYSICAL
RELATIVISM

Even what is soft likes to dissolve that which is different from itself. It is satisfied with mere counting, grasping, naming, it amounts to nothing more than this. That which is grasped may be and remain mush, one which is felt to be constantly fluid. In the so-called ego or the soul this glance began factually at first, and has been continuing moderately since then. Verworn,[108] for example, diminished all psychological concepts, a long time ago, to mere names which signify nothing that is. Here as everywhere, thinking sets up mere signs which are simply added to that which is felt to be endless as the only thing that is, or rather hovers. Mach's model influenced this at first and was applied: the ego is not tenable, but even everything in and outside it is only what is felt to be weaving. This weaving shakes off the hard, arranging concept every-where, as a dog shakes off water or rather as water does the dog, as not belonging to it. There are no psychological states outlined for them-selves, nor is there any real scarlet fever, let alone any psychologically closed diseases, but only the view, the name of them, which heaps together symptoms now here, and now there. Nor are there any sepa-rate bodies, workers, entrepreneurs, classes; this is the further conse-quence of such a purely 'phenomenal' glance. All this does not exist in the endlessly fluid character of given feeling, it is scooped from it only into handy vessels held up close. Concepts thus become reflexive as never before, moreover all concepts, without exception; the idea makes itself small. Not small enough not to reveal in it and its consequences the sly Cretan who said all Cretans are liars. By slandering itself and cancelling itself out, it intends to defeat and cancel out every real statement. And yet only clears away that bourgeois language which has become too weak to say more than that it does not say anything any more.

108 Max Verworn, 1863–1923, German physiologist and philosopher.

Social reflections

This thinking again endlessly loosens things up in order not to have to act. It understands every position so well that it does not need to decide in favour of any one. This system is dubious if, as in the case of Mannheim,[109] it tries its hand at *historical* driving forces. It is then less 'experimental' than contemplatively defusing, namely defusing history into the standpoints which ages adopt towards themselves one after the other. 'History', *Mannheim* and his school thus say, 'is only visible through history itself', there is no leap from the necessarily partial, 'perspective' glance to an objectively ascertainable, sweeping course of events. Mach's model appears here as a kind of destiny of history as a science, namely as 'sociology'. So the model with which history becomes ascertainable today is above all that of ideology, i.e. of economic classification. But respective economic classification determines not just the contents but also, according to Mannheim, the *economical-materialistic concept* which history nowadays, as in the industrial age, has of itself. This modern 'perspective' is for him itself only an economically classified and conditioned one, consequently not a definitive or constitutive one; for him there is no definitive one at all. Thus bourgeois relativism is still associated with the concept of ideology which it learned from Marx, in order to 'apply' it to – Marx himself. Marx is corrected with Max Weber's[110] nominalism and 'positivism'; a good deal of Lukács is added to this and is made suitable for bourgeois use, while Spengler's cultural groups and Scheler's[111] 'theory of types' again serve the purpose of their being a stop on the way for the system of perspective. Thus that theory of ideology which in Marx is a key to previous, but even more so a lever for future history, becomes solely a key, moreover one for a set time; and even one which removes the lever itself. All theory, even the Marxist kind, thus turns, according to its own 'premises', into a so-called sociology of knowledge and perishes in it: there is likewise an economically classifiable and consequently relativizable structural theory of the proletarian idea of today, just as there was one of the conservative idea in Metternich's time or of the chiliastic idea in Thomas Münzer's time. The ideologists of every class, even of the proletarian one, live here as discussible, as in logical terms totally equivalent ones in the butterfly collection of contemplation. If this relativistic social philosophy overdoes historicism, it abolishes every appearance of historical process all the more, and with it the continuous

109   Karl Mannheim, 1893–1947, Hungarian-born German-British sociologist.
110   Max Weber, 1864–1920, sociologist and philosopher.
111   Oswald Spengler, 1880–1936, philosopher of history, with an influential organic view of cultural development. Max Scheler, 1874–1928, philosopher, founded a philosophical anthropology centring on the relationship between spirit and life.

content which corrects itself in history more or less concretely. The content of history was recognized in Marxist terms as the relationship of human beings to human beings and to nature; the process is the dialectic of class struggles. Mannheim, on the other hand, does not just define the earlier ideologies, which duped and, being unfathomed, had to dupe people over class rule, in purely formal terms: namely as a classification of certain contents of consciousness with certain groups, as the sum total of conceptions which mirror and justify existing society. But since this relativism believes even Marx to be subject to its wholly formal concept of ideology, it supposedly uproots Marxist truth and reality itself; there arises the all-comprehending insertion even of proletarian 'ideology' into group conceptions of which one is as true as the other, namely sociologically true and no more. There remains only the stomach which does not digest itself, the scepticism which shades into itself as a final, emptiest terminus, without being able to resolve itself into anything other than scepticism again. There remains the so-called passion of research and a drive to reflection which sees everything in history except what happens; there also admittedly remains the joy of those parties which have not founded their programme on insights, but on a will for blood and on faith, i.e. fascism, the Catholic Centre.[112] Whereby this interpretation had to put up with a critique even from ABC-learners of Marxism, as one which forbids the relativizing defusion of Marxism even in 'theoretically' evident terms. The proletariat, as was justly retorted to Mannheim, has a totally incomparable 'ideology', but not because it merely believes it has a different one, let alone because it is so exceptionally much more clever than earlier classes. But what objectively distinguishes the proletarian 'ideology' from others is the fact that it is the *material interest* of the proletariat not to develop any veiling of reality, but rather to gain insight into the real driving forces and the real tendency of this reality; while it was likewise the material interest of all earlier classes that false consciousness should be formed and its limits should not be exceeded. Of course, Mannheim's sociology is also acquainted with something more than ideologies: it adopts the *concept of utopia* from the 'Spirit of Utopia'[113] and places it alongside the ideologies; utopias then become conceptions which do not mirror and justify the given society, like ideology, but undermine and explode it. If this correct definition also reaches beyond the mere reflexive 'fairytale of an ideal state' as which utopia was alone understood and criticized until recently, it is still itself incomplete and lacks above all – in its formalism – every distinction in class terms between genuine and dead utopia. Petit-bourgeois utopias of today, for instance, under-

---

112 Bloch is referring to the German Catholic Centre Party, founded in 1870, dissolved by the Nazis, and the basis of the post-war CDU.
113 The title of Bloch's own early Expressionist work *Geist der Utopie* (1918).

mine and explode only very approximately after all, and they certainly do not fulfil Mannheim's criterion that utopias 'are always in advance of reality' or become the reality of tomorrow. Solely the 'ideology of the revolutionary proletariat' precisely defined in class terms, as which Lenin defined Marxism, ought also to contain genuine utopia enough and enough utopia of today to 'become the reality of tomorrow'. The concept of utopia of the all-*comprehending* sociologists has at any rate neither 'undermined' nor 'exploded' the social *relativism* in which indeed present society 'mirrors' and 'justifies' itself; it even becomes a mirror of mirrors. It is the most certain sign of sociological false doctrine, and not fear of a recognition for instance, if even Marxism 'relativizes' itself, if the discovered lever of history regresses to the mere conception of the lower proletariat, and behind it there is little more than a thousand differently possible group-dreams too. If the ruling class has already become chaff and if nothing saves it from this recognition, then it is of course useful to this class also to think of all future things as chaff and unreality. And yet it cannot avoid issuing to itself the historical death certificate; and it circumvents the dialectical, the concrete-utopian spot so exactly, as if it could see it.

Physical relativism

A thinking ultimately dismantles in a different way, the proof of which is thoroughly directed towards external things. Such a thinking certainly has concepts due for demolition, in order to figure out a physical view by means of them. Atoms, ether, the basic *physical* concepts become models in the most authentic sense, which can be continually perforated and rebuilt anew, to which at best something 'similar' in the world corresponds. Mach thoroughly triumphed in relativistic physics; Mach's model structure had always denoted atom, ether, and causality as a mythical addition to pure experience. The most effective form was given to Machism by Duhem[114] and Poincaré;[115] here calculation does not even appear as logically necessary any more, let alone as naturally necessary. Geometrical axioms and physical principles become mere agreement, theories supply only 'symbols' for practice, lay no claim any more to mirrored physical reality. This mixture of impressionism and a relativistic crisis of thought has admittedly subsided somewhat in most recent physics; physicists like Planck,[116] Laue,[117] and others are drift-

114 Pierre Duhem, 1861–1916, theoretical physicist and philosopher of science.
115 Jules Henri Poincaré, 1854–1912, French mathematician and philosopher.
116 Max Planck, 1858–1947, physicist, founder of the quantum theory.
117 Max von Laue, 1879–1960, physicist, contributor to the theory of relativity.

ing away from Mach towards a more 'realistic world-view', one which grants reality to the atom, on the strength of its possible visibility, and validity to causality at least in the Euclidean environment. However, this 'reality' succeeds only at the price that since *Planck* and *Einstein* physical relativism has been growing with *regard to the whole universe*. The universe itself now falls into three parts; the closed system of physics, with all its basic principles, cracks in a threefold and disparate way precisely in the new 'realism'. The *atomic* processes inhabit a microcosmic area in which the quantum theory prevails, in such a way that events in miniature are inconstant and irregular, only statistically ascertainable any longer, not causally. The *astronomical* processes inhabit a macrocosmic area in which the theory of relativity prevails, in such a way that clocks and yardsticks which are usual on earth fail in celestial space, that in cosmic dimensions neither simultaneity nor the structure of Euclidean geometry is to be found. Euclidean space neither conditions cosmic motions nor does it extend into these at all; instead, the connections of cosmic space are variable, and it is gravitation which first determines the geometrical proportions of their space for masses and thereby creates a corresponding possibility of motion for them, from place to place. But *previous mechanics*, the Euclidean-classical kind which has also become that of technology, the mechanics of causality and simultaneity remains confined to the mesocosmos of the human environment, centre-world. Thus in this threefold division – far from being relativistic – both the 'modes of thought' are expanded (and therefore the 'a priori tenets' of the past themselves made historical), and the concepts of constancy, causality, space and time reduced to mere 'approximations' in the face of different experience. Closed calculation and its world governed by uniform laws is thus thoroughly forced into models here too, both into the problem of a priori tenets which were supposedly valid for every experience, and into capitulation to a more and more uncontrolledly onrushing matter, a rationalistically less and less producible, systematically more and more difficult to deduce experience-content. Another question is, of course, ultimately this: if there does not correspond to the natural philosophical relativism of these times, as undoubtedly as it is one, something 'real' in the object after all, namely something which possesses *debris as a possible object-state*. Undisturbed relativism is after all much more improbable in physics than in sociology (which with its civic problems is so to speak alone with itself). The 'object' in the metabolism between man and nature makes an incomparably much more penetrating contribution, after all, than in so-called intellectual science and its free-floating 'perspectivisms'.

It will only do here to indicate this question, not to pursue it, leading far afield as it does. It would also concern a quite differently instructive decay than that of the mere *concept* of external things. It would be directed towards a tottering of things themselves, whether this is only now recognized, or instead only now 'appears', in such intensity. Though of course even the concept of nature primarily expresses the society in which it appears; its order or disorder, the changing forms of its dependence. These forms also recur in the concept of nature in superstructural terms; thus the elemental, the magical, the qualitatively graded, and ultimately the mechanical one is largely to be understood as ideology. Mechanical natural science was even to a particular degree an ideology of the bourgeois society of its time, and ultimately of the circulation of goods; in this respect, with the crack in this society, with the surging of uncontrolled matter against calculation, its concept of nature is also now becoming porous and fictitious. But there is already the difficult question whether this concept of nature, as a reifying and mechanical one, did not further represent, beyond mere ideology, a piece of world-content which was itself reistic and mechanized. In Marxist terms this question is partly positively decided already, precisely bourgeois natural science, qua science of nature, is credited with having really recognized a piece of nature; although everywhere else in bourgeois art and science only ideology appears, with the economy as the sole core. In the 'decay' of bourgeois natural science, however, in the relativism of Poincaré, even in the revolutions of most recent physics, a metasocial relation is often denied in Marxist terms or only reluctantly acknowledged. The old bourgeois-materialistic image of nature occasionally remains in Marxist terms; not just as – in the eighteenth century – hallowed by revolution, but exactly in the form which satiated bourgeois natural science, in the nineteenth century, before its crisis, possessed without exception. It was precisely for the old materialism, apparently still in its form conceived by Haeckel, that Lenin wrote his book 'Materialism and Empirical Criticism'; against Poincaré and Mach. Or rather against their emulation amongst Marxists, against that 'modernity' which sought to abolish even Marxist materialism as 'metaphysics in natural science', and dialectics (in so far as it was still known at all) in particular. Lenin incessantly stresses, against the Machists: 'Bodies are not symbols of sensations, but sensations are symbols (more correctly – likenesses) of bodies' (Materialismus und Empiriokritizismus (1927), p. 316); Lenin praises Haeckel's world-riddle both as 'a weapon of the class struggle' (p. 358) and as a proof that for genuine natural scientists no 'other epistemology is possible than that of scientific materialism' (p. 362). But it is characteristic of Lenin's greatness not to have found comfort in the merely ideological character of physical relativism. He sensed the class odour of pure, non-metaphysical 'empirical theory' in a unique fashion of course, but in a truly dialectical way Lenin simultaneously discovered in this 'reactionary philosophy' a changed attitude, one elastic of necessity, a model attitude in a more concrete sense; at least on the basis of a changed object-relation. Lenin emphatically repeats Engels's demand: dialectical materialism has to absorb every epoch-making discovery in the field of natural and intellectual sciences and to enrich itself with it. This demand holds good for Lenin even with regard to late-bourgeois physics, in so far as it is not just 'sociologically' interesting to him of course, not just ideological decay, an idealistic theory of decay; indeed this demand holds good, in a clearly defined sense, even with regard to the physical Machists. 'They indicate the limited nature of such a view' (of the atomistic-mechanical view of nature), 'the impossibility of acknowledging it as a barrier to our knowledge, the rigidity of many concepts among the supporters of this view. This shortcoming of the *old* materialism is also beyond doubt; failure to appreciate the relativity of all scientific theories, ignorance of dialectics, overestimation of the mechanical viewpoint, – Engels too accused the earlier materialists of this.' Only Engels renounced 'the *old,* metaphysical materialism in favour of *dialectical* materialism, but not in favour of the relativism which slides over into subjectivism' (p. 315). 'What fun', Lenin continues, after he has examined Duhem's evidence that every physical law is provisional, 'what fun to kick at open doors! – thinks the Marxist who reads the long meditations on this subject. But this is exactly the misfortune of the Duhems, Stallos,[118] Machs, Poincarés, that they cannot see the door opened by dialectical materialism. Because they cannot give any *correct articulation of relativism*, they slide from the latter into idealism. In a word, the physical idealism of today ... only signifies that a school of natural scientists in a branch of natural science has slid down into reactionary philosophy, because it was not able to raise itself, directly and from the very beginning, from metaphysical materialism to the dialectical kind' (pp. 315, 317). But precisely this step will be taken by modern physics, according to Lenin, being on the point of giving birth to dialectical materialism, in an admittedly painful and complicated delivery. 'Apart from a living being capable of surviving, certain dead products, some waste products inevitably also appear, which belong in the rubbish pit. Part of these waste products is also the whole of physical idealism, the whole of empirical-critical philosophy together with empirical symbolism, empirical monism and the like' (p. 318). In short, for Lenin the problem is already such that mechanical materialism admittedly 'reflected' a piece of nature in many respects, even though defectively and one-sidedly, but relativistic 'decay' in particular, apart from its ideological nullity, has a piece of *constitutive* nature at work within it, namely that of dialectical materialism. Thus Lenin not only gives the undecayed, mechanical concept of nature the honour, the undoubted and relatively concrete honour, of having rediscovered materialism and grasped it more clearly, even

118   John Bernhard Stallo, 1823–1900, American educator, jurist and philosopher of science.

though defectively and one-sidedly. He also distinguishes actually *physical* relativism (which loosened the mechanically closed and uniform rigidity) precisely from its miserable *philosophy*, namely empirical criticism (which allowed no concept whatsoever to be concretely applied to nature). Lenin thoroughly recognizes in the growing elasticity of physical concepts and principles a transition, an inquiring transition to dialectical materialism. The nature-content itself of course has always existed for Lenin, exactly as it is, independently of every human concept of nature. Just as the consciousness of all times is only the more or less cloudy reflection of real class struggles and contents, so natural processes unwind independently of consciousness in dialectical-real necessity. The historically successive concepts of nature are particularly only a reflection of them, reproduce them particularly only according to the respective social system and its control of nature. The progressive transformation of things in themselves into things for us (as Engels expresses it) does not affect the real order of things, but only the recognition of this order; whereby materialistic ages were the most adequate for this recognition. But of course precisely this standpoint of reflection demands its dialectical subject-object-completion: for if 'natural necessity' is correctly recognized in objective terms, then it is controllable, and if it is controllable, then it is changed; thus the concept of nature of an age, in fact even of the capitalist one, certainly intervenes in nature here and causes it to participate in history. Furthermore, the ideology of an age likewise contains, apart from the veiling of class rule, an undoubted surplus qua superstructure, qua cultural production, that surplus which raises the problem of cultural 'inheritance' even with regard to the non-revolutionary past: could there therefore be a problem of inheritance *even within nature*? Such that in the individual historically successive concepts of nature – the elementally animistic ones, the magical ones, the qualitatively graded ones – apart from ideology superseded elements of the great tendency system of nature could have been denoted and informed as well? Dialectical materialism is undoubtedly the highest real insight into nature up to now; in relation to nature it is an attained merging of tottering and necessity, of object-based 'relativism' and 'law'. Whereas the physical relativism of today, as the decay of mechanics *from the viewpoint of the object*, also sensitizes to the possibility of earlier determinations as relative real determinations in nature; so that the dialectics of nature could have not only the mechanical natural science of yesterday, but also certain earlier, actually qualitatively graded elements as material to be superseded, superseded material, if not material overshooting mechanics. This is the content of the most difficult and also most dangerous question which was posed at the beginning of this section: what the decay of the mechanical concept means for the natural objects themselves. This question admittedly arises in dealing with physical relativism and its significance on the move, but it can be no more than indicated, no more than distinguished here; for it explodes the framework of late-bourgeois decay just as it explodes the framework of every mechanism, just as it makes 'omitted elements' in the mechanical state of ruins perceptible again. The late-bourgeois spirit has at least brought a hollow space here too; it has become a flight over air pockets and the closed, enclosed arc no longer its own. Very differently than in the case of the sociological decay of the real, much more directly and positively, from the natural philosophical one a decay, a purpose of the exercise is gained, a purpose for Marxism itself. The new nominalists have not destroyed any Marxist content as well, but only one which Marxism had highly improperly touched upon as well or occasionally still touches upon as well, which Engels himself pursues with fire and sword, namely the content of quantitatively *mechanical* materialism, as one which is finished and closed. As *materialism* it destroyed the mythical notions of the other world in Christianity; but as *mechanically closed* materialism it had itself become mythology again. An astral one at a reduced price; for the hypostasis of fate, of 'necessity', of classical 'Ananke' revived in these finished determinisms once again. But no human being has to complete the circle of his existence in accordance with eternal, iron laws; in the long run they are not eternal, either in history or in nature. Hence if the natural philosophical relativisms and intermittences have certainly not brought any solid base for future man, they have at least deprived him of a false one.

FOUNDATION OF PHENOMENOLOGY

Thinkers have not often begun without themselves. The dismissal of oneself is usual only in the individual sciences, does not turn out to be difficult then either. For research scientists do not need to be personally significant, do not themselves need to signify a piece of existence outside their work. Their best quality is diligence, accuracy, fidelity in detail; the sole fortune for which they are fitted is that of discovery. This selfless element is true not merely of those who are average, but also of those who are very high up; it has after all been essential to scientific work up to now to be independent of the experiencing and interpreting subject. One's own colour or perhaps depth remains at best incidental; as does a local sense of oneself and of one's bourgeois location in time. Hence the possible appearances of nullity outside their work; hence too the naive judgements as soon as scholars speak of events of the day or historians become political. Only in recent times did the class, at least, become sharply defined to which they belong.

But the actual thinkers rarely looked so faceless. Indeed, it is perhaps the case for the first time with *Husserl*[119] that one of them 'achieved' something significant without having it. Through laborious work to begin with in the field of linguistic and sign analysis, a purely individual scientific one. (The disciples of the first Husserl school particularly liked to call themselves 'research scientists'; thinking was even more grammatical, 'the rose is red' its most frequent content.) Then the non-existing personal being was concealed, if not replaced, by the neo-scholasticism which had come down to Husserl via Franz Brentano.[120] A whole herbarium of former vitality, the profusion of the ancient overall conception was thereby transferred to research. Thus in a certain sense a philosophical

---

119   Edmund Husserl, 1859–1938, philosopher and founder of phenomenology.
120   Franz Brentano, 1838–1917, Austrian philosopher.

personality was not necessary here either, but once again only the fortune of discovery; the absorption of forgotten intentio and adaequatio. The plus sounding through, without which there are no retainable philosophical ideas, is thus replaced by a kind of loan on security: and Husserl worked with the loaned sum. But all important thinkers had their plus as sounding through, as 'personans', as 'personality' in itself; not in an individual or even wilful way, but as a 'philosophical plus', referring to an overall conception and above all to a basic content which determines and coordinates with itself the thinking of the smallest part. There is this philosophical plus just as there is a poetic one; despite the very different attitude, despite the cogent will to knowledge and reality which separates the philosophically deposited surplus from the poetic one. In short, the significant thinkers were always just as much 'great minds', as such they not only stand 'on the summit of their age', they not only display the strongest possible awareness of the contents of their age and the next, they also raise facts in their age which are only inherent in it and are thoroughly in need of the philosophical 'sounding through'. Naturally Husserl in no respect belongs to the significant thinkers (in this precisely familiar style) and yet will probably survive, for the reasons cited above, for a fairly long time as 'method'. Husserl has nothing in common with the eclectic beggar's soups which five hundred 'philosophers' pour out in every age to be likewise poured away. It is strange too what different features, here those of Scheler,[121] there those of Heidegger, were pre-formed in a simple semantic theory.

But the weak ego would still not be wholly denied in this way of thinking and made its influence felt. As an average one beneath the summit of the age, as one which bears with it all kinds of discarded things in an unrepresented manner, without a commitment of its own. There is a bourgeois ego which only apparently omits itself in the naive acceptance of everything which seems to become 'insightful in itself' and yet is only the insight of a commodity thinking. The lacking overall conception avenges itself above all in the means with which the 'subjective', and hence floating idealism is to be 'overcome'. Husserl's 'Logical Investigations' began descriptively, against every psychological-genetic explanation of a fact (Lipps),[122] but also against every transcendental production which has its being only in the thinking process (Cohen).[123] Phenomenology was directed against psychological, relativistic idealists as well as against transcendental ones, against the quaestio fiendi of knowledge as well as against its quaestio juris. The quaestio essendi alone was regarded as wholly remote from these always still subjectivis-

---

121 Max Scheler, see 'Social reflections', n. 111.
122 Theodor Lipps, 1851–1914, German psychologist and aesthetician.
123 Hermann Cohen, 1842–1918, philosopher, co-founder of the 'Marburg School' of Neo-Kantianism.

tic movements: as a description of indeducible given mental facts, and then as the actually logical investigation of *'truths' in themselves*. The quaestio essendi detached itself in the whole as an attempted contemplation of the thingness in things, in short as an order of being grasped through 'essential seeing'. Consciousness in general of course, as 'Protestant' subjectivity, was just as much preserved in this apparently objectivistic philosophy, indeed was just as much stressed in the later Husserl as the circuit of a closed reason graded in caste and 'Catholic' terms. But of a reason which did not so much abandon bourgeois idealism as augment it with the much older Platonic-scholastic kind; the slight personans left both unresolved side by side. The 'Catholic' objectivism is certainly stronger; but the catastrophe which it ultimately found in Husserl's school is already inherent in the 'Protestant' consciousness in general. From Husserl's school came the nihilistic Scheler after the objective one, and finally Heidegger put phenomenology on inside out so to speak, with its inside turned outwards, as Kierkegaard viewed ontologically – and all this in the name of Husserl's method. Only because no personans is at work in Husserl's basic conception, but different ones have merely been adopted from different ages, could such different 'relations to being' also explode in his school. This admittedly came to light only after phenomenology *sought to wage war* even in *material* terms on *relativism*, as the subjectivistically smashed ontological coherence of today. It ended in Scheler's final phase with the defeat of 'Catholic world-profusion', in Heidegger at best with a small victory, with a Pyrrhic victory of the existential subject, nominalistic object in phenomenology. From Scheler to Heidegger: it is the retreat of the expansive, world-happy ego to the introverted one, to the lonely soul in the devil's inn as which Luther had described the world. There arose the 'concretization' of consciousness in general (which in Husserl had been only a very generally idealistic point of reference) into the ontology of an *inner* being: perforated by motion, but a nihilistic one, crowned with a view, but to death. But before we go into this, there follows a short review of the inheritance of Husserl's method in its various modes and possibilities. How these appeared in 1917, when Husserl's school was still by itself so to speak, and how they continue to appear for the most part. For the lessons of a method which seeks to apply the heaviest scholasticism to the spectre of a vacuum are not inconsiderable. 'Impersonant' as this philosophizing is (or precisely because of this), there are still handholds in it, partly ones unused up to now and ones whose time is perhaps not yet over.

Firstly, we know more exactly since then what supposing and thinking themselves are. They were described as acts, not first deduced from scientific fruits. *Secondly*, Husserl made the meaning of words sharp, just as it exactly befits them. Language was clarified on the basis of its prescientific meaning, for instance of the jagged, the leonine and other things in it. Whoever merely clarifies concepts, of course, still knows nothing about their real objects; otherwise even the word-splitting Eulenspiegel[124] would be a good, if not the best, phenomenologist. The mere semantic analysis of the leonine naturally produces no real knowledge of lions (if only because the leonine is not in fact merely to be found in lions, there are also leonine men, there is, as Keller[125] says, the 'golden lion of wine'). But even if the real world is not a picture book of 'meanings', it still remains very desirable to know what is to be understood by the leonine, or rather by piece, contract, obligation and similar concepts even below their 'application'. The cognition of this most formal 'sense' is useful, although its re-cognition occurs only in material terms, and possibly also, as an economic-historical recognition, leaves nothing over of the formal-evident sense. *Thirdly*, Husserl's phenomenology rose, over such meanings, towards the thing itself anyway. The intending referential act towards something disappears, and likewise the 'Protestant', the neo-Kantian reference of consciousness in general recedes at this stage. But above all the existence of what is seen is 'bracketed'; what then still remains is the objective *fact*, is the 'essence' which always claims to be the same in the various tiers of sensation or memory. The glance drives totally outwards here, into the wide realm 'of simple and categorical graphic intuitions', into an 'essential world' exactly prearranged in structural terms and withdrawn from all subjectivity. Though it is withdrawn not only from subjectivity, but in fact also from existence; hence with phenomenology all objects can be dealt with, and it 'decides' in favour of none of them, it does not need to 'believe' in any of them. The primacy of the graphic intuition over the concept, of ontology over endless methodizing, does not cancel out the idealistic undernourishment here. The discussibility of everything and anything becomes only 'graphic'. The wall which is hallucinated by a madman and the real wall here to the right of the desk is the same in its 'essential constituents' (just as in Kant a hundred possible and a hundred real Thalers were 'logically' the same). Indeed, a phenomenology of the devil was supplied by interested parties in Husserl's school, with all the determinations of his essential character – as it was to be found in reports, legends, and theologies; only the question of his existence was not touched upon in fact, in contemplative restraint. And as far as the primacy of the graphic intuition over the concept is concerned, it is certainly an interesting and also seemingly concrete inversion that graphic intuition no longer stands at the beginning as something to be overcome, something cloudy, but at the fulfilling end; that the concept of bare currency becomes, in order to buy graphic

---

124   Till Eulenspiegel (see 'Songs of remoteness', n. 233), a peasant prankster famous for taking metaphorical commands literally (*Volksbuch*, *c*.1500).
125   Gottfried Keller, see 'Rough night in town and country', n. 18.

intuition, a bare species of intention which is 'fulfilled' only in the simple or categorical graphic intuition. However, even the constructive method is not so wholly lacking here as claimed, the bourgeois cannot totally leave constructions aside in order to become a pure world-eye. Husserl only sought to improve the *productive* construction (against which the problem of the thing-in-itself arose ever more inexorably) through certain borrowings from the *contemplative* construction of the scholastics. He only surpassed neo-Kantianism, which perished from the 'impertinence of the given fact' (Cohen), through the certainly more qualitative and more materially relevant Ratio of scholasticism. 'Reality' did not thereby appear, however, but solely a kind of sensory logic, a visual categorical theory of a scholastic-caste order. *Fourthly* and finally, this description believes itself capable of an insight which in the case of certain high concepts automatically leaves the external graphic intuition behind it. Loyalty, for instance, and all moral-religious concepts whatsoever, are fulfilled not as an external essentiality, but only as an internal one in itself; for every external one they remain 'exemplary'. If Richard of St Victor[126] asks whether it is the touchstone of perfect love that both lovers wish a third person could participate in their mutual love such that the latter were loved by both to the same extent as they mutually love one another, then this essential definition denotes an illumination of an 'environmental', 'ontically normative' kind, a point where thinking is on a par with a being which not only external graphic intuition but every realization only follows. No outwardly aiming supposing and thinking intends here, but a 'mindfulness', and it has its evidence only in its own place and in its own position, namely in moral-mystical form, a sense of phenomenology which has become very remote, no longer existing in it today, but nevertheless inherent in it.

Such open questions can be asked of this way of thinking, it is after all itself fourfold or even more divided. But the effect of the Platonisms was at first less open, was more covered up, namely a filling of the scientific hollow space with *forms*. As forms of so-called shape-seeing[127] they cancel out not only abstract calculation but also every tendency: where the palm-like, leonine, Apollonian, magical, Faustian entered into the 'real', it immediately became something 'grown' or a 'destiny' for tendency. Shapes are logically, even historically undeniable, but not as motionless ones (as these they deserve the command 'Fire!' – for they are the shibboleth of the purest reaction and 'overcome' relativism at the cost of the most retrograde ideology of statics and the corporate state). Shapes in history exist only as figures of tension, as tendency-shapes, as experiments of the unknown life-shape, which so little exists that precisely for this reason shapes crack again and again and history con-

126 See 'The gospel of this world'.
127 'Gestaltschau': a reference to a notion in Gestalt psychology.

tinues. As essential seeing was practised with or without Husserl, feudal houses and a whole ring of reactionary castles of history and destiny were built into the retreating coherence of calculation. But the leonine and the other worldly kinds of 'Morphe' are finished neither in concept nor in their real fulfilment in particular, are ultimately not existent at all, and thus no shape of that which is really taking shape in tendency. Yet even the 'unworldly' manner of the fourth and final sense of phenomenology, in which the definition already seems to be the content and above all the process seems to lie behind in the past, as if there were a moment of total shape here, even here there is not yet any contact with the latter, not yet the thing itself in its natural size, not yet that 'congruence' which Makarie[128] in the Wanderjahre intended to assume with the solar system (let alone with a mystical one). The seriousness and depths of such an authentic visio beatifica is not in question here: what is important is that phenomenology sought to fill space with substantial forms one last time, with strangely secularized 'visions', without a lower material limit, in concrete endlessness. More important is the crack which occurred soon afterwards in the ontological theory of forms in the world, in the attempt to maintain it against relativistic hollow space. Materiality came to an end, Husserl's 'general truths' and the 'essential laws of specific objects' retreated with increasing relativization to so-called existence and existential analysis – the 'eidetics of the spheres' collapses. And instead of the purely idealistic undernourishment there remains solely a more impure nourishment: through demonstration instead of proof, through shadowy graphic intuition instead of the concept.

128 The mystical old woman in the final volumes of Goethe's *Wilhelm Meister* series. This 'congruence' is described in chapter 10 of Book I of the *Wanderjahre*. See 'Novels of strangeness and theatre of montage', n. 48.

'ONTOLOGIES' OF PROFUSION AND TRANSITORINESS

Since there was nobody behind it, this new seeing remained dim for a long time. It contented itself with claiming that twice two is four or simply that roses are red. Only ten years after Husserl did the path lead further outwards, moreover with people who wanted what they got to see. Instead of division and dissolution the concept aimed at wholeness; this was at least sought in detail. There came, as noted above, seeing of 'shape', this spread at first only in individual scientific and harmless terms, in simple sensory perceptions, in the course taken by diseases and mental processes. For gestalt theory the whole is here simply more than the sum of its parts and remains, as a melody, even when all its parts have become different ones. The whole also enters, as a bodily constitution, into a kind of causal relation with the parts, so that when two shapes suffer the same thing it is not the same thing. Whereby analytical thinking is nevertheless retained and is interchanged with the shape-seeing kind in a way which is reminiscent of alternating models. So that in fact bacilli and accident-prone people, analyses and constitutions, Virchow[129] and the four humours are appreciated at the same time. Shape still hangs rather meagrely in the air here, without the world, the fairly ancient world being visible in which it would alone be possible. A strange attempt to inquire ruthlessly and yet to be able to be complex.

It desires really to be founded on various kinds of being. This alone maintains shape as such, as one which is neither apparent and compound nor fading in the flow. Above all *Scheler* pushed Husserl further here in material terms, beyond the merely conceptual vision. Admittedly he did not give the signal, but rather determined the space in which the whole of gestalt theory, begun by Gelb, Wertheimer, Köhler, and even Kretschmer,[130] spread as far up as Spengler. And from here it becomes

129   See 'Occult fantasticality and paganism', n. 216.
130   Adhémar Gelb, 1887–1936, Max Wertheimer, 1886–1943, Wolfgang Köhler, 1887–1967, psychologists, Ernst Kretschmer, 1888–1964, psychiatrist, were all founders of Gestalt psychology.

completely clear why, to what end the scholastic-objectivistic component in Husserl has become useful today. The scientific gestalt theory of
the Wertheimers and other psychologists has to be detached from this
(Meinong,[131] for instance, already distinguished melody and similar
groups as 'qualities of shape' when no statics was yet visible far and
wide), model thinking was intermixed, and also a restriction to very
specific phenomena. Kretschmer, of course, or the manifold constitutional theories already stand in the fascist transition; this becomes complete with the veritable shape 'visionaries' like Spann,[132] then (geog-
raphically) with Banse and Passarge,[133] then with Dacqué[134] and his
biological dominant species, and then naturally with Spengler and precisely with Scheler, in his anthropological and differently numbered
ethical theory of types. All this cultivates misunderstood Goethe, gives
him a superstructure of scholasticized Plato, if necessary adds a genealogical, linguistic, state and other 'stock' theology from the romantic
Vormärz, makes use of the undeniable seduction of the concept of rest,
the more transparent one of the concept of 'order'; thus 'shape' is fixed
as a substitute for 'law', as an absolutely invariant essentiality, as a
feudal weir in the historical flow. We repeat: there are naturally shapes
in the logical-categorical sense, they likewise exist, although very relatively, in individual scientific 'experience', not just as melody but also
as 'period' in historical time, as 'species' in biology, as 'aesthetic figure',
if not 'figure-tendency' in the observed landscape. But we stress as well:
all these are only relative constants, indeed more than half, nowadays,
reflections of commodity images and unfathomed product fetishes; and
we underline what is said in Husserl: genuine shapes exist in history and
the world only as figures of tension, as tendency-shapes, as experiments of the unknown life-shape, which so little exists already that
precisely for this reason the nodal formation cracks again and again, and
history continues. So much for this shibboleth and the – admittedly
temporary – role it plays in Schelerism.

With Scheler himself the entire process of seeing first revived, became
current in the world. He brought not a genuine, but an interesting
'personality' into the essential seeing of today. A contradictory and
marked one, a slightly diabolical one from the upper middle class, from
the class of order, a broadly interested one and not without phosphorus.
It paid in its colour of phenomenology (instead of formal consciousness
in general), and it also reluctantly demonstrated what has already been
noted in Husserl: namely that construction is not lacking in pheno-

131 Alexius Meinong, 1853–1920, Austrian philosopher.
132 Othmar Spann, 1878–1950, Austrian economist and philosopher, see 'Re-
     minder: Hitler's force', n. 176.
133 Ewald Banse, 1883–1953, and Siegfried Passarge, 1867–1958, geographers.
134 Edgar Dacqué, see 'Science drolatique', n. 222.

menology, that the epistemological concept which precedes the graphic intuition, depending on how it has been employed and above all elaborated before, determines the graphic intuition which fulfils it. (Bergson,[135] for instance, 'likewise puts himself into the thing', but encounters nothing but flowing life where the school of Husserl, which does not have Schelling but a scholastic Plato in its cognitive construction, 'sees' nothing but statues.) Scheler admittedly left this construction unspoken, implicit, as if it were totally in the intended objects themselves, not in his feudal idealism; he gave the epistemological categories at best only a 'selecting' or 'discovering' function, with regard to the 'eternally pre-ordered' essentialities. But precisely this selection or discovery so often changed in Scheler's development, and the graphic institution so totally followed the changed individual and basic species, that the 'eternal' is seen 'pre-ordered' only in Scheler's reactionary epistemology, not in his so variable statues. Scheler began with investigations of psychological acts, then added individual scientific findings which filled the formal semantic analysis and were made 'essential' depending on Catholic requirements. After that Scheler followed a planned 'world phenomenology', of a walk into the 'cosmic divine garden of pure essential determinations', whereby Goethe had to combine superbly with all possible images of rest. Precisely here there opened up the space of the palm-like in the palms, of the moulded form which develops while alive, of the self-shaping Morphe, and Spengler later illustrated it quite surpassingly in cultures and opposed it to analytic research, as well as to everything unfinished in history. Scheler, however, pursued this divine garden less in the world than in ethics; thus, instead of Kantian formalism, he brought to light a material order of Catholic-moral values, an 'ethics of content'. This material ethics was regulated partly by bourgeois, partly by medieval-feudal evaluations as the perception of a personal value-existence; from vital and spiritual grades up to the sacred, from the will in the world up to the blessing heaven of ideas. Scheler's metaphysics of religion ('On the Eternal in Man') added the re-experience of natural-religious acts accessible to everyone, the reception of revealed acts and act-contents; an escape into highest substantial values, an attempted cathedral in the marshes of relativism. The many paths to Rome had here been joined by one of metaphysical semi-giftedness or that relation which inserted the ancient-transcendental order into its second-shearing one not out of faith, but out of a weakness of system. With historical splendour, and even corrective force, the hierarchies of feudal-Catholic idealism now lit up whose repose reigns over the world pacified or satisfied in Catholic terms. But immediately afterwards the crack arose in this very cathedral, there arose Scheler's final change of direction and the decline of objectivism:

135 Henri Bergson, 1859–1941, French philosopher.

unfulfilled acts rebelled against sacred being, the divine garden of eternal totalities withered around the Castle Grail, Klingsor's[136] magic garden advanced, Parsifal brandished no cross above it. The 'urge' superseded the Catholic basic construction, the possibility of an ideal-real ontology in the world; relativism, against which it was founded, had triumphed. Moreover, since the dialectics of history was still absent, and statics continued to prevail, relativism triumphed even as a theological final condition, in accordance with the decline of the bourgeois class world, even in its medieval armour. In his final phase, Scheler had to surrender the divine repose of contemplation, the pensioner's existence of assumed piety to a 'moral-heroic atheism', to a God who does not exist and now has man only as a fighter and hoper without guarantees, no longer as a believer. 'The great seeing which goes through the world' lost its objects, the entire after-glow of graded harmony. The lonely man in a collapsed world of ideas: this 'anthropology' remained the last word and the refuge of a phenomenology which had literally set out with God and the world. Which, with regard to all subjectivisms and relativisms, had sought to found the strictest ontology, a doctrine of the ontic fortress.

Soon afterwards another seeing went inwards, but then immediately economized. From the start, *Heidegger* enlisted possible being only as one 'located' within, indeed as a questionable one even here, as being of anxiety. He loans not from Thomas Aquinas, but from Kierkegaard; thus in fact Protestant features break forth in the vision of being (which had known only Catholic ones for so long). Protestant, even Augustinian inwardness (of nowadays), time instead of space, are now emphasized in phenomenology. Though in such a way that mere words, even though of that within, are squeezed even more strongly than before. Whole experiences occur in newly made or old traditional symbols, in a hyper-German language which reinforces feelings of today with lost ones. Certain psychological refinements, and also a stolid peasant seriousness, strangely unite with the desire to describe it, to make it really discoverable in words; Heidegger has the anxiety even as he lectures on it. This seriousness is strangely upheld by a pedantic rambler, who is joined by a professor of anxiety and worry, as if this were a subject like others too. There thus arises a kind of learned lecture-desk sorrow which, although it has totally subjectivized 'consciousness in general', does not cease to be pure conceptual vision. Heidegger nevertheless had a stimulating effect: 'anxiety', as Heidegger's one existential category, touched on the condition of the petit bourgeois, who has no job and prospects any more; 'worry', Heidegger's other category, affected upper middle-class citizens who are indeed 'held out into

136   The magician Klingsor appears in a fairytale in Novalis's unfinished Romantic novel *Heinrich von Ofterdingen*. The fairytale is also used by Wagner in *Parsifal*.

nothingness' exactly as Heidegger defines the 'human situation in general'. Above all, subjective ontology aspires to a certain proximity to the zero point of modern being, namely to naked life; it thus recommends itself to a general emptiness and bourgeois ordinariness as 'existential'. This 'existential' or even 'indifferent' outcome is at the same time positively none other than that of private industrial being: being-myself and only this rises up in a conscientious-isolated, Lutheran-sombre fashion against the 'disappearance into the They' and the public world. Thus Heidegger reflected the interior design of sinking strata, in an alleged 'analytics of existence in general'; but thus he also dug out for the irrational of the forces of reaction to which he belongs a channel of blood (or higher 'existence'). For the existere of anxiety and worry likewise appears as heroic in the 'analysis', namely as 'unprotected resistance towards fate'; but the elements of analysis remain the pre-logical ones of 'mood', of 'condition'; the logic of existence is the contemplation of a subjectivity which has become incurable, one of dull, decayed emotion. Just as this existential theory is now already beginning to rot, it did not lack vitalisms from the beginning; subjectivity and temporality, those categories to which phenomenology itself at first sought to oppose its firm rational edifice of non-contingent essentialities, have alone remained here, indeed have become ontology itself. Husserl's many 'noetic-noematic' ideas have gone; the great seeing, which was going through the world according to Scheler, has completely withdrawn into dully dark existing. The categories of essential seeing are shrinking into those of posited 'authenticity'; they are all also transcending, in so far as they remain merely in blind 'life' empty of meaning, simply towards death and no further. 'Thrownness' is the last existential category of man, moreover thrownness into death, as into an irrevocable, static condition, as into the only future which is approaching man. Heidegger had gone into the subject in order to escape the relativisms of the external world of essence from the start, in order to have the state of being human as the beginning of a question and not, like Scheler, as the outcome of catastrophe; but he already succumbed to the first danger here, to *vitalism* and its consequences. As Wiesengrund[137] rightly observes, Heidegger was also able to evade the second great threat to every material phenomenology of ideas – that of *historicism* – only by ontologizing time itself; whereby Scheler's notion of the eternal in man paradoxically dissolves; there arises the *fundamental ontology of transitoriness*. The 'essentialities' have not thereby vanished though, but passed from their heaven of ideas into a kind of dim hell of ideas, composed of anxiety, worry, thrownness, and death – the eternal is now merely this temporality. A contemplated temporality as well, a 'time' in the centre, which attains neither history

137   Patronymic of Adorno, see 'On the Threepenny Opera', n. 32.

nor dialectics; a 'practical philosophy' (as related to the 'concrete distress of human existence') which simply contains instructions for accepting positedness, never for action. The final question arises, of course, as
to why the bourgeoisie, which in other respects certainly adds diversion
and intoxication to 'inwardness', tolerates so much Kierkegaard and
gloom in one of its most fashionable philosophers, even though mitigated
by the strict pleasure of contemplation. But *firstly* Heidegger's philosophy, as noted above, has certainly remained a conceptual one, one
discussing sorrow, which it is possible to live with. No matter how
strong the 'ontic' experience, the Luther experience of creatureliness was
in it: it becomes apparent what contemplated questioning of worry, sin,
and guilt 'knows'; namely everything and thereby nothing. Conceptual
seeing, even though emotionalized, still triumphs in the end over dully
dark existential being; self-reference is employed for the purpose of a
contemplative science, namely of onto-logy, even though one with sheer
vitality-content. Heidegger's worry is not self-reference, self-accusation
in Kierkegaard's existential sense, but the object of an analytics of
existence; it is not an 'interest' any more, but interesting, learned,
objective, it is called 'the unity of the transcendental structure of the
inmost neediness of existence in [!] man'. If Heidegger thus recommended himself to the liberal bourgeoisie through a seriousness which
does not seriously go ahead, through reflective feelings which do not
even remain feelings, let alone become practice: then, *secondly*, he recommended himself to a bourgeoisie which had become *fascist* through
the old Protestant heritage of human nullity and the gloom of that
posited for it. All existence is a state of being thrown into death; but
towards the latter there is only the attitude of 'forerunning resolution',
which does not change anything at all in the chance 'down-fall'. Which
simply confirms the continuance of the individual self once again, with
respect to the disappearance into the They: the grasped death as the
grasped being-to-the-end is radical individuation. And even in this death
is not, as in Kierkegaard, a sign of existential paradox, it does not shock
subjectivity into acceptance of the biblical word; it is rather a mere
running out of existence, the mere gloom of the solemn chance down-
fall. If Heidegger formulates 'existence in its unhomeliness',[138] if he
defines 'the original thrown being-in-the-world as non-home', then he
formulates this surrendered element at the same time as identical with
the chance down-fall of the whole of existence in general; he recognizes
no element in it which is opposed to the unhomeliness and the non-
home. Thus existence itself is its own unhomeliness, thus it is completely

---

138 'Unheimlichkeit': the central meaning of this is 'uncanniness', but it takes
on a second, more dominant sense in Heidegger, and can also be seen here
as the direct opposite of Bloch's concept of 'Heimat', the 'home' of
fulfilled existence.

surrendered to death, all 'forerunning resolution' only comes under the eyes of death and nothing else, there is no consolation against death as the positively recognized and acknowledged 'downright nullity' of existence itself, which does not annihilate itself in death, but represents itself. Thus, along with non-commitment, absolute nullity also becomes the peace of the bourgeoisie, the peace which is created by the discouragement of the will to change, by the metaphysical act of rendering its own uneasiness absolute. Eternal death at the end makes the respective social condition 'of man' so important that it can even remain a capitalist one. The affirmation of death as an absolute fate and the only Where-To makes the same contribution to the counter-revolution of today as used to be made by the consolation with empty promises of a better other world. Infinitely remote and not even touched upon in this 'ontology of the subject' is the tendency to found *rebellion* in despair, to find *hope* in rebellion (hope which has not yet been wrecked in the world). There is a lack of every 'understanding oneself in existence' which could burst out against the blind concept of life, against the humanly unmediated status of nature – precisely through 'inwardness'. The pathos of the subject is simply suffering and individual in this ontology and goes, with a totally reified 'fatalism', towards death. A different subject from that of the individual and reified class will perhaps not find with Heidegger that no scientific rigour can equal the seriousness of Heideggerian metaphysics, but rather that the seriousness of every metaphysics has to prove itself in the liquidation of vital thrownness, of mortal fate. As a new element the 'subject' admittedly stands out in this ontology (instead of the Arcadian divine repose in the world-garden). But as a Heideggerian subject, despite its 'existence in general', it only has the character of being a very ephemeral one; it is the subject of the introverted bourgeoisie in decline or of the doggedly maintained one in its accepted nullity. The 'surprisingness of existence', the grounding with anxiety and death, the state of being held into nothingness, the metaphysical question as to the ground or however else Heidegger renders the empty and spooky character of these times absolute, can by no means be concretely experienced in this subject. The genuine 'subject' is not this late bourgeois man (beneath the mask of existence in general), but today only the oppressed, missing and for this very reason turning man (whose strongest overturning point is designated by the proletariat). And likewise, as really timely the subject does not exist in isolation, is not reflected in formalized feelings, vitalized Lutheran corners; but the time of its being is the dialectics of history, the dialectical hope out of nothing but class history. Instead of this (and also instead of the former divine garden, of course) Heidegger has only the labyrinth of late-bourgeois, very squeezed, very incurable subjectivity. It is all a labyrinth, including a guiding thread through to the Minotaur at the end – and the thread of Ariadne is missing.

EXISTENTIAL ILLUMINATION AND SYMBOLIC VISION 'CROSSWISE TO EXISTENCE'

Even many an older glance seeks what has still remained to it here. Fastens its gaze on itself, reflects in an even more lonely and reminiscent way. If the economic circumstances are secure, says *Jaspers*,[139] then the mind expands and forgets to be conditional. If they are insecure (as they seem to be today), then Jaspers, as the last phenomenologist, turns away from them all the more – into what is purely human, higher in a lonely way and educated. The 'mind' is then alone conditioned by the respective representative, by the freely choosing human being, it no longer imposes itself. Science as a profession must not be confessional anyway, but even philosophy is now only recognized as philosophizing, and at most as the Socratic kind. Indeed, in his 'Psychology of World Views' Jaspers had not even granted that much, but was still totally non-valuing, and positive in an individual scientific way. He described the great ideas as purely mental constructs, which are just simply there, assigned them to certain types, glanced at the world only through these types, led mind to selection, did not decide or only imperceptibly, and apart from psychological truths believed in none. Since then of course Kierkegaard has gained ground, the university experienced the 'crisis of reflection', i.e. both the bankruptcy of the bourgeois Ratio and the drowning will for a support; thus, instead of philosophizing, philosophy itself appears again and, as in Heidegger, as an 'existential' one. The existential, however, here becomes – in accordance with its psychologistic origin – a torn and simply advisory[140] phenomenon; this crisis of reflection seeks – with a liberalism which passes into bourgeois anarchy – merely to show every individual how he is doing or (concerning belief) how he is holding on. Instead of risked ontology, there remain ethically only appeal and choice, metaphysically only possible capacities for being affected by ambiguous 'ciphers'. This 'existentially' mitigated

139 Karl Jaspers, 1883–1969, existentialist philosopher.
140 'Ratend' carries both the sense of 'advising' and 'guessing' here.

and coloured agnosticism is advisory, we said; it is so both in the unobtrusive sense of an appealing advice (namely of searchers by a search which itself comes to its senses while philosophizing only through ignorance), and advisory in the final sense of an advisory guess, of a cipher-interpretation of the world-being. 'Existentialist philosophy' at this level therefore knows no certainty, neither a scientific one (this applies only to impersonal consciousness in general and its positivist objects) nor that of a prophetic pathos at the lecture-desk. It also abandons the apodictic claim of 'evidences' which phenomenology, by virtue of a medieval image of the community and of faith, had still maintained for its world of sight, world of single insight. 'Existence', particularly in Jaspers, has become totally Protestant; for it is found only in individual human beings receiving communion, it makes itself sure even methodically always only as *self-affectedness* of mind. In this subject-space, of course, a very strange breadth occurs, one which on an 'existential basis' attempts to fit in at least an educated shape-system; this then touches so to speak, in Protestant narrowness, on a kind of catastrophized Catholicism. Instead of Scheler's shape-vision, a 'symbolic vision, crosswise to existence' appears; Jaspers calls this 'fused into the movement of the existential making sure of transcendence'.

Thinking begins here as a question as to what, still as to what, being is per se. It is quite unimportant to dwell on this, and the moral cry to people 'on the same path' is also quite weak. For not everyone strolls on the path of these worries, nor everyone in an Orphic dressing-gown through the 'law of the day and the passion for the night'. Only bourgeois feelings greet one another in these parts from house to house, eerily unworldly; no light of real analysis falls in. Even the 'world-orientation' with which Jaspers starts has not heard a word about the only positive orientation, the Marxist one. The 'existential illumination', with which a moral volume continues, immortalizes instead the 'antinomies of existence' (of the bourgeois citizen) as existential determinations 'of human imperfection per se'. Here is the parallel to Heidegger's being unto death or to the total devaluation which even liberal fascists, if they do not relish the boom, still keep at their disposal. But the *third* volume of Jaspers's endeavour is more speckled; for the 'transcendence' which appears here is at least torn and wildly animated, wildly patched at the same time. Thus it may be considered as a more genuine sign of the times, as phenomenology in full criss-crossing; it is just as groundless as, in this area, it is surprising as a tangle. Here unconditional obligation has become untenable even as a formal cadre, and in particular Jaspers, as the honest late bourgeois, lacks any leap into religious reality, any binding *ontology* of being as being. There remains only the existential state of being affected by signs, 'ciphers', symbols, by means of which the totally ungraspable transcendence (that is, being as being) manifests itself in 'floating' fashion to an inner preparedness. Hence scientific consciousness, as consciousness in general, cannot 'even hear, let alone understand' the ciphers; but the abyss in these, empty for the intellect, is able to fill up 'for existence'. 'For the transcending temporal existence of man is able as possible existence to become the *unity of present and searching:* a present which exists only as the searching which is not cut off from what it is searching for.' The metaphysical object is therefore never the ens absolute absconditum of transcendence, but only in fact its cipher, with which it touches the existential man in the moment, and also in the midst of world-being, 'in order to confront him directly with the unknown'. The mythical images in which original vision had expressed itself are extinct; positivism, says Jaspers, has rightly expelled them from the world of the knowable. But if this world of scientific consciousness collapses at its limits, then the world of myth-images, this at first only authoritative objectivity, is newly graspable *in the language of existential tornness and fusibility* (as a language becoming general). Unity of the substantial ground is not attainable to this language, but rather that genuine symbolism which is not sent round from one image to another like mere 'symbolic interpretation', in order finally to land in something already known (be it the libido or primitive agriculture or even former stellar constellations). But *genuine* symbolism breaks through its history straight across the already ordered and empirically real; it knows only an *inexhaustibly self-devouring whirlpool of the depths* and lands, instead of in being as a recognized matter, in an abyss of the indefinite. The means of deciphering this language is therefore no longer the concept, but the genuine physiognomical imagination: for it all existence has 'an uncertain vibration and speech, seems to express something, but it is questionable what for and what about'; for it there is 'in the puddle in the road and in the sunrise, in the anatomy of a worm and in a Mediterranean landscape ... something which is not exhausted by mere existence as an object of scientific research'. That which in Jaspers then admittedly, after so many modest-cheerful words, appears as an example of his ciphers would not always have needed such enormous-hidden space. Jaspers, as the former logician of psychiatric diagnosis, undoubtedly understands more of physiognomical understanding than many a Klages, of course; also, an honest thinker of existence is captivated not so much by mythological images (from literature) as those that can be really experienced (from modern existence amd immediate reality). Likewise the drive to fit ciphers crosswise into the world is certainly surprising in the old classifier; if the second part of this 'philosophy', so-called existential illumination, was mainly just spiritual welfare from the pre-war period, the world as cipher is indeed a present-day problem. Nevertheless, the ciphers specifically cited here, such as those of nature, are certainly not fresh visions of images, but likewise full of stale bourgeois feelings, full of prearranged associations, moreover in a language which, despite its metaphysical spiritual welfare, could still not be that of the intended whirlpool depths; for, together with its contents, it has been said a thousand times since the Romantic period, and better. Here there again appears the groundless attempt to pursue 'metaphysics' with late-bourgeois Ratio, just because it lacks the ground under its feet; and above all there again appears the hopelessness of substantial mediation (which is hopeless only to the totally undialectical thinking of this 'transcendence') as 'eternal fate'. Like the alleged nullity of earthly existence, the night-mysticism of 'failure' (which here surrounds the experience of the substantial ground) is also actually a mere act of rendering the bourgeois decline absolute, and equally reactionary; the same is true of the 'eternal inscrutability' of ontic being. But, unexpectedly at any rate, existential phenomenology went from 'judiciousness' to 'docta ignorantia', from the apparent profusion of adequately visualized shapes to the picture at Sais.[141] Now it stands there with empty hands, though also stands there, ultimately, with lines in the palms of its hands and ciphers appearing in all directions. First ontology conquered psychological relativism, and then the *object-based* relativism of hollow space forces ontology itself to take refuge in symbols of isolated detail and transitoriness; indeed ontology in general fades away, its pretended firm *knowledge* of being shatters into *torn, into tearing and kaleidoscoping experience* of being as *suspension*. It is thus in order, and an instructive swan-song, that precisely phenomenology still experiences hollow space, that shape-vision ends as – reading ciphers (in a ruined expanse of subject-object-based ontology). Questions come to an end cheaply for it with its ciphers, and even more cheaply it persists in mere single-layered contemplation with regard to the respective cipher meaning; gratis, even, the 'inscrutable' remains completely beyond historical-dialectical subject-object mediation. But such phenomenology reduced the appearance of finished shapes themselves to absurdity; it knows nothing about them any more, it rips them out of all hierarchy, it places them as written characters (no longer as statues) into an attempted 'this world as miracle'. If late-bourgeois feeling hunts down nothing but itself here, if the problem of a dialectical 'image-theory' in the individual part and the whole will pass over this 'metaphysics', then not in the problem of the cosmic script (to which phenomenology pays its due).

141   See 'Expressionism, seen now', n. 68.

TRIBUTE OF VIRTUE TO VICE

All these many different thinkers strove to be unequivocal. They started, as noted above, allegedly from scratch, and hence with doubts about anything and everything. But this hollow-spaced feeling soon comforts itself with their *own* findings, whether they were logistical or ontological. The empiricists came to the aid of their abstract doubt with clear and distinct knowledge, and thus still with the old calculation, even though with one which confined itself to logistical equations. Phenomenology, on the other hand, believed there was unequivocal ground in simple or categorical graphic intuition, in a kind of higher 'empiricism' as it were. Which raised graphic intuition in contrast to the mere experiences of individual science, which promised a *material* certainty, a material a priori in the objective essentialities themselves. Both so entirely different doctrines are still agreed – despite relativism – in their apodictics, whereby the empiricists were nevertheless a model case in non-logistical, in open 'experiential knowledge' or at least susceptible to relativism. Common to both is also the cult of the 'immediate given fact', in the sense of something ascertainable there and then, unhistorically, undialectically; whereby not only the subject to which something is given is grasped ahistorically as identical, but also the given object in particular (here of the empirical, there of the phenomenological 'findings'). But now the surface has cracked so much further that it can no longer bear any calculation, let alone any ontology of the immediate given fact. The empiricists already had double entry book-keeping, simply that of logistics on the one hand and of open experience on the other. The phenomenologists drew their conclusions in a broader field: Scheler resorted to the immediate urge and vacated the heaven of ideas; Heidegger confined the question as to the unequivocal ground to the question as to the 'actual' self. He admittedly posed this question only for the sake of 'relaying the foundation of being in man', but the immediate 'basic condition' is here nothing but anxiety, worry and other ephemerally appearing experience, hanging out into nothingness. All these thinkers beginning anew, or Jacobins of the late bourgeoisie, thus got out of abstract doubt only at the cost of a more concrete kind: of the chaos in late-bourgeois hollow space. Finally in Jaspers even, in this 'metaphysics', the strangest mixture already appeared, a blend of 'symbols' or an empty montage; here there is almost a tribute of academic virtue to an unknown and unfamiliar, but irrefutable vice. 'One must', teaches *Kierkegaard*, 'be cleverer than the cleverest and then act against cleverness'; our phenomenological thought-officials are not the former, but the latter seems, in places, to be their 'fate'. It was stated above, in the transitional chapter 'Berlin, Functions in Hollow Space' ('Montage, direct', p. 203): 'Directly of course, in their own bourgeois truth, all these crossed emotions or hieroglyphs are only equally crossed and obstructed background.' Now that it is a question of the use of these ragouts, of their dialectics against their will and concept, we are interested in the tribute of virtue to vice or the influence of hollow space on that very 'ontology' which set out to cover it up. Strangely, above all in Jaspers, an eclectic beggar's soup[142] occasionally turns into a soup of letters, also goat rhyme,[143] also cipher-montage. *Genuine* philosophical montage naturally comes from a very different side; but it cannot avoid being dialectically surprised at ontology as cipher-interpretation, at true temple-swamps in the academy. The guarantor of all *genuine* philosophical montage is of course never any other than the recognized dialectical process; and the 'inscrutable' liquidates itself as soon as its 'symbols' are finally read in the right direction, namely from top to bottom, namely from their by no means transcendental 'heaven' down to the earth. Bourgeois thinking is not sufficient for this; it remains, even as far as 'montage' is concerned, in a mere vague, pre-logical 'mood'. The ciphers play a confused, and at the same time isolated tangle, and the 'cipher code'? It is none, except as a dialectical interlacing of 'images' of decay and their objects of decay. As such the decay brings it up, but only in a new, even though wholly inverted order does it become, possibly, decipherable. Decipherable in tension-shapes, tendency-figures from on the way, but all full of attempted signification of that outstanding content which could be no 'housing', but rather the house.

142   Bloch also has the figurative sense of 'Bettelsuppe' in mind here, a paltry intellectual effort.
143   Rhyme based on the transposition of consonants of rhyming syllables in succeeding lines.

APPENDIX: SPENGLER'S PREDATORS AND RELATIVE CULTURAL GARDENS

It is not just mournfully that this man sees how everything passes. He is just as content to create a very fierce stir in the void. Spengler took blossoming paths in historical terms, for the present day only the wild man remains to him. Who begins coldly, and then continues as if there had never been historical cultivation and clothes. The cultivation passes away, in increasingly animal fashion so-called life steps forward.

First of all, modern man was admittedly supposed to be cold, but also very businesslike. Spengler, contemplating everything himself, does not grant others this approach, but praises action. That of big business in fact, and also that of the technological intellect; in 1918 the desire for wilderness seemed to be over. But even a bloodless wilderness was not allowed; since the summer of culture was over, it was senseless to paint, to make music or to write. No 'time' in the West any more for dreams; this thesis was posited by a bourgeois citizen for whom his declining class is every class and his defeated country the West per se. The thesis of decline was to be disturbed by no larking about in lessons, by no imaginative choice of profession; Spengler's curriculum, and chronological fate, demanded this. In the lump, all future talents received, for centuries, without respect of person, an office stool and polytechnic tailor-made for them. Whereby the soldier is not lacking, the victor over 'money and mind'; but in fact, even he does not come from the bright and cheerful war, is no longer a demon who believes in the stars, but a technologist, a Caesar of the mechanical battle. This was the *first* image of modern man and his peak; later, in 1921, in the work 'Pessimism?', some *permits* were added, but without changing the 'Roman face'. When Spengler protested against being merely decline, he permitted, as an 'optimist' – not roses, but asters on the grave. Cheerful asters of course, in keeping with the merriment which the German illusory boom spread after the war, and which it needed as window-dressing. The 'Caesar' admittedly still holds good to whom 'we Germans will yet give birth', though a German novel is likewise permitted, also a 'farce on a grand scale', indeed even a 'German Carmen music, full of dash and spirit, sparkling with melody, tempo and fire, of which Mozart and Johann Strauss, Bruckner [?!] and the young Schumann would not be ashamed to be named as ancestors'. A cheerful last dance without doubt, and so wildly enjoyable that even Offenbach would not be ashamed to appear as an ancestor; he had, after all, already composed into one, *ironically*, everything which Spengler causes to dance around the steel helmet. Or rather, in fact, around big capitalists and directors; for Spengler's 'man of action', his great model, is and remains the heavy industrial robber, the imperialist. With the longing of the senior primary school teacher, Spengler looks at Cecil Rhodes,[144] the 'first representative of the final western style', but here there also already begins the *final pathos* in Spengler's present age, proclaimed in 1932 (the right year), in his work 'Man and Technology'. This final pathos is no longer aimed at the old businessman, but the bloody one: man appears as a *predator*, and in fact as a renewed one. Thus the pleasure of business, and also the prize for technology which Spengler had awarded in 1918, is dismissed once and for all. In keeping with the crisis and the changed interest of profit, curbed invention, burnt coffee, and machine wrecking is ideologized from now on; as in Klages, only considerably more wildly, a 'primeval man' steps into the night. With the praise of the office stool there was still the question as to whether it would have needed such a – detour, whether it would have needed three 'cultural souls' to stabilize such rochers de tombac.[145] Yet this question appears even more strongly justified in view of the predator philosophy into which Spengler's vision ultimately decays; and even less remains of all western culture. Spengler's man of the late period is not even a beast of civilization, as Cecil Rhodes still was, but a completely naked one, above all a steaming one; indeed, a kind of freak, a warm-blooded crocodile. So superficially and summarily, to an extent unusual even in him, does the Spengler of 1932 decree 'vitalisms' whose falseness is surpassed only by their banality, and their banality only by the cynicism of unrestrained exploitation. The sheep are now separated from the goats once and for all, the 'noble ethics of sight' of the predator now prevails over the 'cowardly ethics of smell' of the prey. Now 'the actual human soul is everyone's enemy', for 'it knows the intoxicating feeling when the knife cuts into the enemy's body, when the smell of blood and groaning penetrate the triumphant senses'. Now, in barely credible hysteria, all atrocity propaganda about Germany is confirmed; and zoological nonsense of all kinds comes just at the right time to ideologize in advance the 'night of

144   Cecil Rhodes, 1853–1902, British administrator and colonialist financier in South Africa.
145   Cheap jewellery.

the long knives' which the Nazis proclaimed. 'If the eye were not like the sun, how could it perceive the sun', sang Goethe and knew nothing as yet of the 'ethics of sight' of the final German or the l'art pour l'art of murder. In 'Decline of the West', as an antiquarian, Spengler was a song of elevated styles, a collection of cultural gardens right through the cultivated and thoroughly formed earth; now the antiquarian who has been compared with Herder and Hegel teaches man as teeth, his fellow-man as raw food, and everything else, the medal of Athene, the Arabian dome, the western geometry of night – is so much a thing of the past, it is as if it had not even existed. Windelband[146] once spoke of the 'writer F. Nietzsche' as the 'nervous professor who would love to be a wild tyrant'. This statement is a scandal applied to Nietzsche, but applied to Spengler's last phase it strikes home. With him there lives, as the subject of the 'Germanic end', not even the blond beast, but the sick one, not the dreaming primeval man of the Romantics, but the decadent murder-er, not Caesar, but Nero. Thus in 1933, in the 'year of decision' and his very last, similarly named work, Spengler welcomes the 'national up-heaval' as a 'longed-for' one, and he is worried only by the fact that it might not show enough 'strong spirit'. 'When the workers came home from the war, despite the massive loss of life a housing shortage arose all over the world because [!] the victorious proletariat [!] now wanted to live in the style of the bourgeoisie and achieved this'; and with similar strength of feeling, and depth of knowledge, Spengler in his last phase specifies the gist of his position: 'Unemployment is everywhere in exact proportion to the political standard wage.' Thus the philosopher of the gentlemen's club fears too much 'socialism' in Thyssen,[147] he fears that the 'national upheaval' might rest on the premature laurels of a predator which has not yet bitten anything; that it might not break out on a sufficiently 'grand scale' against the 'white world-revolution' or the class struggle, against the 'coloured' world-revolution or the racial struggle, and both together. 'The disgust of deep and strong human beings with our state of affairs and the hatred of deeply disappointed ones could in fact intensify into a revolt which seeks annihilation.' The first true word in the 'Prussian' ideology, but not meant as such; the first disowning almost of Hitlerism, but only because Spengler does not credit the demagogue with the beast and the great mouth of mass jubilation with aristocratic teeth. Big business with its Spengler does not want any 'apotheosis of the herd instinct', wants itself to be the solitary ruling beast, indeed the only *life* on earth, and the working masses to have died into machines. For 'German Carmen music', with Bruckner as an ances-tor, the dance around such monsters would not be easy. The music of western culture does not suffice for this 'decline' of its own, indeed the

146   Wilhelm Windelband, 1848–1915, neo-Kantian philosopher.
147   The Thyssen brothers, see 'Inventory of revolutionary appearance', n. 45.

latter does not even stretch to Spengler's 'Decline of the West', in which western music had not garnished any slaughter-house anyway, but 'morphology'.

Though there was a contemptuous tone even here, something there to be taken only for the cautious hand. The nothingness of coldness was involved linguistically at least, in the falsely stinted sentences which are supposed to be masterful and are merely brash. What had been called a brilliant style in the nineties here became the cliché as order of the day. The highly contestable thereby appeared exact, the highly general precise: 'Form is anxiety' or 'world history is urban history' or 'optimism is cowardice' or 'cultures are plants' or even 'cultures *are* plants', 'life *is* war' and countless similar examples, so that summary mush stood as if moulded. Yet the basic attitude, behind the military mask, was thoroughly contemplative, savouring and appreciative; this attitude did not, for instance, make history run up to the present day (which in fact knows only the practice of the prehistoric beast), but lingered collectingly, synoptically, historically by all means at a particular place and time. Thereby, fortunately, the brutal and idiotic nonsense of the *journalist* Spengler is also lacking; it is often hardly possible to suspect that the latter and the sensitive antiquarian are the same. Royal courts of the eighteenth century appointed as a separate court official the 'custodian of the turtles'; such an official is the *historian* Spengler with his many miscellanea, and of course also a consumer of turtles and an amusing transformer of collected history into simultaneously laid tables. The historical driving forces themselves were destroyed, something so unrefined as economics not accepted, ages expired, ultimately unmoved, in autarky. Here relativistic sociology (Mannheim)[148] has points of contact with Spengler and vice versa: like the former he abolished every semblance of historical process, and particularly every continuous content, every extensive and comprehensive 'unity in history'. What the various sociological structures in Mannheim performed in *time*, Spengler's culture groups, the isolated landscape gardens of prevailing culture, performed in *space*: namely the explosion of history, the removal of dialectically continuous links. The primacy of space over time in general is an infallible characteristic of reactionary language; beginning with the illustrated supplements which call themselves 'Nation and Space' (supplements of left-wing papers were called 'Nation and Time'), down to Nadler's[149] 'space-historical method' and Keyserling's[150] geographical meditations. In Spengler 'space-historical fate' is, at the most, not so directly connected with the soil but more with the 'cultural soul', which

148   Karl Mannheim, see 'Social reflections', n. 109.
149   Josef Nadler, 1884–1963, Austrian literary historian.
150   Hermann Graf Keyserling, see 'Result for a part of concrete-utopian practice', n. 159.

travelled over such different countries and united them. Baghdad and Cordoba lie in the same spatial sphere in Arab terms and adapt themselves to it; also on Italian soil, beneath pine trees, classical civilization prospers just as well as Faustian culture. Nevertheless, the primacy of space certainly prevails in Spengler, if not by means of landscape, then by means of 'cultural physiognomy'; the latter even brings an excess of 'shape', of 'morphology' and precisely of that statics which, under the appearance of life, adheres to every 'shape-seeing'. The law under which a culture starts is in Spengler more than ever an inner spatial fate and as it were a raised soil: with fixed flora, with the natural determination of the organic blossoming and withering of its fruits, with four seasons over it as in the edifice of nature. There is thus no time at all in Spengler outside the respective cultural space; and this time of his is nothing but the feeble shadow of a pre-ordered development which takes the same fateful path in all cultures, the same beginning, the same end, and only the cultural symbol is different in each case. Even the 'mythological primeval times', which Bachofen could not place far enough away at the beginning of history, are here lifted out of the uniform succession of time; they begin in every culture anew, in the 'misty Merovingian period' of every culture, 'where its symbol is born out of the twilight of an ahistorical dawn'. Here in general there is no distinction of a succession between Egypt, Greece, the West: Alexander and Napoleon, Granada and Rococo, Pergamon and Bayreuth are 'synchronisms'; that is also why the times themselves are not in time, but whirlpools of space in the eternally unmoved, fundamentally untouched substance. 'All urging, all struggling is eternal rest in the Lord God': with this maxim of Goethe's, cultural time, indeed even every cultural symbol is isolated on its own; at the same time the decayed suspension of these symbols is falsely consecrated, namely as suspension in untouched, in eternally unrecognizable space. In this way creative time and unknown future remain all the more excluded, process decays, gets caught in static patterns, without the slightest reference of their relatively true contents to a comprehensive one. This multiple and interrupted element thus corresponds not just to the relativism of separate 'social structures', but cum grano salis, as a 'world-view', also to physical relativism; the latter placed (with more 'justification') several worlds even into *nature*, micro-, meso-, macrocosmic ones, with their own laws and without recognizable reference to comprehensive 'mechanics'. Spengler's 'morphology' is a sum total of variable but settled historical figures, and these figures hang like constellations unconnected in the eternally transcendent universe.

Thus many false glances already went into life here which has none. Economic reasons, and especially causes, are disregarded anyway, as we have seen. But there is also a lack of every other reference to becoming, to the experience of becoming, to the question of the New. Spengler knows no other contents than those which can be pinned up in a museum, indeed for him they are already mounted on the spot. There is a lack not just of the feel for economy but also of that for more beautifully formative driving forces which have released what has culturally become and are not discharged with it. The historian Spengler is thus no backward-looking prophet, but a forward-looking antiquarian. And this whole static prison as well, the reflex of depersonalization, bourgeois-mechanical reification over the whole of 'history'. Given so much 'masterful' rhetoric, so much predatory gesturing, how much historical whipping there is at the same time, how much automatic fate in words and doctrines like this one: 'Only dreamers believe in escape routes; the fate of man is taking its course and has to be accomplished, optimism is cowardice.' Even in motor terms therefore, not just in 'visionary' ones, a total unconnectedness with the phenomenon of time prevails, a 'heroic'-scornful joy in the imposed spell. As Spengler thus exorcizes time, he admittedly comes in time for a bourgeoisie which was increasingly abandoning both history and especially causal-genetic thinking from below. In this respect Spengler has become not only relativistic sociology, with isolated 'structures', but a centre of all reactionary-static ones; for he showed how to make even historical flow – apparently precisely in full 'history' – *congeal*. Likewise 'physiognomics' is a means to this detemporalization, and 'morphology' the medium of space; it is this morphology which relieves 'symbolic constructs' most soundly of causal genesis and most particularly of dialectics. It is also strange here how far back this obvious fascistization of history already goes, the extent to which conscious reactionary thinking of today plucks an unknown one of yesterday. With specifically historical 'understanding' the genetic-causal aversion had already begun in Dilthey,[151] and it led to Windelband and Rickert's 'limits of scientific concept formation' (namely to the limits of natural science alongside history, alongside the 'idiographic value constructs' of history); it finally even received a scholastic contribution through phenomenology or the vision of 'Platonic essentialities'. This 'essential knowledge' contrasted particularly sharply with all merely 'inductive knowledge', and hence with the analytic-causal method of the nineteenth century (which fascism so 'organically' despises). Above all it removed as 'integral knowledge' dangerous Marxism from the discussion much more sublimely than merely relativistic sociology à la Mannheim, than the mere application of 'Marxism' to itself; there thus even arose, beyond Spengler, so-called 'sense-based sociology' (in Sombart,[152] Freyer,[153] Gottl-

---

151 Wilhelm Dilthey, 1833–1911, philosopher who sought to put the humanities on a methodical scientific basis.
152 Werner Sombart, 1863–1941, economist and sociologist.
153 See 'Inventory of revolutionary appearance', n. 53.

Ottlilienfeld[154] and other fascists), which settles totally outside the genetic-causal stream, indeed outside rational deducibility (of the symbolic constructs) in general. Unfortunately the catastrophe of shape-based essential knowledge in the world existing in bourgeois terms (a catastrophe which already began with Scheler, continues in Heidegger and also Jaspers, and the necessary details of which have been heard about in the previous chapters) – unfortunately this more advanced phenomenology still remained unknown to the sociological beneficiaries of the older one. But even so it is a sunspot of 'non-causal morphology' – before and after Spengler – that its appearance at this point of time is so very 'understandable' precisely in *economic-causal* terms; nothing proves causality more strongly than fascism when it denies it. And a second sunspot is the confinement of genetic hatred to causality alone, instead of also attacking dialectics expressis verbis; for the latter is at least as peculiar to Marxism as the despised inductive-causal method. Dialectics, of course, is less of a scientific subordinate than causal thinking, and also by no means a fruit of the nineteenth century, but one of Plato and Hegel; nevertheless – however unpleasant a battle of the new idealists against Plato and Hegel may be, the rejection of simple causality is unfair if it avoids its counterpart, dialectics which is very refined even though it has become materialist, as if it were wholly unknown to the morphologists. Be that as it may, *Spengler's morphology* was for causal hatred the most convenient fulfilment, the most finished portrait, was the most complete barring of the dialectical idea of movement and unity above all. Hence Spengler admittedly fosters the most massive belief in the respective points of unity, in the 'symbols' of a culture; but he knows no point of unity in cultural production in general, which may actually first have called these 'symbols' forth and to its assistance. He admittedly looks – inconsistently enough – into totally isolated cultures, indeed he certainly works with comprehensive concepts of spheres like art, mathematics and religion, he even has such a comprehensive notion as 'Christianity' in a triple version: namely an Arab, Faustian and Russian one. But the historical process itself decays into cultural gardens or 'cultural souls', which are just as unmediated among themselves as they are with man and his work (as the *continuous* matter of history) and with nature (as the differently continuous or comprehensive element in which this history is placed). Historical relativism here – with great skill – becomes static, by getting caught in cultural monads; that is, in cultural souls without windows, without connection with one another and with nature, but full of pier-glasses on the inside.

Thus Spengler inherits so little of the lustre which he presents. He is left with the predator, otherwise there is forgetting or a brief, past,

154   Friedrich von Gottl-Ottlilienfeld, 1868–1958, political economist.

hopeless taste, perhaps a predator with taste. The closer Spengler comes to the Now or to 'existential' questions of the Altogether, the more absurdly the standard sinks which he certainly still observed as an antiquarian. The philistine of bestiality is despicable, the statesman Spengler laughable, but even the morphologist from on the way loses dignity if light of today falls anywhere at all into his antiquarian shop. Then our statesman calls Marcus Aurelius[155] an 'old woman', the predator does not find Lao Tzu and Buddha life-affirming enough, whereas Bernard Shaw appears as the last – Faustian philosopher. Thus Spengler has nothing left at all from foreign cultures, and from his own, Germanic, Faustian ones only the beast, the joker and the 'transitional phenomenon' of socialism. Our obligingness is proverbial, but when Tycho Brahe's[156] coachman had lost his way one day and the astronomer wanted to show him the way, 'Sir', cried the coachman, 'you might know your way about the sky, but on earth you're a fool.' Spengler admittedly only knows his way about the museum of history and not at all about the sky, or at most about one which reduces history to rotating drums, run by stars of fate. Nevertheless, as far as the Now is concerned, Spengler's prescriptions are likewise put to shame by every organized coachman; and the Altogether? 'Cultures are plants, nothing else', says the furious philosophy of history and cuts them. There remain the *details* of morphology, many a fine chapter, many a bright remark, many an amusing parallel, many a crosswise glance above all, reluctantly, and the discovery of 'Arabic culture'. The herbarium character of these educational gardens is evident, as is the biological regression, as is the stability without windows, without utopia. Only if a conqueror were to enter, who knew how to take a different approach to the 'symbols' and many symbolic witnesses from an unconcerned and isolated contemplation of them; only if the 'dome and alchemy', the 'Gothic deep space and analysis as geometry of night' could be examined in a *collected* and *occupied* semantic space, would an inheritance be there, but one which contradicts precisely the new-closedness of this relativism, namely the inheritance of possible crack-symbols of our *common* and *unknown* face. Only then could the relative 'statics' be defined, without lies and hesitation, which certainly also raises whirlpools in the dialectical process, knots of a historical 'surplus', meagre paradises composed of various 'cultural symbols'. There is an undoubted crosswise glance here too, an encountered merging of *details*; the plunging, mixing late period – despite all 'morphology' – cannot help it. Picasso's picture of the *Apollonian* crosswise glance is attractive: pine, coin, polis, statue, close colour, flat ceiling, Euclidean geometry. The kaleidoscope of the *magical* crosswise glance is dreamy: cave, dome,

---

155   Marcus Aurelius, 121–180 (Roman Emperor 161–180), Stoic philosopher.
156   Tycho Brahe, 1546–1601, Danish astronomer.

Arabian fairytale as dome-like suspension of the other world in this world, gold ground of the mosaic, gold ground of Arabian natural science as alchemy, sacrament of baptism. The Rimbaud mixture of the *Faustian* crosswise glance (of the distant and deep dimension) is exciting: Wild Hunt, tower clocks, nave, apse and soaring fan vault, sacrament of penance, perspective and the blue colour of distance, counterpoint and analysis, invention of the telescope, of cheque transactions, of the world economy, of processions of lines into immensity. The basic substance of these syzygies remains at variance, if only because of the appreciative, contemplatively born art of analogy which makes a 'synopsis' here; the attempt at any rate is from a late mixed perspective, and it would in fact be impossible to perform if *side-parts*, *ruined fragments* of meditation had not betrayed certain meanings which the closed summit glance of earlier contemplation could not see. But they are only ruins of *meditation*, and they are framed into nothing but 'cultural souls' that have become still; they are moreover in a night whose Faustian 'infinity' has become pure nothingness for the bourgeoisie. Spengler adds up the 'cultural symbols', despite their inner syzygies, only lifelessly side by side; above all, none of them has anything other to say or to sing out than its own, immanent, aestheticistic 'sense'. In short, only when the dead no longer bury their dead will a very different 'morphology' also form a body, a far-reaching one or one for which the inheritance *lives*. Only then is there no longer historical but incorporated sequence, a sequence of *continuous* human and cultural symbols which takes disappearance from history, a sequence of experimental shapes of the human shape, in Schelling's terms: of silver glances of the extracted human metal. Until then 'morphology' is only a sign, in no uncertain terms, and a dangerous one, of the fascist enemy. But at the same time it advises that dialectics, on its march and during the acts of its disenchantment, should not forget to occupy the treasure-houses which remain real. Apart from the caves of the unbecome and of fermenting uncertainty, apart from the heirlooms of revolutionary consciousness there are, mysteriously, also the treasure-houses of *standing culture*. Of which the enemy makes a desperate inventory after it no longer belongs to him.

PHILOSOPHIES OF UNREST, PROCESS, DIONYSUS

THE CLEVER INTOXICATION

In other respects as well the ego does not keep still. Hence its burrowing; from here there now begins, again, a search from the front. But with a different desire from the pale one of doubt. Instead of this drives compose themselves which nothing disintegrates. Room must rather be made for them.

All this was already in the intoxication, in muffled form. Light fell in only obliquely, as it were accidentally. Here it now appears on the spot, as a separate one which *thinks* darkness so to speak. This thinking passes into its opposite in order to come to an end there. Draws its sleep not only over the weary, but also over the wakeful, in the morning, when it is already getting light. When all images reflect a Today, even where they turn away. Such late sleep rarely fortifies, dreams only restlessly. Thin walls everywhere, confused noise breaks in.

THE SPECKLED PRIMEVAL FLOOD

Many a person already seems right to himself without a glance. Advises the mind to subside, to subside into dream. Klages above all moved in this direction, comfortably, with paper song, and also thoroughly seductively. The conscious ego is to be abandoned, then an abyss will appear so to speak. In which everything is intoxication; one which does not move forward, which marks time on the spot, or rather wells on the spot. Every kind of wakefulness, the whole of civilization is denied as a mere inhibited drive. The thinker Klages seeks to remove it together with the root.

The latter is for him rational per se, from the start. The original man stands against the conscious, cultivated, well-bred one, soul catches up on mind. The modern, wholly run-down enterprise is only the end of destructions which were inherent from the outset in the will and reason. Everything thus cultivated is decadent, wakefulness disease as such, mind an overgrowth of the grey cerebral cortex. Klages employs countless words against the consciousness which disintegrates life again and again into egos and parts; from the start it has a subversive, destructive, analysing, atomizing function. Only the ticking of the ego kills the stream, only egoism and the ego-consciousness which corresponds to it bring the break with the wholeness of life; intellectual culture in general is a single wrong track away from the sources of life, the modern city the punishment for a ten-thousand-year-long destruction of instinct. Man is the only being to have escaped from instinct and the stream of life, precisely as homo *sapiens*. Even the primitives do not master their soul, but feel themselves to be fed by and dependent on it, as a general one, as a stream of images, as an objective power. But in 'history' the Moloch-like character of consciousness gained ground, locked human beings up in themselves, devoured the community with the like of it and with the universe pulsating with life and flooded with images. Only children, poets, seers, sages are occasionally still an echo of the original fullness of life, of the world-soul when this was still to be found on earth, of the earth-soul when this still streamed through people. But otherwise thinking has replaced seeing, the concept the symbol; even in Plato 'the constant apparent world of reified concepts' buried the 'reality of continually momentary images'. Klages admittedly forces his way through a conceptual preliminary consideration himself in his book 'On the Cosmogonic Eros' (moreover with very careful distinctions), yet the drive preaches with quotations from poets and with archaeology against the mind and closes with a passage which at the same time unbeatably reproduces the frothy style which characterizes this sermon. 'We will give a retrospective summary: in the ecstatic surging, life marches towards liberation from the mind – perfection consists in the awakening of the soul and the awakening of the soul is seeing – but it sees the reality of the archetypes – *archetypes are appearing souls of the past* – for their appearance they need the connection with the blood of bodily living beings – this occurs in the event of seeing, which is therefore a mystical wedding between the devotedly receiving soul of him who sees and the generating demon – once he has come round again, the ecstatic *knows*, even if he is able to remember differently, that the world of facts is merely a fantasy which is hard to tear to pieces, that the world of bodies signifies a world of symbols, but absolutely really the monstrous products – of the seeing fertilized by the primeval world, signifies *change* in view of their fading and dying.' In short, the soul frees itself in all kinds of blissful surging; the ego and the reason (mind) are enchanted in this, but the Panic life is alone enchanting.

It is stressed again and again that this life is everything at the same time. Namely the soul of the true interior; though where and how does it express itself? Bleak Wandervögel[157] are occupied with it, whose moths fly into the light. Or elderly intoxicated types or unimaginative bald-headed types who praise a hair restorer which does not help them. This happens to the withered wood, but even Klages, a decided weekend philosopher, has times when the depth of his enthusiasm becomes or betrays a similar depth of niveau. Then sentences like this appear: 'So may this book win this and that new friend to join the old ones!' Or: 'Thus we may express the hope that the new edition may have gained in comprehensibility without loss of content.' This may still be connected with the conceptual preliminary examinations of the anti-concept; although one would sooner expect a dictionary on Xenophon's Anabasis to be introduced in this way than the Cosmogonic Eros. But even within his vision of images, which is ecstatic in the continuous song of praise, precisely 'images' of the following kind appear: 'the captivating

---

157   Bloch is referring to the 'Wandervögel' youth movement here (literally 'birds of passage'), whose members wandered in the countryside and espoused varying kinds of nature-philosophy.

blood circulation of a matter', third-hand metaphors appear and stale examples of bad taste, provincial pathos of the day before yesterday: 'On a lilac-scented summer night in an uncertainly flickering glow of lights'. Sentences of such force appear, to distinguish what is genuine and what is false, of such genuineness themselves as this one: 'Whose heart was moved even once to beat more quickly by the cloud-shadowed ocean distance which Böcklin's [!][158] brush awakened in the painful drunkenness of his Triton's glance' and the like. If this sentence (written as late as 1930) stands for many and if it shows the significance of Böcklin in terms of ecstasy, then even the better are mainly only an echo of the turn of the century, of its 'living it up' and the style of a Dionysian bourgeoisie so to speak. The wonderful Franziska Revent-low[159] already wrote the parody of this Klages age in statu nascendi; of an age in which 'Eros' and 'cosmos' had adorned studio parties, before they became ridiculous salon words and serious windcheaters. The 'Pelasgian primeval stage of life' thus stands revealed as Munich diluvium of 1900: the hollow space of today fills with moods from art and literature of that time; Böcklin has already appeared, he is mixed with Wagner in Art Nouveau style, indeed with Stefan George, as if the latter were Bruno Wille.

What remains is the obsession to become original, which is the same as finally living. The late-bourgeois hunger finds in this all kinds of things which proletarians, who are most urgently in need of them, by no means hit upon as yet. The fact that the conscious human being of today is not the whole one is noticed by him in his bourgeois form in decline and he now wholly submerges; of which more in a moment. What remains in addition is the obsession against the being-oneself of today, against an artificial existence in which there is no blessing any more. Happiness is back in total relaxation, in the bohemian world which turns night into day, and particularly in the outdoors which permits escape from urban unreality. Capitalists willingly go along with this, if only for the sake of the proletarians for whom the Forwards is slandered and the collective 'naturally' falsified and turned around; but also for their sake they love a moratorium on technology (as a Luddism of the proprietors), and sun as well in order to fill the vacuum. The path into the living interior, inside and outside, even has a further continuing effect: it attracts women, as lovers and as mothers, the weary manacle of misery decks itself out in greenery, that primal feeling deceives which makes even men into women, namely fading before Pan. Pan's appear-

158 Arnold Böcklin, 1827–1901, painter.
159 Franziska Reventlow, 1871–1918, writer. Her work is much concerned with bohemian life in Munich. Bruno Wille, 1860–1928, was a similarly progressive author in Berlin who founded the *Volksbühne* theatre association in 1890.

ance steps out of Sunday morning into the centre of life; where professors had treated only so-called 'natural beauty', Klages lures absolutely,
posits the climax Böcklin, Wagner, Nietzsche, teaches a Nietzsche
mixed with winter storms and May, the month of bliss. How far this is
compatible with the caves of matriliny (which are likewise not lacking in
the work of the expert Bachofen) is debatable; it is enough that a cosmic
flood washes selective fruits of reading ashore, branches, quotations,
mythologisms. Indeed, it poses as a stream of images, flowing from the
primeval world and in the manner of an *archaic* kaleidoscope; of which
more in a moment as well. Of course quoted images are never as fresh as
new ones, but precisely they fill, indistinctly, an indistinct gap, old
replacement rages as if it were an age-old one. Strange times, which are
so shaken that even antiquarian dust forms sound-figures. Which are so
in flood that even the tame Sunday morning wildly bursts its banks.

ROMANTICISM OF DILUVIUM

So it is this that claims to be sheer colourful drive. A sheer old and broad one, which apparently omits the Today. At first Klages was not so universal or timeless; he definitely had a look round at life, in his own way, precisely among the individual egos of today. Using graphology, investigating character, isolating tiny parts of an individual existence. Other driving forces behind the Today were not noticed, other authorities were not interpreted. Hence if Klages climbed over the walls of handwriting, and of character, the castle he found no longer lay in the times, but completely backwards. The drive without disguise, the character without a bridle then admittedly stamped prehistorically. Namely just as the weary bourgeois wishes and conceives himself to be a former human being, just as what is wild and colourful goes on glowing for him. The good features of this beginning were thus painted from embittered dreams. Not so much from fullness, which is itself one, and thus gives a good likeness of a past one, articulates it.

The human being is supposed to be a whole one here only when he raves. He was allegedly so complete and original ten thousand years ago and more, namely as *intoxicated*. But did this 'original' human being, this untreated new wine ever exist? And even if he should have existed, is there a living witness to the fact anywhere to be found, is there a way back to this unknown Adam anywhere to be found? Even the last bushman is no old Adam, but notched, broken, cultivated, tattooed in his own way. Wherever human beings appear, in primitive, Greek or whatever other terms, they have been directed towards a guiding image only after puberty; 'original' nature is nowhere to be found in this. Only what has been bred in the way of roses and pigeons, only these 'decadences' or 'sublimations' or 'paradoxes' go back, when left to themselves, to the wild dogrose, wild rock-pigeon again. But the human being, separated from his origin by so many cultures, finds no path to himself as a prehistoric creature. If he seeks it with libertinism, then nothing emerges but a kind of dog from the streets of Constantinople, in which the residue of a thousand breeds is to be found, but no prototype. If he seeks the path with romanticism, then a bottled primeval forest arises, with contents which stem from an empty longing, disordered literature, and full philology, yet from no intuition which is itself the result of primeval growth. For in fact, unlike the dogrose and rock-pigeon, the primeval human being never existed, as a conscious one or even already definitive one at the start; precisely the 'true' human being was always a mist, indeed a *problem* of his consciousness. As such he has passed through ever new radical changes of his attempted solution, precisely through ever new *rational* guiding images of his identity. Precisely through ever new 'clarifications', and attempts at a definition of his 'nature'; we know the sequence of these definitions, we see how the human being in his various 'cultures' always had his changing guiding image. The human being has never been a finished possession, but always a variable of *x*; even the Dionysian state is not 'origin', but the attempt at a definition which has been preceded by others just as others have followed and will follow it. If the real human being had already appeared anywhere, in Dionysian terms, then 'existence' would not repeatedly face the question of how it should live, what it has to do, which unknown dish is cooking on the stove of life. Our world has at any rate, precisely in the radical demolition of all complex and mythological ruins, even of the 'Dionysian' ones, reached a pure zero mark which, if it cries out, does not cry out for masks alien to the times. Neither for the glow of blood nor for the earth myth (which can now merely churn out Hitlerism), nor for celestial myth (which now merely says sunlight, yet with all its idols cannot celebrate any Ostara[160] festival any more). Precisely the genuine metaphysical activities which have remained and are dialectically useful to the upper middle classes (as in Bergson, the authentic vitalist) are associated today with wakefulness, indeed with 'civilization', not with annoyed provincial soul, not with Lenbachism[161] which copies diluvium instead of Titian. The poorly disenchanted who therefore appear to themselves to be enemies of consciousness have never found anything other than archaeology in the Dionysian remnant of consciousness, and if they sought substance here, then they met all the more with an incurable bygone. Precisely the root of all 'myths', the astonished mystery of man and the world, repeatedly wanders anew through the space of consciousness and is today more closely excavated, more unconcealed by false spaces than ever; just as the real substance of man and world only composes, realizes and corrects itself in the light of history, not at the 'beginning'. Klages simply

160   Ostara: a German goddess of spring.
161   Franz von Lenbach, 1836–1904, the most successful portrait painter of his age.

has the merit of having shown 'life' too instead of 'anxiety' and 'worry'; in the existence of a 'subject' which in bourgeois and upper middle-class terms has no 'life' any more, and therefore digs beautiful corpses. But only the class with a future will also be able to use and possess a Dionysian past. Only this future will hammer out of intoxication that which is not beast or cliché, but still possible fermentation.

The human being is further only supposed to be a whole one when he enthuses. He thereby becomes sighted, night-sighted, entranced from the ego, the soul becomes seeing. This occurs in a solitary way in the happiness of children and poets, but the authentically *creative* intoxication, the erotic one, totally fuses bodies, souls, world into one. These in general are the three great fusing methods of intoxication: the heroic, the erotic and the magical; their orgiastic nature always leads ego and mind into *entrancement* again. The ego-death of heroic intoxication passes through the warrior-death of the body, the ego-death of the magical Eros through 'voluptuous-blissful ecstasy', in which the soul liberates its image like that of its visionary contents from the veneer of the millennia. The heroic intoxication has given the name of the heroic age to an entire age of late Pelasgian humanity; the magical intoxication likewise culminates in pure devotion, thus not in willpower and magic for example, but in a cult of the dead and service to the stars. Klages thus even renders heroism and magic effeminate; he halves Nietzsche's heroisms by depriving them of the will to power; he 'halves' Nietzsche's teleology: man is not something which has to be overcome, but merely something which has to be archaically circumvented, de-goaled. Klages also halves Bachofen's pantheisms by essentially only accepting their night-side, namely matriliny and the earth goddess; Apollo is accepted only without 'Apollonianism'. Even the night-side is also halved in so far as Klages removes from it all suffering and negativity, all harshness and misanthropy; his pantheistic-mythical vitalism is equally a – monistic one, a monism of life with the contentment of Böcklin, almost of Haeckel.[162] The contrast is merely the mind, and this stands, as a daemon ex machina, outside life; biocentricity is without pain, as in dreams, is a connection of the earth-soul with unconscious workings, is total harmony with the rhythmic shaping of the stream of life and its images, its pure images. According to Klages the heroic thinking of the 'moral philosopher' is also 'cultivated', whose object constitutes the personality of the human being in its *resistance* to the world: originally solely the cosmic-organic pictorial seeing of the 'metaphysician', whose object is the *demise* of nature. We have Mesmer's[163] 'universal fluid' again, without healing power, but aesthetically; we have the 'sidereal

162   Ernst Haeckel, see 'Mystery-mongering as a large-scale enterprise', n. 223.
163   Franz Anton Mesmer, 1734–1815, founder of the theory of animal magnetism.

storm' of Paracelsus, without medical practice, but with a fascist one. For here too the enemy remains reason, both in its moral and intellectual capacity, both as self-control and as 'intellectualization swindle', both as Socrates and as Jesus. 'That which the intellect seizes possession of is infallibly disenchanted, and it is therefore destroyed if in its essence it was a mystery. Intellectual possession is a *crime against life*, and that is why the criminal is hit by the avenging recoil of life. This statement will remain true as long as a human race exists, and it will have terribly held good when the degenerate human race has perished of the rationalistic disenchantment of life.' In Nietzsche too, Socrates and Jesus were the shibboleths of this destruction; but Socrates becomes in Klages the first representative of 'racially hostile and international rationality' as well, and Jesus especially not only slandered the 'splendid human animal', but his watching and praying also buried according to Klages the 'birth-giving zone of *sacred* myths, which a thicket of *horrific* myths hid from the gaze of the uninitiated'. The mind of the 'metaphysician' may think of these myths as a primeval possession and of the people who are entranced by them as archaic; but in Klages they rather become Wagnerian ones, those who are described in 'The Spirit of Utopia'[164] as being 'dancing ships which unresistingly join in the suffering, the struggle, the love and longing for redemption of their subhuman ocean, and over whom the world-wave of Schopenhauer's Will passes at every decisive moment'. Thus in fact Klages logically stresses the 'voluptuous-blissful ecstasy' as the sole source of genuine illumination, as an authentic marriage of the will to live, which is here called the life-drive, but runs away with man in the same fashion as resistance sets him down. Though this becomes the gain for the seer: 'For anyone who bursts the form of being a person in ecstasy, the world of facts sinks at the same moment and the world of *images* arises for him with an all-suppressing power of reality.' These images then – *the most central part of enthusing vision* – have four attributes in Klages; all four seek to distinguish them from mere concepts, and also ideas. They are firstly seen *inwardly*, man is with them dreaming in the inner blossoming and growth of a flower itself. They *secondly* exist only in the *momentary* experience and one single time, flowing with the moment of their being experienced, and an instant which fuses man and the world in the same beginning. Images are conceived by the soul, and what fertilizes them, fertilizes them in a flash, is the soul which appears in an extra-human way; so that images are not the conceptually recordable water-thing or forest-thing, but appearance of the soul of experience: as a wave which swells and rises from within, as the storm-tossed element of the tree, as the forest 'while it blazes in glowing flames of the evening sun'. *Thirdly* the image tolerates no possible nearness, no tangibility like the thing, but is *dis-*

164   By Ernst Bloch, see 'Social reflections', n. 113.

tance per se, its mountain ranges are always misty blue. But what appears in this image distance, the peculiar tone colour of the longing in it, what shines in the stars precisely *through absence* and forbids us to desire them – this distance is always at the same time the *age-old past*. In the spatial distance of an object its temporal one appears (time is the soul of space, space the body of time); moreover it appears not as distance of the future for instance, which becomes in Klages the most unreal fantasy, but simply as an ancestral image, as a cult of the dead of the distant image seen in the object: 'wandering like clouds over perpetual mountain snows, in the deceptively remote twinkling of stars, prehistoric times eternally drift past eternally taking their leave.' Because of this peculiar and overcast 'distant fragrance', images according to Klages can also be conveyed only by *symbols*; these are the characters whereby it is possible to remember ecstatically envisaged images in the intervals of sobriety: 'if the concept is the starting point of scientific research, then the symbol is the origin of myth.' And finally *fourthly* the life of the image is not quiet, but shoots in confusion ever anew on its age-old spot. Images do not 'exist' like things, they are rather in constant transformation; instead of the dead conceptual things of reason 'the essential feature of the entire character of myth is *metamorphosis*'. Thus Klages describes – Orphic Greece: 'Everything is in motion and wanders, announces itself, unfolds and floats away, and thus it is *alive*; drives and wishes, desire for satiation or copulation, war and fraternization conglomerate the airy, dissolve the solid, draw the celestial fire into the embrace of the swamps, send as mist the nourishing waters into the glowing flames of the sun. The belief in universal liveliness, in panmixia and incessant change is the life-blood of myth and the systems of the earliest thinkers.' Kaleidoscopes even here then, in the new 'swamp age' which Klages reflects in the hollow space: 'The image of man dissolves into the meteorilia, the meteorilia coagulate into the image of man. Colours, forms, sounds, noises, smells seem fused in it into the pandemonium of all image elements; and nevertheless it shines shimmering and over-clear, like a now threatening, now promising face.' Metamorphosis is thus the last attribute of the image; metamorphosis on an imaginary stage on to which primeval times send their hashish, and also their Proteus of course. Once again a tribute of shape-seeing virtue to hollow spatial vice is unmistakable; and once again this tribute is not payable on the basis of mere contemplation, indeed of an effeminate aestheticism. Once again only a class with a future can use the 'distant fragrance of the *horizon*' and the 'images' which stand in it, and blast out the encapsulated element: namely the future significance of the images encapsulated into an undischarged past. Once again, above all, the late bourgeoisie releases – *metamorphosis*, that well-known structure which might be called dream-montage here, if there were not so much (apparent) unconsciousness in it. In Klages only what is past utopianizes itself as such and eternally; the dream of what is past becomes the past of the dream, a cult of the dead, even less: a cult of the dead of – cults of the dead themselves. Future, says Klages, is simply a past projected forwards; this is totally correct in part, but must be amplified by the fact that a past which *lives*, the dead who can be *resurrected*, and *shining* choirs of the former world do not otherwise exist at all either.

The last word on this drive, above all on its images, has not yet been spoken. Not by any means; for this is a charged field, and it extends much further than late enthusing or even than the old memorials. This bourgeoisie seeks to escape the reified concept in a very dreamy way; but it is obvious that it does not get much further beyond beautiful smoke. The reluctance of this approach to take images seriously is evident; it is minutely connected with the mere intoxication of distance. This is admittedly welcomed by Klages as the vehicle of longing itself; but precisely the old times when genuine images were still alive, or those new times which genuinely possess them, demonstrate the wish to fulfil them as well in an *actively near* way. As we know, the genuine tone colour of longing burgeoned in the folk song as follows: 'If I were a little bird, *I'd fly to you*'; and the Greeks in particular, in whose life-cult Klages participates, recognized no Eros of distance whatsoever, their world is body, polis, coastal shipping of the concept. Indeed, even Romantic distance still spoke of *future*, of *attainable happiness*, it did not draw, like Klages's carnival, mere apparent annuities from a long past capital, fictitious even in the past. If Klages's theory of images attempted to thwart the thing in a very vital way, its aestheticism nevertheless gives the image itself the character of a thing again, namely that of the fact: no longer in the sense of something 'made', but rather of something which has long since 'become' and been. The bridge to the future, on which precisely all of Nietzsche's dream abodes had been situated, is broken, teleology shrinks to the Tao of primeval times, the land of children becomes a flourishing antiquarian bookshop, future in general – with a courage of paradox bordering on nonsense – is denied out of the world. And the universal life, the Romantic universal life, to which the vast metamorphosis repeatedly returns, in an equally broad and hopeless uncertainty of being and goal? Of this liveliness it is first possible to say with justification what Jean Paul had once remarked of Schelling's world-soul, in a letter to Jacobi: 'He does not know how to specify the positive element for which I was hoping throughout the whole book any further than to state that it is located everywhere in the general and reveals itself on happy occasions as livestock etc.' So biocentric is the senselessness – not of Schelling, but rather of a panvitalism which leaves man out of life and makes out of man werewolves, dream images, an ancestor cult, and an animal cult. The question of true and false is unpopular with fascists anyway; it does not apply in the dream, it lapses in aestheticism, and Klages's mythology causes it to lapse all the more. The panmixia of the mind lacking a sense of direction even perceives among its elements no difference in the 'images': namely whether they are of 'demons' or of that which scares them away. Where everything is accepting, everything just primeval past seeing, everything also becomes legend and spell; such that the *fairytale* for instance, this fire against the predators of the myth, appears only as a diminutive myth in Klages, only as 'the childlike subsidiary shoot of the visionary life'. Even less does any *dialectic* live as yet in the kaleidoscope of aestheticism; which in fact does not occur where objects themselves become the archetypal one and all, but (even mythically) is only to be found where the one and all in every object equally develops the latter as a contradiction to this allness and sends it on its way in contradiction, on a way frequented by figures, not lit by distant images. Nevertheless, we repeat: the last word on the theory of images, precisely in the archaic encapsulation and 'panmixia' in which it appears to hollow space, cannot yet be spoken. Klages, a Dionysian death knell of bourgeois culture, is equally the most elaborate, the most consistent romanticism of an older one, indeed of the oldest known one – sub specie of late-bourgeois hollow space. Not without reason does the phenomenon of panmixia appear even in this instance, at the centre of this instance; an 'Orphic Greece' in late capitalist fugitive and mixed space. A soft phenomenon and wholly composed of masks, yet the masks bear symbols and remind from the apparent flood in which they exist that even the genuine one is full of attempted images, full of metaphors of an *All in the On The Way*. Concrete poets have always noted such images, thinkers only incidentally or as aids: but their far-reaching cognitive faculty, after the withdrawal of calculation, is near at hand; for the reflections of an unknown end, of a not yet existing All are often in the smallest detail. The merely archaic images, and above all those kept contemplatively archaic, of a Klages are not suitable for this, but rather the genuine ones: partly unwrapped from archaisms, partly newly arisen in the On The Way, precisely from the exodus of the On The Way. In this respect they emerge from the unrest of dialectics, they already embed themselves on the way as both forward-driving and 'meaningful' images, not just as tendency-forms, but almost already as possible final tendency-forms; such 'symbols' are and remain knots in analysis, little Azores in process. If one asks after these genuine images, this is not the place to expound them; we will only say this much: they are already the wishful images contained in the fairytale, they are above all the hopeful images of startled astonishment (only this 'shuddering' is 'the best part of mankind'), they are also those 'forms' of sublimity which, as Kant says, convey a premonition of our future freedom. And precisely these images become concretely visible only from the heights of travelling consciousness, from the standpoint of that newest element which solely carries the 'oldest' element with it in order – in total wakefulness – to dissolve and to inherit it. In Klages himself this does not occur by any means, his backward view is, on the spot, just as separate from the genuine image as the moratorium of technology (for the sake of capital) is from the socialist two-hour day. A false forest-weaving enthuses in his breast, a 'demonically ecstatic relation with the world' makes business easier only for the less ecstatic relations. The sum of existence has become too difficult for capital; as when a schoolboy has to solve equations, but the x becomes an enormous fraction, and he realizes the false approach in the fact: so the complexities are too much for capitalist calculation, and its irrational adherents leave school, and move to the primeval countryside of the drives or of the Eros who started it all. But no 'primeval man' who existed and was already 'real' ever lived, every supposedly old Adam was always just the 'Jesus' of a preceding breaking and determining of the human creatural darkness; hence everything 'first, really oldest' is still unknown, is, as we said, a constant *problem* of consciousness and exists only at the end as a solved one, as the 'primeval reality of man', as the whole 'primeval reality' itself. Precisely the real beginning (which at best haunted the archaic one or circulated in it in shrouded form) always lives only on the peaks of the most wakeful consciousness, not in the infusion of the unconscious, which is rightly called 'relaxation'. Or as an Arabian philosopher, Ibn Tofail, the same one who wrote the first Robinson Crusoe (the man beginning afresh), said: 'The living man is the son of the *man who is awake.*'

IMAGO AS APPEARANCE FROM THE 'DEPTHS'

Sometimes I pestered my father to have the folder brought to him. And sometimes I could not be induced to see a single further sheet, ran off in the middle of things and was scolded. I could not say even today whether the memory of these black magic sheets is dear and precious or hateful to me. But they affected me, I was penetrated by a power emanating from them, and I think I will still be able to say on my deathbed what kind of background the sea-marvel has or the hermit with the skull. 'That is the old Germany', said my father, and the phrase sounded almost spine-chilling to me.

From the Romantic period

Since then the dreaming drive circulates even deeper. The day is dismantled even *psychologically*, in order to thrust down to this darkness. Doctors, for example, often admire the darkness in the insane more than they cure it; as in many a recent school, in that of Jung above all, which has erupted from Freud. Here too the lower man is the real one and the head is correct only when it can sing again what the liver intends. Or the heart; for the lights are changed round and they illuminate very old things. Various dreams wash them up from below, they cannot be unconscious enough.

Admittedly Freud too had gone down below, indeed he first took the dream as a path. He even more decisively posited the drive as a base, the intellect as a reflex; his world is also dark and the drive as libido sufficiently 'irrational'. But if Freud dismantled towards the base, this did not occur with the *means* of the base, but with the most lucid, analytical consciousness. And the passage into the unconscious was for him less than ever the cure, but solely the sharpest consciousness is capable of curing, in so far as it pierces the 'complexes', i.e. precisely the unconsciousness of the unconscious. The lovers of dream-darkness are now attacking this today, the Prinzhorns,[165] Jungs, Klages, the open or crypto-fascists of psychology. It is very interesting here how the fascisticization of science had to change precisely those elements of Freud which still stem from the enlightened, materialistic period of the bourgeoisie. This already begins with the drive itself, in Jung it is not only sexual but greedy, wild and dreaming per se. Above all, the unconscious here is no longer individual, i.e. no acquired condition in the single, as it were liberal human being, but a treasure of the primeval humanity starting to revive; it is equally not repression but successful return, not the origin of neurosis but possibly its cure. For these friends of darkness Freud does not go nearly far back enough; for he sees only the falsified individual of the nineteenth century and thinks it is cured if he brings it to the level of the bourgeois-normal person of today. He sees the mendacities of the age of plush along fairly similar lines in theoretical terms to the poetic or religious 'lie', namely both merely as 'sublimations', with repressed libido as their core. Whereas Jung skips this enlightened, even all too enlightened disenchantment and seeks the right, indeed precisely the primeval right of the artistic imagination, of religious myths; he seeks it precisely in the unconscious, as the 'indispensable' primal value of the dream world. Even the sexual libido is embellished in bourgeois terms here. Jung calls it 'love', sometimes also 'psychic energy' per se; this no longer sounds offensive. But therapy is a return into the unconscious *at the best profit*, i.e. the neurotically amoral person has to take back his repressed decency, but the neurotic out of morality (the most frequent case) must tackle his subterranean demon precisely by joining it. The 'Acherontic' element which Freud had prefixed to his interpretation of dreams merely as a motto is thus brought into the heart of the temple itself by his fascist or crypto-fascist successors, by the exploiters of Bachofen and Romanticism. Whereby of course the equally indispensable significance of an individual plays a trick on the friends of darkness which they sense even in the temple itself. For precisely the old Freud, the teacher of the 'death-drive', occasionally plucks fruits of growing old by virtue of his significant individual status, goes precisely into 'depths' which had been hardly formulated since the late Goethe; whereas Jung, with his 'oceanic feeling', with a depth which incessantly professes to be such, which from sheer depth still 'affirms all religions', either brings home only fruits of antiquarian reading or discusses the depths in such generality, in such abstract all-consternation, and therefore non-consternation, as if precisely here there were pseudo-enlightenment and Forel,[166] even

165   Hans Prinzhorn, 1886–1933, German psychiatrist.
166   August Forel, 1848–1931, Swiss psychiatrist.

though a Forel of mysticism. Finally the Jungs find so many good seeds in National Socialism that the latter almost looks like a sunflower and – illuminates them. In dreams there appears, from dreams there begets itself the lost land of the 'instinctively sure meaning of life'.

At any rate, an older man than the modern one is attempted to be woken here. Jung's patients do not complain because they have not explained their sexual drives. Their existence rather lacks 'meaning': up to the age of forty they suffer from the inability to tackle their lives, and afterwards they cannot come to terms with what has been accorded to them. But Jung does not cure these patients by viewing them for the very most part as patients of the modern economy and society. But only by creating mythical associations for their 'cut-off soul' (and reinforcing capitalism all the more by this 'completion'). The result is a 'transfer of the personality in the sense of a new centring, in which the ego then no longer forms the focal point of the personality'. The capitalism-patient has rather found a contact with the universe, ultimately with that universe which rests in the collective unconscious of an archaic humanity and is our loss, i.e. our illness. The mother fixation, for instance, in many neuroses is not one on the individual mother alone, as Freud teaches, but on an age-old, general mother-image. In Jung's school this is not removed by enlightenment, but reinforced by mythicization so that it can develop its healing power: it is 'imago', even more than this: the 'archetype' of the earth-mother which comes to life in each individual complex. Thus, through mechanized existence, and even more through 'childish enlightenment mania', fundamental needs are everywhere robbed of their gratification and their correlates, namely the mythical ones. And just as the nineteenth century 'lies only as a thin layer of dust over the primeval age of the soul', so the awakening of this archaic universal feeling furnishes younger people precisely with the transition into activity, and older people with the contact with a lost 'meaning of life'. From this standpoint the curative value of artistic or religious 'imagination' is monstrously stressed; for it above all leads up those forms which the prevailing spirit of the times lacks. It above all revives the 'archetypes of the old world of drive images' and 'translates them into currently understandable language', so that mere consciousness can grasp them. 'Whoever speaks with archetypal images speaks as if with a thousand voices, he stirs and overwhelms, and at the same time he elevates that which he describes out of the unique and transitory realm into the spheres of the always existing, he heightens personal fate into the fate of humanity, and he thereby also releases in us all those helpful powers which have always enabled humanity to escape from all peril and to survive the longest night.' In short, the 'sweet madness' in art and religion is no *symptom* of disease, but a *symbol* of healing; in the opiate of ancient past dreams there is here the last, the most substantial

compensation of an 'unsatisfied present'. Jung is little encumbered by
the fact that not all neurotics are philosophers whose brooding is the
'meaning of life'. That there are also – unemployed people among them,
for whom not just neurosis impedes the transition into 'activity'. But
that a Marxism lives which does not remedy the disease of the 'meaning
of life' with spiritual welfare but destroys it with revolutions. Be that as
it may, this crypto-fascism offers art as a substitute for religion, religion
as a substitute for life and both for a weary bourgeoisie; it is David
Friedrich Strauss's[167] 'Old and New Faith' in a mystagogical edition. It
is an aestheticism which indiscriminately loves all 'archetypes' as long as
they are buried very deep in *antiquity*, in a possibly ancient past, a
timeless and process-removed one. There thus arises 'psychosynthesis',
namely synthetic gathering and guidance to the 'hereditary treasure of
original emotional thinking'; thus all categories of creative imagination
are contained in the archaean period in advance, cannot be increased.
Though if such a deep primeval soul also effortlessly shakes off 'the thin
layer of dust of the nineteenth century', indeed 'five thousand years of
civilization', it is still astonishingly affected by the few years of fascism,
and they have obviously increased the categories of its imagination after
all, namely with that of this shaking off itself, with Tarzan in psychology. Among archaisms it is easy to spread rumours, to brag loudly, and
to realize little, above all *nothing new occurs beneath their night*. 'In
each of these images', says C. G. Jung, 'there is ... a piece of sorrow
and pleasure which has happened countless times in the ancestral line
and on average also always took the same course.' Imago is thus not
simple appearance, but appearance from the 'depths'; and these 'depths'
are in C. G. Jung hopeless, allegedly primeval past ones. They therefore
not only restrict artistic imagination, they crush the revolutionary kind
all the more or the advance into the not yet conscious, never yet
thought, never fulfilled. All healing as well as all creation is *reconnection*
with the old powers and images of life, is precisely – non-creation.

Even this escape, if it really came to an end, would not arrive where it
is going. The Jungs are very mawkish and enjoy the darkness only
indiscriminately from the outside, otherwise they would notice its loop.
For the archaic is not as stupid as the myth of blood (which is prettier in
return), not quite as insubstantially constructed ad hoc as the latter.
These psychiatrists, of course, have the 'primeval' imagination merely as
a cultured cliché and chiefly as an opiate; they have the 'fluid' of Klages,
just as he has it from Romanticism or at most from the 'dithyrambics of
destruction'. That is why, in the third volume of his book on the mind
and soul in 1932, Klages rightly says of dithyrambic deeds (although he

167   David Friedrich Strauss, 1808–74, theological and political writer.

means liberal ones): 'The earth is steaming with the blood of *the slain* as never before, and the *ape-like element* is flaunting the spoils from the smashed temple of life.' While the first part of the sentence depicts capitalism plus murder, its final part does not illustrate the telepathic theft badly either where 'primeval souls' anticipate genuine ones, and Tarzan 'prototypes' copy mystery. But where the bourgeoisie was less weary and thieving, in the revolutionary beginnings of its imagination, in the Sturm und Drang, above all in Hamann,[168] as the real magus of the north, precisely the most complex dialectic appeared in the archetypal. It appeared that every path into the 'unconscious of the beginning' is equally, in places, an encapsulated one *into the not yet conscious* of that which lies in human beings and has not yet become in their history. Precisely in the collective-archaically unconscious which a reactionary psychiatry plays off against Freud's merely personally unconscious, something not yet become known – alongside immemorial nonsense and superstition – is itself encapsulated; something unbecome in man which has not yet emerged even in the greatest 'revelations' of historical art and religion. Even this element which has not yet become known is admittedly enveloped in a brooding spell of a very different, namely totally sunken and clogged kind; the reactionary usefulness of the 'myth' stems exclusively from this spell. Yet beyond this, indeed in the encapsulation of some mythical images themselves, there is occasionally a fairytale cipher of still unbecome light and of the utopian lands of happiness, lands of significance which it illuminates. Hence the emergence of this 'primitiveness' in all times of genuine revolution and in fact also in the deceitful times, mixed times of fascist 'revolution'. But hence also an existence of this 'primitiveness' in all not yet seasoned cultures, even if they were fundamentally one of the ruling stratum. This even created, on the basis of the breath of the migration of nations, the mysterious ornaments of the Gothic period, its forests and sturdy dream-lions, the entire overcrowded dark lustre, above all in ancient Germany. But precisely the Gothic period also shows that genuinely recovered 'primitiveness' does not remain or have to remain an age-old past one; its dream-lions lie at the feet of Mary, not of a Cybele of the Stone Age. If the Gothic period also adopted large sections of the 'mythical primeval memory' (or of gnosis), it adopted them in *Christian* terms, and therefore precisely from the standpoint of a *new original leap*[169] of the beginning. Unquestionable 'archetypes' like the mother and child, Holy Night, the vine and the tendrils, and the Ascension of

168 Johann Georg Hamann, see 'Myth of Germany and the medical powers', n. 111.
169 Bloch is here playing on the literal meaning of the German word for 'origin', 'Ursprung'.

the Son of Man were by no means left in the diluvium by the Gothic period or even simply, as Jung would say, 'translated into the language of the times', but utterly transformed. From such archetypal images the Gothic period merely knocked out 'promises' for which it believed it possessed the revelatory 'fulfilment'. Its key is not ours and certainly not the last, but the indiscriminate lovers of the archaic as such possess no key whatsoever, do not want and are unable to have one. For the only elective affinity to the fruitfully archaic as well as its only possible key space is *the hope of the future as the still fermenting reality.* Autochthonous presence in the 'chthonic' world would not place itself on the side of the age-old past, like the sentimental doctors of today or the Romantics of the Romantic period or the philosophy of both together. Hamann for example, whom we have already mentioned, must have been more genuinely at home with 'Irratio' than Jung or Klages; also above all he still lived in the bourgeois Sturm und Drang period, not in the machinations of the period of reaction (which hears only that which has long since been in the Sturm und Drang). But precisely the 'magus of the north' says: 'Who can expect to take proper ideas from the present without knowing the future? The future determines the present and the latter the past, just as the intention determines the nature and use of the means.' And likewise: 'The field of history has thus always appeared to me like that wide field full of bones, and lo ! they were very dry. Nobody except a prophet can prophesy upon these bones that sinews and flesh will grow on them and skin will cover them.' Thus Hamann thinks that just as only poetry provides the true primal element of language, so prophecy is the primal element of all historiography. This is of course the purest idealism from a haughty standpoint (in keeping with the limits of the contemporary, the bourgeois revolution, especially in Germany); yet how differently than in Jung and Klages the archai fermented in the genuine Sturm und Drang, fermented over to the *future* and into nothing but this. Only for the reactionary Irratio, as the 'Sturm und Drang' of reaction, is the archetype which it touches on not the beginning, but conversely primeval beenness per se. The reactionary Irratio remains in the prison of merely mythical archetypal images, as of the solar penis or the great earth-mother; other archetypes as well live on for it in vain, such as the certainly no less imaginative ones of the *flight from Egypt to Canaan* or the considerably more Germanic one of the *Land of Cockaigne.* Such archetypal images however – as those of the 'fairytale' in the 'myth' – are thoroughly avoided by an indiscriminate eulogizing temporis acti. Because the catchword could be heard in them which really placed the dreams of primeval times at the 'beginning', namely into the socialist revolution. Only the beginning which the latter makes with human history also recovers 'primitiveness' concretely, in accordance with *the power of its fairytale images, happy dream images.* This genuine beginning throws away the cinders which reaction recalls together with the fuel, and recalls them together only so that one should not discover the fuel archetypes. The fuel archetypes are exclusively those of human happiness; they thus have utopias within them and seek less to be recalled than realized. The Land of Cockaigne, for instance, then really cures 'of the harmful effects of modern one-sided society'. Yet not by supplementing them, but by removing them; for a proper archetype presses out of the image towards existence, out of opium towards the light. In short, the proper archetypal image does not lie, as having been, below consciousness, whether of the individual or of historical humanity; it is rather journeying, a summum bonum of a revolutionary-dialectical journey, and changes with it.

BERGSON'S ÉLAN VITAL

From here the whole living pleasure first started. As a related glance at what is flowing, as much in the midst of it as possible. The experience in which a piece of sugar dissolves has become a thinking one in Bergson. Has its source in the undivided inner stream, the same one which rises in the interior of all living things. By means of it it is possible to surface in this interior at the same time: living alongside, understanding along-side, empathizing, sympathetic. The enterprise which is doing well pre-sents itself as flourishing and thriving.

Thinking here seeks to be as fluid as life, even more fluid. A surging and flooding of instinctive knowledge which adapts itself to every change. Real experience was struck by this first of all, the confusion of its Now and Over. But then a concept set in which both adjusted and filled the discretion of merely real experience: that of the fermenting, generating, infinite life-impulse. This concept stems from German Romanticism, and thus first and foremost of course from the liberalness of the French Revolution. Schelling had already generally vitalized Fich-te's 'infinitely active ego' (since he was not allowed to do anything else at all in Germany), and Schopenhauer condemned the same process. Then a hundred years later Bergson fetches the old impulse back to its first, admittedly very changed basis: the Romantic universal life becom-es the entrepreneurial élan vital. The 'reason', as a function of expiring life, itself meets only that which has expired, namely things, atoms, matter, in short 'geometric ballast' in life. Only 'intuition' does justice to life with tailor-made suits (instead of with quantitative ready-made clothing); it strikes as élan logique the same zest of life outside in real terms. For the Bergson of the élan vital there exist no things, no calculable causes, not even purposes: just as the ego is free, the mind creative, so its course outside (the way of the world) is constant change, constant novelty of becoming, a curve of freedom without a plan. The world spirit is according to Bergson 'the rocket whose expired cinders fall down as matter'; consciousness remains behind as its spark, penetrates some cinders and causes them to glow into organisms, into plants, animals, people, into just as many streams of life which flow through the bed of matter, richly ramify, experience resistance, deflection, reverses, until one day the primary impulse has succeeded without capita mortua. Bright, so to speak youthful, forward-directed elements are obviously not lacking here. But even more clearly the empty, self-flourishing zest is precisely that of the entrepreneur who succeeds; as such it was in all the cones of fire and heroic lives of the young century,[170] from the Glow-la-la of Dehmel[171] to Richard Strauss; as such it finally entered − with a deducted boom and therefore as force − into the 'willpower' of fascism, into the theories of the Bergson disciples Sorel[172] and Gentile,[173] into the practice of the 'control of the moment' and 'spiritual freedom' which can allegedly do anything at any time. Elan vital in Bergson himself is still that of a bourgeoisie which trivializes its contradictions; which places the 'matter' of its growing alienation in the debit account of the whole universe in order to bear it more easily; which leaps over the dialectic of its destruction with a salto vitale. Elan vital at this level still has the entrepreneur in the fullest bloom of zest, but in a decreasing one of his 'experience', his calculation; thus the zest remains empty, becomes an antithesis which strikes out sideways into the jungle and makes itself absolute without content. This is the curious case of a new Schopenhauer with reflexive cerebral functions (which do not really recognize anything) and the thing in itself as the will to life. Only driven into time and history, only affirmed by a philosophy which knows and acknowledges no suffering, no power to change, no human depths and thus no constituent human spirit above life either.

But in the meantime man himself has risen above so-called life here. For in his last book Bergson himself entered on a surprising curve, an unforeseeable one which actually brought something 'new'. This book teaches an 'open' society instead of that restricted in terms of the family or clan and ultimately choked with mustiness. It teaches animated, 'open' religion instead of the fables about spellbinding and finished powers of the other world; the little spark in man rises in an explosive capacity. 'Les deux sources de la morale et de la religion' (a little legacy, not just a late work) displays an élan in which the citoyen remembers, and the entrepreneur does not simply race into vacancy. Above all the jungle is abandoned, the same one which the philosopher of life had been the first to stage; Bergson's late work literally sets its brow against

---

170   Bloch is alluding to Richard Strauss's tone poem *Ein Heldenleben*.
171   Richard Dehmel, 1863–1920, poet.
172   Georges Sorel, 1847–1922, French socialist co-founder of the doctrine of revolutionary syndicalism.
173   Giovanni Gentile, 1875–1944, Italian neo-Hegelian philosopher.

intoxication. All the bright elements of before are now newly emphasized: the impressive élan which always struck out forwards, never
backwards; the cult of consciousness as a refreshed or preserved fragment from the bourgeois revolution. Curiously even the starting-point
of this philosophizing touches on its present final point; the extremely
idealistic 'independence of the mind from the brain' touches on an
almost Marxist 'surmounting of natural barriers by planning consciousness'. Thus Bergson's philosophy has attained two faces; and the second
one, even in 1932, does not extol any flight from technology or consciousness (as would surely have been expected of the great vitalist).
Bergson's first philosophy remains essentially one of entrepreneurial
zest, one of the many apparent impulses of the pre-war period, behind
which there was nothing but record-breaking, purposelessness and concealment of the only real goal: profit. His second philosophy, on the
other hand, reduces the entrepreneurial zest – quixotically and rather
splendidly – to goal-contents of the French Revolution; indeed, the *late*
Bergson recognizes *controlled technology* (in contrast to the 'tragicomic
half-measure of the situation today') and *goal-thinking*, even if one of an
amazing kind. That which was the most alien thing of all to the eternally
new, and therefore eternally empty element of the élan vital, namely
planning and goal-content, ultimately triumphs, in accordance with
Bergson's fantastic definition of the world: 'l'univers une machine à faire
des dieux'. The transition from 'organic' social modes takes place, and
the leap out of the 'société close' into the humanized one of the 'société
ouverte' occurs, precisely by means of technological reason. For according to Bergson social development has become encapsulated in
the société close of family, tribe and nation, in a community isolated
against everything alien, desiring only itself and not totality. Precisely
with regard to this natural state, a deadlock which fancies it is sovereign
or even organic fullness itself and yet is only habitude, Bergson affirms
explosive technology, as one which is both guided and rationally organized. As one which is organized with the aim of conveying the élan
vital out of the sociétés closes into a société ouverte, of liberating the
stream of life from partialities of mere dependence on nature into a
freedom which is not even one of half human beings, but of whole –
gods. 'Dynamic religion' thus corresponds to the open society: just as
the proper life contrasts with family and clan, so proper piety turns
away from the gods of the spell. The 'love' of the New Testament rises
exaggeratingly against the (totally legally interpreted) 'justice' of the
Old; dynamic religion is mysticism, not mythology, is a fight against all
hypostases of dependence, against all fabulous creatures of ignorant
self-alienation, against all transcendency of becomeness. It is mysticism
of the life to be discovered within one's own self: thus its subject, in an
abstractly severing way, detaches itself from the natura naturata of the
become, attaches itself in an equally abstractly vitalistic way to the

natura naturans of the explosively real, to the 'Joan of Arc of productive faith' or the god-becoming of ourselves. But the société ouverte gives the first space for this and technology – precisely as a postulate, if not a function of the 'mysticism of freedom' – the broadest signal. The fact that the stream of life encountered the restraint of matter is the reason why it sufficed only for the creation of human beings and not of gods. The fact that guided technology totally abolishes the restraint of matter, in a société ouverte beyond mere profit advantage, beyond partial and isolated egoisms, beyond individuals and also beyond the 'organic' sociétés closes – this is the mobilization for the realm of freedom (as the late Bergson interprets it for himself: as a cross between anarchism and Catholicism). A romantic perspective of course, but almost also an animated, exciting one in the manner of colportage (Evanston in Johannes V. Jensen's[174] Chicago novel 'The Wheel' could have created the 'world as a machine of the gods'); there is no longer the slightest *anti-intellectual* romanticism here or irrationality of life per se, as in the former 'cosmic' Bergson. Whereas his imitators stop at 'organic growth', or even returned to the diluvium, the creator of the philosophy of life is no stranger to the courage of the most advanced technology, indeed he aims, even if in mysterious terms, at an equally anti-individual and anti-national – planned economy. The new élan vital contrasts both with bourgeois and with folkloric associations, both with calculation and *dark* demonism; for this is only a bad life-form for it, a 'matter' whispered through in pagan terms or glowed at, but not glowed through and therefore overcome. Quite differently from Bergson's 'philosophy of nature', therefore, his 'ethics' is still filled with the impulse of the bourgeois revolution; even the eloping virgin, even the last, the apparent emancipation of the bourgeoisie, the 'Jugendstil', are audibly echoed in it. The Marxist Horkheimer[175] remarks totally correctly: 'Even today Bergson is even closer to the impressionistic origin of his philosophy than to the political function which his basic ideas have assumed in the meantime by virtue of the historical development.' The aestheticism of entrepreneurial zest is over, but without Bergson also having abandoned the élan (namely the proper one) along with aesthetics and entrepreneurship. A Ratio of intuition was not lacking even before (the primal impulse was always highest consciousness, light), and now even a kind of interference with the world-rocket is at work. No Saul has become a Paul here (Bergson is not that central and his transition is certainly not that precise), but the Irratio has, so to speak, a kind of red-letter day in its late-bourgeois calendar.

174 Johannes Vilhelm Jensen, 1873–1950, Danish writer, Nobel prizewinner, 1944.
175 Max Horkheimer, 1895–1973, philosopher and sociologist of the Frankfurt School.

We, with our constructive powers, are now more than mere life. It is up to us powerfully collected people alone to advise, to help, to *decide*, what 'impetus' is. Thus it opens out precisely on to actions, indeed on to the at first despised machine, on to the rape of life so that it should be life. L'homme vital does not resemble that Horatian peasant who waits in vain for the river to drain away; even less will he wait in the anteroom before the eternal doors of eternal aliveness instead of over-taking time and filling the lack of its Where To. The accelerating accompaniment in order to arrive plunges just as well as and better than 'intuition' into the river, into the duration and the risk of process; but it deprives it of the vanity of the unfinished emotion, the aimless apotheosis of disorder. Action, which logically elucidates and really controls 'tendency', leads precisely into different depths of life, of life irradiated by the rationalism of the irrational, than the mere assertion of the still purely *vitalistic* Bergson had gained, who had defined 'life' always only in contrast to 'concept', 'force', 'ballast' and 'mechanism' or as helplessly negatively as Ovid had defined chaos: at that time no brown cow as yet gave sweet butter. Though since Bergson introduced *human* resources into the élan (even if they are superhuman ones), the 'creative disorder' (that is the non-sense: to equate purpose or goal with causal spell as 'mechanical') has also almost disappeared. The declaration of a freedom existing everywhere, only 'menaced by the sleep of world-matter', was still grotesque; employees knew little of this, and it was not world-matter alone which had hindered their zest in life. Yet that which was radically anti-Marxist as an *ontological assertion*, this same 'indeter-minism' by no means. looks merely abstract as a *hopeful image* of the world, as a *surmounting* of its natural barrier. The Marxist concept of controlled necessity differs fundamentally of course from the spiritual anarchies and fantasies of Bergson. Nevertheless, the contrast of the new Bergson to vitalisms à la Klages, and even to his earlier purely natural celebration of freedom is considerable; it is greater than that of the société ouverte, of the 'centrally controlled and organized machinism', to the Marxist 'final goal'. The *quixotism* of Bergson's utopianizing is obvious of course: the citizens to whom he turns, the same ones who previously allowed themselves to become voluptuously and experience-darkly immersed in the eternally new (eternally old), make no social revolution; and there is decisively no mention of the proletariat, let alone of class struggle. If nations do themselves set free, says Schiller, then welfare cannot thrive you see; in response to the question who else is to set them free, Bergson also merely points to the 'dreamed-of genius of a great creative personality'. Thus not merely the naivety of the stream of life is preserved here, but above all its 'heroic sense', its Carlyleism, its personality still on the threshold of the société ouverte, if not further. Since proletarians and dialectics are lacking, Bergson en-trusts the centrally planning and organizing leadership of the industrial apparatus (which is to set 'humanity' free) to saints and heroes, who are capable of demonstrating the 'leap of the mind' to 'masses paralysed in a thousand-year-old torpor', hoping 'that these, shaking off their torpor, will follow'. Thus this is very far from robbing from Nicodemus his different opinion; it very closely suggests, however, the insight into the partly liberal-anarchistic, partly personal-popish limits of French vitalism, even if, as 'organized human life', it blossoms in Catholic terms. Yet this does not prevent us from grasping in the final Bergson one of the most surprising capitulations of organic vitalism to the – let us say – organizing and anthropological kind; and an unrest which hastens the 'de-reification' in an admittedly dreamy way, yet with escape forwards. This kind of life-cult by no means lands up in the primeval forest or Pan, nor in its French parallels; it abandons the 'natural' warmth of the family, the enthusiasm of the nation which has become second nature. And the 'great geniuses'? The misunderstanding of the masses? The alliance of the French Revolution with a church of intelligence à la Auguste Comte,[176] the anarchy with a popish impulse-head? The 'leap of the mind' abandons even in the curiosity the incubation-warm or raving Ananke, settles into the open life of all, not into the infinite all-life; this Paris is worth this mass.

176   Auguste Comte, 1798–1857, French philosopher, the founder of positiv-ism and modern sociology.

THE IMPULSE OF NIETZSCHE

The badly living ego attacked itself here. The bourgeois ego which wants and does not want itself, depending on whether it has enough of itself or cannot get enough of itself. The cry of life, it says so little and means so much, emanated from Nietzsche. He shouted the emptiness which otherwise only suffered from itself.

This seized soft people at first, they pinned a man on to themselves. A ruling ego which one would like to become in dreams, which one serves when awake. But the masters themselves soon found what was theirs in the superman, the naked and transfigured exploiter. Without feelings of sympathy, without humane phrases; that is how the superman seemed, that is how he actually felt. Nietzsche meant this differently: he portrayed the noble (instead of the good) as indeterminate in the future. 'Do not throw away the hero in your soul'; the blond beast however, preached in these times, could not have any soul at all and was imperialistic. In this respect the superman is honest; from his claws we do not recognize the lion but rather the monster, and what we have to expect from him. The lie already fell away, the lukewarm centre ceased in an age which had only used the whip when it dealt with women.

But otherwise the hard man is just as relaxed as he is burning here. In man the always wild x renews itself beneath the domestic animal, namely the 'drive' which does without. At the zero-point of mechanical existence there are not only the various superhuman beasts, there is also a recollection of *Dionysus*. The predator in tropical, not cold terms, the Thracian forest against the cold reified bourgeois citizen. Dionysus as a symbol of abstractly fantastic escape into anarchy: only here do we grasp Nietzsche's *serious* impact on the age. Only here did Nietzsche express his age in watchwords, in watchwords of an indistinct counter-movement of the 'subject' against the objectivity which it finds to exist. Socrates, Apollo and civilization, even Jesus, moved closer together in their negation; Dionysus ran amok against all 'domestications', however remote. Since then sport, dance, the Fury of war, youth organizations, 'primeval demons' (revived or invoked), and feelings for nature flourish in his name; this was 'the dismantling of the moral and intellectual phenomenon'. Thus Dionysus is also not merely the unrestrained reflex of the capital which causes discipline, moderation, justice, and bourgeois virtue to be dismantled in good time, but he is a formal dissipation into an indeterminate being beside oneself, being-outside-time per se. Even origins of the bourgeois revolution, namely Rousseau, appeared again, yet orientated in a completely opposite way, as if transposed to the antipodes: the pastoral morning was replaced by a Panic one, the Arcadian little garden by a roaring palm-grove, the coolly beginning light by the primeval, nocturnally hot one. Thus romanticism was applied to fire, archaism to the beast, philology to a ship drunkenly putting to sea. The ship has arrived; now it is a question, not in view of the 'superman' (he is already crystal-clear fascism), but rather of the Dionysiac elements, *of sharing the spoils*.

The escape from the age, the desire to be wildly disguised, does not fall to our side. Glowing words, particularly old ones, replace modern feelings, so that nobody knows what the clock says any more. The mask, the formal carnival procession as which the protest against the age does in fact start and move, does not fall to our side. In the previous century Makart[177] was also to be found where he was being combated, and also where a person in disguise accused another of play-acting. Nietzsche against Wagner:[178] when Parsifal and Zarathustra crossed in the post, it was not only swords that were crossed, as Nietzsche thought, but also masked processions. In how Wagner-related, mask-like and decorative a way Zarathustra in particular exhibited his Greek-Persian-biblical gilt edging: intellectual honesty in the form of a Persian founder of a religion teaches the Antichrist with biblical language. A language of utmost intoxication (even though with Romance taste and pure foundation) praises Carmen contra Wagner, mountain air contra Wahnfried,[179] bravery contra baroque cross and kingdom of heaven: and is nevertheless the same copy-dream in which the bourgeoisie lay at the time, or a mere Carneval de Venise against the stout, German one. Even the majority of the great historical figures through whom Nietzsche seeks to teach reverence for the man rolling of his own accord and contempt for the masses, and through whom he moreover curbs the genuine Dionysus, are rather legendary images of the contemporary Renaissancism than 'exempla of nobility'. Even the genuine mask does not fall to our side, namely that of the *drunken* and *cave-like* Dionysus, in which Nietzsche pounced. It was not one of the mere carnival

177   Hans Makart, 1840-84, painter of elaborate historical pictures.
178   Cf. Nietzsche's work *Nietzsche contra Wagner*.
179   Wagner's house in Bayreuth.

procession but a shamanistic one, one which drew down forgotten powers on to its wearer. But this mixture once again of blasting powder and incense, of tomorrow and the primeval day before yesterday, of 'free spirits' and Thracian Ring of the Nibelungen, of revolt and archaisms. Dionysus stands for a very general placeless subject which has not been satiated in the determinations by morality and intellect up to now, least of all in the bourgeois ones; yet how dark he remains in the merely archaic, apparently lively protest. The 'Antichrist' in particular totally presents himself as an enemy of light, if not as an even much older mythologist; thus the rosy dawn of Nietzsche's concept of life is not 'Apollo's reddish sister who illuminates the globe with a raised torch', but totally the opposite of Apollo and remains in the night. Dionysus does not move, like the real one, from India to Greece, but remains in the jungle; Socrates, Apollo and Jesus (with a blurring of all degrees) are not seen as the *opened* eyes of Dionysus (of the fermenting human subject), but only as the agents of his destruction; indeed, the far-striking Apollo stands there as a mere god of the human domestic animal. However: 'Thunder in, O you, with your flaming steeds, Phoebus, bringer of day, into infinite space!' – Kleist[180] sings this, although he was at home with Penthesileas, and also with the 'granite road of victory', and precisely for this reason: for Dionysus is in reality the *brother* of Apollo, and his *tension* is that with 'Zeus', with *pressure*, *sedateness*, and *spell*, with rest, not with light. Not corybantically clouded noise, in drunken caves and artificial origins, but revolutionary dialectics of history is for 'Dionysus' – as the basic contradiction of man to alienation and estrangement – the cult which is a path for him at the same time. Thus what comes to the *right side of the spoils* is not Dionysus as a mere earlier level of consciousness, smeared with blood, an Ananke in labour and a murderous nature, a cave-contrast to light. But precisely a Dionysus as a symbol of the unarrived, unbecome in man, as a god of fermentation, but of the wine-seeking, light-calling kind. This god also becomes audible in Nietzsche, for the first time again after a long silence; though in a different Nietzsche from that of masks, bestialisms and mythology, in that teleologist who has taken up his post in vain on the bridge to the future, whose visions are lit with wild dazzling by a world which is not yet there. The hymn of barbarism, the paradise beneath the shade of (past) swords, the agitation of the Renaissance beast and of all even more transposed 'instinct' fights in every word with the 'I want to go *There*', with the *wide blue yonder* of the Genoese ship, with the sailing out into oppressed expanse, with a better world than that granted to the slaves and – the masters. Then the music of a not yet lived life lights up, the incapacity for renunciation,

180   Heinrich von Kleist, 1777-1811, writer and dramatist, author of the play *Penthesilea*.

the insatiability of hope makes itself creative in order to pour its thousand bottles and essences into the work; then a turning volition, a motor thinking of the New approaches, which sets a goal for the world. An abstract goal in Nietzsche, a private one, one tinged with aristocratic reaction and disguised, a romantic utopia, without contact with history, let alone with the decisive class today; but history takes its contact for itself, the cunning of reason is great. The dance of death of the romantically reactionary frozen meat teaches nothing, yet precisely for 'slave morality' 'Dionysus' is not unknown, a cheerful, and above all an explosive god. The festivals of the slaves of antiquity were called Saturnalia, and Jesus the vine, totally reduced as he was by the Church, displayed in the supremely Christian Peasant War less slave morality than the masters like. 'Dionysus' is one of the most powerful symbols, if not the most powerful symbol, of the man who is still beside himself, and smashes false forms: and he is so not at a finished beginning of history gauged in terms of big business, but always only within it, at its new points of intervention and turning-points.

Admittedly even further out a darkly restless person hears what is his here. Partly, as we saw, the bourgeois person of today, as an employee who dreams of the whip, as a master who has it. Will to *power* is therefore the last word on which 'life', that which blurs everything, decided in Nietzsche. As indeterminate as 'life' is also the power content in which it culminates; equally indeterminate is the 'will' into which the Dionysian 'drive' now sharpens itself. Neither monopoly capitalism nor imperialistic war lack an understanding of this will to power, of course. Yet even in this final phase – after superman and Dionysus – Nietzsche ideologizes not merely imperialism, but a formal upward tendency, with indeterminate content, as well. One against happiness, against the non-tragic person who intends happiness in the world, and of course also against every power which seeks to change the world, instead of ruling it – unchanged. There thus arose the da capo of the hero to the world that has become; there thus arose, in order to consecrate the moment, in order to potentiate life with oneself and only with oneself, the strange doctrine of the *recurrence of the same*. This doctrine is actually by no means new, much rather banal and has often recurred itself, down to the wisdom of bilking students, in Hans Sachs[181] and Hebel;[182] but its domineeringly physical application is unique. Now the points of life are mirrored and multiply backwards and forwards into a veritable spear-forest of themselves; if there was not also the past which repeats itself in the today, then of course every deed would be a creative act which contains the free will for the da capo. But since – which Nietzsche's will for the future very strangely refuses to admit – but since the today, in

181   Hans Sachs, see 'Jugglers' fair beneath the gallows', n. 85.
182   Johann Peter Hebel, see 'Rough night in town and country', n. 17.

eternal recurrence, has in fact equally long since been determined, the hero of the da capo becomes the servant of what has long since been, indeed of the past of all pasts, and the storming of the future heaven merely attains the spell of long since expired, repeatedly expiring earthly days. The upward tendency of mere points or grand heroes without a bond between them, without a dome of general contents, thus produces, in the will to vault this tendency with oneself, only a desolating this world and a terrible other world, namely one without any break-through; there arises the image of an eternity imitated from endless repetition. This is an anomaly in the fluvial word life in which Nietz-sche's philosophy usually shoots forward; an anomaly in particular in the expeditionary character of this philosophy, in the fiery nature of the world-core with which the explosive Dionysus may be in league. The all too much already existing 'predator' the superman, the individualism of heroic historical figures, especially the totally establishing recurrence of the same: all of a sudden Dionysus knows too precisely what he wants here, because in reality he knows too little, knows too indeterminately what he wants. As the formal upward tendency grasps itself in feudal images and those of statics, it abdicates to a kind of barbaric classicism. Also only this static Nietzsche allows just such an interpretation, that of Bertram[183] for instance, to convey him in the best of health even to Weimar, to gods, heroes and George.[184] The other Nietzsche seeks not merely an unbleached this world, but one placed in utopian fires: 'There are a thousand paths which have never been taken, a thousand healths and hidden isles of life. Man and human earth is still unexhausted and undiscovered.' Precisely this (unredeemed) teleology of this world over-grows the point-command to human history, the circle-command to world history; the heart of the earth is of gold and everything in this world, but this this-world has least of all already been discovered and paid out. Thus Dionysus teaches, precisely in the long run, no solitary points, no eternal recurrence; for he is rather too much than too little foamingly the problem of the unfinished man and his world. Only as this Nietzsche, not as the statuary for whose celebration his consoli-dated On The Way gives false cause, is Dionysus there, is he the end of the closed world-view and likewise already, positively, a symbol of – anti-nothingness. Only in this respect is it certain that Nietzsche, and indeed, summarily speaking, that the 'subjectivists' of modern times in such various forms as Münzer, Kant, Kierkegaard, Feuerbach, Nietz-sche, that the thorough humanists and atheists in whom the exting-uished other world is fruitful and has been brought back to the future of man – that therefore even the Nietzsche sailing out to the Where To and

183   Ernst Bertram, 1884-1957, German literary critic.
184   Stefan George, the poet, see 'Myth of Germany and the medical powers',
       n. 109.

Altogether will still live when the great systematic thinkers of the closed world have long been experienced and finished with. The lumen naturale here became fiery, cognition no longer contemplative, the world ceased to be a mere puzzle for the scientific intellect. This Nietzsche is hardly air from another planet, but nor is he familiar air from the bourgeois one. If there is no will to power any more, none determined in bourgeois terms, not even an indeterminate one in bourgeois terms, then we encounter Dionysus or the glowing core in 'man' anew.

This will to live fervently fell back on itself, namely on the wild element. Partly, for the most part, because as a bourgeois one it has only to lose by thinking, by historical continuation. But partly also because 'consciousness' is actually only a light on the path and not the traveller himself. Dionysus appeared in Nietzsche as the traveller, that is the mythological name for the historically repressed, suppressed, weakened, or at least distracted 'subject'. Only in the god of life who did not get involved in consciousness at all, who did not heed any analysis whatsoever, who did not understand its language a limine, did nihilism seem to be without power. Indeed, precisely from the dismantling of the dismantling element itself, from the radical, namely pre-logical beginning itself did the ground water seem to rise which no concept can evaporate any longer. Though from which 'beginning' did it rise? Surely only from one which the flight from every concept seems to uncover, in an imaginary Outside of history and reason. Furthermore, which 'subject' appeared in Nietzsche's 'drive', 'life', even in Dionysus? Surely only the itself badly determined one (if not determined as a 'predator') between monster and superman, in short, as was to be experienced, an approximate subject and not the exact zero-point which cries out. The 'subject' of Dionysus in man, if it is certainly not totally graspable in class terms, namely in the revolutionary class in each case, and thus today in the proletariat, is less than ever all classes or even the ruling one in each case. That is why super-fascist 'Nietzsche-interpreters', such as Bäumler[185] for instance, instructively seek to eliminate Dionysus even in the indeterminate version which he found in Nietzsche; ruling force here becomes his abdication and 'determination'. But Dionysus can *create* only as war against *every alienation*, as the fiery-revolutionary element of every uprising against 'Zeus'; and only in this respect, as directed against every Inside, Outside and Above which is not that of the *totally liberated* man, is Dionysus at the same time the – *Antichrist*. Nietzsche admittedly directs the Antichrist only against Apollo and the consequences, only against the clever god and god of light; he separates, biblically speaking, the tree of 'life' from the tree of 'knowledge' here

185 Alfred Bäumler: a staunch Nazi academic philosopher who edited an edition of Nietzsche's works.

too. But who is the *true* Antichrist whom Nietzsche so strangely cele-
brates in Dionysus, as the vine of the rising life? Antichrist *in this sense*
is the first serpent which caused the eating of the apple, yet also that
second, light-bringing one whose head 'Zeus' crushed underfoot on the
stem of the cross for the second time: the true 'Antichrist' in the
Dionysian sense, of the Eritis sicut Deus,[186] is – Jesus. This is 'Dionysus, the crucified one', it is on this that the only realization insists, from
the depths of Christian heresy, and in fact of the oldest, 'ophitic',
snake-informed one, which does justice to the 'resurrection and the life'.
This Christ is the preacher of an unknown human glory, too bright for
the given body still to be able to equilibrate it, let alone the now existing
world. He is the conquest of the human glory even behind the smallest
and most unexpected window, and precisely there, precisely in the
paradox of the utterly unexpected, not in the contented measure of the
already appeared, ruling, and satiated into which the Church has falsified and defused him. The Jesus of the heretics, thus the genuine one,
the Jesus of whom the 'Ophites' as basic heretics had believed that the
serpent of paradise had been his caterpillar, just as this one, hanging on
the tree of knowledge, is the caterpillar of the goddess of reason: in this
image of Jesus there is also the life of Dionysus or the draught of a
kingdom which is neither of this (become) world nor of that (far from
human, fateful) one. Such allusions and 'ophitic' memories, hostile to St
Paul, suppressed in the history of 'victorious' Christianity, were highest
of all in Nietzsche's last visions, in 'Dionysus, the crucified one'. There
are traces of this serpent again in modern ruins; for Dionysus is not the
ruin or the night to which reaction flees, not steaming nature 'at bottom', but – as planted on the banners of revolution – the fiery serpent or
the utopian flash of lightning. Thus that intended by Nietzsche in the
superman, and especially in the final Dionysus, can be understood very
relevantly, indeed strikingly from the point of view of early Christian
heretics. Together with the Zeus who is dead, and thus no longer binds
Prometheus to the rock. So strongly does the old Eritis sicut Deus
emerge here again, even with all intertwining of hubris and human-
superhuman piety sui generis. This kind of challenge in Nietzsche could
be more food for thought precisely in Christological terms than is
agreeable to the 'blond beast' and other banalities of brutality, but also
to cringers. For not everything which calls itself 'Antichrist' is so totally
remote from Christos who does not eat dust all his life, does not remain
in the grave his whole imposed[187] death long.

---

186 'You will become like God'. Cf. Genesis 3, 5.
187 'Verhängt' also carries the sense of 'veiled'.

THINKING SURREALISMS

A HAND IN THE GAME

Here there is continuous intersection of the collapsed Before, After, Below, Above, and behind this a darkness.

'Novels of strangeness and theatre of montage'
(p. 222).

Too much is seen around this. That which disintegrates above is very colourful. Shouts, dreams, strikes out to the left and right at the same time. Does not emerge from the void, but makes it grotesque. Ruffles even the escape which seeks to go back.

If everything goes wrong, then the flow does not remain straight either. Forms break and shimmer, smoke of today surges up, incidentals assume an air of importance. Thus precisely the 'revue' returns, above the masks, in thinking terms; it is logically used as a form in order to reflect intertwining. A philosophical hand like that of Benjamin[188] reaches into this lower element and into the incidentals which identify it, produces things from it which would hardly have occurred to a sensible man ten years ago. As in literature, so in thought wondrous things appear, refer to themselves.

And not merely the twilight haunts which is above today. But also the times from which we come, those of our parents; they walk eerily up and down. Yet the previous century became strange just as indirectly; namely pictorially, poetically, philosophically, as a surrealistic discovery. It supplies irritants, we do not yet know for what; it fertilizes a

188 Walter Benjamin, see 'Romantic hook-formation', n. 182.

scornful magic, we do not yet know what for. This occurs in a guard which broke out of the upper strata, which manures fields for them with the times just past. That which pleased at the time receives the expression today of gruesome, yet important dreams; that which was an unfeeling mixture of all styles at the time is montaged crosswise today. All the more strangely as most of these users are Communist-orientated; the file on them is by no means closed. More can be contained in it tomorrow than the phenomenon shows today.

REVUE FORM IN PHILOSOPHY (1928)

Where it develops we very cheerfully go along with it. Then something disturbs us, becomes different right alongside, bends round anew. This is how we fare in the first experiment which Benjamin has undertaken of this kind. Playful comparisons are not lacking, although they could be. Even the serious ones do not always come home, or rather out on the street which runs here.

Different things are partly our own, and partly they unnecessarily touch on something old. Precisely in the work 'One-way Street' which Benjamin published and which stands here as a model for a surrealistic way of thinking. Its 'I' is very near, but variable, indeed there are very many 'I's; likewise almost every sentence starts anew, cooks differently and different things. The work uses highly modern means, with late grace, for often remote or missing contents. Its form is that of a street, of a juxtaposition of houses and shops in which ideas are on display.

Something like this could grow only today, without itself being an incidental. Only today can an inner, and above all objective quirk be taken seriously, without it remaining solitary, incommunicable, incomprehensible. For the great form is largely stale; old-bourgeois culture with a court theatre and closed education does not even thrive in epigonic terms. From the street, the fair, the circus and colportage other forms advance, new ones or those known only from despised corners, and they occupy the field of maturity. To be precise, the clown broke into the dying ballet, the light living machine into the already long dead styles, openwork revue into the old, beautifully closed stage set. Revue admittedly contained little directly apart from its 'loosening' (and even this can be screwed tight again). No new 'mime' arose from the revue, it predominantly served the nightclub populace and was amorphous like the latter. But indirectly of course 'revue' could be used, as one of the most open and, against all intention, most honest forms of the present, as an imprint of that hollow space in which nothing can be closed any longer without lies, in which only parts now meet and mix. The indirect impression of the revue came precisely from the sensuous power and liveliness of uncemented scenes, from their changeability and trans-formation into one another, from their contact with the dream. Thus this form entered as an aid into very different art, from Piscator[189] to the Threepenny Opera; even new aspects of 'ad-lib', of feats with the right hand tied behind your back, were not lacking. In Benjamin these feats became philosophical: as a form of interruption, as a form for impro-visation and sudden cross-glances, for details and fragments which do not seek any 'systematic manner' anyway. Epigram, instruction, dia-logue, treatise – these had always been philosophical forms outside the system, long before the modern systems and even within them. Now, with the bourgeois rational principle a priori, the system also departs which had supplied and developed its idealistic coherence solely from this rational principle. The closed system of theories passes away in the same act as the abstractly closed calculation of the bourgeoisie; such that Nietzsche could even dub the system 'the will to dishonesty'. Thus there was room for Simmel's[190] questioning-questionable impressions; thus a kind of Hörselberg[191] even broke into the academic pilgrims' chorus which is constantly singing of 'systems': in the form of so-called existential philosophy – with complexes, but without a system. 'Revue' appears in Benjamin's little formal experiment in a very differently determined fashion; it appears as considered improvisation, as a falling away of the broken coherence, as a sequence of dreams, aphorisms, and passwords between which at most a crosswise elective affinity wishes to exist. Thus if 'revue', in terms of its methodical possibility, is a journey through the hollowing times, then Benjamin's experiment offers photos of this journey, or rather at once: photomontage.

Constantly new 'I's, we said, are to be seen here and extinguish one another. Indeed, in objective terms nobody at all really walks in the street, its things appears with themselves alone. That which portentously fills the heart is expressed only in external fragments; these form them-selves into signs and displays. Into the one-way street in fact, not as an arbitrary creation, as an empty street leading to a square like those which exist in mere dreams, but as a philosophical *guideline* and bazaar. This produces the strangest form in which ideas have ever been un-folded; the chapters are titled: 'Petrol Station', 'Breakfast Room', 'Syn-chronized Clock', 'Taxi Rank for no more than three Cabs', 'Fashion Accessories', 'No. 13', 'Lost Property Office', 'Theatrical Dressing-Room' and so on. Corresponding to this are the philosophized frag-ments which are accommodated at these points, in these displays, and

189   Erwin Piscator, 1893–1966, Expressionist theatre director.
190   Georg Simmel, 1858–1918, philosopher and sociologist.
191   Mountain range east of Eisenach, the Venusberg of the Tannhäuser legend.

yet are in turn equally interchangeable, with the highest variability. Cathedrals for instance appear as 'railway stations of religion', immediately appear again veiled with allegory-glances like this: 'Sleeping-car trains to eternity are dispatched here at the time of the mass'. Criticism of the 'railway station of religion' of course, but the train equally runs in the opposite direction, namely from eternity and its mythical structure into the railway station, in order to unload contraband here. This linguistic style has that profusion of couplings in terms of thought which constitutes surrealism from Max Ernst to Cocteau: the coupling of There with nearest Here, of brooding myths with the most exact everyday routine. Thus the question of the 'I' or 'We' arises anew, which may not after all change or be lacking in such an inhuman way in this street. The enduring 'I' in the street is admittedly only the strolling body, and thus primarily not ear or eye, not warmth, kindness, astonishment, but climatopathic sense of touch and taste. If a category of Bachofen's[192] can be applied here, then a chthonic spirit has found its casing in this street-thinking, or more precisely: arcade-thinking. Just as sailing ships are stuck in a bottle, just as blossoming trees, and snow-covered towers seem enclosed and kept safe in those toy glass spheres that can be turned over, so philosophical assertions of the world are stuck here beneath the glass of the shop windows. This spirit has even the cosmos only with an inner tasting glance or glancing taste, indeed expresses it with physical intoxication (the 'Planetarium' chapter). A physically near dream-street with shops in which the taste of the times, with houses in which mixed contents of the times are condensed – this is or could be the landscape of this experiment. That is why there is not merely a new opening of a business of philosophy here (which formerly did not have any shops), but an orgy of flotsam and jetsam as well, a fragment of sur-realism of lost glances, of the most familiar things.

If we look back at the little whole, it stands for a good many things which have not come today. A thinker tracks down particulars with the utmost precision, mints them sharply, in order nevertheless hardly to say for what the coin is current. He gives script-face values without a bourgeois exchange rate, without even a tangibly different one; what is apparent is anarchic significance and the significance of collecting consternations, wallowing in decay, rescuing, yet substantially unorientated. The same glance which decays causes the diverse flow to freeze at the same time, consolidates it (with the exception of its direction), Eleaticizes[193] even the imagination of the most variant intertwining; this makes this philosophizing uniformly Medusan, in accordance with the definition of Medusa in Gottfried Keller as the 'petrified image of

192 Johann Jakob Bachofen, see 'Rough night in town and country', n. 20.
193 Cf. the Eleatic school of Greek philosophers, founded by Parmenides and developed by Zeno.

unrest'. But if 'revue' goes through surrealistic philosophizing with a current, then a different 'kaleidoscope' certainly comes to light, in the rescued significances from the ruins. For the hollow spaces of our times (as already of the nineteenth century, whose spooky allegory everywhere looms into surrealistic philosophizing) do not lie in what is itself empty, but in the realm of concrete intention, material tendency, as one which is by no means indeterminate. Benjamin's philosophy causes every intention to die the 'death from the truth', and the truth is divided into stilled 'ideas' and their court: the 'images'. Whereas precisely genuine images, the sharp details and exact depths of this literature, its central remoteness and the finds of its cross-drilling do not dwell in snail-shells or caves of Mithras, with a pane of glass in front, but in public process, as dialectical experiment-figures of process. Surrealistic philosophizing is exemplary as polish and montage of fragments, which however very pluralistically and unrelatedly remain such. It is constitutive as montage which jointly builds real series of streets, such that not the intention but the fragment dies from the truth and is utilized for reality; even one-way streets have a goal.

RESCUING WAGNER THROUGH
SURREALISTIC COLPORTAGE (1929)

What is near has always been best seen obliquely. This is possible on both sides, but the younger eyes are on the left. The glance from this side loosens what is familiar or bends it anew. Hinders average enjoyment, separates what was matted, is not shy of freshness, but expresses it. By this means things move closer together which seemed very remote from one another.

Today much that is beautiful crinkles up, also rolls up. Not at worst from the viewpoint of childlike impressions, they often become particularly correct in decay. The feeling of a boy who had to endure six hours in Wagner's Ring thus becomes instructive. From then on he hated this music; it looked like the *parlour*, was also just as sedentary and boring as the visitors in it. Then later he heard, quite by chance, the sailors' dance from The Flying Dutchman, the splendid ninth,[194] the piccolo flute as bosun's pipe. The piece immediately became wild, colourful, colonial; Karl May and Richard Wagner shook hands.

A word beforehand, so that the handshake is not correct too early on. Neither Wagner nor Karl May are in this connection what they are for the reader who is surprised, simply annoyed or even simply delighted at their conductio. Wagner is an embarrassment, that is obvious, but irony over it is cheap, shameless and helpless, is nowhere intended. And Karl May, actually one of the most exciting, most colourful story-tellers, well stands for *fair, colportage*, i.e. for phenomena whose improvisation and garishness have to be taken importantly, almost seriously. 'Rescue' of Wagner by Karl May thus does not imply a joke at a funeral meal, but a living piece. Indeed many a surrealistic experiment sees the *parlour*, the *grandiose salon* of the nineteenth century in the *fair*; in short, there is a sharpening of due tendencies here. Wagner in colportage is the transfer

194 The ninth interval of the diatonic scale.

of the most ingenious questionableness to the level of a modern question.

Let us first consider the parlour from which every boy fled. It has remained repulsive, but has become an enigma, Wagner along with it. The first felt characteristic of the parlour is the *dream* in which it stands. This covers the image of its knick-knacks today; the childhood from which it stems had a very good place in the itself hollow and spooky element of the previous century. Indeed, even the adults lay in bed at that time, the bourgeoisie lay in the aristocratic bed; incapable of having its own form, it dreamed an imitation of old culture, with a glutted stomach, without connection with the very sober working day. Capitalism and its technology, which had destroyed the traditional culture, did not confess itself as yet; new forces which could have operated precisely out of the cultural hollow space had not yet arrived, of the collapse there reigned only the dust it created, which formed itself into decorative clouds. There thus arose this dream-kitsch (to use Benjamin's term), composed of all styles laid on top of one another, this unspeakable overlapping of historical faces, this actual kitsch-mythology in which there is not even ideological truth any more. There thus arose above all the *second* characteristic of the parlour, in and above the dream, namely the *completed appearance*. But this, apart from the merely subjective lie, is not only escape and the most repulsive forgery, but it disenchanted the myths which capitalism destroyed, again through completed 'aesthetic' non-seriousness in them. Without the equally dissolving and raising, objective element of this false tone, music would have perished in the Biedermeier period or formal epigonism, private, without society and content; Mendelssohn, Schumann and better composers are the indication of this. In this way, however, music joined forces with the dream collective of the times, came together with its apparent symbols: with frontages and interiors which not without reason were alcoves, hiding-places in fright and voluptuous, with trade and industry as veritable gods, carved out at the portal of the bank, with Renaissance which had no portières in the sixteenth century, but which was understood only as portière in the nineteenth, with Ludwigshafenia[195] as 'believed' town goddess, with dream-tangle and emblems of breaking, with the Edda as masked content of the times. From decoration there arose this strange form of 'allegory' which is not one at all, at least not in the usual sense, as we know it from the viewpoint of classicism. In the overcrowded appearance of the nineteenth century dream-potions, Kyffhäuser,[196] and Fafnir[197] are no symbolization of abstractions, as the allegory of the Biedermeier period still was, and hence no exhaustion of seen symbols

195   See 'Ludwigshafen-Mannheim'.
196   See 'Amusement Co., horror, Third Reich', n. 33.
197   Treasure-guarding dragon in Norse legend, killed by Siegfried.

into clothed concepts. But the profusion of a historical-mythical kind in fact is the immersion of apparently symbolic afterbirths in dream-kitsch; this is deserted by all gods, in the good and bad sense, but nevertheless hovers in an intermediate stratum of 'masquerade', which reproduces symbol-myths with full non-seriousness, and does not think of allegories with semi-seriousness. Even the peculiar 'largeness' of the times, of their rooms, picture-sizes, furniture, and above all of Wagner himself, stems from masked appearance or rather from the decorative myth in it, which cast its Pan-like space through it. Appearance itself is already at work in the first decoration of Schwind,[198] satiates itself on theatrical and historical painting, becomes three-dimensional in the grand opera, culminates four-dimensionally in Wagner, allegorizes itself again in Klinger[199] and Böcklin,[200] brightens up into the light glowing fragrance in Strauss,[201] stabilizes itself into the so very different, frozen Wagner-haze in the George circle,[202] into the high gilt edging. But the basic work of parlour, of grand salon appearance is and remains the Ring: it stands in such dense theatricality that it almost has something of reality about it, which is why Wagner was also able to play off his absolute appearance against Meyerbeer's[203] half-measure, i.e. against mere theatrical effect as 'effect without a cause'; Wagner fought against Meyerbeer with almost the same arguments with which Nietzsche in turn unmasks the 'actor' Wagner. Wagner's music has its 'genuineness' precisely in this completed appearance; not only from its illusionistic but, of which we are now *thirdly* to speak, also from its physiognomical side, towards the *problem of sense* and sight. As a completed one of the parlour it is at the same time an enigmatic appearance, one which has become an enigma, a *hieroglyph in the hollow space of the nineteenth century*. Only the brevity of its life prevented even Expressionism from discovering in petit-bourgeois wallpaper of 1880 expressions which apart from crude mixture and naive copy are something else as well. The happiness of kitsch, of the arbour,[204] of the posed and yet not completely unreal beautiful façade likewise belongs here; this age had an eye for the also objective mixed light surrounding things. As a life-style unbearable, as a 'style' that which is remotest from us, the nineteenth century still continues to haunt the hollow spaces which the twentieth has in common with it; these and an admittedly more honest knowledge about

198   Moritz von Schwind, 1804–71, Austrian Romantic painter.
199   Max Klinger, 1857–1920, painter and sculptor.
200   Arnold Böcklin, see 'The speckled primeval flood', n. 158.
201   Richard Strauss.
202   See 'Myth of Germany and the medical powers', n. 109.
203   Giacomo Meyerbeer (actually Jakob Liebmann Meyer Beer), 1791–1864, composer.
204   'Gartenlaube' – literally 'arbour', but it also refers to sentimental nineteenth-century kitsch, as published in the journal with the name.

them, also a more concrete 'appearing', have remained from the collapse of the old culture. In France, where Wagner never died out, and also the 'decoration' was never so remote from life, surrealism is curiously going into this dream-bazaar again, into a tumult of symbols in all directions, which it would like to give the blood of real things to drink so that their tendencies appear and the material heart of the symbols should beat. Thus if we understand the art of refinement, not just the beehive of real old culture but also Wagner's waxworks still ought to contain much strange honey. In the chaos of kitsch schemata there is among other things a pseudomorphosis whose days are literally not numbered, and a hieroglyph which awaits interpretation.

So much for the parlour, how it gives cause for surprise, and this is ultimately already enough. How very seriously when (as is to be shown) the *fair* breaks into it; for the latter does not consider the kitsch but overturns it. Formerly the fairytale saw to this, with regard to mythical powers, with the helpless yet victorious Hansel, and also Punch. The heir to the fairytale is *colportage* (which is so close to the fair); the mythical powers have become the apparent kitsch of the proprietors for it, and it plunders the parlour, twirls the demons of the plush curtain until the maid can drape it round her as a bridal cloak. *Colportage* is therefore the most authentic rescue of Wagner, above the dream-kitsch in him; it is the bosun's pipe with which the fresh Wagner-impression began, in which there is nothing enigmatic, but nothing dusty either. Colportage also stems from the nineteenth century, is likewise a dream, yet (as explained in the chapter on 'Intoxication' and here recallable) not one of those who are satiated, but of those who are eager and waiting. It likewise telescopes old subject-matter and reproduces it, but the romances of chivalry, and even myths, which it transforms are inserted into a wishful dream which intends everything in cash, not into one composed of memory and pathetic escape. The colportage dream is therefore a sound one in revolutionary terms, a thundering pictorial mist of gratified revenge and fulfilled wish, with a lot of excitement, action and splendid triumph at the end. Long journeys, very distant or very lustrous scenes of action are essential to colportage; it by no means earns its living honestly at home, it is not the quiet funny story, contemplative calendar story of the settled populace, but a product of freedom of movement, having only originated with it. The antipathy of the modern bourgeois not to smut but to trash[205] thus becomes comprehensible; colportage allows non-adults and proletarians to dream lustre in advance, in short it always provokes even more than (which is only its bourgeois function) it consoles over the industrial prison. Thus if we already understand the fairytale as *anticipation* of freedom of movement,

205   An allusion to the German phrase 'Schmutz und Schund', 'obscene material'.

as battle and victory of Hansel and Gretel, of the clever soldier over witches, devils and mythical entanglements per se, then the hero whom colportage chooses for itself will also always be fairytale-like, a brave, clever Punch on a gigantic (but never big-headed) scale, even where he has equipped himself from 'myth', or rather from the completed *appearance* of myth. Even the as ever problematic 'redemptions' of Wagner pass into the happy end of a wishful dream, in which there is a lot of India, a lot of blurring and quietistic splendour, but no authentic 'myth' any more, which as such always stands against or at least outside human beings and for the heavenly powers. If we take off its stilts, then precisely the circenses of the human break-in, colportage-like lustre ought to be extractable from Wagner's dream-barbarism, hence those circenses which so excitingly pipe or even thunder in it or float off with sounds of the harp into the nirvana-like count's castle. Colportage in general is that element of our times which can be almost directly fruitful; for nothing is mendacious any more in the lustre of the fair, colportage is truly close to the populace, has become our soil and air, folk song and hymn. We understand great works hardly other than in fairytale terms with the appearance of colportage any more, and 'Fidelio' became the pillar of orientation of all colportage, from the Threepenny Opera, which does not lack the king's messenger, to the birth of a new metaphysics from the spirit of colportage. But more than one path also leads from the robber's bride to Wagner's sultriness, from the dream-tangles of old colportage, those extensible at will, to the infinite melody, from Captain Marryat[206] to the pounding, menacing, restless sea of The Flying Dutchman and the female heaven above its flooding. More than one path also leads from the Haddedihns, whom Karl May likewise never visited, to the Teutons of the Ring, from Winnetou's silver rifle to Nothung and his fight against the white father, from the dream-Orient to the kitsch-Edda: – these paths also ought to be usable in the opposite direction, so that Wagner can wholly board his pirate ship, with eight sails, fifty cannon on board and the strange harbour-boudoir of the stilled waking dream. Wiesengrund has already remarked (in his 'Berlin Opera Memorial' (1930)): 'Anyone who has seen Klemperer's Dutchman will have to admit how little blasphemous such a classification is; that it alone is able finally to cleanse Wagner of the dust of the metaphorical, hollowed-out symbolic, mustily consecrated and romantically dressed-up element and to mobilize the foundation of topicality which is quite evident in Wagner today.' In this way Wagner's 'idealism' would perhaps prove dangerous and material, that is, the originally revolutionary element would be retrieved and the colportage of revenge and utopia sharpened out of appearance of 'mythology'.

206 Frederick Marryat, 1792–1848, English writer famous for his sea novels.

Admittedly this freshness is easier generally to advise than definitely to do. It is very curious that we cannot yet be more concrete about Wagner, that everything said about him is certainly in the air, but also remains in the air. The entire attitude of the times to Wagner up to now is embarrassment or negation; nevertheless (or for this reason) in practical terms every director and conductor of the Ring remains a medium through whom the unchanged age of Makart speaks. We are totally incapable of playing The Magic Flute, Fidelio, indeed even the chronologically so close Carmen as they were played in their times, although this would not be the worst thing; but Wagner remains, although it is the worst thing, a Makart bouquet, a Klara Ziegler[207] museum. Such a state of affairs stems not only from the fact that the Bayreuth fund is so totally preserved and is oppressive; nor only from Wagner's tyrant's gesture which allegedly does not have loosened features, and thus does not renew itself and call up the future. Wagner's symphonic opera was an absolute explosion precisely of its age, whose sensation we do not need to recall. If this explosion also soon subsided and became dogmatic in Wagner's work, unlike other old hands and time-bound compilers Wagner is still a musical genius per se, and therefore a figure who per definitionem genii does not remain on the spot. For only talented people remain on the spot, are finished, fully exhausted past, and thus can be past even for us; whereas genius in a work is the element which still carries on working in it, that which continues to concern us, the contribution of an age to the future and to the still unbecome Altogether. Consequently it is not so much the Bayreuth fund which seems to be oppressive as the fact that Wagner's 'mode of genius' has not yet been found, and we accordingly remain in his past mode, play it as a strange mixture of box-office draw and ballast, of marvel, tarted-up mediocre value and most repulsive epoch. In addition to this there is Wagner's contrast to the number opera which is springing up again, to music as plum performance, to the delight in variety, abundance of action, the scene lasting a few minutes. This blocks him off all the more and keeps Wagner, despite the most obvious irritation, in his age, as if he were Meyerbeer or Spontini[208] (about whom we do not need to fret, of course, because they are indeed 'past'). That is why routine and abstract silence prevails, a leaving alone of Wagner, even a rotten 'patriotism' with his Makart bouquet and imperial march, yet no inheritance whatsoever. The only attempted topicalization is that through deletions, ultimately even through the suggestion to speak the greatest part of the Ring and only to have the highlights sung. 'Anyone who watches this film', it said on a poster for 'The Brothers Karamazov', 'will spare themselves the time-consuming reading of the extensive novel'; little else

207 Klara Ziegler, 1844–1909, actress.
208 Gasparo Spontini, 1774–1851, Italian composer.

is intended by the cramped anti-pathos of the new Wagner-objectivity either. If Wagner's Ring is not Dostoevsky's emergency, his individual acts are still symphonically constructed, so exactly balanced in accordance with the sonata movement that the deletion only drives Beethoven, not Wagner, out of Wagner. The merely *diminished* quantity does not yet turn into the quality which we need, and perhaps sense here. Only for the decided fresh and left aspect is the time already ripe: that is to say, Wagner can be decontaminated today from his immediate condition. He needs a different 'tuning', even Bruckner and Mahler, in whom a lot of Wagnerian elements were purified, do not yet help the become fat-music to become the dynamite, the sacred kind, which it occasionally deserves to be.

First the beloved corpse would therefore have to be washed with vinegar. Wagner needs his Offenbach, whom he already has in him anyway, and towards whom he therefore had no sense of humour. The bickering and empty pathos scenes must be driven out so high that they fall down of their own accord. It is not possible to love what is bad, or even Saxon, in Wagner, as we love banalities in Verdi for instance, indeed particularly love him for the sake of these things, the genially profound spirit. Wagner is too presumptuous for this, in the weak spots of a violent despot there is nothing touching as there is in the failings of someone we love; above all even the failings of Wagner are Saxon, not Italian. Much already seems like Offenbach parodied again, so that, as in the case of double inversion, the emergency seems to appear; this would have to be brought back to the involuntary Offenbach in Wagner. This would result in 'parody' and genuine pathos in the same work, often in the same figures, graduated and certainly strange, but at least as a genuine condition in the work which is now simply covered up. This makes no quantitative, but a qualitative deletion in the Ring. the solely meaningful one. Then the really 'significant' bombast would have to be utterly varied, precisely the Klara Ziegler museum, the one which has become alien, the kitsch mythology of the parlour. We have removed all these items precisely from our surroundings, and it is one of the best deeds of modern engineering construction to have liberated us from the kitsch-mythical structure of 'delightful household effects'. But as we noted, one step further this lives on in space, not with regard to its cosiness but its *uncanniness*, as a *hieroglyph*. If the engineering construction of our times serves to ensure that the arrived hollow space now at least does not collapse, then – among other things – the nineteenth century forms enough symbolic material which hovers in the hollow space, also dialectically shines, also denotes fragments of new substance. Experiments with open stage space would therefore be instructive, with visible T-girders around the kitsch mythology and its props; total emptiness of illusion all around, log cabin, Rhine terrace, Brunnhilde's rock, vu par un surréaliste, in the middle. And at all events *colportage* can now already break into Wagner, fair, circus, fairground within it; this made the Klara Ziegler museum criminal even in its day or bore it into the big wide world. We must learn to listen to Wagner, as we devoured Karl May, go with him to the fair. Then the clichés cease, because they become even more garish, and also lose the chaste element which calls itself solemn. In Leningrad Lohengrin was performed behind veils and as a children's play; so they say, with the purest and most proper effect. This would then be as it were a rescue of Wagner by Christoph von Schmidt,[209] by the author of 'Easter Eggs' and 'Heinrich von Eichenfels'; one bend further in the riddles of childhood: and the Ring appears as prairie music, as surrealism of full dream appearance, as liberated colportage in the auditorium and in the direction. The 'unrefined' nature of this music which one always felt, the 'non-legitimate' element of which it was accused precisely by the parlour, displays the noise of the fair in Wagner, obvious colportage enough. By the beard of his prophets, he did not intend the festival ground thus, there and then, but this there and this then only stand as a task and problem. Nor does the sought 'mode of genius' of Wagner yet blossom at the fair by any means, but better at any rate than in the plush cities and their representation of something which no longer exists. The little woodland bird sings its picture postcard song, Siegfried wanders through wild Kurdistan, big dipper music resounds beneath Valhalla, the suburban cinema poster reaches with the most garish scenes, pastoso destinies on to the stage – the Nibelungen fan notices the intention and is not disgruntled.

209 Christoph von Schmidt, 1768–1854, priest and writer of children's books.

HIEROGLYPHS OF THE NINETEENTH CENTURY

Where much is falling, some things are caught hanging crookedly. They
then become more clearly apparent than before on the wall or hanging
together. The fringe trembles, the man surrounding the boy steps forward. Forgotten things push forward and get caught in the jags of
formerly smooth feelings. Even familiar things lie crooked, then look
disturbing.

Thus the days split open from which we come, indeed the body of the
previous century begins to be in labour again. Also brings fresh kitsch
alongside fruits of a merely backward taste. But this *new* parlour,
although very apparent today, is mostly only belated or caught up on;
in petit-bourgeois strata it is still *directly* alive, not indirectly quoted.
More instructive therefore and solely intended here is the *indirect* consternation caused by the things of the nineteenth century; as such peculiar
precisely to the avant-grade. Since Aragon's 'Paysans de Paris', since
Benjamin's strange stamp collections and arcades the times of our parents (moreover in the way we were immersed in them as children)
emerge in ever more adult form. What was formerly only the nightmare
of school-dreams has become the voluntary pleasure of a spellbound
return. Every feature, every device is suitable for this: a vase from those
days at the window, between the tassels of the curtain – and the adult
finds it easy to connect his childhood horror, childhood dawning with
the riddles of this kitsch. For the nineteenth century is actually already
full of dreams, jumbles and rumours; today's memory simply further
interprets what has been. The form in which this century after-dreamed,
copied, mixed and replaced past times comes together into a hieroglyph.

Most small people wanted to seem different than they are at that time.
'Enrich yourselves' was the cry of the 1850s, it remained for the following years. Bourgeois citizens, having grown big overnight, did not
know how to keep this up, their kitsch thus became even greater. It

should not be forgotten here, but let it be noted right at the beginning: the will to enrich oneself also released something real. As the most important thing first: the bourgeois victory in 1789 unleashed the industrial forces of production, from 1830 on the machine revolutionizes life. With new forms too industry put out feelers quite far ahead; through the whole century there run, often amazingly, experiments in glass, iron, undemarcated, thoroughly air-washed space. Giedion[210] excavated as it were this 'building in France': 'Where the nineteenth century thinks it is unobserved it grows bold.' A great exception is finally the science of this century, its will to positivist accuracy and the services it was able to render almost directly to Marxism with its enormous collection of material. But apart from the exception of science (to demonstrate the limits of which, its peculiar transitions to contemplative appearance, would here lead us too far afield), openness in all ideological statements is the century's anomaly and plush its rule. Academic architecture thoroughly hindered the so-called functional kind, bulky styles deposited themselves over the 'combinaisons aériennes' (whose possibilities Octave Mirbeau[211] had already recognized in 1889); 'ornament' above all masked (in the most literal sense) construction. The contradiction between the more and more powerfully beginning social mode of production (of industry) and the private capitalist form of appropriation – this contradiction appeared in two aspects: the technological engineering one on the one hand, the decorative-individualistic one on the other or the anarchy of 'styles'. Except that they were not two aspects at all; for the former was ashamed of its existence, did not prevail at all, whereas historical decoration dominated room, house, way of life, art, and culture from the cradle to the grave. The same world economy which caused the iron exhibition halls to be built also likewise facilitated a historical trade market, namely the mendacious world exhibition 'of all ages and styles'. The *swindle* which had been covered up since the introduction of fixed prices in business dealings now at least broke forth in life again. The *historical imitation* however, another basic feature of the century, sprang from the desire of the parvenu to dream in the conquered bed of nobility, to tart himself up in feudal terms. In Germany above all, with a politically continuing nobility, in the antiquated decoration of this Reich, the bourgeois gentilhomme blossomed, 200 years after Molière, with undreamt-of splendour; his inner *uncertainty* and his historical *dream-appearance* determined society and culture. In short: if most people of the time acted in a sober and bourgeois way, they concealed it or found no form for it. Hence the peculiarly mendacious, mawkish or silly game, the lady-loves that they picked, the

210 Sigfried Giedion: see 'Objectivity, indirect', n. 21.
211 Author of *Le Jardin des Supplices*, an influential book in the *fin de siècle*.

rubbishy bracelets which they gave one another. Hence the gilt edging, mine hostess and the song-loving hunting lads (while the railway had already been running for half a century, the poet Scheffel[212] gave 'his steed the spurs' and rode into the Neckar valley). Hence the bright red housewife at the stove, but outside the kitchen her bubbling laughter, in crinoline with puffed sleeves; hence the compliments of moustache-stroking philanderers. Hence the rift between everyday life and decoration, the apparent life on plush chairs, lit by the glow of gas chandeliers; hence the vestibule of the eighties with carvings, marble splendour and a pneumatic door-catch which locks itself with a sigh and muffles reality. Hence the turned little table in the drawing room, with an opened book on it and dainty little chains which hung down from the top; hence the lifesize photograph on the – easel, with a reefed curtain over it. Hence the golden apples of art in silver bowls of papier mâché, the deluxe edition and the Bavarian royal castles, erected against a reality which best succeeded in escaping from itself in aesthetic terms. The financial splendour also supplied something special of its own of course: namely an *effeminate festive enjoyment*, in life as in art. To the cry: 'Enrich yourselves!' there finally corresponded a hedonism which in Schopenhauer and Hartmann[213] pervaded the entire philosophy of life; it reduced almost all world problems to balance-sheet questions, to the account of desire or aversion, to optimism or pessimism. Hence again women had to be 'feminine', with bust, hips, waists, fat arms and veiling full of presentiment. Bootees ran oppressively and tormentedly with curved edges in heart-shaped patterns; vaginal ruches trimmed parasols, coatees, trains, culs de Paris, even in the grass of the park the lilac of the rhododendron sat no differently from the ruche on the train of a large dress. The age of portières swelled out so voluptuously that its women all look towards us like figures from the 'Pschütt' or the 'Vie de Budapest', despite the pervasive bourgeois mentality in their main occupation. The gentlemen were no different, with tight trousers and full beards: in their beards there nested hairstyled sultriness, in their bedchambers there burnt the hanging lamp, in the whole age there swelled, muffled, and lied plush. It was the century of sobriety and equally of the bombast which was to stifle it; the century of lascivious manufacturers and their dream-blend in the bed of the nobility; the century of a 'stylistic art' which stood as a historical mask-shop on the bleak and opposite street.

This phenomenon sent a greeting from house to house, but also dimly and covertly. Human beings veiled themselves, even things all lay in cases as in a bed. How exactly in general fear and hidden deception were associated with these dwellings, how dangerously something criminal

212   Viktor von Scheffel, 1826–86, popular poet and novelist.
213   Eduard von Hartmann, 1842–1906, philosopher.

found expression in them. Benjamin saw this element of the century beautifully: the 'singing gas-jet' or the 'long corridor which dictates the escape route to the victim'; thus the palatial dwelling was not only the rich arena of taking, but also the illuminating one of being taken, of the detective novel. In addition to this, as the thickest lustre of the drawing room of profit, there was the fact that the rich of that time, not satiated by the drawbridge, spinning-wheels and other renaissance features, also needed the Orient, also needed kilim sails across their rooms, Persian carpets on the floor, the indoor palm-tree in the middle, camel-bag patterns on all cushions and sofas. Whatever had discovered the Orient in the Biedermeier period, the cashmere shawl and the turquoise walls, this Balkanized here, the Balkans in capitalism became the 'khanate of humbug'. Such was the drawing room, and the *street* continued the artificiality, at the same time with a new variation of the basic motifs of the century, which are *falseness and lavishly great dream-appearance in the bed of the nobility*. When we look at these enormous windows and balconies, the stone knick-knacks as monsters, the cast-iron coarse stuff and the caryatids in front of bank-palaces, a new people seems to have migrated here, a barbarian civilized race instead of the gently cultivated one of the Biedermeier period; in order to devastate Germany in the space of a few years with horrors which sought and did not find their parallel, except in the dream-pinchbeck, in the stylistic blend from all ages and peoples. It is the street of world exhibitions and a historic-ism in which everybody could do everything, the architect did not merely build on an enormous scale but in a Romanesque, Gothic, Renaissance-like jumble, according to his commission, and the external size corresponded to the internal boundlessness. The French Impress-ionists a solitary exception, the honestly great old craft of the Leibls[214] or Gottfried Kellers without influence: the art of that time consisted of a masked ball. It extended from the teasing genre to the equally theatrical giant format; only the genius of a Wagner made an almost mythical, scarcely still mythical mask out of this. The last (already speckled) apparent world of the nineteenth century was Art Nouveau, was this glowing lilac in weariness, as such still lingering on in Wagner's epi-gones and noticeably down to Klages. Art Nouveau was the apparent emancipation of a bourgeoisie which – now social-democratically, now Nietzscheanly goaded – still found nothing more in itself to emancipate than escape and living it up, as strange swamp motifs at the same time, as swamp appearance of the breeding beginning in the rotting end. The ornaments of earlier centuries were an internal figure which externalized itself; the decorations which the nineteenth century took from ancient ornament did not even become good counterfeiting. Though this was also for a hieroglyphic reason and one which is precisely connected with

214   Wilhelm Leibl, 1844–1900, German realist painter.

the wishful and compensatory dreams of the bourgeoisie, with the added ingredient of the collective dream. For the nineteenth century did not only copy, in a learned way, the past, but at the same time materialized its dream-appearance out of it: it is historical copy plus architectural dream of a deceased history.

Where much is falling, we said, some crooked things are caught hanging. This is noticeable above all in the previous age, mere disgust no longer expresses it. After disgust had come laughter, the often very artisan amusement at the strange clothes and manners of plush. Disgust and laughter had not gone very deep, they lay in a certain zone of silence; but now the previous century becomes audible as a *riddle*, louder though even spookier than before. The listening subject is first of all, still without interpretation of the consequences, the child of that time in the adult; his reaction is horror and itself angular consternation rich in echoes. For childhood, as we said, never found so many jags and embellishments as in the nineteenth century, so many hiding-places which frightened and concealed, so many dreams of lateness which caused archaic ones of earliness to crystallize. But above all the zone of silence is passed because the things of the nineteenth century are only now decaying, because they are rotting and phosphorescing like dung. National Socialism is doing its bit as a spectre to use the parlour very *directly*. It rejects precisely those elements of the nineteenth century 'pointing to the future', hence its first or engineering aspect; but it lives closely in the second one, in plush. And the more clearly the previous instruments of power for suppressing real socialism fail, the more exactly big business needs fascist dictatorship and narcosis as well, as dictatorship in a different form: the more frequently too it topicalizes the festive appearance and masked ball of the previous century, the more skilfully in turn scene-painting can triumph. The *indirect revival* on the other hand, the strange avant-garde of surrealism, which distils haut-goût for equally strange, neo-symbolic purposes, presents the nineteenth century in forensic terms: as shock and object, as formerly living waxworks and spookiness, as excavation and 'antiquity' with post-mortem lividity. Gaslight in petit-bourgeois terms above the dining-table and the Vertiko alongside it; gaslight in upper middle-class terms above bearded dress-coats and plush circular flowerbeds. Gaslight in petit-bourgeois terms on the engravings and oleographs of the age, on the girl-angel who protects a child from the abyss, on the Savoyard shepherd boy, on the water-lily lake and the adorned gondola woman, on the red and green lit ballroom of the background in which couples dance in décolleté dress and dress-coat; gaslight in upper middle-class terms above Makart pictures whose alabaster arms are corrupted to corpse-white, whose composition decays as wild junk. These areas are only now, through shock and decay, releasing their meanings: as hieroglyphs of appearance and overfilling, as mixture of styles and bottomless mythology. Thus surrealism has in the nineteenth century its sensitivity, its field and its colosseum. But the content of the yield is precisely the totally decaying mixture of dream-styles, and the means whereby its hieroglyphs are reinforced in order to be strangely relevant, perhaps even legible, is diabolical montage of the ornaments shot through in all directions even then. The photographs on easels, the thermometers on halberds, the mysterious chamber of horrors of the times: this century is closer than childhood, more remote than China. But surrealists like Max Ernst, Chirico, Aragon, and Benjamin light a log-fire in the Great Wall of China, draw up the little gold chair from the confectioner's, and the Great Wall of China encloses a time which is the experiment *of the man of dross*. Touts at fairs are in the habit of whispering to people outside many a booth that 'the mysteries of Greece' are to be seen there. In the nineteenth century they are not, but the age contained other mysteries, namely the adolescent ones of the adults of the time; it was a bourgeois conformist temple composed of alcoves, a neo-mythical Old Mexico composed of nothing but 'Budapest'. Without doubt: rejected cornerstones (not always in a blasphemous sense) still ought to be discoverable in the expanse of ruins. The fauna of ornaments is also large, and the lion's head on the sofa no longer grips the ring. The mine of this nineteenth century yields no works of art like the previous ones, but primal images, archetypes (of human expression) out of collapse.

MANY CHAMBERS IN THE WORLD-HOUSE (1928)

Out there too much stirs without us. It is not always bad that what has been named runs away again. It stands out all the more particularly, no longer belongs together in such an agreed way. Grows green or fades away quite differently than one may think.

Indeed, this very green occurs only in its own realm. The flowers are fragrant perhaps and 'dream', as this was called, but who knows what for and what in. Most animals live far off, not in our world, in which or even towards which they hardly move. Nobody has the paths of the fish, how it swims them, what it seeks and sees on them. There are also considerably less domestic animals than people admit to be true or rather false. The cat never crosses our path, not even to bring bad luck, and even the dog does not go along. However much its barking denies the beggar, affirms the money which it is protecting.

In us as children things do not look much more straight. In the little, surging condition which we hardly dream any more, at the time when door handles looked like flies' heads. And again the women around us, however much they may have suffered, experienced and finally even seized male language as their own: in them there remains fragrance enough from totally foreign gardens. The naked, voluptuous woman, a dangerous foreign wonder, and at the same time the girlfriend, the alter ego in the truly dialectical act of love. Even the misty aspect of women, very clearly to be felt, is different from the male one, and equally the direction in which it seeks to be questioned. Women were not devalued when they were called sphinxes without riddles or their 'unfathomable halfness' was cornered, our concept of the riddle, even this, was thereby merely devalued through them. Not the chaste maid, not the donna graziosa, not the sister of reform with equal rights, not the chorus girl, not the female comrade elucidates the indefinite aspect of woman, hardly that which is already given to her herself. The female feeling of love has a strangely averted glance, even in lust, precisely in this; motherhood seems as if it is initiated into obscure circles, a reserve, not to be communicated, hardly to be included. At least in the direction of love and motherhood, the female distaff side lies beyond the male glance. It is placed alongside and often above the latter's sword side, not added to it as a variant.

Closer to us, the order is hardly right in the human body, not even as a crooked order. The bloody muscles directly beneath the thin skin, immediately we look different, do not resemble ourselves at all. Think of all the other things which are packed up in the body in the way of twitching, throbbing tubes, lumps, worm-shaped motions of the bowels; this barely tallies with man as he presents himself, to say nothing of his excretions. It is hardly credible that human life is brewed in this bloody interior or thinking in the brain; in a Geissler tube[215] the transition would be more 'understandable', more homogeneous as it were, or in a flashing machine – l'homme machine, he is not this. Even above this deep sea, on the surface of the body as its covering mirror,[216] with such very different expression, there is still interruption enough. The genitals, for example, are foreign to the canon of the naked human being as we have it since the Greeks. The mollusc and snake circulate in it, are expressed only pornographically, on the margin of language, crudely, racily or bombastically. The genitals interrupt the Apollonian outline, and the baroque one, which is closer to them, clothes them. The act of love in particular has its own realm, a room with an open floor and open ceiling, but without windows and daylight, circles in it with reflex-like 'barbarism'. In the modern city shocks from the power of sexuality are not audible, as least on a 'workday'; or only in the evenings, in luxury streets and dazzling lights, inauthentically, in the manner of foreplay, defused into colourfully scattering pranks. Perhaps the bourgeois world is animated by hunger, but certainly not by love; even into its art and religion love-glances have been mixed only inauthentically and not as the most important driving forces. Among the Greeks there was at least still *tension*, and in Gothic Christianity *enmity* between Dionysus and Apollo, between the underworld demonism into which Eve burst and Mary-Christ. Sensual happiness still at least vied with peace of mind, in the modern world it stands at a totally crooked angle to the mere working day. Mary-Christ was still the robbing attempt to escape from Dionysus, the superior experiment of pouring purified water into a new life even from Dionysian phials; courtly love stemmed from this and permeated a whole culture, down to the rococo period. For the 'mind' which has become bourgeois, however, Dionysus is totally disparate, though thereby also all the more keenly perceptible

215   A fluorescent tube named after the mechanic Geissler, 1815–79.
216   Bloch is using the word 'Spiegel' here in the sense of 'Wasserspiegel', 'water-surface'.

as something omitted. Yet 'Dionysus' is only one, even though a powerful example, among many instances where our habitual sense of life and
abstract rationalism fails.

If the night of love does not become clear, then its fruit becomes even
less so, although it is carried in broad daylight. The child in the womb is
bizarre, the unutterable sleeping world of the embryo, carried by pregnant women into the street, into shops, to dances. The beginning of a
world, indeed of the world in general, dulls and glows here in a wakeful
woman; the zero-point of prehistory possibly travels between two tram-
stops, in the cool everyday life of the year 1928. This incomparable
simultaneity can of course be homogenized; either in modern terms, by
gynaecologists dealing with the embryo as if there were a tram running
in the womb too, or mythologically, by cabbalists having seen a little
flame on the head of the foetus, the 'angel' which guides it. But the
latter classification burst long ago (just as Dionysus burst as a god in a
'system of gods'); and it also gave only a more colourful house, with
colours of the primeval world mixed in, where no possible house at all
yet occurs. Moreover: if the gynaecologists cannot classify the mysteries
of the beginning, cabbalists conversely did not accommodate the existence of the highly earthly world in which the work of the angels is, after
all, enclosed. The shock which overcomes Reinhardt, a young scientist,
in Keller's 'Epigram' when he hears the love-story of his parents to
which he owes his origin is the *experienced*, not just contemplative
concept of this his own beginning, as a world-beginning in the midst of
the civilized wedding-house, indeed in the midst of the familiar,
apparently self-sufficient urbanity. The love-period of one's parents
creates this shock not just for Freudian but also for metaphysical
reasons. The loathing of children to imagine their parents in the act of
love, but also the horror of parents at the incipient love-life of their
children, has these darker reasons too, apart from the understandable
ones: there are trapdoors in the world here, places at which the bottom
drops out of habitual reality. Even church culture cannot give shape to
the embryonic existence of all human beings and again and again of all
human beings, a shape which does not place apparently continuous
history, continuous even in its revolutions, over bottomless depths. It
has baptism only for the moment of transition; but the monstrous world
of spooks beforehand, an inverted realm of the dead, carried around in
the midst of the living, remains without light.

It almost goes without saying how much death really breaks and
darkens. The axe-blow to the quick, so that the same flesh rots which
first formed so strangely. The bitter corpse now lies there, no longer
enclosed in the world like the foetus, like the baby calf in the body of
the cow which is being driven to the slaughter: but the thinking man has
himself driven to the primary site of the illogical, close beside the town
in the graveyard. Death has been included in the organic substance itself,

placed at the head of a separate drive as it were, the death-drive. Not just as a longing of old age, but precisely also as a tendency of youth, as a mineral tendency as it were which seeks to extinguish the ego, to make it pass away cosmically or rigidly. Even in asceticism such an annihilation-drive is supposed to be at work, not in the asceticism of work which takes great pains, nor in the asceticism of escapism for the sake of an inner light or the supernatural world, but rather in the pure desire for mortification which can be a gluttony of the death-drive as it were and in which religion is an ideology. Likewise there are certainly several ways by means of which death was included in the psychological substance or at least used by it. Either directly, as among the Egyptians, as the worshippers of rigidity, of statuesqueness, of the teachings of Osiris, or indirectly and as it were dialectically in the phenomena of the 'love-death', most of all of the 'sacrificial death', and also of genuine asceticism. In aesthetic terms the phenomenon of tragedy belongs here, the way it makes death into the framework of an expelled meaning of life. Yet however correctly or falsely these phenomena may be inter-preted, even their interlacings always occur only on the *margin* of death, on its arranged show-side, not in the centre. It remains the alien non-ego per se, the irrational in the Ratio of every culture, even of the Egyptian one, even of the Christian one; death is the prototype of every 'imposed fate', as one which is equally undesired and alienly intervening and uncomprehended. Even more alienly than the previous man the later man and his realm of corpses thus reaches into the conceptual day, is not surpassed by it at all any more or only with the most enormous alienation. The enlightened consciousness of life capitulates in the face of death, the ecclesiastical one cuts through it, but nowhere is the Gordian knot really entwined into victory.

So much could be added to the simple green with which our astonish-ment began here. A sketch, less than this: a little catalogue would thus have to arise, very incomplete and deliberately unarranged. *A catalogue of what has been omitted, of those contents which have no place in the male, bourgeois, ecclesiastical conceptual system.* But which have to emerge again to the same extent as the system is exploded in revolution-ary terms of 'relativistically' bursts itself. And consequently – against *abstract* rationalism – existential contents appear which certainly do not explode every Ratio, but need a more existential and concrete one. Wretches come forward who are kept worse than cattle and do not stir against it because they stand completely outside. Maidservants so weak and speechless that they do not go with their suffering, but their suffering goes with them into the water. Prostitutes, pimps, undefined people in bourgeois terms and underdefined ones through crime, stench, maggoty life and in fact 'unspeakably' depraved colourfulness in the southern seaports. And in the settled, more dangerously omitted realm: even the peasants are not marching in rank and file, in their sobriety which is none, in their property which is not capitalist and thus is not overturned. The nobility is even less a thing of the past, overrun by the bourgeoisie in linear terms, but the nineteenth century is still a scuffle between prevailing forces, not the least of which was and remains the restoration,[217] even within the bourgeoisie. And back up again, to resources with deeper darkness or light: have the Jews become chaff after the wheat of Jesus has been removed? Lower, and even the highest religions still abound in the fullest juxtaposition, in the lagoons of the South Seas, infected with cannibals, in the secret monasteries of India; they land neither actually nor substantially in the 'primacy' of Christianity, as if it were already the day to end all dawnings.[218] The 'numinous' is contained in them frighteningly, but frighteningly in religious terms, a portent to all theology which knows what mere rationalism of the heart and mind means. The 'natural barrier' is by no means surmounted either as capitalism would wish, which is here the descendant of ancient sorcery in vain. The mere causal nexus, on which our life, our encounters and the destinies commencing from them depend, does not look like a concrete production budget which surmounts the rank growth of 'nature'. And just as little, on the other side, surmounts the abyss of the accident: the collapses, collisions, explosions in the field of technology, that which is still abstract and pierces nothing; let alone the cosmic defencelessness beyond all the neo-magical triumphs. And in other respects too: how disparately in itself what is natural still stands, even in small details, in relation to the growing common denominator which does not concern it. The water rises so bleakly and heavily, the rock broods, is silent and stares in its nameless way, the procession of waves rolls endlessly out of the night into the night, unbusily on dark business, the pale streak of lightning flashes, which poets see and philosophers do not penetrate, formed in such haste down to the finest detail, yet of inconceivably short duration; the stars burn as Argus eyes which are none, as gods which are none, as lumps of fire, radiant bodies which are none, in the midst of the vast otherness of the world-night: no concept, either empathizing or poetic or qualitative or quantitative, set a goal for this excess of riddles; even the formulation of the question remained blind with Irratio here: as the enormous demand on reason, which cannot solve the mystery without doing justice to it. Even mysticism, with all its sun-formations or depths of God, gave no house to 'nature'. If we grasp the world on the one side, then it escapes on the other, shifts its bad uncornerability again and again. That which is electricity today, this broadly rationalized phenomenon, was for the Greeks certainly just rubbed amber, but in return all ancient magic has returned to a small

217 I.e. the political restoration in the nineteenth century.
218 Bloch is here playing on a variation of the phrase 'es ist noch nicht aller Tage Abend', 'it's early days yet'.

piece of amateurish amber again, and ancient magic was only an unfinished piece of patchwork too. The core of nature darkens all the
more, with human beings at its heart. The mover of human destiny is
unknown, even the mover of hunger and the economy as well, all the
more so the subject of 'culture', of all the illusions and also glittering
images of a varyingly adequate consciousness in which the genuine one
is hidden. In small, tiny details the heart of existence often still dawns
most exactly; even in the way this pipe may be lying there this has the
authority of its beat: yet only a great *astonishment*, even though the last
and highest, reaches composure through it. The subject of existence in
general is totally shrouded in mist, still without a lamp of the concept.
This world-Odysseus is still unknown not just to philosophy but thereby to himself, is still called Nobody[219] or a subject without a face, a
tendency without provided matter; his Ithaca lies below the horizon.

So hard does something amply different push forward, on the left,
and also on the right. Cannot be reconciled, stands crosswise, blocks an
all too quickly or prearrangedly collecting concept. The latter thus
appears as abstract, it omits, with a kind of numerus clausus,[220] what
does not fit into its context. Into its well-worn and thereby doubly
smoothed context, into a frame of reference which, as a male, bourgeois
one, as a continually quantifying one, has very much subsumable conceptual material in the various. The various roams around here as the
individual, which is not accommodated as something particular; especially the qualitatively particular is then just as little also the particular
of something general as the general can be the general of this something
particular. The modern decay of the surface context particularly sensitizes to this kind of thing; but not of course for the purpose of an
abdication of the general, the continuingly whole, the finally even One.
If the whole is not the truth, then simply not the closed whole in all too
finished terms but rather that which is kept open. As one which admits
both below and in front what was previously underprivileged in conceptual terms, which, out of real nobility, does not put on noble airs
towards the merely 'incidental', as even Hegel occasionally says. Such an
experienced pluralism is then precisely a *demand* on the Unitas and
towards it; it first makes the latter unprearranged through impediment.
The whole of this unity is thus not the already comprehensively true,
but solely the true that is still outstanding; this Totum does not yet
exist, except in utopian experimental disposition. Its One Thing[221]
(which is needful, and thus not yet achieved) stands only in the fre-

---

219 In Book ix of the *Odyssey*, Odysseus is able to escape the clutches of the
Cyclops Polyphemus by the ruse of telling him that his name is Nobody.
220 The restricted number of students allowed to enrol for each subject at
German universities.
221 Cf. Luke 10, 42.

quently attempted process-direction towards it. Only thus, but precisely thus, can pluralistic wealth be no disturbing factor, does even its contingent element, seen experimentally, not remain something chaotically incidental, but conversely becomes a pointing and witnessing element from on the way for the whole that would be true. Such a witnessing element gives, instead of the lopping pattern, assisting fullness for depicting the process, and above all strengthens the conscience-knowledge that the world is still unfinished and its All-One, precisely this, least of all finished and dealt with. Which then has an effect not least on the *dialectical* method, as that of the unconcluded process-content itself. Instead of comfortable material, concrete dialectics calls for the uncomfortable sort, and thus not just one in contradictions, and also resistances, which have become homogeneous or are even homogeneous ab ovo. It finds this uncomfortable yet particularly concrete material even where everything does not run in rows, where there is criss-cross confusion, along with non-contemporaneities, indeed disparities. In the many chambers of the world-edifice, those unroofed and hence discovered precisely through decay, those pushed together not only subjectively in montage, such peculiar being beside oneself or possibly being negative lodges a lot, even without a premised thesis. Instead of the always identical triple cadence of thesis, antithesis, and synthesis, in which there is always the same and an all too certain blessing, there then appears a richly variable and also strongly syncopated rhythm. Instead of the one-way process, there lives a multi-temporal, multi-spatial one, in which its by no means homogeneous matter shapes itself and emerges through experiment. Precisely in the dialectical method the world thus operates pluralistically, but all the more so as a multiverse versus Unum nondum inventum. Hence devoted to a unity which equally circulates and is latent as the *perfect*, lacking anyhow (not totally absent though), in the imperfect for this very reason, i.e. in its perfect, inappropriate element. Thought must be open to this day and night, a rationalism of contingency moved into openness and of dialectical chargedness at the same time, a utopian experience which neither abstractly flees nor irrationally capitulates.

But for this the concept must be both sensitive and mindful. This too can be learnt from the collapse in so far as one does not belong to it oneself. And just like society, the world dependent on it also opens at new pages again and again. This can even be the case, even though to a not yet determinable extent, in the world relatively independent of us, inducing it, corresponding to it. Hence not only through technological mediation of today (which by no means needs to be one which is already concrete), through its often merely cunning detour, artificial combination of law-governed natural connections. But there were times – and they could return at a highly rational level – when human beings had a more *cosmomorphic* relationship than that of cunning, than that of mere 'mastery', 'exploitation' of natural forces. Pending this still very outstanding, indeed very hypothetical relationship though, most of the inorganic world, seen in humanistic terms, will admittedly remain a no man's land; i.e. it will be by no means concretely mediated with man and his history, although it totally surrounds them, by no means linked up with them. Indeed, the agent of things itself, the x which drives them and in which their essence is latent at the same time: this was in fact denoted as a 'world-Odysseus' who is himself still called Nobody, togther with an 'Ithaca' towards which this travelling element still by no means has a channelled future of arrival, which even rises only out of its tendency-latency during the proper journey and through it. But the *self-problem of unfinished existence* has many stones in the building of its possible solution which previous builders have rejected. Philosophizing must thus be able to take a lot along with it in order, on the other hand, to keep that mindful one-sidedness in testing terms again which sharpens for the purpose. Not with chambers which remain very remote in the end, but with the unity of a dwelling as world, which only thus would no longer need recherche de l'espace perdu. This is a still totally unreal borderline concept of the Unum; beyond it the glance at what is unincorporated therefore remains a good remedy against poverty of encompassing. Totum relucet in omnibus: yet not in fact as a reassuredly generalizing one, but only as a centring one in utopian terms can Totum shine back. Whereby it is beneficial to the concept if it seeks and is able to collect witnesses in the slightest detail.

TOPICAL CROSSWISENESS: FEAR OF 'CHAOS' (1932)[222]

It widely inhibits today. It is, after all, the eleventh hour, they say. After it the abyss before which one stands or has just stood. Before which the carriage was pulled back at the very last moment. Gratefully one therefore becomes brown,[223] also glances above again and again.

That which had to dwell below had to endure more than merely mockery for its affliction. Below there was supposed to be a stupid rabble almost without exception, riff-raff, the lazy, cheeky, unmusical slave. A contemporary portrayer relates of the purposeful peasants in the Peasant War that when they set out they 'did not know why, the blind, wretched, stubborn bunch'. Whatever wears rags, drinks schnapps, does the heaviest and dirtiest work, and shows neither education nor manners, has this minus as a consequence of its innate brutality and not the brutality as a consequence of its social minus. Odi profanum vulgus et arceo,[224] sings Horace, the son of a freedman; this senior primary school teacher sentiment has remained wherever people of the servant class appear who forget to be respectful. Cheeky servants, spiteful beggars, not to mention mutinous sailors find no mercy from Horace to – Jack London.[225] 'Woe betide those', sings Schiller, 'who lend the celestial torch of light to the eternally blind'; the knight also has no desire to see in the social abyss what the gods have graciously covered with night and with horror. Women of the revolution, ringing the alarm-bell, are out and out hyenas; sexual fear and the mistrust of the petit bourgeois towards the always disorderly woman thereby contri-

---

222 The title of this section echoes that of a work by Bloch's close friend Joachim Schumacher, *Angst vor dem Chaos*.
223 Bloch is referring to the Brownshirts here.
224 'I hate the vulgar mob and avoid them.'
225 See 'Ludwigshafen – Mannheim', n. 10. An odd choice of example here, as London was ostensibly a socialist.

bute a particularly chaotic note to the revolution. Conze,[226] in his many-sided book 'The Thesis of Contradiction', compiled the most instructive of these examples, they all present the 'rabble' as inferior by nature. For centuries the ruling class has been repeating that the masses have no understanding, no judgement, that they are, as Sombart[227] puts it, 'intellectually limited, short-sighted, gullible', even uncritical. Ortega y Gasset,[228] the flattering prattler and disgruntled fascist, declares: 'Today we are witnessing the triumph of a super-democracy in which the masses act directly, lawlessly [!], and impose their wishes and tastes on the community by means of material pressure.' The masses are literally defined as 'the totality of the not particularly qualified' (for it is obvious to the bourgeois who formerly came from lower strata himself that it is only 'the lack of their own initiative' which keeps people in the masses); Ortega y Gasset continues: 'The basic condition of their soul is inadequacy and incorrigibility, it is their innate failing [!] not to consider anything which is beyond their horizon, neither facts nor individuals.' But Macaulay[229] already completely depicted in advance the modern fear of chaos, or rather the terrifying image, mitigated only by contempt, of a social popular front. He prophesies the 'Bolshevist chaos' completely as homo homini lupus: Ausgabe, p. 398: 'There would then be many millions of human beings, herded together in a cramped space (?), robbed of all those aids which would alone make it possible for them to exist in such a cramped space. Trade, factories and credit will be dead. What else could they do but fight for the simple preservation of their lives and tear one another to pieces, until famine and epidemics in the wake of famine turn the terrible commotion into an even more terrible calm?' [Translators' paraphrase.] Macaulay, also Luther, also Schopenhauer – the list would be long and could be continued with countless variants; but the ruling class in each case is agreed that the masses are only wolves or asses or a hybrid of both.

Mentally too, so to speak, the opponent becomes worse than nothing. If *fear* depicts him in bloody terms, *ignorance* does so in pessimistically black terms. The laziness and greediness of the rabble cannot be anything other than – materialistic. This word is served up to the petit bourgeois solely in the tritest sense, and he detects the nastiest one in it. Whatever the petit bourgeois is fleeing and what he is surrounded with, he ascribes precisely this to the 'materialistic' proletarian. Every concept

---

226   Eberhard Conze: Marxist philosopher who applied the method of dialectical materialism to logic.
227   Werner Sombart, see 'Appendix: Spengler's predators and relative cultural gardens', n. 152.
228   José Ortega y Gasset, 1883–1955, Spanish philosopher and writer.
229   Thomas Babington Macaulay, 1800–59, liberal English politician and writer.

therefore gets confused: 'materialism' as gluttony; as an egotistical attitude, intent only on its own advantage; as a returning of the world to
mechanical death. It does not matter here that gluttony is the least
failing of the proletarian, that the martyrs of the Commune took very
little account of their personal advantage, that dialectical materialism
smashes mechanics to pieces. The petit bourgeois gets rid of all adverse
aspects of capitalism by calling them 'materialistic'; and the 'Bolshevist
chaos', as a practice of the materialists, is thereby doubly incriminated.
Two generations ago this was different, when the liberal bourgeoisie still
had its apparent struggle with holy water and sabre. Whereas today, no
longer interested in such a struggle, it has made materialism contemptuous of itself, though of course: merely theoretically contemptuous, and
emancipated the impulse of the ideal, and ultimately of the irrational.
Since then all mention of materialism occurs condescendingly from
above, always with the emotional aim of hurting the labour movement;
this materialism is dismissed as flat, crude, crass, shallow, arid, banal,
soulless, mindless, uncultivated, grey, boring, dead, long overcome, in
short its characterization consists solely of summary insults. The days
are far off when Windelband[230] could still treat Democritus as a thinker
equal to Plato and Aristotle; and the foreboding seriousness is certainly
past with which Hegel had distinguished the French materialists. Materialism is not only understood purely as a mechanical one, and in form of
the Büchners[231] and Moleschotts[232] which is barbaric anyway, it is also
turned into a hopeless misfortune, indeed into grey misery per se. Not a
word comes to the ears of better-class gentlemen about the Novum of
dialectical materialism, not a word about the differences which the latter
sets against bourgeois materialism, and especially against the epigonic
kind of the Moleschotts and Haeckels. The petit bourgeois would be full
of world-riddles if he knew the genuine emotions which precisely dialectical materialism turns against the fully flattened apes of the mechanical kind. Against the 'itinerant preachers and caricaturists Vogt,[233]
Moleschott and the like', against their 'flourishing at the time of the
deepest humiliation of Germany and of official German science' (Engels,
Naturdialektik, p. 151). The petit bourgeois in need of light could certainly expect the 'most ideal' surprise if there were no such obstruction
by the clumsy propaganda of the vulgar Marxists, and the cunning
propaganda of the ruling class with regard to materialism. Totally remote from its historico-dialectical shaping, reshaping, reshapability, de-

230   Wilhelm Windelband, see 'Appendix: Spengler's predators and relative
      cultural gardens', n. 146.
231   Ludwig Büchner, 1824–99, German doctor and vulgar materialist philo-
      sopher, brother of Georg Büchner.
232   Jacob Moleschott, 1822–93, Dutch physiologist and mechanistic material-
      ist philosopher.
233   Karl Vogt, 1817–95, German materialist philosopher.

tective and hopeful at the same time. But the materialist conception of history, from the academic textbook to the newspaper article, is thus only defined à la canaille; if the 'educated' man wants to take counsel here, then he learns that the 'craving for money' is regarded in Marx as the sole motive of man, the movements of history were reduced by Marx 'exclusively to those of the substructure, to a mechanical [!] system of laws'; economics and nothing but economics is the 'content of history' and will remain so (!). Recently, besides the smell of carrion, Marxism is even also being distinguished with that of – decay, in a unique reversal of the real situation in which capital and Marxism find themselves. The untamed Irratio of the vitalists, and the more restrained one of the so-called Gestalt theorists are writing the obituary of Marxism as a 'product of the liberal century'; in such a way that the 'educated' man, when he looks at forms, disgustedly dispenses with merely 'haptic'[234] materialism, with this vulgarity of the sense of touch, and totally sticks to 'optic' idealism, to the world of shapes, forms and ever more distinguished personalities. Enough is stolen from Marxism because it is reality and because not even deception, in so far as it occurs in reality, gets by without it. But the doctrine becomes taboo, an abyss, vulgar philosophy, the end of culture. Just as for the peasant and petit bourgeois, although he has nothing to lose but his debts, the republic of the 'have-nots' is sheer horror, a so-called movement of the godless becomes for him, although he does not believe in any real God at all any more, a zero, indeed a minus per se. There thus appears to him in the Marxist 'abyss' no blossoming this-world, no unknown miracle of liberation, but an icy chaos.

From the situation itself in which the little man lives everything does not become clear here. It admittedly veils the path into the open for him, but it does not downright demonize it. This is achieved only by an older, non-contemporaneous structure, a – beside all the rest – *superstitious* fear of the 'below'. Age-old *mythologies*, the very latest renewals of them ultimately still come to the aid of ignorance, are mobilized into the service of a new fear of the devil, join the former one. For the latter, evil was always down below and the light with the masters who tame. Here the biblical serpent crawls along the ground, has to eat dust all its life, bites man in the heels, and he has to crush its head underfoot. Here, resulting from the Fall, is the lascivious woman, she must be firmly restrained like all covetousness, is the company of Korah[235] and the great Whore of Babylon[236] who likewise seeks to ascend from the abyss. Here is chaos itself as a condition right from the start, the cosmic

234 'Haptic': concerning the sense of touch.
235 Korah, (in Numbers, 16), the great grandson of Levi, swallowed up in the earth for rebelling against Moses.
236 Cf. Revelation, 17.

underground of the world and as such threatening wherever the band of honest awe, pious awe disperses. Even Dionysian reversal of these valuations is no match for the old-established, so to speak patriarchally established basis of reaction. All the less so since 'Dionysus' has been completely turned into a master's god, into a particularly unscrupulous one, and 'slave morality' thoroughly remains for the people, among irrational clichés which are solely supposed to stupefy it. But precisely the fear for his life of the usual petit bourgeois seeks security; precisely the non-contemporaneity of the demonized petit bourgeois, which actually touches on earlier states of consciousness and stands in a frenzy of blood, at least in archaic dreams, does not want shapelessly represented chaos, but combats it. In subordinate form it wants leadership and followers, in demonized form a dragon victory and German star; jubilation by 'pan-chaotic' types per se is rare. It is difficult to distinguish whether the religious value-feelings which accompanied the concept of *matter* in its long prehistory are not also revived in places in the modern fear of chaos, fear of materialism; at least in the 'educated' variety. The verdict which the Church bestowed on matter is already enough; for the Church hands it down to consciousness (and today to the unconscious) as 'non-being', as all the 'imperfection' which 'night' adds to the figures of the Creation. It hands down the patriarchal, the Platonic-mythical equation of matter with flesh, darkness, suspicious material of the abyss, just as it hands down 'idea' as form and sole light. All this is a contribution to the fear of chaos wherever it lies in the interest of the ruling class. The Christian 'reverse movement of love' whereby the soul does not reach for the shining God of the summit but has its Eros and its objects in the nether realm: this reverse movement seems less in the interest of the ruling class today, although Scheler speaks of it. The petit bourgeois is frightened by the proletarian condition to which he sees himself to be close, which he regards as an absolutely eternal one, like everything in his world. And the upper strata promote all reflexes of mythology which shrink back from the abyss – as if it was one.

But even the feeling of the eleventh hour lives on. A social order in which all little people suffer bears its end within it, both subjectively and objectively. In order that it should not appear to them in such a mythically obscured form, the so-called abyss cannot be illuminated adequately enough. This will not be achieved by a cult of the proletarian or by a dismissal of bourgeois culture because it is one of bourgeois citizens. The cult of the proletarian is for the most part only the equally abstract answer (even though the interested dirt of blindness is lacking) to the abstract blindness with which the ruling class judges the proletariat. Vulgar Marxism is just as little use for the purpose of illumination; for, as far as 'lack of ideas' is concerned, it only underlines the Hades which the ruling class presents as 'Marxism'. If Marxism is no abyss, it still does not lack 'depth'; so it is no help to dispel the fear of chaos with the pathos of shallowness. The will to National Socialism could be long since punctured if it were only certain of the superstitious non-will to genuine socialism, the terror of the 'abyss' in which man is in fact more certainly to be found than on those heights which live off him. The intellect casts the demonizing myth only where it has already become weak, but an exact imagination of reason attacks it where it dazzles and conceals. It is not without reason that all arrived terror acts as fascist and, where it appears as socialism, acts as its destruction and never, as with fascism, as a logical consequence. Thus to the exact imagination of reason there also belongs the power to give the lie to every diagnosis of a *socialist* abyss; for it is always the *fascist* element itself, the broadly threatening element per se, which warns of it and leads into it.

FLAG RED AND GOLD (1932)

The day is empty. Work is lacking. Service is hard. The populace needs stimuli. The Nazi paints them in the stuffy air as the 'populace' wishes and capital commands. 'Workers' of the brow hold out their hand (nothing else) to the worker of the fist; big owners of small mining shares shout 'Good luck!' and know it all, as brave miners. To everyone else, behind the excesses of revenge, the portal of clichés, there always just appears the same sad unstopped reality. Technologists see machines curbed which could create bread for millions, see inventions prevented because they stand in the way of profit. Doctors have to make people healthy and productive for a hell, cure diseases which always return from the living conditions of modern society like wounds in war. Lawyers dispense justice as a naked expression of violence; the fascist state tolerates them solely as butchers of a higher order or as sophists of crime. Teachers, artists, writers find no culture any more on the basis of capital, unless it is an ironic or strange one, one which is homelessness, direct objectlessness itself. Nevertheless, petit-bourgeois habit stands in the way of each of these insights. Nevertheless, a very small stratum of people with a vested interest shapes the revolutionary situation in reactionary terms and makes use of those whom the nineteenth century had called 'desperadoes'. Nevertheless too, however, the forces of reaction would never have been able to seduce people so far if their methods were not speckled and contradictory like the situation itself, if their art had not remained so undisturbed, to whisper in the dark. The 'irrational' needs of today, of course, also ultimately stem from the economic situation, but not so smoothly and simply, and they therefore cannot be so smoothly and simply treated and remedied either. During the few years of 'Objectivity' many a friend of progress had claimed: 'Our times are an infertile soil for ghosts'; it has become apparent what a fertile one they are. For if there were not just as much starved imagination as offended snobbery, economic ignorance and real deprivation among the pauperized strata, then it would have been impossible to conduct the 'revolution' in such reactionary terms, and the reaction in such lemurean[237] terms, with God, Führer, fatherland and fireworks. The bleak phenomenon of decline phosphoresces both receptively and 'elementarily'; this phosphorus still brightens the deception for its believers, and particularly causes the iron constructions and montages of the upper strata to glow in the hollow space. Without this wild and wholly crosswise phenomenon neither would the 'soup logic with dumpling reasons' (which Heine regarded as the most effective with the populace) be prevented so injudiciously from day to day nor would the 'spiritual lack' be capable of being so totally turned against Marxism instead of against capitalism, against the cure instead of against the disease. In the (undisturbed) irrational there lies the apparent means which is supposed to remedy the 'diminution of man' (Nietzsche) and which, as we have seen, is swallowed so dangerously, so fantastically or instructively. But it would not be swallowed so 'totally' if in the enthusiasms of intoxication, in the experiments of collapse, there did not also lie a susceptible 'element', whose susceptible side Marxists have in fact left unstressed for far too long. Apart from the fact that red is alien to bankrupt bourgeois citizens, they are even less familiar with the gold on the red flag, the golden figure of sickle and hammer in the red. The poetry of prose is alien to them, the poetry which ceases to be fraudulent only through prose. The dream (even without sleep) is alien to them, the image of happiness (even without contentment in the mustiness), the renewal of all existence (even without revival of the stale one), the imagination of the horizon (even without shady swindling), the Fata Morgana of the Where To and What For (even without perpetrated lies). But precisely in Marxist terms the path with the tendency is never exactly a path unless it is entered, as into the 'totality' of the momentary situation, into the true totality of human hope and latency as well. There is countless National Socialist deception; there are religions whose 'heaven' only consoles poverty with empty promises, there is philosophy whose 'metaphysics' is only the physics of the exploiters, high above. This heaven and this metaphysics stand revealed, moreover with ninety per cent chloroform behind them instead of roses and the scent of roses. But the field of 'lacks' has not yet thereby become empty, either of present seductions to what is false like those demonstrated by National Socialism, or of future ones. Marxist dialectics itself is no immanent mechanism; this dialectics itself has – quite apart from the subjective factor – as its most material driving force the fact that the main thing, namely real human life, has not come into being as yet in any class condition. Hence the will, the humanely augmenting and not

237   Lemures (Latin): spirits of the unburied dead exorcized from early Roman homes.

just economically exposing will, to lead class society across into the socialist society, after all its external conditions have fully ripened. Hence the watchword to keep the What For and Altogether which is not yet known as a permanent question. Man does not live by bread alone, particularly when he does not have any. If he does have it, then the dream of the More is all the more due and red.

FAITH WITHOUT LIES

Only the discontented person can be devout. It is futile to cling in a neo-pagan way to an allegedly already lavishly given life. It is a total lie to refresh oneself with images of a traditional other world, which depicts non-existent lives over there as existing and finished, as a substitute and compensation. We will say nothing of the withered Jewish law from which not just the Jews who have become lax are fleeing. We will say even less of the watery soul of fire of so-called liberal Protestantism, which sells faith at a reduced price. Which has not remained, for instance, a tormented report of modern half-heartedness, relaxation, and remoteness from faith, but cheap contentedness with this and evasion into the emotions. The liberal-Protestant individual has also very quickly ceased to stand in the pathos of the 'decision' or of the ever new 'crisis'. He capitulated almost even more quickly than the orthodox one as soon as the fascist power-state decreed to him the correspondence, if not the heaven to such a kind of inwardness. This last Protestantism recognizes race and state as 'canons and ordinances appointed by God' and knows only that 'in a world of sin all these ordinances have no *exclusive* validity and no *redeeming* force'; whereby thin inwardness or the soul in the bag joins forces with the authorities, consoles itself in a Christian manner with itself afresh. Whereby the Luther state mythologizes itself afresh in its harshness, brutality and totality: as a God-appointed reprisal against the servant of sin, as a reprisal above all against the proletarian servant who possesses so little that he does not even have a faith and an inner mode. Very recently an emergency federation of priests has admittedly been grumbling because it is confronted with too much of its state. But the Lutheran anger itself is reactionary from the master onwards; that which was identical for the beginning cannot escape the sequel very far, loyalty is the soul of honour. It would likewise be best to pass over the great Catholic Church in silence with completed experience. Its spirit, formerly cunning, also bold, colourful and broad, but today 'harmonious' and without its bite, has become one of the savings bank, not of transubstantiation. The questions and impulses of will which combat man's becoming a commodity as well as mechanization by means of capitalism, the antinomies which the Catholic Christian experiences in particularly non-contemporaneous terms in this society, are not only remedied, as always, by consolation with the compensating other world, but also by draperies from a long since condemned society, namely the feudal one of the Middle Ages. The papal Church does not even stick to this, at least relative contrast to the Now, but rather it is practically total modernism, it affirms and defends capitalism and curbs only the revolutionary elements in it, namely the proletarian 'excesses', accumulation, dialectics. The Church would like to return capitalism only to certain middle-class stages of economy and thinking, so that it can be perpetuated all the more securely; far from abstractly rejecting practical mechanism or conversely driving it concretely to an end, the Church chooses an unwise compromise, a harmony based on incompatibility, namely practical modernism with Gothic ornamentation. It chooses a devotional capitalism, a mild profit with equally mild gospels, a soft concrete with correct symbols from the Thomist pattern book; thus precisely the 'transcending' element is lacking, the 'transcending' element in the Now which explodes a hellish present. That is also why the Church senses in Bolshevism only the fight against capital, nothing else; it protects an opium of religion which had fumed without exception in the service of the Tsar. The 'social' Rome does not notice the most Christian impulse of all in that materialism which pursues the creation of the classless society; it would rather perish with a capitalist materialism which calls itself Christian than recognize a practical Christianity which is realized with theoretical materialism. The papal Church was often on the point of weakening its connections with Christianity and solely recalling its historical tsarism; hence it became a concordat with all forces of reaction, whether in Mexico, Spain, Austria or Germany. Hence it did not protest against the murder of workers and Jew-baiting, but only against the erosion of its organizations and habits; hence it did not loosen the unholy Concordat[238] because of the Ten Commandments or because of the sacrament of baptism, but because its 'possessionalism' seemed threatened and Ahab disturbs totalities for Saul. What a courageous cardinal in Germany preaches in the way of negations is more than made up for and exposed by the positions of another in Austria, by God's blessing over this Austria. Only Russia remains alien to the always alert class feeling of the papal Church, only the war of faith for a heaven on earth, for a finally concretely mediated heaven.

238   Bloch is here referring to the Concordat between Pope Pius XI and the Nazis in 1933.

Through this clash with Russia (it is more dangerous than the medieval
one with the Empire) the Church will perish or – capitulate on nothing
but ruins; for precisely that which may partly still distinguish it from
the rich of the world up to now is, with dialectical immanence, at least
in the initial lift of the other side. And even the average faith, the
residual faith of this residual world which has become correct and has
been splendidly raised, of this enormous tradition composed of catacombs, Roman imperial antiquity, scholasticism and feudal lords, mystics and diplomats, burning at the stake and an illustrious feeling for art,
the Inquisition and all-mastering mental breadth: they have no God any
more, the cosy mystics of today who subsist on the annuities of the
world with which they have been favoured, they are almost all atheists,
only dishonest ones, ones draped in modern-Gothic terms or believers
of the gesture, because it is cultivated habit and comfortable splendour
conceals the hollow space; but God loves a single honest atheist who
knows what this means more than thousands of these devout people. If
certain religious problems remain longer than their 'clarifications', and
certainly longer than their mythologically concluding dogmas: then a
Church so called ought, if at all, to be 'escaped from time' surely only as
a *locus of these problems* (or unsubdued by the 'gates of hell' which it
has opened up for itself now, more than ever). Even without a clergy the
question of Where To and What For will burn in the classless society,
indeed it will be the most powerful one and more inexorable than today,
when a large part of the bourgeoisie – for the clearest class reasons – has
castrated it. Dams it back on youth and diluvium or also on 'Natural
Right of property', 'corporate state' and other round Thomisms. Then
perhaps – not the Church economically disenchanted and rendered
superfluous, not this old instrument of domination, but rather an educational and teaching power (if not religious power) of the Where To will
decontaminate those worries and elucidate those questions which do not
let people rest easy even after their work is done. Nietzsche says: 'I am
at my wits' end; I am everything which is at its wits' end, sighs modern
man' – this man is also the religiously needy one of tomorrow, the man
in the western chancel of anti-Nothing. The more in order everyday life
will be, the more questionable death will remain, which falls into life
and bleaches its goals; and the more worthy of mediation the space in
which human life drives upwards. It can be missed terribly easily,
indeed not only nominally fascist Molochs have opened up here. Hence
the password, by virtue of utopian conscience and knowledge which
stands on guard, to adopt again and again the unmistakable path of what
is aimed at, the dialectical path to the human house which indispensably
communicates with the path itself, so that it is one. But this cannot be
thought of highly enough, not just morally but in the same breath
metaphysically, precisely with regard to faith without lies, to the What
For which likewise reaches into the exact imagination. With that old

enlightenment which omitted man least of all, and that new, finally due one which, when it comes to light, is precisely also at home with what is latent, without omitting its darker depths. There is enormous duping of ignorance, deception through false imagination, incense via transparent feelings. But there are also red mysteries in the world, indeed only red ones.

INDEX

Dante Alighieri, 125, 182, 205, 253
Defregger, Franz von, 77, 196
Dehmel, Richard, 320
Dehn, Günther Karl, 133–4
Democritus, 362
Descartes, René, 177
Dietzenschmidt, Anton Franz, 180
Dilthey, Wilhelm, 295
Dimitrov, Georgi, 133
Dix, Otto, 77, 242, 250
Döblin, Alfred, 224
Dostoevsky, Fyodor, 58, 127, 344
Dubislav, Walter, 260
Duhem, Pierre, 265, 268

Eckhart, Johann ('Meister Eckhart'),
   46, 94, 135
Edschmid, Kasimir, 34
Ehrenstein, Albert, 243
Einstein, Albert, 266
Eisner, Kurt, 145
Engels, Friedrich, 7 n.6, 60,
   96 n.114, 147, 176, 268, 269, 270
Ernst, Max, 207, 336, 351

Feininger, Lyonel, 77
Feuerbach, Ludwig, 329
Fichte, Johann Gottlieb, 319
Fischer, Ernst, 252
Forel, August, 314
Fourier, Charles, 131
Freud, Sigmund, 205, 312, 313, 314,
   316
Freyer, Hans, 68, 90, 295
Friedrich II, King of Prussia, 46,
   120–1

Gauguin, Paul, 49, 239
Gelb, Adhémar, 277
George, Stefan, 94, 302, 329
Giedion, Sigfried, 200, 347
Giotto, 228, 253
Gobineau, Joseph, Arthur Comte,
   85, 86
Goebbels, Joseph, 66, 67, 71, 74, 78,
   94, 127, 196, 235, 242

Goethe, J. W. von, 2 n.1, 4 n.3, 77,
   81 n.87, 90 n.102, 182, 192 n.4,
   228, 230, 240, 245, 246, 248,
   276 n.128, 278, 279, 292, 294,
   313
Göring, Hermann, 127
Gotthelf, Jeremias, 50, 165, 167
Gottl-Ottlilienfeld, F. von, 295–6
Goya, Francisco, 251, 252
Green, Julien, 222–3
Grosz, George, 77, 242, 250
Grünewald, Matthias, 77, 248
Grützner, Eduard, 77

Hamann, Johann Georg, 94, 316,
   317
Hartmann, Eduard von, 348
Hasenclever, Walter, 243
Hauff, Wilhelm, 101, 155, 161, 167
Hauptmann, Gerhart, 179–80
Hausenstein, Wilhelm, 234, 235
Heartfield, John, 250
Hebel, Johann Peter, 50, 328
Heckel, Erich, 77
Hegel, G. W. F. von, 115, 123, 177,
   228, 261, 292, 296, 357, 362
Heidegger, Martin, 68, 182, 203,
   255, 272, 273, 280–3, 284, 285,
   288–9, 296
Heine, Heinrich, 246, 367
Herder, J. G., 292
Herzog, Rudolf, 155, 193
Hess, Rudolf, 86
Hesse, Hermann, 243
Heym, Georg, x, 243
Hielscher, Kurt, 133
Hiller, Kurt, 243
Hindemith, Paul, 211
Hindenburg, Field-Marshal Paul von,
   32 n.17, 65, 83
Hitler, Adolf, xiii, 61, 66–9,
   70 n.58, 74, 75–6, 78–9,
   83, 86, 95, 97, 103–4, 122, 127–9,
   138–9,   145–8, 162, 170, 196
Hofer, Carl, 77
Hofmannsthal, Hugo von, 217
Hölderlin, Friedrich, 78

Meyerbeer, Giacomo, 340, 343
Meyrink, Gustav, 172
Mirabeau, Comte Honoré de, 72
Mirbeau, Octave, 347
Modersohn-Becker, Paula, 77
Moeller van den Bruck, Arthur, 58,
    118, 127
Moleschott, Jacob, 362
Montanus, 130
More, Thomas, 136
Mörike, Eduard, 246
Moses, 119
Mozart, W. A., 343
Münster, Hanns A., 70–1
Münzer, Thomas, 118, 128, 135,
    136, 263, 329
Mussolini, Benito, 80, 196, 201

Nadler, Joseph, 293
Napoleon Bonaparte, 121, 122
Nestroy, Johann, 168
Neumann, Therese, 100
Nietzsche, Friedrich, 52, 70 n.58, 96,
    107 n.129, 109–10, 292, 307,
    309, 325–31, 335, 340, 367,
    371
Nolde, Emil, 77, 242
Noske, Gustav, 199, 204, 234

Offenbach, Jacques, 52, 291, 344
Origen, 57, 123
Ossietzky, Carl von, 32
Ovid, 323

Paracelsus, 170, 306–7
Passarge, Siegfried, 278
Paul, St, 331
Pechstein, Max, 77
Picasso, Pablo, 77, 205, 216, 238,
    250, 251, 252
Piscator, Erwin, 335
Pitt(s), William, Younger and Elder,
    72
Planck, Max, 265, 266
Plato, 296, 301, 362
Poe, Edgar Allan, 164
Poincaré, Jules Henri, 265, 267, 268

Prinzhorn, Hans, 313
Proust, Marcel, 3, 222, 223
Przywara, Erich, 133

Reventlow, Franziska, 302
Rhodes, Cecil, 291
Richard of St Victor, 123, 275
Rickert, Heinrich, 255, 295
Rimbaud, Arthur, 239, 298
Rosenberg, Alfred, 78, 127, 196, 248
Rousseau, Jean-Jacques, 112, 326
Rubiner, Ludwig, 243
Rudbeck, Olof, 87
Russell, Bertrand, 259, 260

Scheffel, Viktor von, 348
Scheler, Max, 263, 272, 273,
    278–80, 281, 288, 296, 364
Schelling, Friedrich, 115, 127, 171,
    279, 298, 309, 319
Schickele, René, 243
Schiller, Ferdinand C. S., 260
Schiller, Friedrich, 73 n.68, 95, 177,
    193, 226, 323, 360
Schlageter, Albert Leo, 146
Schlick, Moritz, 259–60
Schmidt, Christoph von, 345
Schmidt-Rottluff, Karl, 77
Schmitt, Carl, 68
Schönberg, Arnold, 219, 242
Schopenhauer, Arthur, 87, 307, 319,
    320, 348, 361
Schrimpf, Georg, 199
Schubert, Franz, 49
Schumann, Robert, 339
Schwind, Moritz von, 340
Sealsfield, Charles (Karl Postl), 54,
    164
Shakespeare, William, 253
Shaw, G. B., 297
Simmel, Georg, 335
Socrates, 307, 325, 327
Sombart, Werner, 295, 361
Sorel, Georges, 320
Spann, Othmar, 147, 278
Spengler, Oswald, 57, 263, 279,
    290–8

Heritage of Our Times is a brilliant examination of modern culture and its legacy by one of the most important and deeply influential thinkers of the twentieth century.

Through a montage of separate analyses, Bloch explores the cultural dimensions of our "age of transition," and offers a powerful defense of unclaimed ideas and images from past and present. He argues that the key elements of a genuine cultural tradition are not just to be found in the conveniently closed and neatly labelled ages of the past, but also in the open and experimental cultural process of our times. Included in this edition are the writings which formed Bloch's central contribution to the Expressionism debate of the 1930s.

One of the most compelling aspects of this work is a contemporary analysis of the rise of Nazism. It probes its bogus roots in German history and mythology at the very moment when the ideologies of Blood and Soil and the Blond Beast were actually taking hold of the German people.

Originally published in German in 1935, *Heritage of Our Times* is an astonishingly prescient book, literally before its time. The breadth and depth of its vision, together with the rich diversity of Bloch's interests, ensure its place as one of the key books of the twentieth century.